10/21/15
$ 28.00
B&T
As. 14

11/15

Withdrawn

Also by Tom Gjelten

Bacardi and the Long Fight for Cuba:
The Biography of a Cause

Sarajevo Daily: A City and Its Newspaper Under Siege

A Nation of Nations

A GREAT AMERICAN IMMIGRATION STORY

Tom Gjelten

Simon & Schuster
New York   London   Toronto   Sydney   New Delhi

Simon & Schuster
1230 Avenue of the Americas
New York, NY 10020

First Simon & Schuster hardcover edition October 2015

SIMON & SCHUSTER and colophon are registered trademarks of
Simon & Schuster, Inc.

For information about special discounts for bulk purchases,
please contact Simon & Schuster Special Sales at 1-866-506-1949
or business@simonandschuster.com.

The Simon & Schuster Speakers Bureau can bring authors to your
live event. For more information or to book an event contact the
Simon & Schuster Speakers Bureau at 1-866-248-3049 or visit
our website at www.simonspeakers.com.

Interior design by Lewelin Polanco

Manufactured in the United States of America

10 9 8 7 6 5 4 3 2

Library of Congress Cataloging-in-Publication Data

Gjelten, Tom.
  A nation of nations : a great American immigration story / Tom Gjelten.
—First Simon & Schuster hardcover edition.
    pages cm
1. Minorities—Virginia—Fairfax County—Social conditions. 2. Immigrants—
Virginia—Fairfax County—Social conditions. 3. Immigrants—Virginia—Fairfax
County—Biography. 4. Social change—Virginia—Fairfax County. 5. Fairfax County
(Va.)—Ethnic relations. 6. Fairfax County (Va.)—Emigration and immigration.
7. Fairfax County (Va.)—Biography. 8. Developing countries—Emigration and
immigration. 9. United States—Emigration and immigration. 10. United States.
Immigration and Nationality Act Amendments of 1965. I. Title.
  F232.F2G54 2015
  305.8009755'291—dc23
                                        2015017291

ISBN 978-1-4767-4385-1
ISBN 978-1-4767-4387-5 (ebook)

To Magnolia

The Americans of all nations at any time upon the earth, have probably the fullest poetical nature. The United States themselves are essentially the greatest poem. In the history of the earth hitherto the largest and most stirring appear tame and orderly to their ampler largeness and stir. Here at last is something in the doings of man that corresponds with the broadcast doings of the day and night. Here is not merely a nation but a teeming nation of nations.

Walt Whitman
Preface to *Leaves of Grass*

CONTENTS

x ★ *Contents*

PROLOGUE

The family farm sat on the edge of a pristine glacial lake in Norway's fjord country, in a sparsely settled district known as Årdal, which was therefore the family name. Behind the barn, a dirt trail led up a valley into the mountains. The hillsides were steep and rocky, but the soil was fertile and well watered by glacial runoff. In the summer, cattle and sheep grazed on the verdant slopes. The Årdal family named it Søgnhildtunet—Søgnhild's Place—after one of the early Årdal women. The property had been in the family as far back as 1759, passing from father to firstborn son according to the ancient primogeniture law that guaranteed continued family ownership of Norway's farmland.

By 1864, Søgnhildtunet should rightfully have passed to Johannes. But he was just twenty-two and restless, and the prospect of following the familiar path of his father, grandfather, and great-grandfather left little to his imagination. In Norway, he faced a predictable future, and not an easy one. For all its natural beauty, Søgnhildtunet would never be a farm that yielded abundance. The winter was long and dark and cold. To stay there would be to settle for the narrow nineteenth-century world of the Norwegian peasantry. His forefathers had no choice, but Johannes did.

The talk in Årdal in those days was of going to America, a country wide open to Norwegian immigrants. From towns on the west coast, ships were sailing daily to Bergen or Liverpool or other transatlantic embarkation points. For the equivalent of about thirty dollars, companies offered special "America" packages, covering steamship travel across the ocean plus rail transport into the U.S. interior. Large tracts of tillable land, so scarce in Norway, stood empty in Wisconsin and Minnesota and the Dakota Territory. Dreaming of new lives in a different land, Johannes and his twenty-year-old wife, Brite, said good-bye to their families and headed across the Atlantic.

With Johannes abandoning his claim, the farm in Årdal passed to the next oldest son, Ole. There were two other sons in the family, however—Samuel and a second Ole—and when they reached adulthood a few years later, they had no land of their own and nowhere to find work. Norway in the nineteenth century had one of the highest rates of population growth in Europe, but it still had a preindustrial agrarian economy that offered few employment opportunities. More than two thirds of the population lived in rural areas, the majority of them landless. The Årdal brothers knew what they needed to do, and in the spring of 1875, they sailed to Liverpool. From there, they booked passage to America on the Allan Steamship Line, a route favored in those years by tens of thousands of Norwegians.

In each decade from 1860 to 1910, the country lost about 5 percent (and sometimes more) of its population to emigration. Only Italy and Ireland lost proportionally more. The vast majority left rural Norway and made their way to the rural United States. The Norwegian American writer Ole Rölvaag called it "The Great Settling," and in his novel *Giants in the Earth* he painted a vivid portrait of the Norwegian immigrants' experience as they fanned across the upper Midwest. They traversed the plains in covered wagons, towed by oxen that would later be put to use plowing fields or hauling timber. The wagons were packed with the things they would need to start a frontier life—household utensils, farm implements, clothing, bedding.

Samuel and Ole made their way to western Minnesota, where their brother Johannes had homesteaded a decade earlier. By the time his younger brothers showed up in June of 1875, Johannes had an established farming operation, and he immediately put Samuel and Ole to work. After the harvest season, Samuel and Ole found work in the area as laborers, hiring out to whoever needed help. During the winter, when farmwork was scarce, they attended public school—grown men sitting alongside nine- and ten-year-olds—in order to learn English. Once they had saved enough money to buy some livestock and a wagon, Samuel and Ole moved on to look for land of their own. They headed first toward the Red River Valley in the northeast corner of Dakota Territory. It was a slow journey. The cattle they brought with them were constantly hungry and kept stopping to graze along the way. Nearing the Red River, they found the plain almost entirely flooded and had to wade through the water and muck. Mosquitoes tormented them.

Most of the land they crossed had already been settled, so they pressed on to the west, where there was still acreage free for the taking. The southern part of Dakota featured abundant grassland, but the Årdal brothers, having grown up among fjords and mountains, were not drawn to wide open spaces, so they stayed to the north. As they plodded on, they encountered fewer and fewer sod shacks, until at last they reached territory no one else had claimed. The land had not been surveyed yet, and Samuel and Ole could take it simply by driving stakes into the ground and declaring it theirs.

The terrain was somewhat reminiscent of rural Norway, but this was virgin land. Everything Samuel and Ole built, they built by hand. Most of the work they did, they did for the first time. Ingenuity and enterprise were key. For their first shelter, they turned their wagon box upside down and mounted it on four posts, laying the canvas over the top. Next, they built rudimentary log cabins. After stripping the logs, they stacked them one atop another, filling the spaces between with clay from the riverbed. The roof was made of bark and sod, laid carefully across pole rafters. In Norway, the farm life had been ritualized, consisting of chores done the same way, generation after generation. In America, the sod Samuel and Ole opened with their plows had never been broken before. The land had never been planted, the fields never fenced. The whole venture was exhilarating. This was the Norwegian immigrant experience that inspired Rölvaag: *As Per Hansa lay there dreaming of the future it seemed to him that hidden springs of energy, hitherto unsuspected even by himself, were welling up in his heart. He felt as if his strength were inexhaustible.*

Success in America for immigrants required looking ahead and focusing on what had been gained, not what was left behind. The Årdal brothers would never see Norway again. They had year-round farming responsibilities and soon were raising families. The "old country" was impossibly far away. Inevitably, the immigrant experience included periods of loneliness, especially acute there on the Great Plains. But Norwegians were known for their stoicism. Pious Lutherans and not given to frivolity, the brothers worked hard and skillfully and prospered in their new farming lives, cultivating wheat, oats, and potatoes. They dutifully came to see themselves as Americans, but it was not hard. No one marginalized them as newcomers, challenged their presence on the land, or questioned their loyalty, identity, or religion. With other local immigrants, they built schools and churches. As pioneers, they took that part of America as their own, and no one questioned their claim.

Back in Norway, the emigration continued. In 1883, Samuel and Ole's sister Brita left with her husband, Tollef, and joined her brothers in North Dakota. In 1900, their nephew Nicolai followed, thirty-six years after his Uncle Johannes had blazed the trail. He had also lost the Søgnhildtunet inheritance to an older brother. Like the others, he headed to North Dakota and worked for his relatives, attending a one-room country school to learn English. But the farming life was not a good fit, and Nicolai opted for business school, eventually finding work at a bank in the town of Milton.

There, he met and wed a young schoolteacher named Bessie, the daughter of an immigrant from England. Their marriage produced five children, among them my mother.

The country my ancestors chose as their new home had a political culture that grew largely from the pattern of its settlement. In Europe, the people came with the territory, but in America, the territory came first, and those arriving from other lands became American citizens by swearing allegiance to the new nation and the individualist ideology on which it was founded. "They must look forward to their posterity rather than backward to their ancestors," John Quincy Adams said of the immigrants. By coming to America, they could assume a new national identity based on their adherence to a creed and a set of values.

To outsiders, the American character was shaped on the frontier, where rewards came in return for effort and enterprise. The French travel writer and historian Alexis de Tocqueville, having visited the United States in 1831, was struck by the egalitarianism of American life, which he largely attributed to the country being a "new and unbounded" place where people coming from foreign lands could start over, all on the same basis. It was a country "where the inhabitants arrived but as yesterday upon the soil which they now occupy, and brought neither customs nor traditions with them there." As Adams had noted a decade earlier, the separate genealogies that had channeled people in the Old World into one or another future were irrelevant in America. Class differences mattered little, because the abundance of opportunity produced a degree of social mobility in America unmatched anywhere else in the world. Instead of deferring to authority, Americans learned to be self-reliant. "As no signs of incontestable greatness or superiority are perceived in anyone of them, they are constantly brought back to their own reason as the most obvious and proximate source of truth," Tocqueville wrote.

Comparing America to other countries he knew, he found it unique in almost every way. "The position of the Americans is quite exceptional," he concluded.

Thus arose the American myth that would inspire people around the world desperate for a chance to prove themselves in a new land. "The bosom of America is open to receive not only the Opulent and respectable Stranger," George Washington had famously declared, "but the oppressed and persecuted of all Nations and Religions, whom we shall welcome to a participation of all our rights and privileges, if by decency and propriety of conduct they appear to merit the enjoyment." No country on the planet would be as associated ideologically with immigration as the United States. The foreigners who broke ties with their old countries, pursued new opportunities in this different land, and were willing to be judged on their own merits and achievement personified the model American. This was said to be the nation of new beginnings, where people could be defined, in the words of immigration historian Oscar Handlin, "not by virtue of common descent but rather of common destiny."

The experience of my own Norwegian relatives matched the idealized version of the immigrant story. America was indeed the place where their ambitions were limited only by their own talents, will, and discipline. After becoming a bank officer, my grandfather Nicolai lost almost everything in the 1930s, but his faith in his adopted nation and his pride in what he had become were unbroken. To the very end of his life, he wore a white shirt and necktie seven days a week, every day of the year. It was not some carryover of an Old World custom; in Norway, he was raised on a farm. If anything, his dress served to highlight his break from his own rural background. On a return visit to Søgnhildtunet at the age of eighty-four, his relatives took a picture of him sitting on a hay rake behind a horse, dressed even there in a shirt and tie. It was as if to show he belonged at a desk in his North Dakota bank, not in a hay field in Norway.

For most of the world's population, however, the American immigrant promise was hollow. In reality, it was limited to people of the same skin color as my Scandinavian ancestors. Despite George Washington's lofty declaration, the first immigration law passed by Congress in 1790 offered U.S. citizenship only to "free *white* persons." The foreigners who settled in the United States over the first two hundred years of its history were from Europe and almost nowhere else, except for those Africans who came as slaves or were born into slave families, and they had to struggle mightily to gain membership in the nation. Almost everyone else was limited by poverty or circumstance from moving to the United States, or they were barred under U.S. law from coming at all. Thousands of Chinese, almost entirely men, were admitted in the middle years of the nineteenth century, but only as contract laborers, and with the passage of the Chinese Exclusion Act in 1882, Chinese immigration was officially prohibited. The more people wanted to move to America, the more difficult it became to obtain American citizenship. Even those coming from southern and eastern Europe found they were unwelcome. The Harvard-trained lawyer Prescott Hall, cofounder of the influential Immigration Restriction League, posed the critical question in 1897: "Do we want this country to be peopled by British, German, and Scandinavian stock, historically free, energetic, progressive, or by Slav, Latin, and Asiatic races, historically downtrodden, atavistic, and stagnant?"

So much for the Tocquevillean idea that America's immigrant history promoted an egalitarian and individualist political culture, supported creativity and enterprise, and produced this new nation where one's ancestry did not matter. In the view of the immigration restrictionists, it was not the liberating and energizing experience of venturing across the ocean and into an unfamiliar environment that led my North Dakota forebears to prosper. Rather, they achieved what they did simply because they were Norwegian. That view was reflected in a 1924 law that allocated immigration slots on the basis of the candidates' national origins and effectively excluded most Asians from citizenship. The thrust of the legislation was reinforced with the passage of the McCarran-Walter Act in 1952. Each of the

Asian, African, and Middle Eastern countries was allocated barely a hundred immigrant visas per year, while Germany, the United Kingdom, and other countries of northern and western Europe each received thousands of reserved slots. The evident premise of U.S. immigration law was that the explanation for America's success in the world actually lay in its European heritage, not in its history as a country shaped by enterprising newcomers.

It was only after 1965 that the United States unconditionally embraced its immigrant character, and it did so unintentionally. The 1965 amendments to existing law effectively ended the allocation of immigrant visas on the basis of national origin, putting applicants from around the world on a mostly equal basis. The reforms coincided with dramatic changes in the global order. In newly prospering Europe, economic and social pressures were no longer pushing people to seek new opportunities abroad. At the same time, the developing countries were experiencing population growth, rising aspirations, and heightened conflict. In those regions, more and more people wanted to leave, and improved communication and transportation—across the whole world and not just the Atlantic Ocean—facilitated their migration.

So they came, in far greater numbers than the legislators of 1965 had anticipated. In the next fifty years, the percentage of the U.S. population born outside the country tripled and shifted dramatically in composition, with immigrants arriving from Vietnam, Korea, India, Pakistan, Egypt, Mexico, Central America, Ethiopia, Nigeria, and many other places previously unrepresented. Their experiences were not so different from those of my Norwegian ancestors. They came because opportunities were lacking in their own countries, and they were attracted by what America offered. Like the immigrants of a century earlier, they took risks and were rewarded for their perseverance and initiative. The obstacles they faced, on the other hand, were bigger than anything their predecessors encountered. These new immigrants could not disappear easily into a white Euro-American society, no matter how hard they tried. Language barriers sometimes kept them isolated; even their ideas about God, family, and work could set them apart. Devout Muslims stood out in particular. In this alien environment, some immigrants would experience rejection and a disappointment that cut even deeper than the pain that drove them to leave home in the first place; others discovered that hard work and ambition could actually lead somewhere in this country.

The immigrant influx set up a belated test of America's character and identity. Was its strength and resilience a result of its formation as "not merely a nation but a teeming nation of nations," as Walt Whitman said? Or were its achievements actually due to its Anglo-Saxon heritage? That aspect of American society was fast diminishing in relative importance, replaced by unprecedented racial and ethnic diversity. The country had not yet dared to see whether it could live up to its motto, *E pluribus unum,* "Out of many, one" (an expression that referred originally to the thirteen colonies coming together as one state). At last, America could find out whether it was truly an exceptional nation and what it really meant to be American.

The story unfolded with particular drama in some communities, like one suburban county in northern Virginia that experienced a lifetime of change in a few short years, as immigrants arrived from all sides of the world, with experiences the local old-timers never could have imagined. Some were poor. Some came from professional families. All were enterprising, and together their lives represented the experience of a diversifying nation.

PART ONE

1

TWO FAMILIES FROM KOREA

The second time Jung Jae fled Seoul, she left her son Pong Suk be-hind. They had escaped together when North Korean forces cap-tured the city six months earlier and then returned as soon as U.S. and South Korean forces took it back, but in January 1951 the North Koreans crossed the Han River again, and this time was far more frightening. Jung Jae was certain that Pong Suk would be grabbed, if not by the Communists then by the South Korean troops who were conscripting every able-bodied man they could get their hands on. Her husband had died in 1936, and Jung Jae depended on her twenty-two-year-old son too much to risk losing him. An elder in her church who had vowed to remain in Seoul despite the Commu-nist advance said he would protect Pong Suk by hiding him in the basement of the pharmacy he owned, and Jung Jae felt she had no choice but to trust him.

"Don't move," she told Pong Suk on the day she left Seoul, ac-companied only by her fourteen-year-old daughter, Nam Soo. An older daughter was with relatives in another province. "We'll be back," she said. "Just wait here for us."

It was the last time she saw Pong Suk.

By then, the only way out of Seoul was on a single freight train headed to Busan, the port city about three hundred miles to the southeast, at the tip of the Korean Peninsula. There would be no more trains after this one, and desperate residents were fighting to get aboard. Jung Jae, fifty years old, and Nam Soo managed to climb on top of a boxcar and claim a small space open to the elements. They stayed there all the way to Busan, huddled with others in the January cold, buffeted by wind and rain and snow, with only a single blanket for the two of them. Some of the people crowded around them developed frostbite or hypothermia; some fell off the train; some froze to death. Jung Jae and Nam Soo, clinging tightly to each other for three days and two nights, somehow survived the trip, and in Busan, they found relatives willing to take them in. But the trip had taken its toll. Five months later, weakened by her ordeal on the train and sickened by guilt and anxiety over her decision to leave Pong Suk to his fate in Seoul, Jung Jae suffered a heart attack and died, not knowing what had become of her son.

The pharmacist had hidden Pong Suk well. The North Koreans did not find him during their three-month reoccupation of Seoul, and he was not detected till the day U.S. forces showed up at the pharmacy looking for medicine. Not understanding English and unable to determine what the Americans wanted, the pharmacist reluctantly called Pong Suk out from his hiding place to help him communicate. Pong Suk had studied English in school and was somewhat able to interpret. Impressed by his language ability and much in need of Korean speakers to assist in the war effort, the Americans conscripted him on the spot and took him away with them to work as an interpreter at a U.S. base in Daegu, about seventy miles northwest of Busan. Several months later, on a weekend leave, Pong Suk went to Busan to locate his mother and sister. It fell to Nam Soo, now fifteen years old and alone, to tell her brother that their mother had died. Recalling the moment more than sixty years later, she could not stop crying.

Heartsick, Pong Suk returned to Daegu to work with the U.S. military for the duration of the war, but he vowed to leave Korea the first chance he got. "I hate this country," he told Nam Soo the next time he saw her. "Everything I loved is gone. I never want to see Korea again."

With his fluency in English and his experience working with the American military, Pong Suk qualified for a scholarship to study in the United States and received a student visa. He left Korea on a boat in 1954, with no intention of ever going back. His scholarship took him to Simpson College, a four-year institution in the small town of Indianola, Iowa. It was hardly a place where he could feel at home, but Pong Suk was thrilled by the opportunity. With his visa to enter the United States in the 1950s, he was in a select Korean group of senior government officials, students, war brides, and some Korean military personnel who had been associated with U.S. forces during the war or were pursuing additional military training in the United States. Outside those special categories, it was nearly impossible for Koreans to immigrate. Before leaving, Pong Suk told Nam Soo and his other sister, Soon Sung, that he wanted them to join him. "As soon as I get to America and get settled down, I will find a way for you to come," he promised, but they knew it was unlikely. Pong Suk did eventually manage to line up a Simpson College scholarship for Nam Soo, but getting her a visa was likely to be a challenge and in any case there was no money for her to make the trip.

After the war, Nam Soo returned to Seoul and reunited with Soon Sung, who was fifteen years older and had an eight-year-old daughter of her own. Soon Sung's husband had died before the war, and she and Nam Soo were both penniless, a condition they shared with many others in Seoul. Much of the housing had been destroyed, and after three years of war, a quarter of the population was homeless. The two sisters and Soon Sung's daughter found space in a shelter run by their church and lived there with other women. It could have been much worse. Of the 300,000 South Korean women who lost their husbands during the war, many were left with their children to wander the streets of Seoul or across the Korean countryside, scrounging for food. Such conditions lingered for years. By 1960, the annual per capita income in South Korea was still below $100, comparable to the poorest countries in Africa. Nam Soo was able to get a low-paying job as a clerk in a government office but her older sister, having to care for her daughter, was able only to do some work at the church where the women had taken shelter. When the three of them left the church, it was only to share a single room they had rented in someone else's house.

Their brother, Pong Suk, meanwhile, was thriving. A student of economics, he was able to continue his education at Yale University, and he successfully petitioned the U.S. government to have his immigrant status adjusted to that of a permanent resident, qualifying him later for citizenship. He married a fellow student, also Korean, and in a rare letter to his sisters in Seoul Pong Suk enclosed a picture of himself and his young bride. They kept it and looked at it often to remind themselves that dreams sometimes come true. "We have a brother in America," Nam Soo would tell her friends. "That could be my life, too."

Arranged marriages were common in rural Korea at the time, but the union of Lee Jeom Chul and Seong Nak Man* in 1957 was nevertheless notable for the way it was thrust upon the young couple without any consideration of their wishes. The father of the groom and the father of the bride, occasional drinking buddies in the village of Jimshil, were both practical men. "Hey, you have a daughter, don't you?" Nak Man's father asked his friend one day. The man's wife had

---

* Koreans use their surname first, followed by their given names. "Lee" and "Seong" are family names. In America, Korean immigrants generally adopt the English form and reverse the order, putting their surnames last.

health problems, and though their son was just seventeen, the wife had lately been complaining that she wanted their boy married, so she could get a daughter-in-law to take over her household chores. The girl, Jeom Chul, was already twenty and suitable for the role. When Nak Man's father suggested that the two young people wed, Jeom Chul's father readily agreed, not bothering to consult either his daughter or his wife. The deal was done. Though they had been raised in the same village, Jeom Chul and Nak Man were essentially strangers, and the day of their marriage was one of the first times they had set eyes on each other.

Overnight, Jeom Chul's life turned miserable. As was expected, she moved in with Nak Man, his parents, and his four younger siblings, the youngest of whom was just seven years old. Nak Man's mother informed Jeom Chul that from that day on she would be responsible for all the cooking in the house plus the family laundry, which had to be done in a nearby river. Thus began nearly twenty years of abuse under the roof of her-in-laws. Though it was not a life she had chosen, Jeom Chul accepted it, at least in the beginning, guided by her sense of duty to elders and family. In the winter, when she sat by the river pounding the family laundry against the stones in the icy water, Jeom Chul's hands would turn numb. In the fall, she had to help with the wheat and potato harvest, and during the spring planting season she spent hours bent over in the rice paddies, placing the rice seedlings one by one in the water bed. At the end of the day, she had to pick the leeches off her legs.

The extended Seong family lived in a traditional Korean farmhouse, built around a central courtyard. There was no electricity or plumbing. The water was drawn from a well in the courtyard, and the cooking was done over wood fires. South Korea had yet to escape poverty, and life in rural villages like Jimshil was especially hard. In early 1960, shortly after the birth of her first son, Jeom Chul decided she could no longer tolerate her mother-in-law's treatment, and she got up one night and left the house, heading to her parents' home in the same village. She arrived in tears, knowing that under

Korean law and tradition, leaving her husband would mean giving up her child, but she was nevertheless hoping for some sympathy from her own mother and father.

"I can't do this anymore," she cried. "They are so mean to me." Her father, the man responsible for her predicament, was unmoved by her plea and slapped her hard across the face.

"What are you doing here?" he said. "You don't belong here. You belong there. You are married now!" and he shoved her out the door. From that night on, with her parents refusing to offer support at her most vulnerable moment, Jeom Chul knew she had nowhere else to turn. She went back to live with the Seong family, resigned to her fate.

Over the next ten years, Jeom Chul and Nak Man had three more children, two more boys and then a girl. As the oldest son, Nak Man was obligated to support his younger siblings and his parents in addition to his own children. With no employment opportunities in the Jimshil area, he sought work elsewhere, and in the spring of 1970 he had a job in Busan, the city at the bottom of the Korean Peninsula, where he lived in a single rented room. Jeom Chul by then was pregnant with her fourth child, and as her delivery date drew near she joined him in Busan. She gave birth in that rented room without assistance, holding on to a doorknob for support and cutting the umbilical cord by herself.

They named the girl Gyeong, meaning precious. In traditional Korean families, girls are often less valued than boys, because they do not carry on the family name, but Gyeong was an exception. With three older brothers able to maintain the Seong line, Gyeong's parents were overjoyed to have a girl at last, and they treated her like a princess. Indeed, Gyeong's early childhood was largely carefree. She knew little of the way her grandmother had treated her mother, because Jeom Chul would not complain, nor did Jeom Chul burden Gyeong with chores. She played in the dirt with friends and roamed the nearby hillsides with her brothers looking for chestnuts. When she was a bit older, she was responsible for grazing the family cow, but even that task was an easy one. She did lose track of the cow one day when she was playing in the pasture with friends and failed to notice it getting dark, but no harm was done. The cow, knowing it was time to be fed, had walked home on its own and was eating contentedly in its stall when Gyeong came rushing back in tears, ready to confess her negligence.

As Nak Man's mother grew older and more infirm, she became all the more demanding of her son and daughter-in-law, and their life in Jimshil was increasingly intolerable. Jeom Chul no longer had to work in the fields, but she still had to care for Nak Man's parents, and his mother's criticism was ever sharper and meaner. Jeom Chul could not even give her children a weekly bath without being told she was wasting water. For Nak Man, the moment he had dreaded for nearly twenty years was finally arriving: He would have to choose between the interests of his wife and children and his duty as a son to support his parents. For a Korean man, it was an excruciating dilemma, but Nak Man knew what he had to do.

2

A FAMILY FROM BOLIVIA

The urge to move, a drive that would eventually bring the whole Alarcón family to America, went back to Grandma Edu and her childhood in the hinterlands of Bolivia. Until the day two girls who had been away from the village came back with new dresses and barrettes in their hair, Edu had been content with her simple rural life. Each morning she rose at dawn with her dog to fetch water from the river, take the cows to the *pampa* to graze, and tend to the bulls. Though she had four brothers, it was Edu who helped her father most with the chores. Some days she would go off with him to his orchard to pick peaches and apples. Other days she would stay in the pasture with her dog, singing to him or snoozing in the sun. At midday her father would ride up on his horse to check on her and bring lunch, usually a little pail of *choclo* soup, a tasty corn chowder that her mother made with peppers and potatoes. There was no school in her village, and at the age of fourteen she had not yet learned to read or write, but the idea of schooling never appealed much to Edu anyway. Nor did she care that her clothes were worn and tattered or that she had no decent shoes to wear—not, that is, until the day her two friends showed up in their new outfits, looking so pretty. Edu decided then and there to follow their example.

The girls had gone off to the nearest big city, Cochabamba, about sixty miles to the north, to work as domestic servants. Edu had never seen Cochabamba, but her older sister Benigna had been there to visit some cousins, and once Edu got it into her head to go there and earn money, she pestered Benigna relentlessly to make the journey with her. Their father would never agree to it, so they would have to make the arrangements on their own. They left early one morning while their father's attention was elsewhere, heading on foot to a village where their father's sister lived. She was surprised to see them and admonished them for having left home without telling their parents, but she let them spend the night. After another day walking along dirt roads and then taking a bus, they made it to Cochabamba. Benigna led the way to their cousins' house, and a day later the girls found work as servants. Their father showed up two weeks later, determined to bring the girls home. Benigna agreed, but the woman who employed Edu was so impressed by her work habits and maturity that she persuaded Edu's father to let the girl stay. The days of going barefoot, grazing the cows, and picking peaches were over for Edu. She returned to her village on occasion after that to visit her family, but never again to stay.

With her venture, Edu was establishing the principles that would guide her life and set an example for her future family. One was that the experience of poverty motivates people to self-improvement. "When you start out poor," she said, "you are better than others at rising up." Another was to be enterprising and smart in confronting obstacles, no matter your level of education. Edu would be illiterate all her life, even in America, but she believed that intelligence was not measured only by the studying one does or the status one attains. "You have to think carefully about where you're going to go and how you're going to get there," she told her four daughters. It was that instinct for looking ahead and finding a path that took Edu from her village to Cochabamba and then from Cochabamba to La

Paz, Bolivia's capital. It was why she later supported her daughters and her son-in-law when they wanted to move to America, and it was why she eventually followed them there herself.

Inevitably, there were times when her progress slowed, such as the years after she met and married her husband, Lucho, and began raising a family in La Paz. During that period, Edu was not earning money of her own, and Lucho had only a meager income from his work in a restaurant. She thought he drank too much and did not give her enough to care for her girls properly. For the first time in her life, Edu felt helpless. Sometimes she went without eating in order to be sure there was food for her four daughters. "You have to have faith at a time like that," she said. "I prayed, 'Dear God, Show me what to do. Why is it that other women are earning money and having things, and I cannot? What is it that I have to do? Show me a way.'"

An answer came through her oldest daughter, Rhina. While visiting a friend one afternoon, Rhina saw the girl's mother making carrot juice in her kitchen. The woman peeled and grated the carrots, then wrapped the shavings tightly in cheesecloth and twisted it until juice dripped out. When Rhina related what she had seen, Edu was inspired. Street vendors in La Paz at the time were selling juice from oranges and other fruits, but she knew of no one who was selling fresh carrot juice. Edu promptly went out and bought a basket of carrots, and with the help of ten-year-old Rhina, she grated them and produced a small container of juice. By mixing the juice with water, Edu made some carrot punch, which she brought to her local market the next morning to see whether anyone would buy it. She sold out quickly, and the next day Edu returned with two more buckets, and then three. At last, she had found a potential moneymaking enterprise.

For good reason. It took far more labor to squeeze juice from carrots than from oranges or other fruit. The business took off only after Edu's husband, Lucho, managed to acquire a German-made electric juicer like one that was used in the restaurant where he worked. The carrots still needed to be peeled before they could be fed into the juicer, but it was no longer necessary to grate the carrots and wring out the juice by hand. Over the coming years, her product proved hugely popular, and the money rolled in. Before long, Edu was going through two hundred or more pounds of carrots in a single day. Rhina, her assistant since the first day, continued working for her, even after meeting and marrying a handsome young Argentine by the name of Victor Alarcón.

Not surprisingly, Edu's daughters soon had dreams of their own, bigger than anything Edu herself had imagined. The two middle girls, Aída and Marilu, had a school friend who visited Miami every year with her family, and in 1980 the girl was set to move to America to attend college in the Washington, D.C., area. She wanted Aída and Marilu to come with her, and the girls were eager to go. Their request took Edu by surprise. "I knew the United States existed," she recalled, "but that was all. I really knew nothing about the country." She was not alone in that regard. Only about sixty Bolivians visited the United States on an average day that year, and almost all of them were businessmen, government officials, or wealthy Bolivian tourists traveling for pleasure. Just three countries in South America—Guyana, Paraguay, and Uruguay—sent fewer visitors to the United States. But Edu could hardly say no to her daughters, having set out on her own at such an early age and believing as she did in the importance of taking one's destiny in one's own hands. She took out a loan using her juice business as collateral and sent the girls on their way.

The venture was a disaster from the start. The friend who was to accompany Aída and Marilu could not leave Bolivia because of a last-minute paperwork problem. The man who had arranged the girls' schooling had defrauded them, taking their money but never registering them for school. Aída and Marilu managed to find jobs in the area as nannies, but they were in different homes. With no friends, minimal English, and no idea how to get around the area, the girls were lonely and miserable. On their one day off each week, they would try to see each other, but they spent much of the time crying. As soon as they had saved enough money to pay back the money their mother had borrowed, the girls returned to Bolivia.

Aída was willing to return to her old life in La Paz, but Marilu, a year younger, soon regretted her decision to give up on America. The only job she could find paid a pittance. At night, she dreamed she was back in the United States. "I could see a future there," she said. "In Bolivia, I couldn't. I decided that I would rather live the way I had been living in the U.S. and try to make something of it than struggle in Bolivia with no hope of ever getting ahead." The girls' student visas were still valid, and Marilu convinced Aída they should give America another chance. They flew back to Washington and found work again as baby-sitters. Aída ultimately decided to go back to Bolivia, but Marilu resolved to stay. By then, she had a better sense of how to get around, and she enrolled in school to learn English. She made some friends, and through family connections, she eventually met a Bolivian man, Raúl Plata, who owned his own dental lab in northern Virginia and had naturalized status as a U.S. citizen. Seeing him as stable and reliable, Marilu married him, which qualified her for legal residency in the United States and a path to citizenship.

Marilu's successful experience in America caught the attention of her brother-in-law, Victor Alarcón, the handsome Argentine. Victor was bright, energetic, and enterprising, but like his mother-in-law he sometimes felt vulnerable to forces beyond his control. Though born in Argentina, he grew up in La Paz, where his father had owned a hotel. When business setbacks sent his father back to Argentina, Victor stayed in Bolivia with his mother and younger brothers. Because his mother worked all day, Victor had adult responsibilities from an early age, from shopping and cooking meals to accompanying his brothers to school. He and Rhina married young, and they soon had two little boys of their own, Victor Jr. and Álvaro, born in 1982 and 1983.

Bolivia by then was facing a serious economic crisis. High

interest rates and low commodity prices were pushing the country into depression, but the government was incapable of dealing with the challenges. The annual inflation rate in 1980 was 300 percent, with the country's economic output shrinking by 7 percent. By 1984, hyperinflation had set in. Edu's juice stand was still bringing in loads of Bolivian pesos, enough that she and Rhina had to carry the money home each day in bags, but the currency was so devalued as to be almost worthless. Victor came to Edu's house one afternoon to find heaps of money piled on a bed and Rhina and Edu trying to count what they had. He had told them many times they needed to exchange the Bolivian currency each day into dollars to gain some protection from inflation, but the lines at the banks were so long that people were literally sleeping on the sidewalk in order to keep their place. Private money traders were more accessible, but they sold dollars at more than twice the official exchange rate. At its peak in the spring of 1985, the inflation rate reached an annual rate of 60,000 percent, at which point prices were doubling about every two weeks. Shortages of basic consumer goods meant that Rhina or Victor had to get up at four in the morning to stand in line to buy bread or milk, and even then they often went home empty-handed.

Under the circumstances, Victor saw no option but to follow his sister-in-law's example and go to America, where Marilu insisted there was economic opportunity for anyone willing to work. He had a friend at the U.S. embassy in La Paz who had helped Marilu and Aída get their student visas, and Victor turned to him again for help in getting a visitor's visa for himself, one that entitled him to multiple U.S. entries over a ten-year period. He left for America with what little money he could scrape together. Marilu and her husband, Raúl, lived in Fairfax County, Virginia, on the far western side of the D.C. metropolitan area, and they offered Victor a corner in their basement in exchange for modest rent. Marilu directed him to a Mexican restaurant where he might find work, and he was hired as a dishwasher on the night shift. His tourist visa did not permit him to work, but at least Victor was in the country legally, and the enforcement of immigration regulations was more lenient in 1986 than it would be in later years. He was far from alone in his work and living situation. Foreigners like himself were arriving every day in Fairfax County, finding jobs in the booming service economy, and fast diversifying what just a few years earlier had been a largely white and rural population.

The experience was nevertheless discouraging. There was no convenient public transportation between Marilu's house and the Mexican restaurant, so Victor had to walk the three miles each way. The work in the restaurant was hard and dirty and did not pay as much as he had hoped. Never in his life had he felt so dependent on others as he now was on Marilu and Raúl, and it made him uncomfortable. When Rhina reached him with news that his mother had died, Victor decided to return home.

Back in La Paz, life for a while seemed better. Prices were stabilizing. Victor found a job with Caritas, a Catholic relief organization, and went back to school to complete his college education. Before long, however, Victor came to the same conclusion his sister-in-law had reached: that his future lay in America. "I was not happy," he recalled later. "Always, in the back of my mind, I was thinking, 'I can do better than this.'" Like Marilu, he had learned some lessons from his first experience in America. If he were to return, he needed to be better prepared. He needed to improve his English and save some money. He needed to secure visas for his entire family. After two years in Bolivia, he returned to the United States, this time with a better idea of what he faced. He went back to the same Mexican restaurant where he had gotten a job earlier, this time determined to learn everything he could about the business. He rented a room in a nearby house where other restaurant workers were living, enabling him to work longer hours. He impressed the owner with his intelligence and discipline, and after just two months washing dishes, he was promoted to cook. A month later, he sent for Rhina, and once she was convinced that living in America made sense, she went back to Bolivia to fetch their two boys.

Edu, whose lifelong spirit of optimism and enterprise had inspired her whole family, mortgaged her house to help finance the Alarcóns' move, and a few years later she and her youngest daughter, Gloria, joined them in northern Virginia, leaving the juice business in La Paz to her daughter Aída. Not one to slow down, however, Edu promptly found a job at a Fuddruckers restaurant franchise, where she spent eleven years doing various chores on the swing shift, arriving at four in the afternoon and working until midnight. Next she moved to a Wendy's. At the age of seventy-seven, she was still working and still going strong, undeterred by her own illiteracy. Her mostly Hispanic co-workers at Wendy's affectionately called her *la dueña*—the landlady. Her own daughters and their children called her Rambo, for her strength and independence and for her unrelenting pressure on them to make the most of their opportunities, advice that proved important as her family confronted one obstacle after another in their adaptation to life as Americans.

"You have two jobs, right?" Edu once asked her grandson Álvaro, as he drove her to a family gathering. "Don't ever let me find out you only have one job." She was no easier on her daughters. "They are always whining about something," she told a friend. "If I were like them, speaking English like they do and being able to read and write, I can't imagine how far I would have gone. I'll tell you one thing," she said. "I wouldn't be working at Wendy's."

3

OUT OF KOREA

Seong Nak Man decided he could no longer allow his mother to abuse his wife, but with no money of his own, he had no idea where he could take his family if he abandoned the household in Jimshil. Help finally came from his older sister, Jeom Joo, who was living in nearby Daegu with her husband. Over the years, she had grown ashamed of the way her mother treated her brother and especially his wife. She told Nak Man that her husband's brother, who had moved to America, was helping Koreans to immigrate. The key was to get a special EB-3 employment visa, a subcategory of which included an offer of permanent residency to immigrants who were able and willing to take jobs that U.S. workers scorned.

The program had been in existence since the 1952 McCarran-Walter Act, but as long as Korea was limited to just a few visas per year, almost no Korean could take advantage. When the national origins quota system was finally abolished in 1965, Korean workers had the same right to pursue a visa under the EB-3 program as workers from other countries. For a fee, Jeom Joo's brother-in-law, who lived in Baltimore, could do the immigration paperwork and arrange for Nak Man and his family to move permanently to the United States, on the condition that he and his wife agree to work in a chicken processing plant in southern Maryland. The jobs were hard to fill because the work was dangerous, difficult, and low-paying. Nak Man would need several thousand U.S. dollars to pay the fee and buy airline tickets for himself and his family, but his sister, who was moderately well off, said she would help him. He could pay her back in installments. Nak Man broke the news to his parents in early 1976, and it was not easy. "You're leaving us here to die," they told him. "You are a disgrace." His decision was an act of vision and bravery. Nak Man would have to abandon all he had in Korea, but he knew there was no future for his family there. They would be stuck in Jimshil as long as his parents were alive. They would always be poor, and his children would never be well educated.

Jeom Chul dressed her children in their best clothes, and the family headed to Seoul and flew to the United States. The three boys were 17, 13, and ten years old. Gyeong, who was six, had her first taste of American food on the flight across the ocean and threw up all over her seat. The family was met at the airport in Baltimore by Jeom Joo's brother-in-law. He knew they would be eager for some Korean treats upon their arrival, and he brought bean paste with him to the airport, much to Gyeong's delight. The Seong family stayed in Baltimore for a month, while the final arrangements were made for their work permits, and they then moved to Berlin, Maryland, to work for Showell Farms in a plant where chickens were slaughtered, cleaned, and packaged for sale. The company assigned the family a two-room housing unit in a cinder block barracks along with a dozen other families, with whom they shared a communal bathroom at the end of the hall.

The Seong family stayed in the Showell "motel" for two years. Nak Man and Jeom Chul worked the maximum overtime hours their employer allowed, including nights, and they saved almost all their earnings. The only shopping they did was at the nearby Family Dollar. In future years, immigration brokers would bring hundreds of Koreans to toil in the area chicken plants, and journalists would uncover corruption in the arrangement of the labor contracts (Perdue Farms, which acquired Showell Farms, terminated the program), but the Seong family was one of the first to benefit, and their achievements were exemplary. After two years, they had saved enough money to move out of the cinder block barracks and make a down payment on a small brick ranch house in the nearby city of Salisbury, where the public schools were better. Jeom Chul, who lacked marketable job skills, continued to work at the Showell chicken plant for another eight years, but Nak Man soon got a loan to purchase and operate a gas station/convenience store in the town of Pittsville, halfway between Salisbury and the Showell plant.

Having come so far from Korea, and at such a cost, Nak Man and Jeom Chul made clear to their children that they expected them to take advantage of their educational opportunities in America. Gyeong, raised by loving parents and sheltered by three older brothers, flourished in school, mastered English quickly, and made friends. She did not entirely understand what her mother had experienced back in Jimshil until several years later, when Nak Man's mother came for her one and only visit. With living conditions cramped, Gyeong shared her bed with her grandmother. As they lay next to each other one night, her grandmother turned to Gyeong and told her that her mother was "a terrible person." Gyeong had no idea what she meant and began to cry, but her grandmother persisted, saying Jeom Chul was "one of the worst people in the whole world." Gyeong, who was ten years old at the time, had never heard her mother speak ill of her grandparents and could not understand why her grandmother would say such a thing. The next day she told her brothers, who finally explained to Gyeong how their grandmother had abused their mother. Gyeong, who until that day had nothing but affection for her grandmother, could barely stand to look at her afterward and felt closer than ever to her mother.

In 1986, Nak Man and Jeom Chul bought a liquor store and pool hall in the suburbs of Baltimore. Jeom Chul left the chicken plant where she had been working for ten long years and along with their three sons helped her husband with the new business. Seven years later, after their sons had left home and were no longer available to help, Nak Man and Jeom Chul sold the Baltimore operation and bought a small liquor store in Washington, which they could manage by themselves. They kept that store until their retirement, working long days like so many other Korean immigrant shopkeepers.

From the day they began work for Showell Farms until the day they retired, Nak Man and Jeom Chul saved every penny they could, forgoing all luxuries. Their annual incomes were modest at best, but they never accepted government welfare, and they made sure their children all went to college. Their devotion to each other did not conform to a conventional Western notion of love, with its connotations of romance and passion and sentimentality. Nak Man and Jeom Chul had not chosen to be with each other, and what they shared was not so much mutual attraction as mutual loyalty and a deep sense of duty and partnership. Gyeong, who took the name Alex, told her friends that her parents' attachment to each other was best described by the Korean word *jeong*, which implies a connection that is less ego-centered than a relationship based on love, but arguably more durable. A couple with *jeong* does not depend on either partner's fleeting emotional investment, nor does the relationship require constant validation to be sustained. The attachment is almost involuntary, approaching mutual bondage.

Gyeong/Alex admired her father and mother in the way that many immigrant children do, knowing what the parents have endured and sacrificed to give their offspring the opportunities they never had. She was impressed by her mother in particular, who insisted that she pursue as much schooling in America as she could. When her father said she should look for a husband as soon as she finished college, saying her attractiveness to a potential mate would diminish each year she didn't marry, her mother told her to ignore his advice. "You don't need a man," she said. Having experienced the drawbacks of depending on someone else, Jeom Chul wanted to be sure her daughter had options, and Alex followed her counsel. After graduating from high school with high honors and completing college on a full scholarship, she went to law school, passed the Maryland bar, and became an attorney. In a few years, Alex Seong would end up in Fairfax County, Virginia, one of the jurisdictions in the United States most transformed by immigrants. She would marry another young Korean lawyer whose life story was almost as dramatic as hers.

Nam Soo's harrowing escape from Seoul on top of a freight train followed by the loss of her mother and then the postwar years of poverty left her traumatized and dreaming of a life somewhere else. Though only a few Koreans in the 1950s had family members in the United States, the knowledge of what her brother, Pong Suk, had achieved by emigrating left her determined to follow in his footsteps. Little did she know it would take twenty-five years, first because of U.S. immigration restrictions and later because of her personal circumstances. In 1960, she married a Presbyterian minister by the name of Kim Sang Woo, who like her and many other Koreans had lost both his parents during the war years. No sooner had they begun planning their future than Sang Woo was drafted by the South Korean military and sent to Saigon to serve as a chaplain for South Korean forces stationed there in support of the Vietnam war effort. He was permitted to visit Seoul once every two years, but his deployment in Saigon extended until 1969. Nam Soo remained behind, raising a girl and then two boys. When Sang Woo was finally released from military service and returned to Seoul, he found a country that still had not recovered from its postwar devastation. With few attractive options, he decided the family should return with him to South Vietnam, where he spoke the language and had extensive contacts in the expatriate Korean community.

In Saigon, Sang Woo established a Korean church and community center for the roughly five thousand Koreans who lived there. With its colonial heritage and hundreds of thousands of U.S. government and military personnel, the South Vietnamese capital provided a multicultural setting, and the Kim children learned French and English. But the war came ever closer, and when Saigon fell to the Vietnamese Communist forces in April 1975, Nam Soo and her three children were forced to flee. Sang Woo stayed to oversee the evacuation of his congregation members and was stranded on a rooftop when the last helicopter left without him. As a former officer in the South Korean military, he was soon arrested by the Communist forces and imprisoned. Back in Seoul, Nam Soo was left to care for her children on her own. She moved with them into a small apartment and worked when she could, but depended on charity and welfare payments and some support from Sang Woo's military friends. Her youngest son, Sun Yeop, was just four years old when he last lived in South Korea, and in school he had difficulty with his reading and writing assignments in the Korean language.

With no news of Sang Woo's situation, the family was prepared to believe he would stay in prison indefinitely or even be executed, and it was a surprise when he suddenly returned to Seoul in May 1975, having been released in response to international pressure. Not having lived in South Korea for fifteen years, however, Sang Woo once again wanted his family to move. The new legislation in the United States would permit Nam Soo, as the sister of a naturalized U.S. citizen, Pong Suk, to immigrate with her family, but there would be a waiting period, and in the meantime Sang Woo suggested they move to Australia, where he could establish another Korean church and where the children could get good-quality Western schooling. The Kim family spent the next five years in Sydney. Ten-year-old Sun Yeop flourished in his new environment, becoming fluent in English. He decided on his own to change his name to Mark, in part because it sounded like Mahg, the Korean nickname his family had always used for him, from the words "Mahg-Dong-Yi," meaning the youngest child.

In 1980, twenty-six years after her brother had left for America, Nam Soo finally got her turn, along with her husband and Mark. The two older children joined them after finishing their schooling in Australia. They settled in Los Angeles. Mark had lived already as a foreigner in Vietnam and Australia, but never had he experienced a place of such human diversity as he encountered in southern California. He enrolled at Rancho Alamitos High School in Orange County, where the student body was divided between whites, Latinos, Asians, and African Americans. His father took over the ministry of a small Korean Presbyterian congregation in Orange County, and his mother went to work on a factory assembly line, alongside other Asian and Latino immigrant women. Their family income was meager, and Mark himself started working as soon as he turned sixteen to bring in a little more money.

At school, Mark took an early interest in current affairs and U.S. politics, inspired by the American promise of a system open to all. He was moved in particular by the Reverend Jesse Jackson, who spoke directly to a young immigrant's idealized notion of what the United States represented. "Our flag is red, white, and blue," Jackson told the 1984 Democratic National Convention, "but our nation is a rainbow—red, yellow, brown, black, and white." To Mark, no other politician laid out a civic vision that so clearly included people like himself and made them feel welcome. The United States, Jackson said, was less a blanket of unbroken cloth than a quilt, with "many patches, many pieces, many colors, many sizes, all woven and held together by a common thread. The white, the Hispanic, the black, the Arab, the Jew, the woman, the Native American, the small farmer, the businessperson, the environmentalist, the peace activist, the young, the old, the lesbian, the gay and the disabled make up the American people."

Jackson competed for the Democratic presidential nomination that year and again in 1988, by which time Mark was a political science major at the University of California at Irvine and an enthusiastic follower of Jackson's Rainbow Coalition. By then, he had changed the spelling of his surname to "Keam" in order to distinguish himself from the multitude of Korean immigrants named Kim. He quite literally intended to make a name for himself in the political world. He was awarded an internship in the nation's capital in the spring of 1988 and chose to spend it at the Democratic National Committee (DNC), where he performed impressively enough that he was hired to work that summer at the national convention in Atlanta. Politics had infected him. During his three months in Washington, he stayed in an apartment across the river in suburban Fairfax County, Virginia, where the political landscape was rapidly being reshaped by immigrants like himself. He would return to Washington seven years later as a young lawyer and political activist and would eventually run for office with Fairfax County as his political base.

4

BOLIVIA TO AMERICA

Rent is often the biggest expense for new immigrants, which is why so many start out living with relatives or friends or anyone they meet who wants to share a living space. Victor Alarcón, who had followed his sister-in-law to America, was standing on the platform at a Metro station in northern Virginia one day in early 1989 when he heard someone shout his name. It was Juan Encinas, a childhood friend from La Paz who had left for the United States seven years earlier. Victor knew he had moved to the D.C. area, but he didn't have his contacts and hadn't made an effort to track him down. Juan and his wife were cleaning houses for a living, and he told Victor they were struggling. Victor said he was, too. Rhina had just come from La Paz, and they had gone back to living with Rhina's sister Marilu and her husband. Juan suggested they move in with him and his wife, who was also from Bolivia. Both couples could save on rent. Such crowding was not unusual in immigrant communities in northern Virginia, though the practice violated zoning laws and drove property managers crazy.

It would be a squeeze. Juan's apartment, in a low-income part of Fairfax County known as Seven Corners, had just one bedroom. His plan was to divide the living room with a partition and give half to Victor and Rhina as their private area. He and his wife would keep the bedroom, and the two couples would share the kitchen and bathroom. It wasn't much, and the arrangement got a lot more difficult a few months later, when Rhina brought their boys, Victor Jr. and Álvaro, to live with them in America. Now the tiny space had to accommodate a family of four. There was just enough room for a bed for Victor and Rhina and bunks for the boys, plus a small TV. The Alarcóns lived and ate separately from Juan and his wife, taking turns in the kitchen. With no table, Victor and Rhina and the boys sat on the edge of their beds at mealtimes, eating off TV trays. The atmosphere in the apartment was tense, especially between Juan's wife and Victor. While he and Rhina valued cleanliness, Juan's wife often left clothes lying on the floor and dirty dishes in the sink. Cockroaches ran freely around the apartment, driving Victor crazy. He kept a bottle of disinfectant handy and was constantly spraying along the walls and in the corners, but to no avail.

It was August when Rhina arrived with the boys, and the Fairfax County schools opened just a few weeks later. Victor was working long hours then—he had a new job as an assistant manager at a 7-Eleven—and it would be up to Rhina to register the boys for classes. Victor told her the closest school was Sleepy Hollow Elementary, and he claimed it was within easy walking distance from Seven Corners, not far from their apartment complex. On the first day of classes, Rhina set out with Victor Jr. and Álvaro at her side, following her husband's instructions. The boys had attended a private Catholic school back in La Paz, and she dressed them just as she would have in Bolivia, with white shirts, neckties, and dress pants. After walking nearly an hour along Sleepy Hollow Road, however, she still hadn't seen any school, and the boys were now grumpy and sweaty and thirsty. "It's here somewhere," she said. They tried some side streets but found nothing. Rhina spoke almost no English and was not yet comfortable asking for directions. Finally, she gave up and headed home.

"So, how did it go?" Victor asked the boys that evening. "Your first day of school in America!"

"What do you mean, how did it go?" Rhina snapped. "There's no school there!" The school was much farther down the road than Victor had said. He didn't know his way around the neighborhood as well as he claimed.

Rhina found the school the next day and had the boys enrolled, but it was just one of many stressful days she had as a stranger in America. She got some part-time work at a Burger King, but without English her opportunities were limited, and she worried constantly—about money, about neighborhood crime, and especially about her boys. She would get upset about little things, like the day six-year-old Álvaro came home from school and told her that ice cream cups had been available at lunch and that he had taken some, only to have to give it back. Not yet understanding English, he didn't realize he had to pay for the ice cream, and he had no money. The thought of her boy being humiliated like that sent her into the bathroom to cry, as she did almost every day. The tension around the apartment only made everything worse.

After six difficult months with Juan and his wife, Victor learned that another one-bedroom apartment had come open in the same housing complex. He had exhausted his savings on immigration lawyers and airline tickets, and an apartment of their own would be a stretch financially, but Victor and Rhina felt they had no choice and grabbed it immediately. With no furniture except for their bunk beds and no money to spend, they settled for what other people were throwing out. They kept an eye on the neighborhood dumpsters and the trash piles along the street and hauled off any usable items that were to left to be picked up by garbage trucks or charity organizations. Piece by piece, they furnished their apartment. It didn't take much. The bedroom was crammed with a double bed for

Victor and Rhina and the bunk beds for the boys, and when a baby came along in 1991, space had to be cleared for a crib. They named the little boy Miguel, but because they were in America, they called him Mikey.

The Alarcón family spent four years in the Seven Corners apartment. Victor and Rhina both struggled to acquire English, but their boys were resilient and fast learners, and their school was accustomed to dealing with immigrant children. Álvaro was the more outgoing of the two and made friends easily. Years later, as a social worker, he would credit his ability to pick up nonverbal cues in a social setting to his early determination to understand his English-speaking classmates when he didn't quite know what they were saying. By the end of their first year at Sleepy Hollow, he and Victor Jr. were comfortable enough with English that they would fight with their mother over which programs to watch on television, preferring sitcoms like *Three's Company* to the Spanish-language soap operas that Rhina wanted to watch.

Outside their building, they had to deal with the gangs. The earliest in the neighborhood were Vietnamese and African American, but by the time the Alarcón family settled in the Seven Corners area, immigrants from El Salvador dominated the criminal scene. Like the Vietnamese, many of the Salvadorans had fled a brutal civil war in their home country, and they were hardened to violence. In the United States, the Salvadoran youth felt marginalized, and their families had often been fragmented by the migration experience. Gang membership offered a sense of identity and kinship. The highest profile belonged to Mara Salvatrucha, a name derived from Salvadoran slang roughly meaning tough Salvadoran fighters and often shortened to MS-13 (the letter "M" being the thirteenth in the alphabet). Many dumpsters, trash cans, and park benches around the Alarcón apartment complex were spray painted with "MS" graffiti, marking the area as their territory.

MS members could be identified by their bandannas, their

tattoos, and even by their New Balance 503 sneakers, 503 being the telephone code for El Salvador. Álvaro and Victor Jr. both had MS acquaintances and encountered gang members regularly, walking home from school or heading to the park to play soccer. "What's going on?" the gangsters would ask, with intimidating looks. "Who are you rolling with?" No answer would satisfy them, even when the boys were barely ten years old. One day, when Álvaro and two friends were proudly wearing some new Nike headbands they had bought with money they'd saved, some MS members stopped them and told them to take the headbands off or they'd be beaten up. They were apparently too suggestive of rival gang sympathies. On another occasion, Álvaro and a friend were fooling around on a neighborhood playground with a friend when two MS members came by and began teasing them. "Let's tie them to the monkey bars," one said, and they did just that, leaving them hanging help-lessly with their shoes tied together until Victor Jr. showed up and untied them. No harm was done; the humiliation was enough to send a message.

Despite the harassment, the criminal activity, and the associ-ated violence, Álvaro and Victor Jr. and their friends came to see the gangs as a natural outgrowth of life in their tough Seven Cor-ners neighborhood, which was known locally as Willston. It was an ethnically diverse environment, and the young people growing up there were most comfortable with those who shared their ex-perience and instinctively wary of those who did not. Across the street from the Alarcón apartment complex was a set of buildings where most of the residents were African American. While Álvaro and Victor Jr. and their friends favored soccer, the African Amer-ican boys preferred basketball. They played loud music and were bigger and stronger than the Latino boys, and they had a gang of their own. Álvaro and his brother always circled around the Af-rican American complex on their way to the local Safeway rather than walking to the store directly. The other side of Wilson Boule-vard was Vietnamese territory, dominated by the TRG—the Tiny

Rascal Gang—and the Alarcón boys stayed clear of that neighborhood as well.

The smallest gang units were more like cliques, organized street by street. The MS guys that Álvaro and Victor Jr. encountered were all associated with their Willston complex; other housing projects had their own crews. Looking back on his childhood, Álvaro would recall how he and his brother and their friends engaged in behavior that could easily have evolved in a gang direction. Four of them once organized a "club," complete with officers and their own clubhouse—an old black Lincoln their father had junked behind their building. They held their meetings secretly in the car, sharing snacks and baseball cards. Before long, four other boys from the neighborhood discovered them and wanted to join, but Álvaro and the others wouldn't let them. The whole idea of a club, after all, is its exclusivity. But this was the Willston neighborhood, and the boys' refusal to let others into their club sparked a miniature gang war. The four who had been spurned went off and found two other friends and returned to challenge the Alarcón brothers and their friends to a brawl. Now it was six versus four, so the boys in the Lincoln club scrambled to find their own reinforcements. The little confrontation ended when Álvaro and Victor Jr. persuaded another friend of theirs to call in some of his genuine gangster buddies to provide protection.

That Álvaro and his brother did not themselves fall into the gang life was due in good part to the attention and support they received from their parents. But Victor and Rhina often worked long hours and sometimes had to leave their boys alone, trusting them to care for little Mikey. Sometimes the boys had to think for themselves, like when the drunk from the next building would try to break in, mistaking their apartment for his own, as he did more than once. On those occasions, the boys would escape through a back window. Victor Jr. would go first, and Álvaro would hand the baby to him. Álvaro would then scramble out, and they would run to a neighbor's apartment and wait for the drunk to leave. When she learned about such incidents, Rhina would be terribly upset, but what could she do?

It was only years later that Álvaro and his brother learned the real reason their dad kept a baseball bat in the van behind the driver's seat. They had figured it was just because he was always taking them to Bon Air Park to play ball. Victor never told his boys he wanted the bat handy in case he got jumped.

Victor Alarcón was a proud man who had been through some hard times, and he was not about to be pushed around by a bunch of tattooed teenagers in bandannas. That attitude nearly got him killed one Sunday morning in 1993 as he was driving home from his overnight shift at the 7-Eleven in nearby Annandale. It had been another long night selling beer and cigarettes, and when some kids in a red Toyota Celica tried to cut sharply in front of him, Victor was not obliging, nor was he amused when one of them flashed him the middle finger. He wondered if they were the same Salvadoran punks he had just yelled at in the store for being boisterous. At the next stop light, as the Toyota pulled alongside, Victor rolled down his window and warned them in Spanish that his big van could do some damage to their little car. The kid on the passenger side just laughed and then showed Victor he had a gun. Not wanting to suggest he was intimidated, Victor reached for his baseball bat and held it up. The light turned green, and the Toyota sped off. Victor, thinking the encounter was over, turned the corner onto Wilson Boulevard and pulled into the parking lot behind his building.

He was driving an old Dodge Ram cargo van he had bought from someone for three hundred dollars. He actually paid for it with nickels, dimes, and pennies he had been collecting for years in a plastic barrel. "Are you joking?" the man said as Victor set the barrel down. "You're going to pay me with this?"

"It's money, man," Victor said. "There's your three hundred bucks, right there." Nothing in his life had come easy.

As he climbed out of the van, Victor noticed that the red Toyota had circled around the block and pulled into the apartment parking lot behind him. The punks in the car were either unwilling to let anyone get away with disrespecting them or they needed to demonstrate their toughness as young gang members. Two had gotten out of the car and were walking toward Victor. One of them, wearing a black bandanna, had a gun in his hand. Without warning, he fired two quick shots at Victor, one of them hitting the van's doorpost, inches from where Victor was standing. He dove back into the vehicle headfirst, just as the kid fired a third round, this time cracking the windshield. But cargo vans have no windows on the side, and Victor was now out of the shooter's sight. He slid over to the passenger side, opened the door, and jumped out, taking cover behind a dumpster. Seeing the punks heading back to their car, Victor dashed around to the front of his building.

When the shooting happened, Rhina was making sandwiches and the boys were playing video games. It was a blustery mid-December day, but the sun was out, and Victor had promised his sons he would take them to the park when he got home, as he did every chance he had. As many as a dozen other boys would tag along. Victor had played recreational league soccer back in Bolivia, and even though he was working two and sometimes three jobs, he always found time to give his boys and their friends a little coaching, something few other fathers in the neighborhood bothered to do. He was fit and fun, and the boys loved that he played with them.

The minute Victor opened the door that day, Rhina and the boys knew something was wrong. With the TV on, they hadn't heard the gunshots, but Victor looked disheveled and faint. He had lost his shoes in the mad scramble to get away and was standing in his stocking feet. The green jacket he wore had a large dark stain on one side, and as he took it off everyone saw that his white shirt was covered with blood. Rhina screeched.

"Oh," Victor said. "I got shot." With the adrenaline rush, he hadn't felt a thing, but now he did, and he sank limply into a chair.

"Call the police," he said. Rhina was too upset and still had trouble with English, so Victor Jr. made the call. An ambulance arrived a few minutes later, but the EMTs didn't even get out of the cab. Victor Jr. and Álvaro ran out frantically to say their dad was inside and bleeding heavily, but the EMTs said the rule in a case like this was they couldn't do anything until police were on the scene.

America was such a strange place.

5

A FAMILY FROM LIBYA

Thirty years later, having taught about two thousand other high school students, Sherry Morgan could still remember exactly where Esam Omeish sat in her biology class. She saw him at his desk a few rows back, a dark-haired boy in glasses, following her every word, always attentive, always listening. She couldn't stop glancing at him, because the look on Esam's face revealed whether her lecture was making sense. He was one of the quietest students in the class, but without a word he would acknowledge everything she said.

Esam had come to the United States from Libya with his family in 1982 at the age of fifteen, speaking minimal English. The adjustment to J. E. B. Stuart High School had not been easy, but Morgan's classroom was one place he felt comfortable. Learning came easily to him—back in Libya, he placed third countrywide on a middle school graduation exam—and biology involved the same concepts no matter the language in which it was taught. He studied for hours every night, half on his homework and half on his English, often going through *The Washington Post* with an Arabic-English dictionary alongside. In Sherry Morgan, an environmental biologist who took up teaching for the joy of it, he had someone who recognized his intellectual aptitude and went out of her way to support him. She started him and other immigrant students in a textbook written at the fourth grade level, but when she saw how quickly Esam was mastering the material, she got him moved into her regular biology class, with native English speakers. Even there he did well, and by the end of his senior year he was in an Advanced Placement course, out-performing his fellow students. Eager to learn and always well pre-pared, Esam was the kind of students teachers yearn to have in their classrooms, and with his Middle Eastern background and worldly experience, he was one of Sherry Morgan's all-time favorites. "You are truly one of the best and most interesting students I have ever taught," she wrote in his high school yearbook, which he treasured.

Esam chose to concentrate on his schoolwork in part because he found the rest of his high school experience unsettling. Much of what went on at J. E. B. Stuart clashed with his relatively conser-vative upbringing in Libya and his beliefs as a Muslim. He had not mixed with girls since he left elementary school, and suddenly he found himself in a culture that seemed to celebrate promiscuity. He could not relate to the high school sports scene or the pep rallies and cheerleading that accompanied it, and because the Quran frowned on alcohol, Esam avoided the partying and drinking that passed for social life in the J. E. B. Stuart world. To the extent he participated in extracurricular activities in high school, it was with the Math Team, the Science Club, the National Honor Society, and other groups that brought together students who shared his academic in-clination. When one student invited him to join a group going to see an Iron Maiden concert, he initially agreed, wanting to show he could get along with the guys, but he backed out when he realized it was a heavy metal group of long-haired, tattooed rockers who employed violent imagery and used copious amounts of fake blood in their stage shows. He did attend a boating party organized by a friend from biology class, but with all the beer and the bikini-clad girls, Esam felt uncomfortably out of his element.

His closest high school friends were other immigrants like himself, of whom there were many. During Esam's years at J. E. B. Stuart, about a third of the students enrolled at the Fairfax County school came from outside the United States. He spent most of his time with Doug Nguyen, an outgoing kid from Vietnam who often turned to Esam for help with his biology schoolwork, and with Steve Hughes, who was born in Ghana. Neither was Muslim, although Esam felt that Steve, as an African Christian, shared some of his conservative values. Doug, on the other hand, was always pushing Esam to get out more. He had his own car, a Mustang, and often volunteered weekend excursions to the movies or the nearby Tysons Corner shopping mall. Esam sometimes went along, though of the three he was the serious one. By the time of his high school graduation, he already had announced his plans to do premed studies at Georgetown University. In their yearbook farewell notes to him, his friends emphasized how much they respected Esam's determination to succeed. "One of these days, we might work in the same office," Doug wrote. "You'll be there from 9 to 5 as a doctor, and I'll be there from 5 o'clock on as the janitor."

Esam's school discipline came in part from his father. Salem Omeish was an economist, trained on a Libyan government scholarship at Ain Shams University in Cairo and then at American University in Washington, and he took his profession seriously. His schooling in Egypt came at a time when many university students there were secretly involved in the Muslim Brotherhood organization, but with its promotion of "Islamic socialism" and its opposition to the established order, the Brotherhood was seen (and forcefully suppressed) by the Egyptian government as subversive, and Salem kept his distance from the movement. His training and family background inclined him instead to public service and to the West. In 1954, during the reign of King Idris, Salem went to work at the Finance Ministry in Tripoli, and over the next fifteen years, the Libyan government sent him routinely to the United States, with assignments either at the United Nations in New York or the Libyan embassy in Washington. As a result of those trips, Salem became fluent in English and was exposed firsthand to life in America, but he remained a patriot and always returned to Libya. In 1963, at the age of thirty-one, he married a fifteen-year-old girl from Trip- oli, Samira Elyazigi, after first getting permission from her father, a school principal. Samira had not yet finished the ninth grade.

The arrangement of the wedding was in accord with the na- tional custom, but times were changing. Salem and Samira prayed more or less regularly and fasted during Ramadan; beyond that they were not overly religious. While Samira's mother and grandmother both wore a *furashiya,* a white robe that covered them from head to toe, younger Libyan women like Samira generally dressed in West- ern style and left their hair uncovered. The 1960s was a decade of greater freedom around the world, and Jacqueline Kennedy was setting international fashion standards. Like other women of her age, Samira took pride in her hairstyle and wore dresses cut above the knee. During her short stay in Washington while her husband was doing graduate study, she learned to drive a car and manage her household affairs, despite obstacles. Speaking little English and frustrated that Arabic speakers or Muslim-friendly establishments were hard to find, she had to adapt. With no place to buy halal meat, for example, Samira did her shopping at a kosher market.

Salem was nearing completion of his PhD at American Univer- sity in 1971 when Colonel Muammar Qaddafi's two-year-old rev- olutionary government, desperate for professional expertise, called him back to serve as one of Libya's ten governors, assigned to the Bayda province. The appointment did not last long. Salem's brother was soon imprisoned due to his membership in an opposition party, and Salem resigned the governorship, taking a position in the Ivory Coast as a deputy manager of the African Development Bank. Salem by then was falling out of favor with the Qaddafi regime, and work opportunities were getting harder to find. When he moved his family back to Washington in December 1982, it was to work at the World Bank as an executive director in representation of Libya and other North African countries. Salem and Samira by then had eight children, six boys and two girls, and needed a lot more room than during their previous stay in the D.C. area. This time, they chose to live in the Virginia suburbs, renting a four-bedroom house between Seven Corners and Bailey's Crossroads, in the area where many other immigrants were also settling. Though he did not realize it at the time, Salem and his family had left Libya for good.

6

CROSSROADS

The bullet that hit Victor Alarcón passed cleanly through his shoulder without hitting a bone or artery. He was taken to a hospital but then discharged after just a few hours, his arm in a sling. His family was nevertheless traumatized by the incident. Rhina's sister Marilu hurried to the hospital where Victor was being treated and found Rhina and the boys in tears. The Fairfax County detective who investigated the case told Victor the incident was undoubtedly gang-related, but Victor already figured that. Within days, the police had three suspects in custody, though their apprehension was due to a separate incident that took place three days after Victor was shot. Once again, a red Toyota Celica was involved, and Victor told police the occupants of the vehicle looked like the same punks who had ambushed him. The three suspects, all teenagers, tried to carjack a man. He managed to escape, identified the three from a photo array, and testified against them in court. The prosecutor was convinced the same three were responsible for shooting Victor Alarcón, but he decided the carjacking made for a stronger case. All three were convicted. To his relief, Victor was saved from testifying against them.

Associates of the gangsters likely held a grudge. Six weeks after the shooting, the Alarcón apartment was burglarized while the family was away. The thieves stole stereo equipment and jewelry, including Victor and Rhina's wedding rings. But many of the items were personal, as if the intent was to humiliate the family and show that even their most intimate belongings were not safe: Rhina's pots and pans were taken, along with Victor's shoes, dirty clothes, and razor, even Mikey's baby wipes. Álvaro had nightmares for weeks afterward, dreaming that bad guys were breaking through the apartment windows, and he insisted on sleeping next to his parents' bed. Juan, Victor's friend, told him he had to get the family out of there. "If you don't, they'll kill you," Juan said. "They're going to try it again. You have to leave."

Rhina and Victor tried to be cheerful and reassuring around the apartment, but the older boys knew what was going on. While pretending to be concentrating on their video games, Álvaro and Victor Jr. could follow their parents' whispered conversations, and at night they could hear their mother crying in the next room.

"We have to move," Rhina would say. "I don't care if we don't have the money, we have to move. I don't want my kids to go through this. This is not why we came to this country."

The Alarcón family's first years in America included many of the elements that make the immigration experience painful. Victor, Rhina, their sons, and Rhina's sisters and mother all came to the country separately, not knowing when they could be reunited, a situation that frequently produces stress in immigrant families. In the early months, they had to share living quarters with others, another typical phenomenon that often brings conflict and can lead to a confrontation with the local housing authorities. They had little money, lacked medical insurance during vulnerable times, were unfamiliar with the bureaucracies that regulated daily life in their new country, struggled to find employment, and had to deal with transportation hassles. The language barrier was a constant problem, and their meager incomes forced them to settle in marginal neighborhoods where crime was a constant concern. Adapting to life in America meant overcoming all those obstacles and moving steadily forward, which the Alarcón family ultimately was able to do.

The governing authorities of the communities in which immigrants congregate cope with their own challenges, from the increased demand for public services to new law enforcement issues. Few places were more dramatically affected than Virginia's Fairfax County. Settled by tobacco-growing colonists in the early eighteenth century, the county through its first 250 years was largely rural. Though George Washington's Mount Vernon estate lay within its borders, the county was more identified with the South than with the nation's capital and points to the north. In 1950, fewer than 100,000 people lived in the county, and the population was 90 percent white. The remainder was almost entirely African American, and those residents were isolated in all-black neighborhoods. Just 145 people in the county fell into the "other" category. Over the next half century, all that changed, with the county experiencing three major transformations: urbanization, desegregation, and immigration. Each of the three phenomena was disruptive; the combination, in quick succession, was all the county could bear. Communities, like people, experience growth pains and identity crises, and Fairfax County was being reshaped with a speed and thoroughness it could barely manage. The way it responded and the way it incorporated its new population might suggest how America could handle the challenges it had taken on by opening its doors as wide as it did after 1965.

The Hispanic families who occupied most of the apartments in the Willston complex in the early 1990s were only the latest of the various tenant populations drawn to the development since it was completed in 1952. For the Alarcóns and the others who settled there, beauty was not a consideration. The entire complex of 1,500 units, stretching block after block, consisted of identical two- and three-story buildings set tightly against each other, so drab and nondescript in appearance that area developers referred to the Willston apartments simply as "the red-brick buildings." They were garden units with no gardens. But the rents were relatively cheap, and in the close Virginia suburbs of Washington there were always people in need of affordable housing. The apartments were built by William Ingersoll, a dentist from Salt Lake City who moved to Washington in 1933 and made a fortune in real estate in the years after World War II, when veterans were returning to civilian employment in the Washington area and young women were flocking to the nation's capital to take jobs as "government girls" in the expanding federal bureaucracy.

The District of Columbia was just a few miles to the east, across the Potomac River, and the area around the Willston complex was soon booming. Three major roads—Wilson Boulevard, Leesburg Pike, and Arlington Boulevard—intersected within a few blocks of the apartment complex, and two more streets originated at that crossing, meaning the intersection actually had seven corners. The surrounding area had been farmland through the end of the 1940s, but growth had then come quickly. In 1953, two D.C. businessmen purchased thirty-three unimproved acres adjacent to the Seven Corners intersection from the descendants of Frederick Foote, a former slave who had bought the land in 1864, and two years later they began building a shopping mall at the site. When it opened a year later, the Seven Corners Shopping Center was the biggest in the Washington area and one of the first indoor malls in the country. Buses ran in all directions from the Seven Corners hub, so nearby residents could easily commute to work. More red-brick buildings went up along Leesburg Pike, down to Bailey's Crossroads (named for circus impresario Hachaliah Bailey, who once had a farm nearby) and west from there to Annandale and distant parts of Fairfax County.

With the D.C. metropolitan area spreading outward, previously empty land was soon taken up by used car lots, gas stations, and convenience stores. The growth in government employment, especially in defense-related areas, was a major factor in the development. By 1970, the county population was approaching a half million, and the ethnic explosion was about to occur. Over the next three decades, the white percentage would plummet. While the African American population in Fairfax County remained relatively stable, the foreign-born share during that period would increase sevenfold, double the growth of the immigrant population in the country as a whole. The 1980 census showed that 9 percent of Fairfax residents had been born outside the country; ten years later, the figure was nearly 16 percent. By 2000, one out of four county residents was an immigrant. Students in the Fairfax County schools spoke more than one hundred languages. The Mason Magisterial District, an administrative unit of the county that included Seven Corners, Bailey's Crossroads, and Annandale, was then the most ethnically diverse of the nine county districts, with immigrants making up more than 40 percent of the population. The used car lots were replaced by halal butchers, Asian fish markets, and pupuserías. The movement of people into, around, and out of suburban Virginia communities during these years jolted and reshaped the region so thoroughly and quickly as to make the area a testing ground for cultural change in America.

First came the trauma of racial desegregation, an experience that would have been wrenching even without the subsequent immigrant wave. Up through the 1960s, African American life in the region was still bounded by discrimination, both formal and informal. Margaret Foote Jackson, who sold her share of her father's property to the developers of the Seven Corners Shopping Center, discovered when the mall opened that as a black woman she was not entirely welcome there. Garfinckel's, the upscale department store that anchored one end of the mall, was known for its attentive service, but its idea of exclusivity was to exclude black shoppers. The store employed no black clerks until the 1960s, and no black woman was allowed to use the store's dressing rooms. If Margaret Jackson went home and found that the Garfinckel's dress she had purchased did not fit, she could not return it. As a result of the store's policies, many African American shoppers boycotted Garfinckel's, but it is not likely the management much cared. The store's target customers came from the leafy white neighborhoods of Sleepy Hollow and Lake Barcroft, not from the black neighborhoods nor from the red-brick apartment buildings where working-class whites lived and where immigrants would soon move in.

African Americans in northern Virginia lived in segregated enclaves, most of them physically separated from the surrounding white-only areas. One such settlement was in the area of Bailey's Crossroads, near the old Hachaliah Bailey property. In 1876, a former slave named John Bell purchased fifty empty acres there with money he had earned working for the government. The all-black Bailey's community that developed from Bell's landholding was accessible by a single street, Lacy Boulevard, which dead-ended in the center of the neighborhood. (Bill collectors and policemen could often be seen waiting at the Lacy corner, knowing the residents all had to enter and exit at that single point.) Like other historically black neighborhoods in northern Virginia, the community for many years lacked the paved streets, sewer lines, or public water supply provided routinely to white neighborhoods.

Public schooling practices were just as discriminatory. For decades, Fairfax County authorities offered education to African American children only if the local community provided a school site. The black teachers were paid significantly less than white teachers, and the "colored" schools often lacked indoor plumbing, central heating, and decent teaching materials. In the Bailey's community, the first school was a three-room wood structure built in the early 1920s on property belonging to a woman named Lillian Hopkins

Carey. She had some college education, so Fairfax authorities made her the teacher. The school had only outdoor toilets, and the water supply was a pump in the schoolyard. Heat was provided by a wood- and coal-burning stove on which Mrs. Carey cooked soup for her students. The boys kept the fire going, and the girls were responsible for cleaning the classrooms. The textbooks provided by the county had been used previously in the white schools, and they often came with missing pages or other mutilations. The Bailey's school was closed in 1948, after which the students were bused to the new James Lee Negro Elementary School in the neighboring city of Falls Church. At the time, Fairfax County authorities saw no need to offer black children any schooling beyond seventh grade. The first secondary school for black students, Luther Jackson High School, opened only in the fall of 1954.

Four months earlier, the U.S. Supreme Court had ruled unanimously in *Brown v. Board of Education* that separate schools for black and white students were "inherently unequal" and therefore unconstitutional, and the school systems in Washington, D.C., and suburban Maryland were moving quickly toward integration. Segregationists controlled the government in Virginia, however, and they were determined to defy the *Brown* decision. "If we can organize the southern states for massive resistance to this order," declared Harry F. Byrd, Virginia's senior U.S. senator, "I think in time the rest of the country will realize that racial integration is not going to be accepted in the South." Under a plan approved by the Virginia legislature, the state mandated the closure of any school under an integration order and cut off state funding for any school that attempted on its own to integrate. When the school board in Arlington County dared to propose a modest integration plan, the state board of education in Richmond rejected the plan and fired the entire Arlington board. In Fairfax County, the authorities did not merely refuse to comply with the Supreme Court's order; they defiantly named their next two high schools after Confederate army generals—J. E. B. Stuart and Robert E. Lee.

The contrast between Virginia's "massive resistance" stance and the willingness in Maryland and D.C. to proceed with integration highlighted the legacy of racism in Virginia, where racial intermarriage would be illegal until 1967, when the ban was overturned by the Supreme Court. Blacks in Virginia had to pay a poll tax to vote, and state law mandated segregated seating on buses and street cars. Until 1949, when a court overturned the law, blacks commuting from Washington to Virginia had to move to the rear of the bus when they crossed the Key Bridge over the Potomac. Through most of the 1950s and 1960s, northern Virginia was represented in the U.S. Congress by two ardent segregationists, Democrat Howard Smith and Republican Joel Broyhill. Smith was determined to use his position as chairman of the House Rules Committee to block civil rights legislation from coming to the House floor. "The Southern people," Smith said, "have never accepted the colored race as a race of people who had equal intelligence" with whites. In 1956, backed by seventy-six other representatives and by nineteen senators, Smith introduced the "Southern Manifesto," decrying the *Brown* desegregation ruling as an "encroachment on the rights reserved to the States" and commending "those States that have declared the intention to resist forced integration by any lawful means." As a Republican, Joel Broyhill belonged to the party of Dwight Eisenhower, the president who appointed Chief Justice Earl Warren, the author of the *Brown* decision, and who sent federal troops to Little Rock to protect black students trying to integrate Arkansas schools. But Broyhill signed Smith's Southern Manifesto, and with Smith and virtually all other southerners in Congress, he voted to kill the 1964 Civil Rights Act.

Wanda Summers, the great-granddaughter of Bailey's pioneer John Bell, came home one evening in 1967 after being away at college and found to her astonishment that while she was gone, the county had installed street lights along the length of Lacy Boulevard. No other street in the neighborhood was lit, but Bailey's activists had finally managed to persuade the Fairfax authorities to move on one of their long-standing requests. Virtually every quality-of-life upgrade for African Americans in the Bailey's community had come only in response to their agitation. When Wanda was a girl, Bailey's residents were still collecting their water from a local spring where crawfish and tadpoles swam. After community complaints, a public water main was installed, along with sewer and gas lines. Other basic improvements came much later. Until the 1970s, many of the houses in the Bailey's neighborhood still faced dirt streets.

Like other Bailey's children, Wanda was bused as a first grader to James Lee Negro Elementary in Falls Church, but in 1956 the neighborhood for the first time got a modern elementary school of its own, built on the site of John Bell's original homestead and named Lillian Carey Elementary in honor of the community's first teacher. The facility was modern, and the Bailey's parents had few complaints about the quality of the instruction, but it was still a segregated institution. Fairfax County authorities did not end their policy of maintaining officially separate schools for black and white students until 1961, seven years after *Brown,* and even then they stopped short of actually integrating their schools. Instead, the authorities gave African American families the option of enrolling their children in white-only schools, if they were willing to accept the transportation difficulties and the inevitable hostility. Only a handful took advantage, but Wanda's parents were among them. On the first day of school that September, she and her younger brother Clarence walked out to Columbia Pike to catch the school bus to nearby Glasgow Elementary. Once aboard, Wanda headed to the first empty seat.

"It's saved," said the white girl sitting alongside. Moving down the aisle, Wanda and Clarence got the same response from everyone, along with cold stares, until they reached the back of the bus and sat by themselves. Wanda was a friendly and self-assured girl, and despite being one of just three or four black students in her grade, she eventually made friends with many of the white girls. But more struggles followed. In 1965, Wanda was among the first African American students to integrate J. E. B. Stuart High School in the Seven Corners area. The experience tested the strength of the transfer students, and several dropped out or asked to be assigned to other schools. The first blacks attending the school faced hostility from white students, especially those who formed clubs from which their black classmates were excluded.

Wanda would remember the injuries throughout her life. "The hardest thing was when kids you knew would pretend not to recognize you," she said, reflecting on her high school experience decades later. "They would be fine one-on-one, but when they were with their friends they would act like they didn't know you. I felt like I was invisible." But Wanda had learned early in her integration experience to deal with such slights, and her parents had taught her not to dwell on rude treatment from white classmates. "It's probably because they were hanging out with people who were against mingling," she said, as if it would have been foolish of her to expect anything different, given the times. It was Wanda's good fortune to have these experiences in an era when civil rights victories were being achieved all around her. The forward movement of the 1950s and 1960s was apparent to all, and the sense that time was on their side encouraged the activists in the Bailey's community and across northern Virginia to continue to push for equality.

The opponents of integration, having lost the battle to maintain de jure segregation, remained determined to keep white and black students separated less formally, through de facto segregation and the denial of equal housing opportunity. The number of black families willing to send their children into unfriendly white neighborhoods for better education opportunities was limited, and virtually no white families volunteered to send their children to historically black schools. True school integration would come only with increased busing, an issue that Virginia's conservative white leaders grabbed as the next cause to oppose. Republican congressman Joel

Broyhill, whose district included the Seven Corners, Bailey's Cross-roads, and Annandale communities of Fairfax County, thundered against forced busing every time he had a chance.

"Do not underestimate the seriousness of this invasion of your rights and freedom of choice," Broyhill told members of American Legion Post 139 in September 1971. He acknowledged that local governments could no longer close a public school to a student on the basis of his or her race, but he insisted there was no evil in de facto segregation. "This means simply that people want to live next to the people they choose," he said, "often of the same race, interests, or ethnic origin. . . . De facto segregation is a fact of life, and it involves the freedom of choice of where you want to live." Such reasoning, of course, did not recognize the reality that for many African Americans in the Bailey's community and other black neighborhoods, the choice of where to live was not yet one they enjoyed.

Northern Virginia, however, was evolving. In 1965, Harry Byrd left the U.S. Senate for health reasons, and a year later his fellow Virginia segregationist Howard Smith lost a primary race to a Democrat who mobilized black voters behind his candidacy. Smith and Byrd and other segregationists represented the conservative agrarian interests that had long prevailed in Virginia, but the northern counties were increasingly connected to metropolitan Washington, and local politicians had to adapt or become irrelevant. Joel Broyhill stayed in office until 1974, but then lost his seat to a liberal Democrat, Joseph Fisher.

Emboldened by the achievements of the civil rights movement, African Americans were discovering their political power. In 1971, civic activists in the Bailey's neighborhood and two other black communities filed a lawsuit in federal court against Fairfax County, claiming racial discrimination in the delivery of public services. Citing the Equal Protection Clause of the Fourteenth Amendment, the activists asked the court to compel the county to pave the dirt roads in their neighborhoods and provide drainage, curbs, gutters, and sidewalks. In an out-of-court settlement nine months later, county authorities agreed to upgrade six streets immediately and seventy-six more within a three-year period, and they recognized "a continued responsibility to maintain these streets in a fair and equitable manner." When the county later backtracked on some of its commitments, the Bailey's activists once again started showing up at public meetings of the county Board of Supervisors, demanding the overdue improvements.

A county survey carried out in 1975 with federal funds showed they had good reason to complain. The neighborhood was found to have "low improvement values" in comparison to the surrounding white communities and "inadequate" roads, curbs, sidewalks, storm sewers, and recreation opportunities. When local leaders learned that federal funds were available for community development, they challenged the Board of Supervisors one night at a public hearing to spend the money on an improvement plan for the Bailey's community. At one o'clock in the morning, following hours of testimony from Bailey's residents about their plight, the board approved a major development plan, allocating funds to improve the streets and build a community center on the old John Bell property, alongside the former Lillian Carey Elementary School. It would be the first community center in the neighborhood's one-hundred-year history and the board's approval of the project was met with shouts of joy from the residents who had crowded into the hearing room. The development plan approved that evening also called for the extension of Lacy Boulevard through a park on the south edge of the neighborhood and out the other side to give direct access to the city of Alexandria. Within a year, the road was opened, apparently ending the humiliating separation of the Bailey's community from the surrounding area.

The victory was short-lived, however. Residents across the county line to the south were not happy to have their white neighborhood connected to the black neighborhood to the north, and they persuaded the city of Alexandria to erect a chain link fence across their end of Lacy Boulevard, reinstating the segregation of the two communities. It took nearly two years of negotiation and protest by Bailey's residents to get the street reopened.

For one hundred years, the Bailey's community and other black neighborhoods in Fairfax County had been neglected and marginalized. To the extent the residents got the improvements they deserved, from mail service to paved roads and street lights, it was the result of petition drives, public demonstrations, and organized pressure on government authorities. The struggles and the consequent achievements left the African American communities stronger and more unified. This sense of solidarity found symbolic expression in the new Bailey's Community Center. The building, with a gymnasium, a lounge, a kitchen, and several large meeting rooms, was as modern as any community center in Fairfax County, and it opened to grand celebration. The people had fought for the center, they had earned it, and it was theirs. The residents whose efforts were most critical to success—a retired U.S. Army colonel named Charles Robinson, Wanda Summers's cousin Houston Summers, Jr., and a veteran activist couple, Edward and Elizabeth Hall, all of them with deep family roots in the community—were treated as local heroes.

The Bailey's community and Fairfax County authorities were soon confronted by a new challenge, however, and they were caught unprepared. For decades, the top social issue in northern Virginia had literally been a black-and-white concern. Suddenly, new people of color were arriving: Asians, Middle Easterners, Africans, and Hispanics. They came in part because of war, revolution, and unrest in the developing world. More than any other country, the United States was willing to accept refugees from the affected areas. Another factor was the new, more liberal outlook of all those U.S. lawmakers who were enlightened by the civil rights movement. Neither race nor national origin, they had concluded, should be a determinative factor in the decision of who should be allowed to immigrate, and so the doors opened.

The only foreign-born students at J. E. B. Stuart High School when Wanda Summers attended were a few Cubans whose families had escaped Fidel Castro's Cuba. By the time Wanda's own children reached Stuart, the school was far more diverse. First came the Vietnamese students, the sons and daughters of South Vietnamese military officers and government officials who fled when their country fell into the hands of North Vietnamese Communists. They were followed by the children of Iranians who had gone into exile in the aftermath of Ayatollah Khomeini's 1979 revolution. That was also the year the Soviet Union invaded Afghanistan, producing another wave of refugees, many of whom chose to live in the United States and settled in northern Virginia. Beginning in 1980, the civil war in El Salvador drove many people north to escape the fighting, and the exodus from that country continued for years to come. All these people, outcasts from Cold War conflicts around the world, found the suburbs around America's capital to be a good place to seek refuge.

Implementation of the 1965 Immigration Act produced still more newcomers, especially from Asia, the Middle East, and other areas where U.S. immigration quotas had previously been highly restrictive. Most were of limited means and they settled in and around working-class and minority neighborhoods, especially those in Fairfax County's Mason District, the closest to Washington of the county's nine districts. The red-brick apartments in the Willston area of Seven Corners and the other low-rent buildings up and down Leesburg Pike and along Columbia Pike and out to Annandale were soon filled with immigrant tenants and their children.

The foreigner influx provided a coda to the dramatic desegregation narrative. Barely ten years had passed since Fairfax County authorities faced the stress associated with racial mingling in their schools, and now they had to deal with new education burdens that were just as vexing. Students were arriving with foreign languages and different learning styles. School officials had difficulty communicating with them and their parents, and teachers and counselors had little experience dealing with issues associated with the immigrant students' home environments. The change in the school population required a significant shift of resources into English as a Second Language (ESL) programs, a capability the schools had not previously needed.

Some African American parents felt their children suffered as a result of the attention going to the immigrant students and the money spent on ESL initiatives. "We were all concerned," Wanda Summers recalled years later. She was the PTA president at Parklawn Elementary, about a mile west of her Bailey's community, where many African American children were enrolled. "I can remember many conversations," she said. "It was, 'What about us?' We were finally getting accepted, and all of a sudden here comes another group, and they qualify as a minority. What did that mean for our kids?" Her advice to other parents who worried that their children got inadequate attention was that they engage more with teachers and administrators and advocate for their children.

But some parents were less understanding, and in the African American community, some resentment of the immigrants was inevitable. The relatively low cost of housing in the Bailey's community soon made it attractive to bargain-conscious immigrants. The new residents had little knowledge of the rich community history nor appreciation of the struggles that had been necessary to bring the neighborhood up to county standards, and when Hispanics and North Africans and other immigrants began showing up at the Bailey's Community Center, they were not always welcome. To some of the longtime Bailey's activists, it seemed like the immigrants were quick to attend community picnics or take advantage of the after-school and recreation programs at the center, but when it came time to do volunteer work or participate in community meetings, they did not show up. According to the original development plan for the Bailey's neighborhood, the community center was meant "for recreational use by the residents of the neighborhood," but some of the most frequent users of the facilities were not even Bailey's residents. When community representatives complained to county authorities, they were reminded that the county had built the center and covered its expenses and that it was open to all Fairfax County residents, no matter their county address.

A decade earlier, Congressman Broyhill, defending the notion of segregated neighborhoods, had argued that "people want to live next to the people they choose, often of the same race, interests, or ethnic origin." There was indeed some comfort in that arrangement, but with the mix of colors, languages, and national backgrounds that was developing in Fairfax County, conflict was inevitable, and the residents and the county authorities had to deal with it.

When a group of Vietnamese Buddhists in 1984 sought approval to build a pagoda on Columbia Pike in Annandale, Fairfax County planners and nearby residents objected, with the planners saying it would not be "harmonious" with nearby houses and churches. One Annandale resident wrote the zoning board to express concern that the Vietnamese would use the pagoda "for the housing of refugees." A proposal from a group of Lebanese immigrants to build a Druze place of worship in Annandale drew even more protest. Druze militia fighters at the time were playing a key role in the Lebanese civil war, often in alliance with the Palestine Liberation Organization, and that Middle East association was enough to stir concern in Annandale.

"I really don't know much about them," one woman told the zoning board, "but just the word 'Druze' at this time is enough to make anyone have second thoughts." Another resident said he worried somebody would try to bomb the place. "That would not be totally unheard of, given what's going on in Lebanon," he said.

"Nobody wants their neighborhood blown up." In the end, the Fairfax Board of Zoning Appeals approved both the Buddhist and Druze requests. The county supervisor representing the Mason District, Thomas Davis, said any petition from a religious group to build a place of worship had to be judged "on its land-use merits and not on the fact that the neighbors don't like the church. You cannot deny an application on the fact that people don't like the religion."

That principle was put to an especially stern test in 1984, when county authorities received a proposal to build a mosque in the Seven Corners area, squarely in Supervisor Davis's Mason District. At the time, the only mosque in Washington, D.C., was the Islamic Center on Massachusetts Avenue, along the stretch known as Embassy Row. Built in the 1950s with financing from the governments of those Islamic countries that were represented in Washington, it featured white marble columns and turquoise floor tiles and was the largest and most lavishly furnished mosque in the Western Hemisphere. The mosque was designed to serve Muslim diplomats and their families, but many of the worshippers by the early 1980s were immigrants and visiting students, and in 1982, a group of radicals occupied the mosque and demanded that it take political stands on the Iranian revolution and the Arab-Israeli conflict. In March 1983, with the protest still raging, the Islamic Center temporarily closed.

The proposal for a new mosque in the Seven Corners area grew out of that protest. Frustrated by the strife that had paralyzed the only mosque in town, a group of young Muslim men started organizing their own prayer services and Islamic discussion groups, gathering in apartments, private homes, and even local churches. One of their meeting places was a rented house in the Seven Corners area, where many of them lived. The house was on a large lot on Row Street in a residential neighborhood just off Leesburg Pike. It soon became a popular meeting place for many young Muslims in the D.C. area. During Ramadan and on other special occasions, the group prepared meals at the house, often roasting a lamb and cooking rice. With the help of the North American Islamic Trust, a Saudi-backed organization linked to the Muslim Students Association, the group purchased the house and the lot and announced plans to build a mosque there. It would be called "Dar Al-Hijrah," meaning "Place of Migration" in Arabic, and it was intended as a place of worship for Muslims who had migrated to the D.C. area. The architect for the project told the Board of Zoning Appeals that there were already thirty thousand Muslim immigrants living in northern Virginia and that the number was likely to grow in the years ahead.

Buddhists and Druze were controversial enough, Muslims even more so. Residents from the neighborhood where the mosque was to be built showed up in force at a public hearing before the zoning board, and most asked the board to reject the proposal. Many cited concerns about traffic and congestion, but others cited fighting in the Middle East and the prospect that construction of the mosque would carry those troubles to their Seven Corners neighborhood. The Muslims who wanted to build the mosque "may be the most peace-loving people in the world," one man wrote in a letter to the Fairfax authorities, "but there always seems to be a dissident group of Muslims that cause conflict." The Board of Zoning Appeals, on a 4–3 vote, nevertheless approved the mosque proposal. Mason supervisor Thomas Davis, though not a member of the zoning board, was again a decisive voice in support of the worshippers' request. "I could have blocked it," he said in an interview years later. A Republican moderate, Davis saw himself as a strong supporter of religious freedom, a view he attributed to his own Christian Science beliefs. "I remember when we tried to build a church, and they called us a cult," he said. "Certain things in life go to the core of who you are, and this was one of those core issues."

Thus was the origin of Dar Al-Hijrah, an institution that would play a central role in the life of the Muslim community in the D.C. area and produce some of the most prominent Muslim leaders in

America. It would also become the focus of controversy as a result of some of the individuals who worshipped there and an imam who preached there.

Salem Omeish, the economist from Libya, heard about the Muslim house on Row Street from a Libyan friend, Abdul Khadr Muttardi, whom he had gotten to know during one of his previous stays in the D.C. area. It was Muttardi who met the Omeish family at the airport when they arrived, and he helped them get settled. The house Salem rented for his family was just a few blocks from the place on Row Street, and Muttardi accompanied him and his sons there one day shortly after they arrived in America.

For the Omeish boys, it was a life-changing event, and they returned often. The discussions that took place on Row Street were less formal than anything they had encountered as students back in Libya; the worshippers were younger, and they were engaged intellectually and politically in Islam. The conversations were mostly in Arabic, and Esam and his brothers Mohammed and Emad felt immediately comfortable there. Their father was not sure what to think. Although the worshippers were not from the same group that demonstrated every Friday in front of the Islamic Center, several had activist backgrounds in their home countries, and some were affiliated with the Muslim Brotherhood. For that reason, Salem became uneasy as his sons began spending more time on Row Street. Though he was an observant Muslim, he had always kept a relatively low profile in his religious life. His wife's decision to start wearing a hijab after the move to America and his sons' decisions to spend time with the Dar Al-Hijrah crowd were ones they made on their own. In Salem's experience, an association with the Muslim Brotherhood had often brought trouble, even prison terms, and he urged his sons to be careful. He did not want any development in America to jeopardize his position back in Libya, because at that point he still intended to return there with his family.

7

A LIBYAN BOY IN AMERICA

Esam Omeish's parents had raised him in Libya as a good Muslim, but it was in America that his religion came to define him. In Libya, everybody he knew was a Muslim. Instruction in the Quran and Islamic Studies were part of the curriculum at his high school in Tripoli; in America, being a Muslim set him apart. At J. E. B. Stuart, there were many immigrant students like himself who spoke little or no English and whose life experiences were unlike anything their white American classmates had known. But Islam was something Esam shared with only a handful of other high school boys (including two from Saudi Arabia, two from Syria, one from Ethiopia, and Esam's older brothers, Mohammed and Emad), and it was largely because of his faith that Esam sometimes felt isolated in this new social setting. Some other young Muslim immigrants in his situation, wanting to be accepted in their high school crowd, turned away from their religion, but Esam's reaction was the opposite: He chose to embrace and explore Islam in ways he might never have done back in Libya, and his parents had relatively little to do with it.

Within months of their enrollment at J. E. B Stuart in January

1983, Esam and his brother Mohammed went to their high school principal, Glynn Bates, to ask whether they could be excused on Fridays to perform their prayers. They suggested finding some quiet place in the school where they would not be disturbed nor disturb others. No Muslim student had made such a request before, and Bates wasn't sure how to respond. To approve any religious service on school property during school hours might be seen as violating the separation of church and state. On the other hand, Bates knew that the top challenge at her high school was to handle the diversity of her student population, and that required great sensitivity to the cultural and religious traditions they brought with them. No high school in Fairfax County had as large a share of immigrant students as Stuart had. If Bates and her staff were to have an environment where all their students felt secure and respected, they would have to make some accommodations that other high schools in the county would not need to consider. After discussions with her staff, Bates decided that the Omeish boys and their fellow Muslim students could organize their own Friday prayer service at the high school during the lunch hour, and she approved their use of a small conference room alongside the school library for that purpose. It would not be an official school activity, though Bates did alert teachers that the students might be a few minutes late to their next class.

Bates and her assistant principal, Nancy Weisgerber, were model administrators in their management of their school—roving the hallways, engaging with students in the cafeteria, riding along on bus routes, and hosting neighborhood meetings with parents—but ethnic and racial tensions were inevitable. For the first few years after its 1959 opening, the school had exclusively served the white and upper-middle-class families who lived around Lake Barcroft or in the nearby Sleepy Hollow or Ravenwood neighborhoods. Integration brought a minority of African American students to the school, and the hostility they encountered in the early years, from white staff members as well as from white students, triggered several violent incidents, some requiring police intervention. After an underground newspaper at the school reported in 1971 that the high school principal had been caught on tape blaming a cockroach problem at the school on the enrollment of black students, he was forced to resign. The biggest demographic changes at the high school, however, came in the middle 1970s with the arrival of foreign-born families, many of whom settled in the low-rent Willston and Culmore apartments around Seven Corners and up and down Leesburg Pike. The impact on J. E. B. Stuart was immediate, because those red-brick buildings for the most part were occupied previously by single tenants or young couples. Now they were taken up by families with teenaged children, and in many cases eight or more people were squeezing into a single unit to save money.

The Vietnamese students showed up at Stuart when it was still recovering from the trauma of racial integration, and they encountered hostility similar to what the black students had faced. Some of the first Vietnamese to enroll at the school were forced to walk a gauntlet as they entered the back gate. A few white students threw eggs at them and demanded that they press their hands together and bow. The Soviet invasion of Afghanistan, the revolution in Iran, and the wars in Central America produced more people fleeing from violent conflict. There were several resettlement programs in northern Virginia, and as a result no school in the Washington, D.C., area was more affected by foreign wars than J. E. B. Stuart. Teachers at the school wryly noted how they could predict an influx: Whenever anything had happened somewhere in the world, a year later a new group of refugee students would show up at their front door.

By the time the Omeish brothers arrived in January 1983, J. E. B. Stuart was in turmoil. The staff that year documented eighteen major brawls at the school, almost all of them sparked by racial or ethnic conflict, in addition to smaller fights that occurred almost every day in the parking lot, the gymnasium, or the cafeteria. The school, which had had one of the largest shares of upper-class students in Fairfax County, now had the greatest percentage receiving free or reduced lunches. Of the 1,400 students, over 500 were foreign-born. The largest group came from Vietnam, but sixty-five countries were represented among the immigrant students, and they spoke more than forty languages. Half of them were receiving instruction in English as a Second Language, and many—like Esam and his brothers—had little or no English language capability when they arrived. The ESL classrooms were clustered at one end of the building, which meant the immigrants were physically segregated. Many Asian students preferred to sit on the floor, and when they congregated in the hallway, speaking Vietnamese or Korean or Chinese among themselves, trouble would often ensue. Other students passing by, hearing whispers in a foreign language, would assume that someone had made a negative remark about them, and the stage was set for a confrontation.

The school cafeteria, where students generally chose to sit with others who spoke their language, was often the scene of fights. Teenagers brought up in war zones, with vivid memories of going hungry and unaccustomed to the notion of standing in a line, did not always comprehend or respect cafeteria rules, and shoving matches were frequent. Asian students were often ridiculed for the way they ate, hunched over their plates or bowls and spurning the use of forks and knives, utensils with which they were not familiar. Gang loyalties or rivalries that originated outside the school would carry over inside, and some students carried knives in their pockets for their own protection. Half of the fights documented at J. E. B. Stuart in 1982 involved minority-on-minority conflict, with especially nasty encounters between Central American and Vietnamese students and between Koreans and African Americans. Each group had its own fighting style. Many Korean boys, for example, knew Tae Kwon Do and could easily intimidate other students with their guttural shouts and quick kicks.

In an effort to contain the tensions at Stuart, Fairfax school authorities installed two "human relations specialists" at the school—Thu Bui, a former commander in the South Vietnamese navy, and Albert Santiago, a Spanish-speaking crime prevention officer with the Fairfax County Police Department. After a big brawl in December 1982, Bui and Santiago organized a new club, Students Against a Violent Environment (SAVE), and required any student who had been involved in a fight to join. The club sessions were often tense, with students glaring at each other across a table and giving each other the middle finger when Bui or Santiago were not looking. Glynn Bates, who had become principal just two months earlier, resisted the temptation to suspend or expel students who were involved in fighting, urging teachers and counselors to identify the source of conflict instead and work to resolve it.

The Fairfax police at the time were beginning to take an aggressive approach with gangs, often parking their cruisers just beyond the Stuart parking lot and monitoring the after-school traffic. Vietnamese gangs were active in the Seven Corners community, and Vietnamese boys came to Thu Bui with complaints that the police were stopping them arbitrarily. A mild-mannered man, slightly built and no more than five feet tall, Bui nevertheless carried himself with the quiet confidence he had acquired during his military career and war experience in Vietnam, and he commanded respect from all the students with whom he dealt. He had become proficient in Tae Kwon Do, judo, and other martial arts as a young man in Vietnam, and although he never used those skills to break up a fight at J. E. B. Stuart, he did demonstrate them once during a previous teaching experience in another school. Facing especially rowdy and disruptive students, he changed the classroom climate immediately one day by bringing in three pieces of wood, laying them across a stack of books in front of the class, and splitting each with a swift chop of his bare hand. During an especially bad period at Stuart, Bui and Santiago organized a field trip for the students in their SAVE group, taking them to inner-city neighborhoods in Washington and Philadelphia to show them what was happening in other violence-plagued schools. In the places they visited, the doors were locked at 8 a.m., armed policemen were posted on each floor, and all the windows were covered by bars. If the fighting did not end at Stuart, the students were told, their school would soon look the same. The visits had the intended effect, at least for a time.

The conflict resolution efforts did not always work, of course. Glynn Bates never forgot the time she brought two boys, one from Vietnam and the other from El Salvador, into her office after they had been caught fighting in the lunch line. She had them sit next to each other, and when one would try to defend himself to her, she would stop him. "Don't talk to me," she said. "Look at him and tell him," pointing to the boy alongside.

She thought she was making headway when the Vietnamese boy turned again to her and said, "Can I say something else?" Of course, she said.

"He think if we get into it again, it be okay, but it not be," the Vietnamese boy said. "I will kill him."

For Esam Omeish, the environment at his high school was one more reason to keep a low profile and focus on his academic work. The daily fistfights and the ethnic insults hurled so freely around the school, however, did not make Esam regret his father's decision to bring his family to America, even after his own sister, Salwa, was taunted when, as a ninth grader, she showed up at the school in a white hijab. Despite all he saw at J. E. B. Stuart, Esam could not imagine how a school in his own country or elsewhere in the Middle East, or in Europe, or anywhere besides America, could have coped nearly as well with a population like Stuart's, with new students arriving almost every week all year long from countries around the world, some unable to communicate outside their family, many traumatized by war, and others in conditions of poverty. He was impressed by the seriousness with which the Stuart staff took their educative mission under the circumstances and how much care and thought went into their efforts to manage the cross-cultural challenges they faced every day.

Esam's own personal triumph was the speed with which he became proficient in English and able to excel in advanced classes. It was exceedingly rare for immigrant students arriving with no

English to graduate in the same time frame as their native-born classmates. Esam did, and with straight A grades at the end. He gave all the credit to his teachers, especially those who specialized in helping the students for whom English was a second (or third) language. The ESL department at Stuart when Esam was a student there was the largest in the school, with fifteen full-time instructors. No other high school in Fairfax County came close, and no school proved more efficient at meeting the individual needs of the ESL students and moving them quickly into the mainstream. A big reason for this success was simply that there were so many ESL students that it was impossible to marginalize them. Given their share of the population, the school could not ignore them the way other schools could. Educating the immigrant students had to be a central mission of the school. Over many years, Stuart had some of the lowest average student achievement scores among Fairfax County high schools, but minority and ESL students did better at Stuart than anywhere else in the county.

Indeed, the focus on ESL students at Stuart arguably made for better teaching at the school in general. What mattered was a willingness to individualize the instruction, monitor each student's progress in mastering the necessary material, and then have the flexibility to adapt the curriculum and course schedule accordingly. New students with no English skills, classified in group A, spent three periods each day in ESL classes and three periods in non-academic classes such as music, art, or physical education. Those who showed improvement were moved as soon as possible into a B group, spending just one or two periods receiving ESL instruction. In the final stage, an ESL student would be mainstreamed for his or her entire class schedule, but with careful monitoring by the ESL staff. Esam Omeish, the quiet but attentive student in the middle row, was the star ESL student in his time at J. E. B. Stuart, advancing through the stages at a pace no one else could match.

By the time he was a senior, Esam had moved into a leadership role at Stuart, at least within the foreign-born group. Having persuaded Principal Bates to give Muslim students a time and place to pray on Fridays, Esam had organized a Muslim students group at Stuart and was now managing it. He was president of the International Club, a group that was made up both of immigrants and U.S.-born students who wanted to highlight and celebrate the foreign contributions to the Stuart community. Bates also asked Esam to serve on her student "cabinet," a group that gave her advice on policy issues from a student perspective.

After high school, Esam attended Georgetown University in Washington, a Jesuit institution. He completed a double major, biology and international relations, intending to go to medical school but also to follow in his father's footsteps and do international work. He still assumed he and the rest of his family would return to Libya, but his attachment to America was deepening. For all its faults, the country to Esam seemed able to absorb newcomers with an ease and grace that other countries lacked, though years would pass before Esam would fully appreciate his own high school experience. "I felt at home almost from the day I arrived," he said later. "Here I was, a little kid from Libya. I look different, I don't have the language. And yet I never really felt like a foreigner. Not for a single day did I feel I could not belong or would not succeed." Nor did his siblings. When their father finally made an effort to return the family to Libya, they all insisted on staying in America.

PART TWO

8

GOOD IMMIGRANTS, BAD IMMIGRANTS

The Alarcón family, the Omeish family, and the Seong and Kim families all arrived in the United States between 1982 and 1992, years of dramatic growth in America's foreign-born population. As immigrants, they all had or soon acquired legal status, and they sought and obtained U.S. citizenship. With the exceptions of Salem Omeish and Sun Yeop Kim (Mark Keam), they did not speak English prior to coming, and their integration into American life was inevitably hard and often frustrating. They came from lands that had not sent many people to the United States during the country's first two hundred years, and in some of their interactions with those who came before them, they (and others like them) had to deal with slurs and taunts and discrimination in their work and school environments. In the communities where they settled, they tested both America's reputation as a welcoming country and their own willingness and ability to acquire a new nationality. America might not come to signify the same thing to all of them, but to each of them, becoming "American" meant something important. Their stories and those of others in the new immigrant generation provided raw material for the debate over the cultural identity of the United States, a debate that dates to the country's founding.

The immigration story has always been more complicated in America than the mythmakers suggest. The founders' immigration policy was conceived with particular demographic and cultural goals in mind, and the question of which foreigners would be welcomed and under what conditions was a subject of intense discussion. The United States was, in the words of historian Aristide Zolberg, "A nation of immigrants, to be sure, but not just any immigrants." The founders actively recruited some to make the move to America, while scheming to deter others from coming. From their point of view, the best immigrants were the craftsmen, farmers, and artisans who could quickly and efficiently develop the American economy. On the other hand, they did their best to keep Britain from sending convicted felons and paupers to their shores. Benjamin Franklin complained that German immigrants were "generally of the most ignorant Stupid Sort of their own Nation," and he suggested that America would benefit "by excluding all Blacks and Tawneys," meaning the latter term to include most remaining people of color.

The more the immigrant profile diverged from the original Anglo colonist pattern, the more difficult was the acculturation process. By the middle of the nineteenth century, more of the new arrivals to America were poor and relatively unskilled, drawn to the new land largely by the prospect of work in the growing mining, manufacturing, and service sectors, especially in urban areas along the eastern seaboard. Among them were Polish steelworkers, Italian or Portuguese construction workers, Irish laborers and domestic workers, Slovak coal miners, and Jewish garment workers. The rapid growth in the foreign-born population inevitably met with resistance from established native-born elements. In Massachusetts, the secretary of the commonwealth reported to the state legislature in 1857 that the Irish immigrant population in the state was characterized by "wretchedness, beggary, drunkenness, deceit, lying, treachery, malice, superstition." The prevalence of such attitudes in the midcentury years gave rise to the anti-immigrant American Party, also dubbed the "Know-Nothing" party due to its members' refusal to answer questions about their movement. They had little electoral success, but their emergence as a political force foreshadowed the rise of other groups that would mobilize around hostility to immigrants.

The biggest official retreat from the promise of an America open to all came after tens of thousands of Chinese laborers came to California and other western states in the 1850s and 1860s. The first to arrive were drawn by the discovery of gold in 1848. Some were independent prospectors, joining all the others who hoped to find gold on their own and strike it rich. Others came to toil for meager wages as farm laborers, ditch diggers, fruit pickers, or mill workers. The Chinese immigrants were willing to take the jobs no one else wanted, and in the booming gold rush economy such jobs were plentiful. The construction of the western part of the transcontinental railroad from 1863 to 1869 opened thousands more jobs, and Chinese men proved to be hardy, healthy, and skillful workers. In largely white America, they stood out by their appearance, with their long hair braided into a single waist-length pigtail called a queue. They favored long, loose-fitting shirts or jackets and pajama-style trousers. On the railroad, the Chinese crews worked and lived separately, with their own food and cooks. Whereas the white workers, most of them Irish, lived off boiled beef and beans and potatoes provided by the railroad company, the Chinese bought their own foods, paying out of their pocket for dried oysters, bamboo sprouts, and seaweed, all imported from China, along with abalone, salted cabbage, noodles, pork, and chicken. In the cities, the Chinese resided almost exclusively in ethnic enclaves.

The isolation of the Chinese immigrant population was in good part a consequence of the racism they encountered in white America. Often referred to disparagingly as "Mongolian," Chinese workers were assigned to the hardest and most dangerous jobs and were paid substantially less than white workers. Those who came looking for jobs in the mines were often driven away by whites. Those who did find work were assessed a "foreigner tax" that most other immigrants did not have to pay. Anti-Chinese hostility increased sharply after 1869, when the transcontinental railroad was completed and as many as ten thousand Chinese laborers were displaced, forcing them into the general job market, where they competed with white, Mexican, and black workers. Racist union leaders encouraged unemployed white workers to direct their frustration against the Chinese.

The growth in the Chinese population was simply too much for this young immigrant nation to handle, and the U.S. government began to backtrack on its commitments to newcomers. In 1870, the U.S. Congress belatedly permitted African Americans to be naturalized as U.S. citizens, regardless of their place of birth, but it did not extend that same right to Asians. The 1876 Democratic Party platform lamented how Chinese immigration had "exposed our brethren of the Pacific coast to the incursions of a race not sprung from the same great parent stock [of the United States]." Six years later, Congress passed the Chinese Exclusion Act, which suspended the importation of Chinese labor altogether. The Exclusion Act formalized a division of U.S. immigrants into good and bad nationalities, and the distinction would only grow sharper in the next few years. Congressman Henry Cabot Lodge of Massachusetts, whose forebears arrived during colonial days, complained in 1891 that "the immigration of those races which . . . built up the United States and which are related to each other either by blood or language or both, [is] declining, while the immigration of races totally alien to them [is] increasing." Good immigrants, in his view, were losing population share to bad immigrants.

The half century from 1875 to 1925 saw two major developments in the United States related to immigration. First was a big jump in the number of people coming into the country. Second was a head-on clash between opposing views of the U.S. identity, the clash that had been building since the early days of the republic. On one side: those who believed America was defined by its openness, where anyone committed to the country's ideals could become an American. On the other: those who believed the United States was essentially a north European nation and should remain so. The first development reinforced the second; as more immigrants arrived, the question of the country's character became more pressing.

Global transport and communication systems were improving rapidly, making migration easier. At the same time, industrialization in the United States was bringing new job opportunities for both skilled and unskilled laborers. The Chinese would be excluded from coming to join the U.S. workforce, but for free white people the door was still open. There were no numerical limits on immigration, and in many foreign countries the pressure to move was building. In 1880, about 200,000 foreigners were admitted. By 1905, about a million immigrants were arriving each year. Leaving aside the Chinese case, the belief that America should be a refuge had endured, at least in some quarters. The Statue of Liberty, a gift from the people of France, was erected in New York Harbor. As her contribution to a fund-raising effort, the novelist and playwright Emma Lazarus agreed to write a poem celebrating the project. A Sephardic Jew, Lazarus at the time was active in a movement to resettle refugees fleeing anti-Semitic pogroms in tsarist Russia, and the most famous lines of her poem—*Give me your tired, your poor, Your huddled masses yearning to breathe free*—reflected her notion of what America's message to the world should still be. In 1892, the federal government established an immigration reception center at Ellis Island, near the Statue of Liberty, and at peak times it processed thousands of immigrants each day.

The Statue of Liberty was built facing east, across the Atlantic to Europe, whence the tired and poor were presumed to be arriving. In theory, the promise of freedom could have been extended to the huddled masses of all world regions, including Asia, but not many U.S. leaders were willing to make that argument. One of the courageous few was George Frisbie Hoar, a Republican senator from Massachusetts who during earlier terms in the House of Representatives had emerged as an outspoken defender of civil rights for African Americans, treaty rights for Native Americans, and voting rights for women. In an extraordinary speech on the floor of the U.S. Senate in February 1882, Hoar countered every argument against free immigration that had yet been made or would be heard in the century to come. He interpreted the Declaration of Independence's assertion of a universal right to the pursuit of happiness as meaning governments had no authority to interfere with an individual's desire "to go everywhere on the surface of the earth that his welfare may require" and then quoted the New Testament (Acts 17:26): "He made of one blood all nations of men to dwell on all the face of the earth." The exclusion of Chinese from America, Hoar said, reflected no more than "the old race prejudice which has so often played its hateful and bloody part in history."

Hoar's was a lonely voice, however. The Exclusion Act passed by lopsided margins in both chambers of Congress. The bigger question was which Europeans should be welcomed to America. The transatlantic flow had shifted, with more people coming from the countries of southern and eastern Europe and fewer from the northern climes. The new immigrants heightened competition for jobs, housing, and social services among the least advantaged segment of the population. Among the most vigorous defenders of U.S.-born workers was the American Federation of Labor. Speaking at a conference on immigration in 1905, AFL president Samuel Gompers argued that "self-protection is the first law of nature, and it is of the utmost importance that the American workman should do all in his power to prohibit the importation of those who would still further press him down."

The uglier side of the opposition to immigration was based simply on prejudice. The late nineteenth and early twentieth centuries saw the emergence of "scientific" research purporting to demonstrate the superiority of some races or ethnic groups over others. Such research was cited in the reports of a federal immigration commission established in 1907 under the leadership of Senator William Dillingham, a Republican from Vermont. The Dillingham Commission was mandated to investigate who exactly was immigrating to the United States and what capacities they brought. Their forty-two-volume final report made the case for a more selective immigration policy, distinguishing between more and less desirable ethnicities. The commission's "Dictionary of Races or Peoples" offered generalizations about Slavs ("fanaticism in religion, carelessness as to the business virtues of punctuality and often honesty"), southern Italians ("excitable, impulsive, highly imaginative, impracticable"), and Scandinavians ("the purest type").

In Congress, Dillingham and others argued vigorously in favor of new immigration restrictions. They achieved partial success with passage of the Immigration Act of 1917, which introduced a requirement that immigrants over the age of sixteen pass a literacy test. It expanded the Chinese exclusion by keeping out persons from a broader "Asiatic Barred Zone," comprising most of Asia, including India, plus the Pacific Islands. Still, the immigration critics were not satisfied. As it turned out, Slavs and Italians were as able to pass the literacy test as other immigrant groups were, and there was still no limit on the overall number of people who could be accepted as immigrants. The Dillingham Commission had recommended that the United States restrict the entry of immigrants from southern and eastern Europe in favor of northern and western Europeans, and the restrictionists proposed to achieve this through the establishment of separate immigration quotas for each country.

Such a policy embodied the idea that prospective immigrants should be considered on the basis of their race or nationality, not their individual qualifications. Its chief advocate in Congress was Albert Johnson, a Republican from Washington state who chaired the House Committee on Immigration and Naturalization.

Johnson's key adviser on immigration policy was Madison Grant, an amateur eugenicist whose writings had given racism a veneer of intellectual legitimacy. In his best-selling 1916 book *The Passing of the Great Race,* Grant revisited the nineteenth-century classification of the human species into Caucasoids, Negroids, and Mongoloids. Not surprisingly, Grant ranked the Caucasoids as superior, but he then subdivided them into three more groups: Nordics, Alpines, and Mediterraneans. Grant saw the Nordics as the elite group, characterizing them as "a race of soldiers, sailors, adventurers, and explorers, but above all, of rulers, organizers, and aristocrats."

In the aftermath of the Communist revolution in Russia, an atmosphere of xenophobia had taken hold, with the U.S. Senate refusing to ratify membership in the League of Nations. The Ku Klux Klan, having terrorized black communities throughout the South during the post-Reconstruction era, was enjoying a revival, this time promoting itself as an all-American organization that opposed foreigners, Catholics, and Jews, in addition to African Americans.

What little support there was in Congress for continued immigration came mostly from members representing urban districts, primarily along the East Coast. Among the few outspoken critics of an immigrant quota system was Emanuel Celler, a firebrand freshman Democrat from Brooklyn, New York. Celler, the grandson of immigrants from Germany, had worked his way through law school selling wine (mostly to Italian immigrants) and brought an outgoing and often combative personality to his politicking. Campaigning in 1922 in a district that had never elected a Democrat, Manny Celler addressed voters from the tailgate of an open truck. An aide would set off a burst of fireworks in order to draw a crowd, and then, Celler recalled later, "you'd get up and harangue them." He won the election by a narrow margin and went on to serve in Congress for fifty years.

When he arrived in Congress in March 1923 at the age of thirty-four, both chambers were ruled by Republicans, and Celler would say later that, politically, he felt like he was looking out "on a sea without a shore." The adjustment from his law practice in Brooklyn was sharp. "I was quite bewildered," he later told a reporter, with the barest hint of modesty, "but it was not too long before I began to chart my bearings." He had come to Washington determined to work for the repeal of Prohibition, but he was quickly moved instead by the debate over immigration policy. Celler's constituents were mostly Italians, Jews, and blacks, the very people then being portrayed as coming from inferior racial stock, and he was outraged by what he heard.

"There were men older than I in Congress," he wrote in his autobiography, "men of more experience, of more learning. Yet the talk . . . did not fit into the picture I knew. I knew the women in the Brooklyn tenements who scrubbed their floors again and again in the helpless fight against squalor. I knew the timid, perplexed son of the immigrant—part of him Old World, part of him New—serious and hungry, filling the free schools and the free colleges of New York. I knew the Negro, kept down in poverty and degradation. The folklore of Poland, of Lithuania, of Russia, of Italy, became part of my folklore because I had heard it so often. I knew their richness and their laughter and the disappointing heartbreak of the struggle in America to adjust. I knew, also, their pride, the unfulfilled dream of independence that had first brought them here."

Later, as a veteran congressman, Celler would counsel freshmen to keep a low profile during their first year, but if he got that advice as a newcomer, he ignored it. A dapper dresser, with blue eyes that twinkled through his round, wire-rimmed eyeglasses, Celler carried himself with self-confidence and a bit of attitude, often with a cigar in hand. His parents had died when he was just eighteen, and he had put himself through college and law school at Columbia entirely on his own. More senior members of Congress did not intimidate him in the slightest, especially if he regarded them as ignorant and provincial, and the controversy over immigration fired him up from the moment he arrived in Washington. When he read in *The New York Times* that John Cable of Ohio, who served on

Albert Johnson's Immigration Committee, had said during a July 1923 visit to Ellis Island that too many Jews were being admitted to the United States, Celler immediately shot off a response. "There is no such thing as superior and inferior races," Celler wrote in a letter to the editor. "One set of people is as good as another." He even took advantage of the occasion to take a swipe at Labor Secretary James Davis, whose own father, Celler noted, could neither read nor write when he arrived in America as an immigrant from Wales. "Was he for that reason inferior?" Celler asked. He had been in Congress for just four months at that point, but he had already joined the immigration fight. It was a cause that would consume him for the rest of his congressional career.

The preparation of a new immigration law was a top priority for Albert Johnson's Immigration Committee in 1924. Johnson's new proposal would establish a visa quota for each nationality equivalent to 2 percent of the foreign-born U.S. residents in 1890 who shared that national origin. The 1890 date was chosen deliberately in order to favor immigrants from northern and western Europe at the expense of those from eastern and southern Europe, most of whom had arrived after 1890 and would therefore not be counted for quota purposes. Hearings on the new bill were held in January. Celler was not on Johnson's committee, but he could not stand idly by while it considered immigration restrictions that he found highly objectionable. In a column published in *The New York Times*, Celler blasted the very idea of prioritizing prospective immigrants on the basis of their national background. "I can see no logic in accepting a criminal Scotchman or a degenerate Swede and in excluding a refined and cultured Pole or an industrious and honest Czechoslovak," he wrote. "Not only is the quota law illogical in theory, but it is cruel and heartless in practice." Celler seemed to take special pleasure in going after Labor Secretary Davis, who considered himself an expert on immigration. In February 1924, when Davis published a lengthy article citing immigration and citizenship data in support of his claim that new immigrants (from southern and eastern Europe) were not assimilating as quickly as the older immigrants had, Celler published his own analysis of the data, showing that Nordic immigrants had actually taken longer to apply for citizenship in America than the newer group had taken.

When Johnson's proposed immigration bill was debated in the full House and Senate in April 1924, Celler and the handful of other opponents found themselves greatly outnumbered. The House Immigration Committee report endorsing the legislation was signed by fifteen of the seventeen committee members. The two members who did not sign, both of them Jewish, came from Chicago and New York and represented districts with many voters from southern and eastern Europe. Some of the arguments in favor of restricting immigration were blatantly racist. "We have in America perhaps the largest percentage of the pure, unadulterated Anglo-Saxon stock," said Senator Ellison DuRant Smith, a Democrat from South Carolina. "It is for the preservation of that splendid stock . . . that I would make this not an asylum for the oppressed of all countries, but a country to assimilate and perfect that splendid type of manhood." For its part, the Ku Klux Klan deluged representatives with petitions urging passage of the bill, pointing out that it would reduce the numbers of Jews, Catholics, and other undesirable groups entering the country.

Celler, three of whose four grandparents were Jewish, was stunned by what he heard during the immigration debate. Thirty years later, his recollection of the hateful rhetoric was still vivid. "I believe that not in the three decades I have been in Congress have I heard such venom spilled on the floor of the House," he wrote in his autobiography. Without identifying any of his colleagues by name, he quoted one as bellowing, "It may be even now too late for the white race in America. . . . I wish it were possible to close our gates against any quota from southern Europe from the Orientals, the Mongolian countries and the yellow races of men." When the member finally sat down, Celler recalled, "wild applause filled the House." There was so much boasting of the racial superiority of white northern Europeans that Celler felt compelled to introduce the latest anthropological research disproving any inherent racial disparities in mental capacity or criminal behavior. The effort was of little use, however. Johnson's bill passed both the House and the Senate by overwhelming bipartisan margins and was immediately signed into law by President Calvin Coolidge.

Immigration from all areas of the world except the Western Hemisphere would be limited to 165,000 annually, less than one fifth of the pre–World War I yearly average. Albert Johnson said the passage of his bill amounted to "America's Second Declaration of Independence." His coauthor in the Senate, Republican David Reed of Pennsylvania, explained in a *New York Times* column that the goal was to restore the ethnic mix that characterized the country before the arrival of so many Italians, Poles, Russians, and other Slavs. Celler summarized the anti-immigrant argument succinctly: "We were afraid of foreigners; we distrusted them; we didn't like them."

The new formula was hardest on southern and eastern Europeans, because most of those immigrants had arrived in the United States after 1890. The new annual quota for Italians, for example, would be 3,845, whereas about 200,000 had come to the United States each year in the first decade of the twentieth century. Germany, meanwhile, would be permitted more than 50,000 immigrants a year under the new legislation. The law kept in place the long-standing rule that limited the right of U.S. citizenship to "free white persons" and African Americans, meaning Asians were still excluded. The Tocquevillean notion that America's immigration policy nurtured an egalitarian and individualist political culture, promoted creativity, and made possible the construction of a uniquely American identity was abandoned, at least for the time being. Maurice Samuel, a novelist who was born in Romania but grew up in Britain and the United States, expressed the disappointment that many immigrants felt. "If America had any meaning at all," he wrote, "it lay in the peculiar attempt to rise above the trend of our present civilization—the identification of race with State. . . . America was the New World in this vital respect—that the State was purely an ideal, and nationality was identical only with acceptance of the ideal. But it seems now that the entire point of view was a mistaken one, that America was incapable of rising above her origins."

Immigration to America dropped off sharply. Fewer than 300,000 people were allowed into the country in 1925, less than half the number in each of the preceding four years, and 45 percent of them that year were from Canada and Mexico. The number of Italians and Poles allowed into the United States dropped by an astounding 90 percent as a result of the low quotas assigned to their countries. Those who wanted to reduce the flow of people to the United States from anywhere other than northern Europe had finally triumphed. By 1930, in the words of historian Aristide Zolberg, "The United States in effect proclaimed to the face of the world, 'We are no longer a nation of immigrants.'"

With some modifications, the attempt to maintain America's nineteenth-century ethnic character through immigration controls remained official policy for decades. Many European Jews fleeing Nazi persecution encountered closed doors in the United States, and Emanuel Celler was again moved to outrage. "There were sporadic speeches on the floors of the House and the Senate," he wrote in his autobiography. "There were editorials, and there were speeches without end on the subject throughout the country. Yet there was not concerted movement that could have compelled the United States to consider the possibility of opening its doors to those fleeing murders." Celler's personal appeal to President Franklin Roosevelt to welcome Jewish refugees went unheeded. In 1943, the Chinese Exclusion Act was repealed, but it was a token move. China was assigned only 105 quota slots per year. Immigration from the other countries in the Asiatic Barred Zone was still prohibited, with a few exceptions. In the aftermath of World War II, a relatively small number of refugees were accepted from Asia as well as from Europe, and some family members of Asian American citizens were allowed to immigrate.

U.S. immigration policy by then had become hopelessly complicated by a hodgepodge of laws, executive orders, regulations, proclamations, and international treaty obligations. Members of Congress from both parties agreed that a new comprehensive law was needed to simplify and clarify immigration policy. After a three-year study, the House and Senate Judiciary subcommittees on immigration launched joint hearings in May 1951 to consider a new law, the first such hearings since the 1920s. Much had changed in the intervening decades. Hitler had made it impossible to talk seriously any longer about "Nordic superiority," and members were somewhat less inclined to make overtly racist comments. Emanuel Celler, a freshman representative at the time of the last debate, was now a congressional veteran and chairman of the House Judiciary Committee, and in Harry Truman he had a reformist ally in the White House.

From the start, however, it became clear that Celler and other reformers would have trouble overturning the immigrant quota system. The Senate Judiciary Committee chairman, Democrat Pat McCarran of Nevada, served also as chairman of the immigration subcommittee, and he was still committed to the selection of immigrants on the basis of their nationality. The chair of the House immigration subcommittee, Democrat Francis Walter of Pennsylvania, held similar views. Celler was not a member of his own immigration subcommittee, and McCarran and Walter did all they could to exclude him from the debate. When Celler asked that he be allowed to explain a liberal reform bill that would have overturned the national origin quotas, McCarran, who was chairing the hearings, gave him just three minutes to testify, an extraordinary insult to a full committee chairman. After speaking, Celler stormed out of the hearing, red-faced and fuming. McCarran and Walter, meanwhile, had their own plan to update but reaffirm the 1924 national origin quotas. Their proposal eliminated all racial references in immigration policy and did away with the Asiatic Barred Zone, thus legally reinstating the right of Asians to immigrate to the United States. But those were token modifications; low quotas meant only a trickle of Asians could come. The McCarran-Walter bill designated a new "Asia Pacific Triangle," roughly comparable to the Asiatic Barred Zone, from which a maximum total of two thousand immigrants could come to the United States per year. Even worse, the quotas were based on ethnicity, not place of birth. A British citizen, born in London, but with one parent of Chinese ancestry, could not enter the United States as a British immigrant but would instead have to compete for one of the few visas reserved for Chinese immigrants, even though he or she—or even the "Chinese" parent, for that matter—had never set foot in China and had no ties with the country. There was a significant exception for immediate relatives (spouses or children) of U.S. citizens, who could immigrate independently of the quotas, but the strong racial bias toward northern and western Europeans was maintained.

Though the U.S. mood had changed since 1924, it still favored strict limits on immigration. After World War II, the fear of Communism was the dominating sentiment, and it further served to fuel suspicion of foreigners, many of whom were thought to harbor Communist sympathies. The McCarran-Walter immigration proposal, formally named the Immigration and Nationality Act of 1952, passed both houses of Congress by a wide margin. Even with the liberalizing changes to the 1924 Immigration Act, the 1952 act preserved the most essential feature of the earlier legislation, the use of quotas to promote the immigration of some nationalities and impede the entry of others. The goal as described in the legislative language was to preserve "the sociological and cultural balance of the United States."

Passage of the McCarran-Walter Act prompted a torrent of criticism from organizations as diverse as the American Bar Association, the American Jewish Committee, the International Rescue

Committee, the YWCA, the National Council of Churches, the NAACP, and the Congress of Industrial Organizations (CIO), which was more supportive of immigration than its fellow labor federation, the AFL. President Truman called the bill "a slur on the patriotism, the capacity, and the decency of a large part of our citizenry," and refused to sign it. In Congress, Democratic senators Herbert Lehman of New York and Hubert Humphrey of Minnesota, the principal authors of alternative reform legislation, denounced the bill, as did several other senators, largely from the Northeast. But Senator Joseph McCarthy and others had roused his followers into frenzied opposition against suspected Communists and other "un-American" elements in society, and Congress voted to override Truman's veto. The McCarran-Walter Act became the law of the land. The United States, by deliberate design, was to remain largely a white European nation, with the warmest welcome reserved for Scandinavians, Germans, the British, and the Irish. At the other extreme, only a few hundred slots at most were reserved per year for each of the Asian, African, and Middle Eastern countries. China, India, the Philippines, and Korea were each allowed just one hundred immigrant visas per year.

9

JFK

Boston's North End was an enclave of Irish immigrants when John F. Fitzgerald was growing up in the 1870s, but by the time his grandson John Fitzgerald Kennedy looked for votes there in 1946, the neighborhood was almost entirely Italian. For the last four years Jack Kennedy had been off fighting a war, and when he launched his campaign to represent the 11th District in the U.S. Congress, he knew hardly anyone in the North End. His grandfather, known as "Honey Fitz" for his affable personality, had once held that congressional seat and later served as Boston's mayor, but Kennedy was determined to make his own Boston connections, and one of his first moves as a congressional candidate was to find some Italian Americans who could introduce him around the neighborhood.

So it was that the twenty-nine-year-old Kennedy met William "Yammy" De Marco on a rainy Sunday afternoon that spring. Kennedy was walking down Hanover Street with Billy Sutton, a campaign aide from Charlestown, when Billy spotted De Marco across the street and called him over. Billy knew almost everyone across the river in Charlestown, which was still solidly Irish, but Yammy De Marco was one of his few North End friends.

"Yammy, this is Jack Kennedy," Sutton said. "He's a Harvard grad just back from the war, and he's running for Congress. He'd like to meet some of your folks and find out what's on their minds."

As Sutton went on speaking about Kennedy, De Marco was thinking that the candidate looked awfully young and skinny. The rain was coming down hard, and Kennedy had neither an umbrella nor a hat. His hair was tousled and wet, and his suit seemed to be shrinking fast on his thin frame. He was not the kind of politician De Marco was accustomed to seeing in the North End and certainly not one he would have associated with the legendary Honey Fitz. Kennedy told De Marco that his grandfather and his mother, Rose, were both born in the North End back when it was an Irish neighborhood and that they still attended mass down the street at St. Stephen's. De Marco said he knew that, because he had seen Honey Fitz at the church on many occasions. The more they talked, the more De Marco liked him, and he told Kennedy he'd be happy to help his campaign. He was the presiding officer at an Italian American social club based on the fifth floor of the Testa Building across the street, and he suggested they head up to the club right then to talk to some of the guys gathered there.

About sixty men were at the club that day, most of them playing whist or scopa, an Italian card game, and drinking wine or beer. Many, like Sutton and Kennedy and De Marco, had fought in the war, and on that Sunday they were celebrating the return a few days earlier of another veteran, Chippy Califani. The party was getting boisterous, and when De Marco walked in with his guests and banged his hand on a table to get everyone's attention, some of the men grumbled. They had come to party, not attend a club meeting.

"Boys, I have someone important here I want you to meet," De Marco said. "This is Jack Kennedy. He's one of us. Some of you older guys might remember his mother, Rose Fitzgerald, who used to live over on Garden Court Street, and surely you've seen his grandfather at St. Stephen's. Jack is a Harvard boy, well educated, and he comes from a family we all know well here in the North End. He's running for Congress, and we can help get him elected."

Kennedy, the son of a wealthy and famous Boston Irish family, seemed a bit shy at first in this working-class Italian American group, but to the men at the 28 Club he seemed gracious and humble, and he soon had them sharing their stories. Like other voters Kennedy had met, the North End men said they were mainly hoping for decent housing, better education opportunities for their children, and some confidence about where their next buck would come from. As Italian Americans, however, they had one issue that bothered them in particular. Under the 1924 law, Italy was permitted fewer than four thousand immigrant visas per year, and virtually every family in the North End had relatives back in Italy who were desperate to move to America but could not get a visa. The quota amounted to blatant anti-Italian discrimination, because Germans who wanted to immigrate to the United States faced no comparable limit.

Kennedy nodded in agreement. Ethnic bias and unjust immigration laws had been concerns in his family ever since John F. Fitzgerald got involved in politics in the previous century, another time when immigration policy was a hot issue. As a first-term member of the House of Representatives, Fitzgerald simmered when his congressional colleagues prattled on about all the "inferior" foreigners being allowed into the country, an argument to which he was especially sensitive given the way Irish immigrants like his parents had once been regarded. He was outraged when Republican senator Henry Cabot Lodge, from his own state of Massachusetts, introduced a bill in 1896 under which any immigrant who could not read or write would be denied entry to the United States. Such a requirement would block many immigrants from southern and eastern Europe, and it would have excluded Fitzgerald's own mother, who was illiterate when she arrived from Ireland. When Lodge's bill was introduced in the House, Fitzgerald pledged to fight it. In a speech he wrote for delivery on the House floor, Fitzgerald declared himself "utterly opposed" to the literacy test. "It is fashionable today to cry out against the immigration of the Hungarian, the Italian, and the Jew," Fitzgerald said, "but I think that the man who comes to this country for the first time—to a strange land without friends and without employment—is bound to make a good citizen."

Fitzgerald later said that Lodge, with his Yankee blue-blood ancestry, was angered that a young Irish American congressman would dare object to the literacy bill, and he claimed that Lodge confronted him one day in the halls of the Capitol. "You are an impudent young man," Fitzgerald quoted Lodge as saying. "Do you think the Jews or the Italians have any right in this country?"

"As much right as your father or mine," Fitzgerald allegedly responded. "It was only a difference of a few ships." Fitzgerald got a chance to challenge Lodge once again in 1916, running against him in a race for his Senate seat. With Congress considering a quota law, immigration was again an issue in the race. Fitzgerald lost the election, with 45 percent of the vote to Lodge's 52 percent.

Listening to the boys at Club 28 complain about how quota restrictions were keeping relatives in Italy from joining their families in America, Jack Kennedy recalled what his grandfather had told him about fighting for his southern and eastern European constituents, and he promised to continue doing so. As they rode down the elevator after the meeting, Yammy De Marco told Kennedy he could count on him to organize the North End for his election, and at least two other men at the club that afternoon—Sal Venezia and Dominic Butera—became enthusiastic campaign soldiers for Kennedy in Boston's Italian American community. Honey Fitz himself was almost eighty and did not play an active role in his grandson's congressional campaign, though he would show up at rallies on occasion to sing a couple of verses from "Sweet Adeline," his trademark song from his own politicking days. Fitz and his wife by then were living at the Bellevue Hotel. Jack, who was still single, had an apartment at the same hotel, and he checked in down the hall with his grandfather every day for political advice.

To the astonishment of political observers in Boston, Kennedy took 40 percent of the votes in a ten-way race for the Democratic Party nomination that summer. Given that it was a safe Democratic district, winning the primary was tantamount to being elected. At a triumphant celebration on primary night, a jubilant Honey Fitz jumped on a table to dance a jig and lead the crowd in singing "Sweet Adeline" one more time.

John F. Fitzgerald died in 1950. Had he lived a while longer, he could have seen how reforming immigration and going after the Cabot Lodges had become family missions. In 1952, Jack Kennedy took a stand against the McCarran-Walter plan to maintain most of the 1924 immigration restrictions. Later that year, he challenged the Senate reelection bid of Henry Cabot Lodge II, the grandson of Honey Fitz's old adversary. Kennedy defeated him decisively, perhaps helped a bit by his campaign calling attention to anti-Jewish comments made sixty years earlier by Cabot Lodge's grandfather.

In 1962, Honey Fitz's youngest grandson, Edward Kennedy, was elected to the U.S. Senate, beating George Cabot Lodge II, the great-grandson of Henry Cabot Lodge. A year later, as the first Irish Catholic president, John F. Kennedy sent Congress a bill to abolish nationality discrimination in immigration policy, and in 1965 Edward Kennedy steered the reform into law.

The efforts to eliminate racial and ethnic barriers in U.S. immigration policy mostly failed in the 1950s, because the effort was seen as a liberal cause at a time when Congress was still dominated by southern conservatives. In a message accompanying his veto of the 1952 McCarran-Walter Act, Harry Truman framed the question largely as a civil rights issue, which may not have been the best way to win over hard-core southern racists. The quota system, in place since 1924 and reinforced by McCarran-Walter, "discriminates, deliberately and intentionally against many of the peoples of the world," Truman said. He was especially scornful of the McCarran-Walter provision requiring that any prospective immigrant who had one parent of Asian ancestry had to compete for one of the scarce Asian immigrant slots, regardless of how many generations removed the parent was from his or her country of origin. It was an "invidious" discrimination, Truman said, inasmuch as it applied only to people with an Asian background.

The leading supporters of an impartial immigration policy in the 1950s were all Northerners. In the House, the indefatigable Emanuel Celler was by then in his fourth decade of battling national origin quotas. He had been joined by Peter Rodino, a New Jersey Democrat, and Jacob Javits, a Republican from New York, among others. In the Senate, the fight was led by Herbert Lehman along with Hubert Humphrey of Minnesota, a strong civil rights advocate who had provoked a split in his party with his 1948 speech urging southern Democrats to "get out of the shadow of states' rights and walk forthrightly into the bright sunshine of human rights." In 1953, Lehman and Humphrey were joined in their reform push by Jack Kennedy, their freshman Senate colleague.

Vigorous efforts to turn back McCarran-Walter began immediately after Congress overrode Truman's veto of the measure. One of the first commentators to weigh in was Harvard University's Oscar Handlin, a prominent immigration historian whose Pulitzer Prize–winning book *The Uprooted* had concluded that the common experience of immigrants in America, regardless of race, religion, or nationality, was one of hardship and alienation followed gradually by Americanization. Handlin was infuriated by the McCarran-Walter Act, and within days of its passage he published a column urging opponents to redouble their efforts against the measure. "There ought to be no place in our laws for the racist ranking of nationalities," he wrote. Handlin recalled a time when people in the United States "had confidence enough in their own society and in their own institutions to believe that any man could become an American. More than ever, do we now need to reaffirm that faith."

When Congress overrode his veto of McCarran-Walter, an

angry President Truman responded by ordering the establishment of a presidential Commission on Immigration and Naturalization. Going far beyond the complaint that existing policy was unfair to southern and eastern Europeans, the commission noted the broader discrimination in U.S. immigration policy against "the non-white people of the world who constitute between two-thirds and three-fourths of the world's population." Outside Congress, the view of U.S. immigration policies was beginning to shift. The controversy over the national origin quota system, inflamed by Harry Truman's blistering criticisms, prompted Dwight Eisenhower to distance himself from the McCarran-Walter Act during the 1952 campaign, and as president he advocated significant policy and legislative changes. Rather than making a civil rights argument, however, President Eisenhower and his administration focused on foreign policy concerns. The State Department was warning that a highly restrictive immigration policy would tarnish the U.S. image abroad and play into the hands of U.S. adversaries.

In 1955 Lyndon Johnson of Texas was elected Senate majority leader. He had gone along with other southern Democrats on most issues, including McCarran-Walter, and the record of his speeches and interviews includes abundant evidence of prejudice with regard to foreigners as well as blacks. But Johnson took the majority leader title seriously, and he knew that if he were to bring his northerners and southerners together, he would have to defuse the issues that divided them, civil rights and immigration among them. Johnson was one of the very few southerners in Congress who in 1956 declined to sign the Southern Manifesto decrying the Supreme Court's *Brown v. Board of Education* desegregation ruling, apparently because he wanted to stay above the fray. His longtime aide Harry McPherson, who worked as a floor counsel for Johnson in the Senate, said Johnson as majority leader could play both sides when it came to civil rights. "He would tell the southerners they were wrong and embarrassing," McPherson said, "and he would tell the northerners they were wrong and intemperate . . . that they just didn't understand, and that it was just going to take a lot of time."

In July 1955, however, Johnson suffered a serious heart attack and had to spend several months recuperating at his Texas ranch. Upon his return to the Senate, he worked with Republican Everett McKinley Dirksen and other senators to implement some modifications to the McCarran-Walter immigration structure. The effort failed. The chairmanship of the Senate immigration subcommittee by then had passed to James Eastland of Mississippi, an ardent segregationist. Eastland was a strong believer in the need to apply racial and ethnic criteria in judging whom should be admitted to the United States, and he opposed any change that would have the effect of boosting immigration from southern and eastern European countries.

Throughout his years in the Senate, Johnson remained close to Eastland and other southern senators. But he was also friendly with northern liberals, including John F. Kennedy, whose vice-presidential nomination he seconded at the Democratic convention in 1956. Four years later, Kennedy in turn named him as his own running mate. On some issues, including immigration, Johnson could be unpredictable. Unlike other southerners, he had Jewish friends, both in Texas and in Washington, and he took an active interest in facilitating the immigration of Jewish refugees from Nazi rule. As a freshman member of Congress in 1938, Johnson personally arranged an immigrant visa for Erich Leinsdorf, a symphony conductor from Austria who was visiting the United States on a temporary visa when the Nazis invaded and occupied his country. Until Johnson intervened, Leinsdorf was due to be sent back to Austria, where as a Jew his life would have been in danger. That same year, Johnson also worked with a Jewish friend in Texas to secure the rescue of forty-two Polish and German Jews. With the exception of the one legislative initiative he undertook with Everett Dirksen, however, Johnson was not especially active in immigration legislation as Senate majority leader.

The only immigration laws enacted by Congress in the 1950s were either "private" bills sponsored by members of Congress to benefit particular individuals or "special" bills to accommodate broad categories of refugees or other persons displaced by war or disasters. Such legislation enabled the immigration of foreigners who would not otherwise have qualified for visas because the quotas for people of their national origin had been exceeded. Reform advocates cited the proliferation of these special interest laws as one more argument for overhauling the whole immigration apparatus. With spouses and children of U.S. citizens also permitted to immigrate regardless of their national origin, two thirds of the immigrants entering the United during the nineteen 1950s were coming in on a "nonquota" basis. U.S. immigration policy was still racist by design but increasingly incoherent in its implementation.

John F. Kennedy had been talking immigration off and on for a dozen years, dating at least to his 1946 meeting with the Italian Americans in Boston's North End. With the 1960 presidential election on the horizon, Kennedy set out to burnish his reputation as an immigration reformer. First came the 1958 publication of his book *A Nation of Immigrants*, written at the suggestion of the Anti-Defamation League, which supplied Kennedy with an outline prepared by a Harvard historian. (One of Kennedy's aides, Myer Feldman, was later quoted as saying he, not Kennedy, did the actual writing.) A year after the book's publication, Kennedy introduced still another bill to do away with the national origin quotas. It stood no more chance in the Senate than those he had cosponsored in the past, but this time Kennedy was contemplating a run for the presidency and needed to underscore his particular commitment to the cause of immigration reform.

The 1960 Democratic Party platform called for the abolition of the national origins quota system, saying it "contradicts the founding principles of this nation," and as a presidential candidate that year Kennedy hit the theme regularly. The party in those days had a "Nationalities Division" whose mission it was to rally first- and second-generation immigrants to support Democratic candidates. The division's chairman, Michigan governor G. Mennen Williams, advised Kennedy that "Nationality groups" could provide a "tremendous impetus" to his campaign but that he would need to work hard because Republicans had been wooing immigrants "to such an extent that we have a job on our hands."

After winning the Democratic nomination and the elections, Kennedy did nothing to advance immigration reform during his first two years as president. To be sure, other issues and crises had grabbed his attention: Cuba, Berlin, Vietnam, and the rapidly escalating civil rights struggle at home. The distractions were serious enough to explain a young president's inaction on a lower priority issue like immigration, but groups who had invested their reform hopes in a Kennedy White House were nonetheless dismayed. When work finally began on a bill to fulfill the immigration campaign pledge, the Justice Department lawyer charged with drafting the legislative language regarded his mission as "almost hopeless," because conservative southern senators would be sure to block any reform legislation.

It was only in the spring of 1963 that the Kennedy White House was ready for a detailed discussion on comprehensive immigration reform legislation. Even then, there was no unanimity within the administration on how to proceed. Kennedy's immigration adviser was Abba Schwartz, a lawyer well known in Washington for his advocacy of an "open society" approach on immigration and his opposition to discrimination on the basis of national origin. But Schwartz happened to be on friendly terms with Francis Walter, one of the leading opponents of immigration reform, and his conversations with the congressman led Schwartz to believe that if the White House produced a reform bill that abolished national origin quotas, it would be dead on arrival in Congress. Working out of the State Department, Schwartz produced draft bills that were only partial reforms, tinkering with the quota numbers but essentially leaving the national origins approach intact. Schwartz's proposals stopped well short of legislation introduced in the House by Emanuel Celler, still as committed as ever to immigration reform, and in the Senate by Philip Hart, a Democrat from Michigan who had taken the Senate lead on the issue. Celler, who had been promoting immigration reform longer than anyone in Congress, was not happy with Schwartz's approach and so informed President Kennedy in a "personal and confidential" letter. "I do not see why you should not submit a bold proposal for a basic change and a complete and definite departure from an antiquated principle," he wrote. Justice Department attorneys, who had been working on draft legislation close to what Celler and Hart were suggesting, also opposed the Schwartz proposals.

Kennedy's decision on which way to go was eased by the death of Francis Walter on May 31 from leukemia. The next most senior Democrat on the subcommittee was Michael Feighan, a dour Irish American lawyer from Cleveland known mainly for his prickly personality. Feighan shared Walter's hard-line immigration and anti-Communist views, but he was initially seen as somewhat more likely to cooperate with the White House, in part because his Ohio district included a large number of ethnic voters, and in July Kennedy forwarded his long-delayed immigration reform proposal to Capitol Hill. The Kennedy plan would have gradually eliminated the allocation of visas based on national origin quotas, with visas given instead on a modified first-come, first-served approach. The overall number of available immigration slots would be unchanged, but they would be distributed according to the applicants' skills and abilities or their family connections in the United States. Ancestry would be irrelevant, except that no more than 10 percent of the available slots could go to applicants from any one country. Spouses, parents, and children of U.S. citizens could immigrate to the United States without any numerical limitation, as could residents of countries in the Western Hemisphere. The anti-Asian bias in existing law would completely disappear. In the Senate, James Eastland ignored the proposal, but the White House had higher hopes for the other chamber.

Chairman Feighan, however, liked neither the proposal nor the way it was presented, and he stubbornly refused to schedule hearings on the legislation. To his detractors, of whom there were many, he was a small-minded man, easily offended and occasionally grouped with "the right wing cranks" in Congress. White House officials made the mistake of sharing their immigration plan with Celler before speaking to Feighan, and when so slighted Feighan "got his nose out of joint," in the recollection of Lawrence O'Brien, Kennedy's special assistant for congressional relations. When they did speak to Feighan, the officials found him irritated and unfriendly. During a trip to Europe in October, Feighan is said to have told guests at an official dinner that John F. Kennedy was soft on Communism and that he had decided not to support his reelection.

A month later, the president was dead.

10

THE 1965 REFORM

On the Sunday following the assassination, Lyndon Johnson, now president, attended services at St. Mark's Episcopal, a church on Capitol Hill he had visited on occasion since his days in the Senate. The church was swarming with Secret Service agents, and snipers were posted on the roof of the Library of Congress annex across the street. The new president took a seat in the seventh row, accompanied by his wife and daughter, Lucy, who were veiled and dressed entirely in black. Johnson stared straight ahead throughout the service, remaining solemn and silent except for reciting the Lord's Prayer and singing "America" with the rest of the congregation. From time to time he wept, wiping his face with his handkerchief. Afterward, he lingered in the parish hall, where worshippers gathered for coffee after the service. People, many of them crying, came up to him to shake his hand or touch his arm as if to comfort him. It was the first time he had been with ordinary folks since the assassination, and an aide who was with him said Johnson found the human contact "immensely strengthening."

Johnson had viewed John F. Kennedy with affection and respect, and he was deeply grieved by his killing. In the weeks and months afterward he made clear to everyone that he intended to complete what Kennedy had begun. "The ideas and the ideals which he so nobly represented must and will be translated into effective action," Johnson told a Joint Session of Congress five days after the assassination. Over the next two years, among other achievements, he oversaw the enactment of civil rights and voting rights legislation, the creation of Medicare, urban renewal, financial assistance for higher education, a war on poverty, plus immigration reform. Some of his achievements reflected his own goals or his personal commitment to the New Deal vision of his hero Franklin D. Roosevelt, but in other cases—immigration being a good example—Johnson was being faithful to the fallen president's agenda. His longtime counsel and speechwriter Harry McPherson said that when Johnson took over as president in November 1963, the White House was like a slow-moving train that had suddenly lost its engineer and gotten stranded in the middle of nowhere.

> Everything had begun to stop. Kennedy was unable to get anything done. Then he's killed. An engineer who couldn't make the train run is now dead. And we passengers are all out in the middle of the desert someplace. And a guy gets up and says, "I'll go up and run the damned train. I know how to fix these things." And he gets his wrench . . . and gets into the train and fixes it. And pretty soon the train starts to roll. Everybody lets out a great cheer.
>
> It was the damndest performance the first few months. It was a spectacular performance.

The importance Johnson assigned to immigration reform relative to his other agenda items is not clear. "He had no real priority among them," writes historian and Johnson biographer Robert Dallek. "He wanted them all." Asked what Johnson personally found compelling about the need for a new immigration law, his press secretary

George Reedy said it was "just that he thought something ought to be done, and he did it. . . . There's not much to say about it." Moreover, it apparently took some time for him to get up to speed on the subject. Irving Bernstein, another historian of the Johnson presidency, said the new president was "uninformed" about immigration reform when he took office and had to be educated on the issue by Myer Feldman, the Kennedy aide who ghostwrote *A Nation of Immigrants*. Feldman told one interviewer that Johnson initially worried that immigration might be too hot an issue for him to take on. But Feldman, Abba Schwartz, and other former Kennedy advisers soon convinced Johnson that if he were really going to produce a civil rights law that eliminated "every trace of discrimination and oppression that is based upon race or color," as he had promised to do shortly after taking over the presidency, he would also have to commit to the elimination of the national origin bias in immigration law.

In his first State of the Union speech, delivered just six weeks after taking office, Johnson envisioned a world "in which all men, goods, and ideas can freely move across every border and every boundary," and he called for the elimination of visa quotas based on national origin. "A nation that was built by the immigrants of all lands can ask those who now seek admission: 'What can you do for our country?'" he said. "But we should not be asking, 'In what country were you born?'" Though President Kennedy was more associated with the cause, he had not mentioned immigration in any of his three State of the Union speeches.

In deference to Johnson's wishes, Senator James Eastland's immigration subcommittee had already scheduled a hearing to consider reform proposals, the first of its kind since 1952. Immediately prior to the meeting, Johnson summoned members of both the Senate and House immigration subcommittees to the White House Cabinet Room to sit down with representatives of private voluntary organizations, religious groups, and other associations with an interest in the immigration issue. He told them that he would be pushing for a new immigration law, and with television cameras rolling, he asked the legislative leaders to cooperate. Eastland, who chaired the full Judiciary Committee as well as the immigration subcommittee, had previously refused to consider any legislation that would have done away with the national origin quotas. But he found it hard to defy a fellow southerner and old friend, and he promised Johnson that his subcommittee would look into the issue "expeditiously," as did Congressman Michael Feighan of Ohio, the immigration chair in the House.

One of the senators at that White House meeting was Edward M. Kennedy, who had won a special election in 1962 to finish his brother's term in the Senate. Eastland, sixty years old, had taken a liking to the young senator from Massachusetts as soon as Kennedy arrived in Washington and told him told he could get him assigned to a good Judiciary subcommittee. In his memoir, Kennedy said Eastland invited him to his Senate office one Tuesday morning. After pushing a glass of scotch on him, despite the early hour, Eastland said, "I think I know what you want. You've got a lot of Eye-talians up there in Boston, don't you? Now, the Kennedys are always talking about immigration and always talking about Eye-talians and this kind of thing. You drink that drink there, and you're on the immigration committee." Next, Eastland offered Kennedy the Judiciary civil rights subcommittee. More drinks followed, only some of which Kennedy managed to empty into a potted plant next to his chair. In Kennedy's own recollection, he was "weaving a bit and reeking of alcohol" when he left Eastland's office, but he had established a bond with the aging segregationist and secured important assignments. Now that President Johnson was prepared to push immigration reform, Kennedy's membership on Eastman's immigration panel put him in position to influence any legislation being considered there and to promote what had become a family cause.

To the surprise of many on Capitol Hill, Eastland even told Kennedy he could preside over the immigration hearings as acting chairman. The Mississippi senator had no stomach to oversee hearings on the legislation that he so thoroughly opposed, but he realized that he needed to let them proceed. Knowing that his position as chairman of the full Judiciary Committee meant he could probably kill any immigration bill that emerged, Eastland figured there was no harm in letting Kennedy run the show at the subcommittee level. Thus began Teddy Kennedy's association with immigration reform in the U.S. Senate. For the next twenty-two months, except for time he spent recuperating from a plane crash, Kennedy would play a key role in managing the legislation, and he would be as responsible as anyone on Capitol Hill for the law that was finally enacted.

At the initial two-day immigration hearing in January 1964, six senators advocated an overhaul of the visa quota system. No additional hearings were held until July, however, largely because the Judiciary Committee was focused on passage of the Civil Rights Act, which was achieved in May. The House had passed its version of the civil rights legislation in February, but in the weeks that followed Congressman Feighan made no effort on immigration. Johnson grew impatient, as he always did when Congress moved at a snail's pace. The only White House bill under consideration in Congress at the time was the one President Kennedy had sent over the previous summer. Johnson had taken full ownership of it, however, and was pestering his allies in Congress to move on the legislation, in phone call after phone call. "I'm mighty proud of you," he told House Speaker John McCormack and Judiciary Chairman Emanuel Celler shortly after passage of the civil rights bill in the House, but then he added, "I hope you get my immigration bill out now."

"I'm having some trouble there," Celler said. He was locked in another feud with his immigration subcommittee chairman, who was being just as obstinate as he had been the year before, despite his promise to Johnson to cooperate. Three months later, there was still no action on the bill, and in another phone conversation with the president Celler reported that "our friend Feighan is still sitting on it." Feighan finally convened hearings on the immigration law in July, with Secretary of State Dean Rusk and Attorney General Robert F. Kennedy and several other witnesses testifying. It was exactly a year after the Kennedy White House had delivered its legislative proposal. Feighan's movement after stalling so long may have been a result of White House pressure, but probably a bigger factor was his surprisingly narrow victory that spring in a Democratic primary back in Ohio. Feighan's opponent had made an issue of his inaction on immigration, and it hurt him among ethnic voters in his Cleveland district. Chastened by his near loss, Feighan suddenly became more cooperative on immigration, though President Johnson had to give him the famously high-pressure LBJ "treatment" at the White House and even aboard Air Force One on a trip to Cleveland, when he pulled him close and forced him to say unequivocally that he would allow the immigration bill to go forward.

Advocates of changing the nation's immigration law were still downbeat about their prospects, however. There was no groundswell of popular support for reform, and it was far from clear that either immigration subcommittee would approve a bill to change the visa quota system. Abba Schwartz, who had been President Kennedy's top immigration adviser and was playing a similar role under President Johnson, had earlier questioned the depth of President Johnson's commitment to immigration reform and on the basis of his briefing the secretary of state, he also said that Rusk seemed, "unenthusiastic, even indifferent," when it came to challenging racial and ethnic discrimination in the visa allocation system. Schwartz was especially alarmed when Rusk phoned him at home the night before he was to appear in front of Feighan's committee.

"Abba," he said, "I'm not inclined to testify on the immigration bill tomorrow, because I'm a reluctant witness. You don't really think we should let in people like . . ." not finishing the sentence but continuing, "on a world-wide competitive basis, do you? After all, we are an Anglo-Saxon country."

Stunned, Schwartz told Rusk that if he really wanted to

withdraw from the hearing, he would need to discuss it with the president, who, Schwartz pointed out, now had a strong political commitment to the Kennedy reform proposal. Rusk testified the next day anyway, and Schwartz said afterward that he proved to be "the Administration's most articulate and effective witness."

Rusk was wrong that the United States was an "Anglo-Saxon country." At one time that had been true, but the 1960 census showed that only 35 percent of the population was of Anglo-Saxon origin. Despite the determined effort of lawmakers over many years to preserve the country's original ethnic profile through the use of national origin quotas, immigrants of other national backgrounds were somehow managing to come in. Some were spouses or children of U.S. citizens and as such were not obliged to wait their turn for an available slot. Some were "paroled" into the country temporarily for humanitarian reasons and then allowed to adjust their status to that of a permanent resident. Others benefited from the private or special interest immigration laws enacted at the request of individual members of Congress. The electoral constituency for a new immigration policy less tied to Anglo-Saxon interests was growing.

Evidence for that development came in the 1964 presidential election, when Senator Barry Goldwater and William Miller, a congressman from western New York, lost overwhelmingly to Lyndon Johnson and his running mate, Hubert Humphrey. As a vice presidential candidate, Miller tried to make an issue of Johnson's immigration reform plan, saying the proposed elimination of national origin quotas would "open the floodgates for any and all who would wish to come and find work in this country." Miller may have been assuming that voters were not in favor of immigrants, but with his comments he appeared to alienate voters of southern and eastern European backgrounds. The Johnson-Humphrey ticket won by huge margins in Polish, Italian, and Hispanic wards. Whether immigration was a decisive factor in the election is not clear, but the landslide win for the Democratic ticket set the stage for Johnson's unprecedented achievements in the next Congress, one of which would be the passage of the most important immigration law in the nation's history.

The prevailing sentiment in Congress on immigration reform shifted dramatically in 1965, making what had looked hopeless before now seem feasible. Much of the credit went to the civil rights movement. Americans had recognized the sickening hatred of white supremacists who would dare to plant a bomb at an Alabama church and kill four black girls. They had seen thuggish policemen turn fire hoses and attack dogs on people peacefully demonstrating for their right to vote. They had been moved by the courage of black students willing to walk a gauntlet of racist jeers and insults to enter schools they were entitled to attend. In Washington, Republicans and Democrats had joined forces to overcome the conservatives who for years had successfully blocked passage of a meaningful civil rights law, and that same bipartisan coalition in 1965 was preparing legislation to support voting rights. It was finally becoming unacceptable to discriminate against people according to their color, and the idea of judging prospective immigrants on the basis of their ancestry alone was no longer sustainable. Immigration reform had become linked to the civil rights movement. "We have removed all elements of second-class citizenship from our laws by the Civil Rights Act," declared Vice President Hubert Humphrey. "We must in 1965 remove all elements in our immigration law which suggest there are second-class people."

It had also become clear by 1965 that the quota system was broken, undermined by more than a thousand private bills and dozens of special laws favoring some individuals or groups over others, quite apart from what their national origin would have dictated. The old law was no longer defensible, even by those who believed in restricting immigration on the basis of nationality. So the ground was finally set for a grand reform, and at this opportune time the country had a president who was a master at getting things done, of fixing a broken train. In January 1965 Lyndon Johnson had a huge congressional majority to work with and he was determined to get a new law.

He wasted no time. On January 13, a week before he was inaugurated for a second term, Johnson introduced his own version of the immigration bill President Kennedy had sent to Congress a year and a half earlier. It was almost identical. No longer would immigrant visas be allocated on the basis of the applicants' ancestry, with a disproportionate number going to those with a northern European background, fewer to those with southern or eastern European origins, and just a token number to Asians, Africans, and Middle Easterners. Instead they would be distributed according to the applicants' individual characteristics. Spouses, minor children, and parents of U.S. citizens would be allowed to come to America in unlimited numbers as "nonquota immigrants." People from Western Hemisphere countries were also exempt from quota restrictions, though they would have to satisfy some basic criteria relating to their character and employability. For all other people around the world, about 165,000 immigration slots would be available, and they would be allocated in categories. The first 50 percent of the slots would be set aside for immigrants with exceptional skills or education deemed "especially advantageous" to the United States. The other half would be reserved for categories of those relatives of U.S. citizens and legal residents who did not qualify for nonquota visas, such as their adult unmarried sons and daughters or the spouses and children of legal U.S. residents who were not yet citizens. Any unused slots in one category would be distributed among the other groups. Introducing his legislation, Johnson said it would underscore the American belief "that a man is to be judged—and judged exclusively—on his worth as a human being." Manny Celler of Brooklyn, the only member who was in Congress when the 1924 Immigration Act was passed, introduced the Kennedy/Johnson bill in the House, and Philip Hart of Michigan was the lead sponsor in the Senate.

Administration officials at the time were still worried their legislation could get stuck somewhere as it made its way through Congress. One potential trap in the House had been Michael Feighan's immigration subcommittee, where three of the five members, including Feighan, had been cool to the administration's bill, if not opposed outright. With their added clout in the House, administration officials and Democratic leaders moved quickly to expand the Feighan subcommittee from five members to nine. Chairman Celler worked with the top Republican on his Judiciary Committee, the relatively liberal William McCulloch of Ohio, to select the four new subcommittee members. They were willing to support reform, at least in some form, meaning Feighan would have a much harder time killing the administration bill.

Meanwhile, the reformers were making progress in the Senate. Judiciary chairman Eastland was letting Senator Kennedy run the immigration subcommittee, and Kennedy had launched a full set of hearings on the proposed legislation. The other two Democrats senior to him on the subcommittee, Sam Ervin of North Carolina and John McClellan of Arkansas, were southern conservatives and defenders of the national origin quotas, but like Eastland they were content to let Kennedy manage the hearings. Between February and August, the subcommittee held twenty-nine hearings, with Kennedy presiding over most of them. Though he was only thirty-three years old and in just his third year in the Senate, Ted Kennedy had already mastered the Senate culture well enough to play his leadership role skillfully. Despite his own commitment to the cause of ending the quota system, he kept a low profile as the presiding chair, allowing opponents of the reform bill to say everything they wanted to say and rarely interjecting his own opinions.

Johnson was pleased by Kennedy's performance. He had a difficult relationship with Ted's older brother, telling biographer Doris Kearns Goodwin that Bobby Kennedy "acted like he was the custodian of the Kennedy dream, some kind of rightful heir to the throne," but Johnson was on almost fatherly terms with Ted and spoke to him regularly. When Ted called Johnson at the White House one night in March, partly to update him on the immigration hearings, he was quick to apologize for bothering him at such a late hour, but the president cut him off.

"I've told you, call me anytime you want to," Johnson said, "because I want to be true to the trust that's placed in me." Kennedy told Johnson that the immigration hearings were going well, but that the prospects in the House were less clear because of the unpredictability of Chairman Feighan, whom Kennedy called "a tough cookie."

"We've got to work on him a little bit," Johnson agreed.

The immigration hearings in both the House and the Senate at that point were addressing such profound issues as what it meant to be American and how open the country should be to foreigners from diverse backgrounds, but Johnson, always the legislator, tended to focus on the process rather than the substance of the debate.

"Why can't we get that immigration bill out?" he asked Majority Leader Carl Albert of Oklahoma during a May telephone conversation.

"Well, I think we will get it out," Albert said, but Johnson interrupted him.

"I think you ought to talk to Speaker [McCormack] and . . . you ought to call [Emanuel] Celler and this boy in from Ohio [Feighan] and just say, 'Now this is January and February and March and April and May . . .'"

"I think we'll get it out," Albert said, but he acknowledged that Feighan could be hard to deal with.

"Just shove it anyway you can," Johnson said.

But there were no shortcuts to an immigration consensus in either the Senate or the House. Even with the new liberal majorities, some powerful members of Congress still weren't ready to approve a sweeping change in U.S. immigration law. In the Senate, Kennedy was mindful that Eastland, McClellan, and Ervin were all senior to him on the immigration subcommittee and all three of them opposed

Johnson's proposal. He could not afford to rush the hearings. In the House, Feighan had been a strong defender of the McCarran-Walter law for years, and even though his views had evolved over the previous twelve months, he would make sure that people opposed to changing the law would get ample opportunity to speak.

Under the proposed reform, the United States would no longer be able to shape the racial, ethnic, and cultural composition of the country's population through immigration policy. No one knew for sure whether such a revision of the law would fundamentally change America and if so in what ways. The question of the country's essential identity had been debated since the founding of the republic. For some, the United States was essentially a branch of Europe, with a Christian or Judeo-Christian character and largely Caucasian "stock." For the idealists, America was more a notion than a nation, a country where race, religion, and ethnic origin should be irrelevant, because one acquired American nationality by adhering to a creed and embracing the values that defined the country. Over the next several months in the U.S. Congress, the immigration hearings and floor debates would dance around those core issues, sometimes addressing them but also dodging them and in the end not quite resolving them.

Among the witnesses testifying before Feighan's subcommittee in both the 1964 and 1965 hearings was John Trevor, Jr., appearing on behalf of a group called the American Coalition of Patriotic Societies. Trevor's testimony linked back forty years to the debate that surrounded passage of the 1924 Johnson-Reed Act, the law that established the basic framework of the national origins quota system, inasmuch as his father, John Trevor, Sr., was credited with providing the basic thinking from which the quota system evolved. Trevor Sr. was close to those who argued on the basis of eugenics "research" that some races were intellectually and cultural inferior to others and that their numbers should therefore be restricted in the United States. Trevor Jr. was himself a director of the Pioneer Fund, an organization founded in 1937 to support research into racial and genetic differences and dedicated originally to "race betterment" in the United States.

Explicitly racist arguments were no longer acceptable by the time Trevor Jr. appeared before Congress in 1964 and 1965, but his testimony recycled the forty-year-old argument for selecting immigrants by ancestry, i.e., that the racial and ethnic character of the U.S. population should be preserved for the good of the country. "The national origins provision," Trevor said, in his 1964 testimony, "holds a mirror up to the people now in the country and attempts to provide that the people who come in shall be a reflection of those who are already here." His "mirror" metaphor was popular with supporters of the quota system, and they went back to it regularly throughout the debate.

Trevor's principal problem with the Kennedy/Johnson reform bill was its promotion of what he called "new seed." By eliminating the national origin quotas, the law would in his view permit the entry of too many foreigners whose ancestry did not match those of most other Americans, and would therefore contribute "new seed" into the American population. At a time when equal opportunity and civil rights were popular causes, Trevor knew he was making a controversial argument, and one way he softened his testimony was by citing provocative commentary by others as opposed to offering his own.

The president general of the Daughters of the American Revolution, Mrs. William H. Sullivan, Jr., complained that eliminating a quota system based on national origins "could result in further unemployment, overladen taxes, to say nothing of a collapse of moral and spiritual values if nonassimilable aliens of dissimilar ethnic background and culture are permitted gradually to overwhelm our country."

The "assimilability" of various foreign populations had been a hot issue in every immigration debate over the previous century. On earlier occasions, the question was whether Jews or Italians or Poles could assimilate into the prevailing culture; before that, it was the Irish who were the outsiders. By 1965, most (though not all) of the immigration restrictionists had accepted that those southern and eastern European people could become fully American, and the question focused now on more distant populations. Democrat Sam Ervin of North Carolina wondered about Russians, for example.

"I really believe that a people that have been living under a totalitarian government like Russia are less experienced in government than the people in the United States," he said during one hearing. On another occasion, he wondered aloud whether immigrants from Indonesia would become responsible U.S. citizens as readily as people from Ireland. It was a game he played with nearly every witness who came before the subcommittee. In an exchange with Secretary of State Rusk, Ervin argued that a reform that reduced the number of immigrant slots reserved for people of British origin (65,000 per year at the time) while increasing the number available for Ethiopians (100 at the time) would discriminate against British people, because—in Ervin's words—"they gave us our language, they gave us our common law, they gave a large part of our political philosophy. . . . The reason I say this bill is discriminatory against these people is because it puts them on exactly the same plane as the people of Ethiopia are put, where the people of Ethiopia have the same right to come to the United States under this bill as the people from England, the people of France, the people of Germany, the people of Holland, and . . . with all due respect to Ethiopia, I don't know of any contributions that Ethiopia has made to the making of America." In another hearing a week later, Ervin made similarly disparaging remarks about potential immigrants from Congo.

Entirely absent in the congressional deliberations was any recognition of the contributions African Americans had made to the country. At the time, they literally did not count. Although immigrant quotas for European countries had been tied since 1924 to the percentage of Americans whose origins were in those countries, there was no such link for Americans with African origins. During the Senate floor debate, Democrat Spessard Holland of Florida asked,

"Why, for the first time, are the emerging nations of Africa to be placed on the same basis as are our mother countries—Britain, Germany, the Scandinavian nations, France, and the other nations from which most Americans have come?" In fact, the 1960 census showed that Americans of African descent outnumbered Scandinavian Americans by a margin of two and a half to one, and there were more African Americans in the United States than there were Americans whose origins lay in Italy, France, Netherlands, Belgium, Austria, and Switzerland combined. For the senator from Florida, however, the nations of Africa were not among "our mother countries."

The prospect of more nonwhite immigrants from Asia and Africa was a central topic of the 1965 hearings. This shift of geographic focus from the earlier concentration on southeastern Europe revealed deep prejudice against people of color. It also highlighted what in future years would turn out to be the key change in the U.S. immigrant population. Representative Ovie Fisher, a conservative Democrat from Texas, said he objected to the reform bill because it "shifts the mainstream of immigration from western and northern Europe—the principal source of our present population—to Africa, Asia, and the Orient," an observation that over the next decades would prove accurate. Senator John McClellan of Arkansas asked whether the new bill would lead to "still more ghettoes and thus more and more acts of violence and riots?" Using language identical to that used by Fisher and others, McClellan advised his fellow senators to remember that "under this bill, immigration will shift from those European countries that contributed most to the formation of this nation to the countries of Asia and Africa."

Rather than challenge the prejudicial view that more Asian and African immigrants were a cause for concern, however, Johnson administration officials and their supporters simply denied that any such shift would occur. In summarizing the bill, Kennedy promised "the ethnic mix of this country will not be upset." Emanuel Celler, the House sponsor, said there would not be "comparatively many Asians or Africans entering this country." Secretary of State Rusk said only about 16,000 or 17,000 people would move to America over the next five years from countries across the entire Asia Pacific Triangle, a flow he described as "relatively inconsequential." No more than 5,400 people would immigrate from Japan during that period, he predicted, and he said the State Department's "best information" suggested that immigration from India during those five years would total about 8,000. When questioned whether such estimates were accurate, Rusk said he saw no indications of "a world situation where everybody is just straining to move to the United States." The most erroneous assertion came in a fact sheet on "Quota Waiting Lists" prepared by the Justice Department. "Even if the national origins system were removed overnight," the fact sheet claimed, "the United States would not be inundated by Africans and Asians. Indeed, over 90 percent of all immigrants to the United States would be Caucasian, predominantly European. Thus, those opposed to large-scale migration from Africa and the Orient at this time should not be concerned on that score by the legislation." The migration flow within a few years would be almost exactly the opposite of what the Justice Department anticipated, with about 90 percent of all immigrants to the United States coming from outside Europe.

The refusal of Johnson administration officials to acknowledge that their reform could bring a more diverse U.S. population meant that it fell almost entirely to liberal members of Congress to say that the country could and should accommodate more immigrants of color. Most of the members willing to make that argument came from ethnic groups that had themselves been the target of discrimination. Representative Spark Matsunaga of Hawaii, of Japanese descent, reported that people in his state could testify to the civic contributions of Asian immigrants, pointing out that Hawaiians were able, "because of our unique geographical location, to speak from the vantage ground of actual observation and experience." Peter Rodino of New Jersey, of Italian origin, stood on the House floor and said, "The American nation today stands as eloquent proof that there is no inherent contradiction between unity and diversity." Emanuel Celler, who recalled a time when the assimilability of his fellow Jews was questioned, made a similar point about the promise of interethnic harmony by telling a joke about an imaginary restaurant scene in his native Brooklyn. A man entering a Chinese restaurant, he said, would be surprised to encounter a black waiter. When the man asks the specialty of the house, the waiter says, "pizza pie." Confused, the man asks why a Chinese restaurant would serve pizza. "Because this is a Yiddish neighborhood," the waiter answers.

Johnson administration officials, however, didn't ask members to set aside their stereotypes and prejudice regarding non-European immigrants. Apparently thinking that such an argument would fall flat, the officials chose to stick with their insistence that changing the criteria for admitting immigrants would have no consequential effect on the ethnic makeup of the immigrant population. In the coming years, when their official predictions were shown to have been wildly inaccurate, a debate arose over whether Johnson administration officials were misleading in their presentations to Congress or simply mistaken.

The short answer to that question is that the administration was looking backward, not forward. With respect to future immigration to the United States from countries in the Western Hemisphere, for example, officials based their estimates exclusively on the immigration patterns of previous years, assuming no change. Attorney General Nicholas Katzenbach, whose staff had largely drafted the immigration bill, told the House immigration subcommittee in March 1965 that the number of immigrants arriving in the United States from Western Hemisphere countries had been holding "reasonably steady" at approximately 125,000 per year and was likely to remain so. "I see no reason to believe that those figures would exceed, five years from now, by any great amount, perhaps not at all, the average for the past ten years." He would soon be proved wrong.

Such judgments did not adequately take into account how conditions were changing across the world, with respect both to the "push" factors that were driving people to leave their home countries and the "pull" factors in the United States and other receiving countries, that is, the cultural, economic, and political conditions that were making those destinations attractive to immigrants. Past patterns could be deceptive. If their assumptions about future migration flows were to be accurate, officials would need to identify trends and see where they would project. Immigration from northern and western Europe had already declined dramatically, because people in those countries no longer saw compelling reasons to move. Administration officials also anticipated that the urge to migrate would soon be declining in Italy and other southern European countries. They did not, however, foresee how many people in Asia, Africa, Latin America, and the Middle East would be increasingly likely to leave home and look for a better life elsewhere.

An example of a missed clue into future trends was a 1961 exchange between Kennedy administration officials and a U.S. diplomat named Gregory Henderson, who at the time was serving as a cultural attaché at the American embassy in Seoul, South Korea. One of Henderson's responsibilities was to keep track of Korean students who were given U.S. visas to attend American universities. The idea behind the program was that the students would gain a firsthand and favorable view of the United States and pass those impressions on to their compatriots on their return to Korea, thus serving U.S. foreign policy interests. Henderson, however, noticed that the great majority of the Korean students were choosing to remain in the United States after completing their studies. A memorandum Henderson wrote about the situation made it all the way to the White House, where presidential assistant Arthur Schlesinger, Jr., saw it and forwarded it to Deputy Attorney General Byron White, saying it was "a matter which you and the Immigration and Naturalization Service might want to brood about."

The memorandum also caught the attention of officials at the State Department, who agreed with Henderson's observation and pointed out that a similar situation was developing with respect to foreign students arriving in the United States from Afghanistan, Taiwan, Iran, Iraq, Pakistan, the Philippines, and Africa. Though the numbers were still small, the trend was unmistakable and illustrated the powerful draw the United States had in the middle of the twentieth century for enterprising and ambitious young people from across the developing world. Henderson and his State Department colleagues had identified what would become a significant part of the U.S. immigration flow. Their observation was apparently disregarded, however. Six months after preparing his memorandum, Henderson wrote a former schoolmate at the Justice Department to say he had received no further response to his concern. Four years later, the situation was apparently far from Secretary Rusk's mind when he said he saw no indication of people "straining to move to the United States."

By the summer of 1965, the battle to eliminate the national origin quota system was largely won. In the House, Congressman Feighan had agreed to support most of the administration's reform proposal, though he insisted on two key changes. First, he wanted a ceiling imposed on immigration from the Western Hemisphere, a provision the Johnson administration opposed as inconsistent with a "good neighbor policy." Second, Feighan wanted to rearrange the "preferences" under which immigrant visas would be distributed. The administration's bill had given priority to visa applicants considered "advantageous" to the nation because of their skills and training, with up to half the available slots reserved for applicants meeting that criterion. Relatives of U.S. citizens and legal residents were next in line under the administration plan. Feighan wanted to reverse those priorities, with the unification of divided families becoming the top priority. His amended version of the administration proposal set aside up to three quarters of available visas for family members, with separate categories for married and unmarried adult children of U.S. citizens, plus another category for family members of legal U.S. residents who had not yet become citizens. The largest number of visa slots—24 percent of the total available—would be set aside for brothers and sisters of U.S. citizens, a far more generous allocation for that group than the administration bill provided.

Feighan had for years strongly supported the national origin quota system as a way to preserve the racial and ethnic composition of the U.S. population. Recognizing that the existing quota system was doomed, he concluded that the same demographic result could be achieved by making family unification the paramount goal of U.S. immigration policy. If priority were given to visa applicants whose relatives were already in the United States, he figured, the existing profile of the U.S. population would be unchanged. In a February 1965 speech to the American Coalition of Patriotic Societies, the group headed by John Trevor, Jr., Feighan said U.S. immigration policy should be dedicated above all to the unification of those families that are "split and divided by peculiarities of law rather than free choice." Trevor and other ACPS leaders found his logic compelling enough that they decided not to oppose the elimination of the national origin quota, as they had previously.

Another group won over by Feighan's argument was the American Legion, which in the summer of 1964 had vigorously defended the principle of selecting immigrants on the basis of their national origin, through the use of quotas. A year later, the legion came out in support of Feighan's revised immigration bill. Two Legion representatives, in an article full of praise for Feighan's legislative work, said that by redesigning the administration's immigration reform proposal to emphasize family unification, he "devised a naturally operating national-origins system." Giving priority to immediate relatives, the Legion representatives argued, would actually bring about the result the quotas were meant to produce. "Nobody is quite so apt to be of the same national origins of our present citizens as are members of their immediate families," the Legion representatives wrote, "and the great bulk of immigrants henceforth will not merely hail from the same parent countries as our present citizens, but will be their closer relatives. . . . Asiatics, having far fewer immediate family members now in the United

States than Southern Europeans, will automatically arrive in far fewer numbers."

That argument was so persuasive that some of the fiercest critics of the old national origins approach were dismayed that its hated nationality bias could resurface under the proposed reform. The Japanese American Citizens League pointed out that Asians constituted just one half of one percent of the total U.S. population, so the number of Asians who would qualify for immigrant visas for family unification would be small. "Thus," the league complained, "it would seem that, although the immigration bill eliminated race as a matter of principle, in actual operation immigration will still be controlled by the now discredited national origins system, and the general pattern of immigration which exists today will continue for many years yet to come."

Supporters of immigration reform, including Kennedy and Celler, accepted Feighan's reversal of the preference categories, lowering the number of slots reserved for high-skill applicants and increasing the set-aside for family unification purposes. The more controversial of Feighan's amendments was the imposition of a new ceiling on immigration from the Western Hemisphere. The Johnson administration resisted this change, especially after U.S. forces invaded the Dominican Republic in May 1965, inflaming anti-American sentiment across the region. It was not the time, administration officials argued, to further alienate governments across Latin America and the Caribbean. When the full House Judiciary Committee approved the immigration bill, the Western Hemisphere ceiling was no longer in the legislation. Members who supported the ceiling filed a minority report saying "the possibility of a sharp increase in immigration from Western Hemisphere countries" made it necessary to establish a numerical limit.

Lyndon Johnson did not have strong feelings about the Western Hemisphere ceiling and deferred to Secretary of State Rusk on that issue. As always, the president was focused more on the parliamentary drama than the substance of the debate. On the day the immigration bill passed in the House, Johnson turned his attention to the Senate. The legislation was still pending in that chamber, largely because Senator Eastland, the Judiciary chairman, wanted a judgeship in Mississippi as his price for allowing his committee to take up the bill. Having summoned Celler to the White House, partly to congratulate the veteran reformer on the House passage, Johnson got Attorney General Katzenbach on the phone to discuss the next steps. He was on a speakerphone, with Celler listening in.

"What are you going to do for me on my birthday?" Johnson asked Katzenbach. "Get the immigration bill reported?" (Johnson's birthday was the next day.) "Tell [Eastland] you're gonna get his judge in Mississippi. Me and you and Celler's gonna get it for him. Manny, can I commit you?" As chairman of the House Judiciary Committee, Celler would have to go along with the appointment of a new federal judge.

Celler agreed. Johnson sensed that the way at last looked clear for enactment of immigration reform. He was in a good mood and already looking ahead to a celebratory signing ceremony. "Tell you what we'll do," he said to Katzenbach. "If you ever get that damn immigration bill past the Senate, if you get Teddy Kennedy to catch up with old man Celler here—he's seventy years old and he's already got his bill passed—then we'll hijack some of these fellows up there in Brooklyn and we'll take the pens that we sign the bill with, and we'll get [House speaker] John McCormack to come down from Boston. We'll get you to come up from here, and we'll bring [FBI director J.] Edgar Hoover to scare everybody. And we'll go up there to Ellis Island with old Manny and get a picture in the paper with him and salute him and click our heels."

It took another month to get the bill passed by the Senate. The numerical limit on immigration from the Western Hemisphere, dropped in the House bill, was restored in the Senate version, largely to win the support of Republicans like Everett Dirksen of Illinois, the ranking member on the Judiciary Committee. The Johnson administration had argued that immigration from the Western

Hemisphere had effectively been limited by provisions in U.S. law that gave visas only to those persons who could be certified as not taking jobs from U.S. citizens or were not likely to become dependent on public welfare. Many in Congress, however, with good reason, anticipated that poverty in Central and South America would eventually cause a tide of immigration from that region unless some limit was established. In the end, the administration decided not to fight the Western Hemisphere ceiling, much to the dismay of Philip Hart and Celler, both of whom saw it as a step backward from existing policy. Though their legislation would go down in history books as the Hart-Celler Act, Hart distanced himself from the legislation, largely because of the restrictive provisions that were added. For the first time, a numerical ceiling was put on immigration from the Western Hemisphere. For the rest of the world, the previous ceiling was maintained, except that parents of U.S. citizens could immigrate to the United States freely, without having to wait their turn in the quota line. The significant change from previous law was that the immigrant visas would no longer be distributed in a discriminatory manner, based on the national origin of the applicants. The achievement was a matter of moral principle, and for the Johnson administration, that was sufficient.

The Hart-Celler bill passed by a large margin in the Senate on September 22, 1965. As had been the case with the Civil Rights Act of the previous year, Republican support was notable. In both chambers, the main opposition came from conservative southern Democrats; the Republican caucus actually gave the legislation a bigger share of its vote than the Democratic caucus could provide. But the southerners' hold on the Democratic Party was weakening, and the more farsighted of them knew it. Senator James Eastland of Mississippi railed against the immigration reform but chose not to fight it, and by allowing Ted Kennedy to chair the hearings, he had signaled his acquiescence. His one condition had been that anyone who wanted to testify at the hearings or submit a statement be given the opportunity to do so, and Kennedy honored that commitment scrupulously. When witnesses—or fellow senators—made outrageous arguments, Kennedy did not object. In contrast, his brother Robert—who was now a senator from New York—was more inclined to speak his mind and sometimes had trouble containing himself, engaging in sharp exchanges with Sam Ervin of North Carolina and Spessard Holland of Florida.

Ted Kennedy knew the votes and momentum were on the side of the reformers, and he figured chances for smooth passage of the legislation would be enhanced if he allowed his opponents every opportunity to make their case. His management of the hearings and the floor action on the bill earned him the praise of his colleagues, including Sam Ervin, who in the end actually voted in favor of the legislation. Though he had led the criticism of the proposed reform throughout the hearings, it seemed he had been largely playing the role of a devil's advocate, and he credited Kennedy for allowing him to do so. "Had it not been for the tact and the understanding and the devotion which the senator from Massachusetts gave to this bill, the bill would never have come from the subcommittee or the full committee in such fine form," Ervin said during the final floor debate.

The Immigration and Nationality Act of 1965—as Hart-Celler was formally known—technically a series of amendments to the 1952 McCarran-Walter Act, was approved by both chambers of Congress on September 30, 1965, and sent to the president for his signature. Perhaps the most important factor explaining its relatively easy passage was that both the immigration reformers and the immigration restrictionists managed to convince themselves and each other that the legislation would not change the immigration picture all that much. In future years, the advocates of tighter immigration controls would look back at the passage of the 1965 Act as a major cause of the immigration wave that followed, with millions of Asians, Africans, Middle Easterners, and Latin Americans moving to the United States. The administration officials who insisted that no such inflow would occur were proved wrong, but they were not alone. Ironically, it was Congressman Michael Feighan, a long-time supporter of the national origin quotas and a close ally of the immigration restrictionists, who was most responsible for opening the United States to more non-European foreigners. Feighan's elevation of the priority given to family unification visas, including his insistence that nearly a quarter of immigrant visas go to brothers and sisters of U.S. citizens, proved to be a decisive element in the expanded immigrant flow. His plan to come up with "a naturally operating national-origins system" backfired. Fifty years later, about two thirds of all immigrants entering the United States legally were family members of U.S. citizens or permanent residents, and the 1965 law was even known in some quarters as "the brothers and sisters act."

President Johnson signed the Immigration Act on October 3, 1965, in an elaborate ceremony on Liberty Island in New York Harbor, in a scene almost exactly as he had envisioned. Ellis Island, where millions of new immigrants had been processed upon their arrival in the United States, was rejected as a site for the ceremony because it did not have proper landing facilities and was not then in good condition. But Liberty Island was a more picturesque location, with open terraces overlooking the water. An ornate wooden desk was set near the base of the Statue of Liberty. October 3 was a beautiful autumn day, with blue skies and a blustery wind, and hundreds of invited guests and interested onlookers gathered around, some of them hoping to get one of the souvenir pens the president would hand out. The White House had invited almost everyone who had had a hand in the preparation and passage of the immigration legislation. Among the invitees was Erich Leinsdorf, the symphony conductor from Austria who had first sensitized Lyndon Johnson to immigrant concerns and who had been able to escape Nazi rule thanks to Johnson's personal intervention. Like many of the other guests, Leinsdorf arrived by boat, but with hundreds of people milling around, he never got close enough to see the actual ceremony.

Johnson took a seat at the wooden table, with his wife Lady Bird, at his right elbow. Luci, their daughter, stood nearby. Gathered tightly around them were Vice President Humphrey and his wife, Muriel, and Manny Celler and his wife. Philip Hart was next to Celler. Ted and Robert Kennedy stood to the left of the president. Around them were top Democratic leaders, including U.N. ambassador Arthur Goldberg, House speaker John McCormack, Ambassador Averell Harriman, Senators Daniel Inouye of Hawaii, and Mike Mansfield of Montana, along with two House Republicans, Ogden Reid and John Lindsay, both of them with New York constituencies that had a stake in the liberalization of immigration policy. Michael Feighan stood off to one side, as far from Manny Celler as he could be. The waters of New York Harbor and the Manhattan skyline provided the backdrop.

The president's remarks, delivered at a podium in the shadow of the Statue of Liberty, reflected the ambiguous interpretation of the legislation. "The bill that we sign today is not a revolutionary bill," Johnson said. "It does not affect the lives of millions. . . . Yet it is still one of the most important acts of this Congress and of this administration." For the president and his administration and for those members of Congress who had worked hardest for the reform legislation, the Immigration and Nationality Act of 1965 was above all a symbolic victory in the battle against injustice and discrimination. Johnson said the bill "corrects a cruel and enduring wrong in the conduct of the American nation."

> The bill says simply that from this day forth those wishing to immigrate to America shall be admitted on the basis of their skills and their close relationship to those already here.
>
> This is a simple test, and it is a fair test. Those who can contribute most to this country—to its growth, to its strength, to its spirit—will be the first that are admitted to this land.

The fairness of this standard is so self-evident that we may well wonder that it has not always been applied. Yet the fact is that for over four decades the immigration policy of the United States has been twisted and has been distorted by the harsh injustice of the national origins quota system.

Under that system the ability of new immigrants to come to America depended upon the country of their birth. . . . Families were kept apart because a husband or a wife or a child had been born in the wrong place. . . .

This system violated the basic principle of American democracy—the principle that values and rewards each man on the basis of his merit as a man. It has been un-American in the highest sense, because it has been untrue to the faith that brought thousands to these shores even before we were a country.

Today, with my signature, this system is abolished.

Following the ceremony, Johnson and his party left the island on a helicopter. White House staff had finally located Erich Leinsdorf, and Johnson invited him to go in the helicopter with him and then ride along in his limousine to the Waldorf-Astoria hotel, where the president and first lady were to have dinner with Ambassador Goldberg, an old friend of Johnson's, and his wife. Nine people were crowded into the car, more than it was supposed to carry, but Johnson was in a celebratory mood and insisted that everyone squeeze together in the limousine, as if they were on their way to a high school prom.

PART THREE

11

TURNING POINT

None of the people involved in the 1965 reform of U.S. immigration policy understood what they were doing. The Kennedy and Johnson administration officials who drafted the reform proposal, the members of Congress who were its strongest supporters, and the immigration critics who reshaped it in ways to serve their own ends—all miscalculated.

In testimony over the course of a year, administration officials insisted that the elimination of national origin quotas and the introduction of new "preferences" for admission to the United States would not bring a big increase in the number of people coming to the country. In fact, the subsequent surge of immigrants from Asia, Africa, Latin America, and the Middle East brought the share of the U.S. population born outside the country back to a level not seen since early in the century. Meanwhile, Michael Feighan of Ohio, the congressman who came up with a plan to preserve the existing ethnic profile of the U.S. population by favoring those immigrants with family members already in the country, managed to produce exactly the opposite result. In 1960, seven out of eight immigrants were white people from Europe. By 2010, Europeans accounted for barely one out of ten newcomers; immigrants from other parts of the world dominated. Feighan's "naturally operating national-origins system" was a bust.

U.S. Census data, collected every ten years, clearly identified when the immigration pattern changed. After decades of decline, immigration to the United States started increasing again around 1970. The shift in the national origin of the new arrivals occurred more gradually, but the data show a steep drop in the European share after 1960, with a corresponding increase in immigration from other parts of the world.

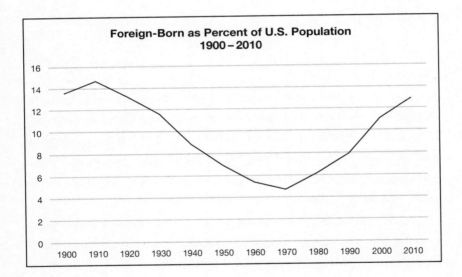

A clear explanation for the dramatic change in the U.S. immigration picture after 1960 is the 1965 revision of immigration law, given that it opened America's doors to people around the world who previously were unwelcome. The 1965 Act committed the United States for the first time in its history to accept newcomers on a nondiscriminatory basis, and the expanded allocation of family visas made it easier for foreigners to qualify for U.S. resident status. The elimination of national origin quotas brought vastly increased

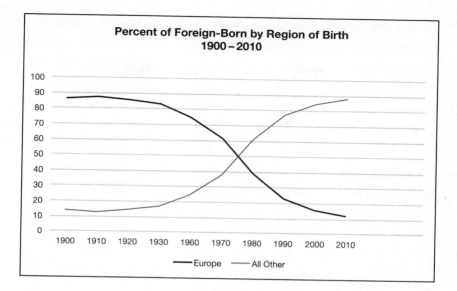

immigration from Asia in particular. As long as Asian countries were allocated only about a hundred quota-based visas per year, the demand far exceeded the supply. The new allotments made an enormous difference. In 1960, barely 11,000 Koreans were living in the United States. Forty years later, the number had grown to 864,000. During the same four decades, the number of native Pakistanis in the United States jumped from 1,700 to 223,000, while immigration from India increased from barely 17,000 in 1960 to more than one million by the year 2000. Those numbers would have been inconceivable without the immigration reforms of 1965.

To be sure, other factors contributed to the immigration surge in the closing decades of the twentieth century. Powerful social, economic, geopolitical, and technological forces after 1965 pushed people out of their home countries and pulled them to America, independently of the new immigration law. Improvements in global communication meant that people everywhere became more aware of the available opportunities in distant lands. The development of new transportation networks made migration easier and cheaper. In the United States, increased employment in restaurants, child care, general contracting, lawn maintenance, and housecleaning offered entry-level openings for immigrants who lacked other job skills or fluency in English. In Mexico and Central America, people migrated in larger numbers because of political violence in their homelands. The 1965 Act was merely coincidental with those developments. Nor did it account for all the refugees or asylum seekers who came to the United States in subsequent years from such countries as Cuba, Vietnam, Afghanistan, or Somalia, most of whom benefited from separate legislation. Still, the 1965 reforms played a key role in the cultural and demographic transformation of America.

In the case of increased immigration from Africa, the 1965 legislation complemented other developments. Prior to the 1960s, the main migratory routes out of Africa were to the European countries that had colonized the continent. Between 1925 and 1965, fewer than 40,000 people from all of Africa were admitted as U.S. immigrants. While it is true that African countries during those years were allocated only a token number of U.S. immigrant visas, the available slots were never completely filled. In every year through the 1950s and early 1960s, more Africans could have immigrated to the United States than actually came. With decolonization, however, some of the links to Europe were severed, as governments there imposed new immigration restrictions on their former possessions, and the United States promptly became the favored destination. Political unrest arising from independence struggles in Africa, meanwhile, increased the outmigration pressures. Were it not for the big increase in available immigration slots introduced by the 1965 reforms, many more Africans would have been frustrated in their desire to move to America. As it was, by 2005, the number of U.S. residents born in Africa was approaching 1.4 million.

The numbers for Latin America are equally impressive. In the forty years prior to 1965, for example, fewer than 20,000 Salvadorans immigrated legally to the United States. Over the next forty years, more than a million came. Again, however, one must be careful in linking the increased flow to the passage of the 1965 Act. The legislation did ultimately facilitate heightened immigration from

Latin America, but it did so in unique ways, and the connection requires separate explanation. Whereas immigration from Asia before 1965 was restricted by the tiny visa quotas for those countries, that was not the situation in Latin America, inasmuch as there was no numerical limit on immigration from the region during that period. The low numbers coming from Latin America were due instead to the absence of an established migratory infrastructure and the relatively low education levels of the population. To qualify for a U.S. resident visa, migrants had to show they would be employable in America and unlikely to become a "public charge." Those were major obstacles to overcome, no matter whether visas were theoretically available.

The most important legal immigration channel for Latin Americans prior to 1965 was the bracero program, which since 1942 had authorized workers from Mexico and other countries in the region to come to the United States on a temporary basis for employment in the agriculture sector. Congress voted in 1964 to terminate the program, spurred by liberal reformers who saw the program as exploitative of the foreign workers. That action had two consequences. First, it led to a major increase in illegal immigration, because the migratory pattern was by then a well-established part of the U.S. economy. The braceros (in Spanish, those who work with their arms, i.e., manual laborers) continued to come across the border to do the same seasonal work they had always done, but now without legal authorization. Second, the cancellation of the program triggered interest in alternative immigration routes. The 1965 Act brought new opportunities for U.S. citizens to serve as sponsors for relatives who wished to immigrate. Latin Americans who were unable to prove they would not become a "public charge" in the United States soon had another way to qualify for a resident visa, thanks in good part to the new law.

In combination with the other forces at work in the world, the 1965 Act helped set in motion immigration flows that almost no one had foreseen. Dean Rusk's statement in 1965 that he saw no evidence of "a world situation where everybody is just straining to move to the United States" suggested that the Johnson administration officials had little idea how consequential their reform would prove to be. The miscalculation on the part of Michael Feighan and his allies, meanwhile, was to think that by putting family unification over the promotion of professional skills and employability they would minimize the likelihood of a shift in the ethnic makeup of the incoming immigrant population. In the short run, their reasoning was sound. Asians, Africans, and other non-Europeans had far fewer family members in the United States than Europeans had. But family unification was a powerful force, and the presence of even a single naturalized U.S. citizen with family members in the home country proved sufficient to set in motion an ever-widening process of chain migration. The first in the chain could arrive with one of the visas that were set aside for immigrants who filled particular employment needs in the United States, with separate categories for "priority workers" and professionals with "exceptional ability," and the EB-3 program offered residency to immigrants able and willing to take jobs that U.S. workers spurned. Hispanics or Asians or Africans who came to the United States with such visas could soon sponsor the immigration of their relatives, including their adult brothers and sisters, plus their siblings' spouses—who in turn could sponsor their own brothers and sisters and their families. A doctor or engineer arriving from India, a technical worker from South Korea, a student from Africa who found employment in the United States, or a refugee from Afghanistan provided an entrée for an entire family network.

From the Vietnam War onward, Virginia's Fairfax County was a prime resettlement area for refugees and asylum seekers. That created a pool of immigrants, each of whom was able to invite family members to join them. Moreover, the county's strong economy and superior schools made it especially attractive to new residents. With its proximity to federal government agencies and defense-related industries, northern Virginia had abundant employment opportunities, and immigrants with special skills were highly valued. Even with its concentration of low-income residents in its Mason District, Fairfax County was consistently ranked among the wealthiest counties in the United States. The rapid growth of the immigrant population if anything added to the county's prosperity, by adding new and energetic workers just as the regional economy was expanding.

Each immigrant family had a story. A Korean man by the name of Sang Duck Yeom and his wife, Ok Um, immigrated to Fairfax County in the 1970s from Seoul at the invitation of Ok Um's sister, who had become a U.S. citizen by marrying an American affiliated with the U.S. military in South Korea. Once Sang Duck became a U.S. citizen via his wife's sister, he was able to sponsor his own sister Sang Sook Kim and her husband, Miyung Jun, who were eager to move to America to get better medical care for their daughter, Un Joung, who was afflicted with cerebral palsy. Sang Sook and Miyung Jun had in the meantime moved to Buenos Aires, where there was a strong Korean immigrant community, but they saw Argentina as only a stop on the way to their desired destination. A similar immigration process was set in motion when Abdul Sayeed Khan moved to Fairfax County from Pakistan in the late 1960s, sponsored by the U.S. company for which he had worked in Karachi. Over the next twenty-five years, Khan in turn sponsored the immigration of six brothers and three sisters, along with their spouses, all of whom were subsequently naturalized and thus authorized to invite their own siblings, with their spouses and families. By 2015, Abdul Sayeed's initial move to the United States had resulted in the immigration of more than a hundred extended family members. Such chain migrations proceeded slowly; an authorization to get a visa only got immigrants a place in line. One of Khan's brothers, Abdul Shaheed Khan, worked as a refrigeration technician in Saudi Arabia for several years before he was able to move to America with his family.

Sang Sook Kim and her husband waited ten years in Argentina for their visa number to come up. But the expansion was nonetheless exponential.

Those immigrants who arrived in America through family connections often had to start out at the bottom, because they were coming without employer sponsorship. Sang Sook worked as a seamstress in Korean-owned dry cleaning shops in the D.C. area, while her husband, Miyung Jun, repaired sewing machines. Abdul Shaheed Khan, who followed his brother Abdul Sayeed to America, had been trained as a refrigeration technician in Pakistan and held professional positions in Saudi Arabia, but upon arriving in America the only job he could find was as a cashier at a 7-Eleven. Lacking their own housing, his family, like Sang Sook's family, moved in with the siblings who sponsored their immigration.

With the allocation of immigrant visas on the basis of family ties and employment criteria, the integration process was substantially different than it was for previous generations. In the years before immigration became so restricted, foreigners generally arrived en masse and settled together in core urban neighborhoods, where they could find factory jobs, or in sparsely settled rural areas, where they could farm. The new immigrants, coming to the country only when their individual visa number came up, generally went where their relatives lived, or they settled in communities of their own choosing. Many were drawn to the suburbs, which offered safer streets, more employment opportunities, affordable housing, and better schools for their children. Fairfax County met all those criteria. In the three decades after 1970, the county population doubled, and it was largely due to the arrival of people born outside the United States. Between 1990 and 2000, for example, an increase in the number of foreign-born residents in Fairfax County accounted for nearly three fourths of that decade's population growth. The county by then had become what human geographers called an "edge gateway," distinguished from previous immigrant settlement areas by its location on the edge of a major city rather than at its core. The steadily growing concentration of immigrants in Fairfax County over the last years of the twentieth century gave them power to shape the suburb. They were not mere interlopers, taking advantage of the superior quality of life they found there; the county's future to a large extent lay in their hands.

This new suburban settlement pattern meant the immigrants' acculturation experience was different from that of their predecessors. In the past, each major city had a "Chinatown" or a "Little Italy" or some other ethnic enclave where a particular immigrant population was concentrated in isolation from the rest of the urban population. In Fairfax County, immigrants making their own residential choices based on their particular values and interests scattered more or less randomly. The Annandale community was sometimes called "Koreatown" because of its many Korean restaurants and shops catering to Korean immigrants, but that was a misnomer. Most Korean immigrants lived elsewhere and came to Annandale only to shop. Hispanic residents actually outnumbered Koreans there.

By the twenty-first century, Fairfax had become the most populous and diverse jurisdiction in the entire Washington, D.C., region. A *Washington Post* survey in 2010 found that only 2 percent of Fairfax County neighborhoods were segregated by race or ethnicity. The county had a "diversity index" of 64, meaning that if two individuals were drawn randomly out of a Fairfax county neighborhood, there was a 64 percent likelihood they would be of different races. The country's stunning demographic transformation presented enormous challenges to Fairfax authorities. Planners had to deal with a radically changed school population and overcrowded schools. Law enforcement and judicial officials faced unfamiliar cultural issues. County publications were distributed in six languages—English, Spanish, Arabic, Farsi, Korean, and Vietnamese—but even that was not enough, because more than a hundred languages were spoken in the county. Patterns of civic participation were upended, with unpredictable consequences for local governance.

The diversity of the immigrant population in the county was

reflected not only in the variety of nationalities and languages represented there, but in the educational and class backgrounds. A
community survey undertaken in 2000 showed that 74 percent of
households where Urdu was spoken (indicating South Asian ancestry) were headed by someone with a college degree or better.
For Korean households, the figure was 58 percent; among Farsi-
speaking households (largely Iranian), it was 56 percent. Meanwhile, only 1 percent of the immigrants from El Salvador had a
college degree; two out of three had not even finished high school.

The challenge in places like Fairfax County was to incorporate the
new immigrants in such a way as to establish commonality among
all the residents. The question of whether and how that could happen had been considered for decades. The Immigration Act of 1965
did not by itself account for the immigration influx that came in
its wake, but the congressional debate that year over the proposed
reforms did anticipate the influx, and it highlighted the relevant
issues. The key question—how far the United States should go in
accommodating cultural differences in its population—would re-
sound for years to come. When Peter Rodino of New Jersey, advocating an end to ethnic discrimination in immigration policy, said
he saw "no inherent contradiction between unity and diversity," he
was making a point about the merits of multiculturalism that would
be heard and challenged over and over in the decades ahead and put
to the test in Fairfax County and other communities where immigrants settled in large numbers.

Notably, it was the opponents of the 1965 reforms, not the supporters, who insisted on talking about increased immigration from
Africa, Asia, the Middle East, and Latin America. Millions of people would soon be arriving in the United States from all corners of
the earth, and the 1965 debate appropriately focused on what such
immigration was likely to signify for the nation. Johnson administration officials vigorously denied that the act would trigger big

changes in the ethnic composition of the American nation, but they and other reformers still had to argue that such changes should not matter in any case, because someone's suitability as a U.S. citizen should not depend on his or her national origin or the color of their skin. The firm establishment of that principle as a matter of U.S. law was an act of historic importance, especially because it came almost simultaneously with other landmark civil rights achievements. No longer would the country try deliberately to maintain an essentially European character. Harvard sociologist Nathan Glazer said the immigration reforms signaled "a revolution in American national identity." As an official statement of principle, immigration reform sent a message to the world that the United States from then on would be committed to an unbiased admissions policy. Potential immigrants everywhere took notice, with new hopes and expectations they may not otherwise have considered realistic.

The 1965 Act also established a new framework for dealing with immigration, one better suited to modern realities. Regardless of how many of the new arrivals came to the country as a direct result of the legislation, it is undeniable that the 1965 law better prepared the country to manage the inflow. A system of preferences specifying "whom we shall welcome" was precisely the approach recommended by the 1952 Truman Commission in its report bearing that title. Immigration policy would henceforth serve the goals of family unification and U.S. economic interests rather than private or ad hoc priorities or racist assumptions about superior and inferior ethnic "stock."

Revolutions, of course, are unsettling. The critical question was whether the immigrants who could qualify for admission to the United States under the reforms would ever become truly American in outlook and behavior. As Robert Byrd of West Virginia had argued during the Senate floor debate, "The reasoning back of the present system is that additional population from those countries [that were favored under the national origin quotas] would be more easily and readily assimilated into the American population.

Naturally, those immigrants can best be absorbed into our modern population whose backgrounds and cultures are similar." Developments in later years countered some of those assumptions. By 2010, the foreign-born portion of the U.S. population on average were more enterprising and less likely to be unemployed than the native-born, even though they were poorer. (Census data consistently showed immigrants with marginally higher rates of entrepreneurship, self-employment, and labor force participation than native-born workers.) Immigrant families also appeared to be generally stable, with lower rates of divorce than native families and a higher percentage of households maintained by a married couple. Half of all the foreign-born U.S. population spoke only English at home or at least spoke it "very well," and for second-generation immigrants good English ability was nearly universal.

For immigration critics, however, these empirical data did not address the deeper concern: Had these new immigrants from what used to be called the Third World genuinely embraced American culture and values? Notably, the same questions were asked at the turn of the last century, when the United States was facing a huge flow of immigrants from southern and eastern Europe, people with life experiences and skills that differentiated them from northern and western Europeans. In that case, the passage of time effectively eliminated those differences, and by the second or third generation, the Slavic and Mediterranean Europeans had become one with the larger group of European Americans. The notion that post-1965 immigrants, almost entirely non-European, might similarly blend into the broader U.S. population seemed plausible. But would it work?

In 1995, thirty years after the sweeping reform of the country's immigration laws, Princeton University sociologist Douglas Massey tackled that question in a paper he titled "The New Immigration and Ethnicity in the United States." Massey, who grew up in the state of Washington and was introduced to Spanish by his third grade teacher, wrote from a position of familiarity with migrant communities in the United States. Fluent in Spanish, he visited Mexico every year and was hardly unsympathetic with foreign-born Americans, whether Hispanic or Asian or African. He nevertheless approached the question of the assimilability of the new populations with an open mind, prepared to address the persistent anti-immigrant sentiments held by many white Americans. Those feelings, he said, were fueled by "a fear of cultural change and a deep-seated worry that European Americans will be displaced from their dominant position in American life." Such a reaction, Massey suggested, was not surprising.

"Whatever objective research says about the prospects for individual assimilation, the ethnic and racial composition of the United States is clearly changing," he wrote, "and with it the sociocultural world created by prior European immigrants and their descendants. . . . What the public really wants to know (at least, I suspect, the native white public), is whether or not the new immigrants will assimilate into the Euro-American society of the United States, and how that society and its culture might change as a result of this incorporation." In his paper, Massey reviewed the successful integration of the once scorned Polish, Jewish, and Italian populations, saying it was natural to consider their experience as a model for the assimilation of new immigrants from Asia, Latin America, and elsewhere. But then he signaled caution. "The new immigration," Massey noted, "differs in several crucial respects that significantly alter the prospects for assimilation and, hence, the meaning of ethnicity for the next century."

Two significant features of the new immigration distinguished it from the earlier flows. First, the great wave of southern and eastern Europeans into the United States was followed by several decades when immigration from Europe was reduced to a trickle. This hiatus, Massey suggested, "gave the United States a 'breathing space' within which slow-moving social and economic processes leading to assimilation could operate." With relatively few immigrants arriving from the old lands during the middle years of the twentieth century, there was no raw material for "the grist mill of ethnicity," and the old national identities weakened in each successive generation. By contrast, immigration after 1965 was an accelerating phenomenon, meaning that the ethnic identities of Asians, Hispanics, Africans, and others were constantly reinforced by the arrival of new people from the same ancestral lands. The second difference, Massey observed, is that the integration of the European immigrants occurred during a period of economic expansion, with many opportunities for socioeconomic advancement, while the post-1965 immigration came in a period of growing inequality, sluggish growth, and rising economic stress. As a result of those two factors, Massey wrote, "the patterns and outcomes of assimilation [for the new immigrants] are likely to be quite different." One danger would be that the assimilation of some new immigrants would be incomplete, with a prospect of being stuck in an immigrant underclass. Though Massey was writing in 1995, the contextual conditions he identified—the constancy of the immigration numbers and the surrounding economic difficulty—would persist in the years ahead.

Other observers raised related questions about the post-1965 immigrant populations, though with less rigor and with evident cultural prejudice. Harvard University's Samuel Huntington argued in his 2004 book *Who Are We?* that America was "Anglo-Protestant" at its core and that the unity of the country was jeopardized by immigrants who did not identify with that culture. Unlike earlier immigration critics, Huntington did not necessarily object to the admission of non-European immigrants; he cared only about their values and outlook. "Throughout American history," he wrote, "people who were not white Anglo-Saxon Protestants have become Americans by adopting America's Anglo-Protestant culture and political values." Someone coming from Korea or Sierra Leone or El Salvador could be as American as anyone else as long as he or she adhered to the Anglo-Protestant way. Huntington said the central issue posed after 1965 was, "To what extent will these immigrants, their successors, and descendants follow the path of earlier immigrants and . . . become committed Americans forswearing other national identities, and adhere through belief and action to the principles of the American Creed?"

Whether Huntington was asking the proper question about the new immigrants, however, was debatable. The notion that America should be a "melting pot" where all newcomers merge into a single cultural type characterized by an Anglo-Saxon outlook was to some a misinterpretation of what it actually meant to become an American. To be sure, the country's Founding Fathers had a common background, but whether the "American Creed" was inherently an Anglo-Saxon artifact is open to question. Huntington defined it in cultural terms, but historian Richard Hofstadter saw the American nation instead as the embodiment of an idea. "It has been our fate as a nation not to have ideologies but to be one," he was famously quoted as saying. Political scientist Seymour Martin Lipset, who wrote extensively about "American exceptionalism," cited Hofstadter's quote approvingly and took it a step further, saying that "becoming American was . . . an ideological act" akin to adopting a new "political religion." Lipset described the American Creed in terms that mostly freed it from any particular cultural context, saying it consisted of a belief in five essential ideas: liberty, equality (of opportunity, not outcome), individualism, populism (as opposed to elitism), and "laissez-faire," by which he meant a noninterfering, live-and-let-live philosophy, both in governance and in daily life. For Lipset and others who shared his views, immigrants could become American by adopting those principles as their own, regardless of their bloodline, place of birth, or adherence to a national or religious heritage. As long as immigrants accepted those basic tenets, they were free to maintain a distinctive cultural, ethnic, or religious identity.

The country's adoption of this "assimilation contract," as some writers term it, showed the United States to be a uniquely welcoming nation and explained its appeal to migrants worldwide. The implicit accommodation of diversity also meant the country experienced constant cultural change, because acculturation works in both directions. Just as immigrants adapt to life in America, the American nation incorporates some of the cultural elements the immigrants bring with them. With nine out of ten coming from a non-European background, the idea that America is essentially a European country becomes progressively harder to maintain.

The passage of the 1965 Immigration Act signified a formal acceptance of this diversity model, but external circumstances to a large extent made it inevitable. Globalization and technological change in transportation and communication mean that populations no longer live in isolation from each other. The immigrants of a century ago found it far more difficult to maintain ties with their ancestral lands; immigrants today communicate instantaneously and at virtually no cost with their relatives back home, and as long as their travel documents are in order they can fly back and forth without spending an exorbitant sum. As a consequence, they are less likely to give up their Old Country identities entirely, and governments recognize this reality by allowing dual citizenship to a greater extent than ever before.

All these developments complicated the construction of a modern American nationality. The U.S. philosophical heritage, once limited to the Anglo-Saxon ideas of its founders, was now imbued with new intellectual strains. Asian immigrants brought with them Confucian beliefs in hard work, sacrifice, and meritocracy, which partly explained their superior educational achievement and disproportionate representation in elite academic institutions. The arrival of immigrants from Muslim lands, a prospect not foreseen or discussed during the 1965 debate, raised additional issues, as they brought with them distinctive dress and religious practices and separate legal and political traditions. The 9/11 terror attacks, the rise of Islamist extremism, and U.S. military deployments in Muslim countries raised issues for Muslim immigrants that other groups did not encounter and that complicated their assimilation. Many immigrants, encountering ethnic or religious discrimination, sought protection as minorities, but the assertion of collective rights contradicted an element of the American Creed, which was that Americans should be judged and rewarded as individuals, not as members of a group. Hispanic immigrants, arriving from nearby countries in large numbers and all speaking the same language, raised the prospect of a separate national subculture. In comparison to other immigrants, those coming from Mexico and Central America were far less likely to speak English "well" or "very well," were slower to seek U.S. citizenship, and were often more burdened by traumatic experiences in the countries from which they had fled.

When Modesto Quintanilla went off to play cards with the other gambling men in his village in El Salvador, he took his seven-year-old daughter, Marta, along for protection. The men were all poor *campesinos*, and none could afford to lose. Some of them drank while they played, and angry words would invariably be exchanged. The potential for violence over a disputed bet was great enough that the men agreed beforehand not to allow machetes at the table. But Modesto didn't trust his fellow gamblers and wanted to be ready in case someone came after him, so before leaving home he tied a machete to little Marta's chest and covered it with her long dress. He would leave her sitting nearby for the duration of the game, which could be an entire day.

The experience did not endear her father to Marta, especially when he was gambling away what little he had earned picking coffee berries on a nearby plantation or doing farmwork on someone else's land. On those occasions, there would be no money left for food, and Marta and others in the family would go hungry. Modesto did not drink, as so many other men did, but his wife, Ana, and their children had enough hardship without his gambling habits making life all the more difficult. They lived outside the town of Moncagua, in a semirural settlement without paved streets, running water, or electricity. Their house had a dirt floor, and the roof and walls were flimsy tin sheets nailed to a wood frame. In the early 1980s, when Marta was growing up, the Salvadoran military was engaged in combat with leftist guerrillas, and sometimes there was fighting in the area around Moncagua. On those occasions, Marta's mother would tell her and her siblings to stay inside the house. If the shooting got close, they would pile rocks around the bed and hide underneath it.

A stressful childhood can be scarring or it can be strengthening. Marta Quintanilla was a resourceful and resilient girl with street smarts and a good heart, and from an early age she was making decisions, rightly or wrongly, with a confidence well beyond her years. There was a rural school in the area, but it was a thirty-minute walk each way, and the older she got, the more Marta felt guilty being away all day when she could be helping at home. Her mother had taught her how to make tortillas, and she often took care of her baby brother while her mother was washing clothes or doing other chores. When her father replaced a tin sheet on the roof, Marta held the nails for him. She helped him make the mud bricks he used to build the well where they got their water, and she would often go to the *milpa* with him to cut the corn or harvest the beans. Her older brother, José, went off to the nearby city of San Miguel at the age of eleven to take a job as a baker's helper, and before long Marta was thinking she should look for work in San Miguel as well. A wiser choice would be to continue her education, but immediate survival needs were more pressing, and her parents made no effort to dissuade her.

So Marta boarded the San Miguel bus one morning and went to the city to find an older cousin who she knew would be selling tomatoes in the market. She was just ten years old and small for her age, but her cousin knew Marta to be a good worker, and she told her of a woman who was looking for a girl to help her around the house in exchange for room and board and a meager wage. The woman hired Marta on the spot and immediately found some better clothes for her to wear. At the end of the first month she paid her eighty Salvadoran colones, the equivalent of about ten dollars. With part of the money, Marta bought some cornmeal and vegetables and headed back to Moncagua. Her mother met her at the bus station, and Marta would never forget the broad smile on her mother's face when she stepped off the bus with a bundle of food under her arm, new shoes, and a few extra pounds on her frame. The feeling of pride and satisfaction Marta experienced that day ensured that her days of schooling in El Salvador were finished. No longer would she be another mouth to feed, even a small one. From then on, she would be a provider.

Over the next four years, Marta went back and forth between her village and San Miguel, taking jobs where she could find them and helping her parents as best she could, while also experiencing some of the adventures of city life. As the departmental capital, San Miguel had its own military command, and Marta became friendly with a soldier there, several years older than herself. He told her he liked her, and even though she was just thirteen at the time, she thought she was ready to have a boyfriend. She let him be intimate with her, and within a year she discovered she was pregnant. Her soldier boyfriend by then was drinking heavily and smoking marijuana. With the arrival of the baby, a boy she named Erick, Marta returned to her family. She was barely fourteen years old.

The conditions in El Salvador by that time were fueling a relatively new phenomenon in the country—mass movement to "El Norte," the United States. The number of Salvadoran immigrants residing in the United States increased nearly fivefold between 1980 and 1990, from 94,000 to 465,000. The *campesino* population, poor and landless, had struggled for survival in El Salvador since the early colonial days, but war and violence through the 1980s had made their lives much worse. The improvement of transportation and communication networks made migration a more realistic option, and the more Salvadorans established residence in the United States, the more family and friends came to join them. Anyone who wanted to make the journey could find a guide who knew the land route through Guatemala and across Mexico to the U.S. border. Those who did it for money were called "coyotes" because of the way they found and preyed on the most desperate and vulnerable in their community.

In 1991, a coyote named Antonio showed up in the village looking for recruits. Modesto Quintanilla heard him boasting of the trips he had already taken and his certainty that he could get anyone across the U.S. border. To Modesto, the pitch was persuasive, and he invited Antonio to come and discuss his venture with his family, including Marta. When they told him there were Quintanilla relatives in the Washington, D.C., area, Antonio assured them he could track them down. One word in their conversation caught Marta's attention each time she heard it: *USA,* spoken in English with a ring of promise and destiny. Her mother and father and her aunt and uncle were similarly impressed. "I've always thought about going up there," Modesto said. "You should go," he told Marta.

And she did, leaving little Erick in the care of her parents. Prior to that, Marta had never ventured farther than San Miguel, not even to San Salvador, the country's capital, but now she was on a bus headed to the United States with a man she didn't know and seven fellow migrants, two women and five men. Marta was the youngest, and Antonio took a seat next to her, promising to take care of her. Sometime during the first night, however, his demeanor changed. Antonio told Marta that she would have to go to bed with him. Having had one rough experience with a man already, she said she wouldn't do that, but then Antonio leaned closer and said if she didn't comply, he would make sure that all the other men he knew could have their way with her. She knew she was powerless.

The entire trip was a terror. Though Marta was small, less than a hundred pounds, and Antonio was tall and strong, she resisted his advances as best she could, but he beat her when he didn't get what he wanted. And then there was the railroad. Antonio directed the group to hitch rides on freights heading northward, and that put them on *el tren de la muerte,* the train of death, named for all the migrants who were killed under its wheels. Guards kept the migrants from approaching the train when it was stopped, so they had to wait until it was moving and then jump aboard. Many lost their grip and fell. Marta saw torn and bloody bodies almost every day, but the more upset she became, the more likely Antonio was to hit her. Fearing being left alone, she nevertheless stayed with him all the way to the U.S. border at Reynosa, and swam with him across the Rio Grande to the U.S. side, where they were immediately caught. Marta pleaded for refuge, telling U.S. Border Patrol officers that Antonio had abused her throughout the journey and that her life would be in danger if she were deported. It was no use. She was sent back to El Salvador. So was Antonio, who showed up at her home a short time later to inform her father that he and Marta were now a couple, that she was his woman. Modesto threw him out of the house, but it was too late. Marta was once again pregnant.

Six months after giving birth to her second son, whom she named René, Marta announced she would again try to make her way to the United States. This time, she was more determined than ever, driven by the realization that she was now responsible for two children and that she would never be able to support them, much less her parents, if she stayed in her impoverished country. Having made the trip before, she would do it alone this time, avoiding all contact with coyotes. Her parents were opposed, but Marta was insistent. "I'm seventeen years old," she said. "I'm a woman now. Whatever happens to me is my responsibility alone." Her parents reluctantly said they would support whatever decision she made and would take care of her two boys until they could join her. Marta's godmother loaned her eight hundred colones, about a hundred dollars, of which Marta kept two hundred for the trip and gave the rest to her parents.

The 1,700-mile journey back to Texas took two months. Still haunted by what she had seen on the train of death, Marta traveled this time only by bus or on foot, stopping along the way to earn money to pay for food or bus fare for the next leg of the trip. Her

200 colones got her only as far as Guatemala, where she stayed for two weeks making tortillas. In Chiapas, Mexico, she stopped to do some field work in a *milpa*. In Veracruz, she gathered fruit and sold it in the market. In Monterrey, she met another migrating woman who agreed to pay Marta's bus fare to the border in exchange for her help crossing the river. On the U.S. side of the border, Marta was again grabbed by the Border Patrol, but this time fortune turned in her favor. The migration officer who interviewed her said she was entitled to apply for asylum on the grounds that she faced a threat of violence if sent home. Because she was only seventeen, however, he told her she would have to remain in detention with other young women until someone agreed to sponsor her in the United States.

Marta stayed in the facility for three months, but it was a house, not a prison. She and the other women were given new clothes and three meals a day. They were relatively free to move about, and once a week they were taken to a local shopping center and given five dollars to spend. It was December, and Marta bought some Christmas presents for her boys. Not in her whole life had she known such luxury, and the fact that she was in the United States gave Marta a sense of security she had never experienced before. In a remarkable coincidence, one of the women detained with her was also from Moncagua and said she would help her. The woman's boyfriend, also from Moncagua, was living in northern Virginia, and when she reached him by telephone, she let Marta speak to him. Hearing she was a Quintanilla, the man said he knew a distant cousin of hers named Mauricio who lived nearby. He told Marta he would arrange for Mauricio to call her, and a few days later he actually did. It was the break Marta desperately needed, and she broke into tears when Mauricio told her that they were indeed related. "Please help me," she begged. "I have no one else." Marta sensed that he wanted something in return, but she did not press him. She cared only that Mauricio was willing to pay her travel expenses to Virginia and sponsor her stay in the United States until she was twenty-one. Her documentation completed and her airfare paid, Marta left Texas with asylum status and a permit to work, good for one year.

After arriving in Virginia, Marta learned that Mauricio expected her to become his wife. For days, Marta could not stop weeping. She had no desire to move in with a stranger, thirteen years her senior, but she felt she was in no position to say no, and reluctantly she agreed. Within a few months, she was pregnant, once again with a man she did not love and did not want to be with. This time, however, she knew it was in good part her own responsibility, and the thought that she would again be delayed in her effort to establish security and independence left her disheartened all over again. Still, she was in the United States legally, with permission to work. Three months after giving birth to another boy, this one named Jonis, Marta found employment as a housekeeper at a Days Inn. Three years later, in 1997, the Nicaraguan Adjustment and Central American Relief Act offered permanent status to registered asylum seekers, and Marta—by then married to Mauricio—became a legal U.S. resident.

Over the next decade, Marta saved enough to buy her parents a house in San Miguel and finance the upbringing of her two sons, Erick and René, with whom she spoke by telephone for a few minutes as often as she could. In 2003, she ended her marriage to Mauricio. He drank too much, and she could not tolerate his jealousy. For the next three years, Marta was a single mother, working long days and attending English classes at night, leaving Jonis with a baby-sitter. While working as a cashier at a U.S. military base in northern Virginia, Marta met a young soldier from Nebraska named Troy Call, and in 2006 they were married. He soon began adoption procedures for Marta's two sons back in El Salvador. As a U.S. citizen he was able to bring them both to the United States as legal residents, which he did in 2009.

"When I left my country, I had one idea," Marta said, "to fight for my family. I wanted to buy my parents a house in San Miguel so they could live there with my sons and not have to live in Moncagua anymore. I did that. My next dream was to get residency and bring my sons here. I did that. Now I want an education. I've had a lot of problems, but I have overcome them." On her Facebook page, Marta posted what she said was her motto: *Primero tienes que sembrar para despues ver el fruto.* If you want to see the fruit, first you have to sow the seed.

12

MINORITIES

Mark Keam's mother had escaped Seoul on top of a freight train, and his father had been imprisoned by Vietnamese Communists, but in America Mark's hero was the Reverend Jesse Jackson, and the highlight of his 1988 internship in Washington was the day Mark met him. Jackson at the time was preparing to withdraw from the presidential race and endorse Michael Dukakis, the presumed Democratic nominee, but in exchange he wanted a prominent role at the upcoming party convention in Atlanta and more minority representation in the party leadership. Those conditions had to be negotiated with Paul Kirk, chairman of the Democratic National Committee, where Mark had his internship. He had been assigned a little desk near Kirk's office on the third floor of the DNC head-quarters, and when Jackson showed up to meet with Kirk, the twenty-two-year-old intern was well positioned to get a glimpse of him. But dozens of other interns and DNC staff were just as deter-mined to greet Jackson, and when the candidate emerged from the elevator on the third floor, he was immediately surrounded.

"How you all doing?" Jackson said, shaking hands all around.

Mark, stuck behind other staffers, could only wave, but Jackson saw him out of the corner of his eye as he passed by and immediately turned around. Aside from a Chinese American woman on Jackson's staff, Mark was the only Asian face in the room, and Jackson apparently wanted to acknowledge him. Reaching back through the crowd, he grabbed Mark by the shoulder and pulled him over. "Hey, how are ya!" he said, grinning. Someone with a camera told Mark to turn around, then snapped a picture of the six-foot-three Jackson embracing the slender five-foot-eight intern. Mark was taken aback. As Jackson continued on to Kirk's office, he went back to his desk, grabbed a piece of paper, and scribbled, "I just met the first black man to run for president," not quite believing what had happened. "This man could have been president of the United States, and he reached out and shook my hand," he wrote. He kept the note, scrawled on the back of a news release, as a memento of the visit for years to come. In the future, Mark Keam would trace his activism back to that encounter, and the promotion of Jackson's Rainbow Coalition, or something like it, would be his core political commitment.

Four years later, in the spring of 1992, the rainbow vision suffered a major setback in Mark's hometown of Los Angeles. On the afternoon of April 29, a mostly white jury in the suburb of Simi Valley announced a not guilty verdict in the trial of four white Los Angeles police officers on charges of assault, despite having been caught on videotape savagely beating an African American man, Rodney King. The city's black community erupted immediately in rage. People poured into the streets, yelling "Guilty! Guilty! Guilty!" and some went on a riotous rampage, starting fires, looting, and violently assaulting establishments they associated with their oppressors. Mark at the time was working as a paralegal in a small L.A. law firm and preparing to enter law school in the fall. He and his co-workers initially followed live news reports of the rioting on their office televisions, but when they heard police and fire sirens outside their own Beverly Hills offices, they ran up to the roof of their building for a wider look at what was happening in their city. Plumes of thick black smoke could be seen over South Central Los Angeles, where the city's African American and Latino population was concentrated. But Mark noticed that smoke was also rising in the sky a few miles to the east of where he stood. He knew instantly where it was coming from—Koreatown, the center of the Korean immigrant community.

Quickly retreating to his office, Mark started calling friends who lived or worked in Koreatown to find out what was happening. He got reports of people trapped in stores, offices, and apartments. One friend said she could see workers at the Han Kook supermarket, directly across the street from her apartment building, moving cars to form a barricade around the store. Some of them then took to the roof of the supermarket, armed with pistols and rifles, prepared to shoot anyone who approached. The woman was terrified, and Mark immediately got in his car and made his way to her apartment to comfort her until her roommate arrived. When he left the apartment several hours later, he found the streets filled with people, some of them carrying weapons. It seemed that all of Koreatown was on fire. The next day Mark learned that his brother-in-law's T-shirt store was among those that had been looted. A friend had been badly beaten when he tried to block looters from entering his store. The mother of another friend had been shot in the thigh as she scrambled to escape a mob, and a store where Mark had once worked was burned to the ground. That was just Koreatown; the situation in South Central Los Angeles was just as dire.

Before the rioting subsided five days later, more than fifty people were dead, and more than two thousand were injured, including dozens of firefighters. About a thousand buildings were destroyed or damaged, with property losses estimated at $1 billion. It had been the most violent urban riot in U.S. history. The event that sparked the explosion—four white police officers acquitted of charges in the beating of a black man—prompted commentators to portray the violence as the product of deeply rooted anger and frustration in the

African American community over institutionalized police brutal-
ity, a white power structure perceived as racist, high unemployment,
and economic exploitation. But whites were actually spared much of
the suffering, in part because the Los Angeles Police Department
gave priority to the protection of white neighborhoods, largely with-
drawing from the more afflicted areas of the city. The worst of the
violence was minority-on-minority. More precisely, it was between
African Americans and immigrants, both Korean and Latino. More
than half of those arrested were Hispanic, and Hispanic as well as
Korean storeowners lost their businesses.

The L.A. riots turned out to be a defining event in the history of
minority-minority relations, illustrating that a major immigration
wave like the one rolling into the country would inevitably produce
conflicts. The construction of a rainbow coalition could come only
if those conflicts were resolved. In an influential and highly personal
1992 article in *The Atlantic,* the writer Jack Miles, residing in Los
Angeles, laid out a persuasive case that at the root of the L.A. riots
was a grim economic competition between desperately poor African Americans and the Latino and Asian immigrants who were
intruding on what little space and prerogative the blacks had finally
won for themselves. Miles said it appeared that African Americans were rioting to reclaim what they had lost to the new minority
groups. "Whatever measure of power and influence they had pried
loose from the White power structure, they now see as being in
danger of being transferred to the Latino community," Miles wrote.
"Not only are they losing influence, public offices, and control of
the major civil rights mechanisms, they now see themselves being
replaced in the pecking order by the Asian community, in this case
the Koreans."

The Koreans had their own perspective on the riots, given that
their shops were deliberately targeted and their losses were so large.
In the Korean language, the shorthand reference to the riots was
Sa-ee-gu—literally, "4/29"—just as "9/11" would forever signify
the 2001 attacks on the World Trade Center in New York and the

Pentagon outside Washington, D.C. The more self-aware Korean storeowners saw how the riots had laid open the cultural chasm that existed between them and their African American customers. Their insularity, their apparent lack of interest in establishing neighborly relations, and the reality of their own racial prejudice helped bring them to this point. A year earlier, a Korean American proprietor of a grocery store in South Central Los Angeles had wrongfully accused a fifteen-year-old black girl of stealing a bottle of orange juice and then shot and killed her during the ensuing scuffle. The girl died with two dollars in her hand, the money with which she was about to pay for the juice. The lingering anger over that incident was a factor in the anti-Korean violence that came a year later. But the fury with which African American mobs had then attacked, looted, and burned their shops left some Korean merchants determined to defend themselves and their property by whatever means necessary. During the rioting, some Korean American leaders made urgent calls over Korean-language radio stations for armed volunteers to stand with besieged Korean storeowners.

For Mark Keam, the riots had a sobering effect, forcing him to confront the limits of his Jesse Jackson–inspired idealism. He had witnessed African Americans and Latinos violently attacking Korean merchants who had only been trying to earn a living. He saw the Los Angeles Police Department holding back, more concerned with the security of white neighborhoods in West Los Angeles than with the restoration of law and order in Koreatown. He would think about those days many times over the next few years, determined to learn from the *Sa-ee-gu* experience. Reflecting on the riots in 2002—by then a lawyer working in Washington and living in Fairfax County—Mark drew two lessons. The first was that his people had to organize politically. "We as Korean Americans must take charge of our own destiny," he wrote, "since no one else will be there for us. It was through brutal lessons of death and destruction that Korean Americans rediscovered our instinct to survive and became emboldened. It was in the face of betrayal and frustration at the lack of government accountability that Korean Americans learned to forge a political agenda of self-empowerment." At the time he wrote that commentary, Mark was already engaged in political activism among his fellow Korean Americans in the metropolitan area, determined to strengthen their political clout. He was also engaged in outreach efforts with other immigrant groups, because there was a second lesson to be learned from the L.A. riots: When ethnic groups turn against each other, they all suffer. "It was from helplessly watching fellow minorities rise up against us," he wrote, "that Korean Americans finally learned the value of building bridges with others in America." The application of those two ideas—empowerment and bridge building—would define Mark Keam's career as an immigrant in American politics. He intuitively understood those principles already in the spring of 1992, but it would take a few years for him to work out how and where he could play a role. First he had to go to law school.

For the Seongs and most other immigrant families, politics was secondary; the drive to survive and achieve security was the imperative. Nak Man and Jeom Chul came to America to work in the most menial of positions, as low-wage laborers in a chicken processing plant. They did not have other immediately marketable skills, and they did not speak English. Their assets were discipline, a disposition to work hard and sacrifice, and a willingness to take the initiative. Nak Man went into business for himself as soon as he could, acquiring a gas station/convenience store with the help of a commercial loan, and he was an independent storeowner for the rest of his working life.

That enterprising ambition was something Nak Man Seong shared with many other immigrants, although in his case it did not reflect an innovative outlook as much as a determination to work in a venture where extra effort brought extra reward. The practical challenges were manageable. Running a little gas and grocery business along the highway in Pittsville, Maryland, didn't involve complex communication, so his minimal English skills were not a major problem. Mostly, he stood behind the counter ringing up gas purchases or selling cigarettes or soda and slices of pizza. There were taxes to calculate, and he had to deal with some paperwork and the occasional county inspector, but it was mainly a cash in, cash out operation. He had no employees, depending only on his three sons for help. The more hours he put in, the more money he collected and the more he could save. Though he had only reached the sixth grade in Korea, Nak Man's natural intelligence was enough to bring him modest business success in America, beginning with that convenience mart in Pittsville and later with the store and lounge he ran in Baltimore with his wife and sons and finally with their neighborhood liquor shop in the District of Columbia. The management philosophy he and Jeom Chul followed in their retail enterprises was the same one employed by many other Korean Americans who owned dry cleaning shops and convenience stores: work long hours, keep the enterprise simple, make use of family members, and save as much money as possible.

Once their three sons left home for college or other work, the Seongs had a harder time managing the Baltimore business, so in 1993 they sold it and bought the store in Southeast Washington, D.C. As long as they were willing to work long hours, Nak Man and Jeom Chul could run the place on their own, and D.C. law required liquor stores to close on Sundays, so they were guaranteed one day off per week. The store they purchased was at the corner of Central and Southern Avenues, S.E., in an entirely African American neighborhood with a relatively high crime rate. Their daughter Alex, who had started law school at the University of Maryland but still lived at home, worried constantly about her parents' safety. Over the previous decade, at least fifteen Korean merchants in Washington had been shot and killed in their places of business. The riots in Los Angeles a year earlier had underscored the challenge of operating in minority neighborhoods.

It was not difficult, however, to see why Korean couples like Nak Man and Jeom Chul would choose to do business in dangerous, low-income communities: It was a setting where they could compete. Bigger and wealthier retailers had little interest in serving those neighborhoods, and the cost of acquiring an inner-city establishment was relatively low. Because they depended on family labor, the storeowners could save on wage costs, even while staying open long hours. Their customer base was relatively stable, because the lack of access to transportation made it difficult for residents to travel outside their neighborhood to shop. Such conditions had prevailed for many years. In the jargon of urban sociologists, the Seongs played a classic "minority middleman" role, inasmuch as they provided a commercial link in a racially or economically stratified setting between the local consumers and the distant corporate producers. Around the world, immigrant groups have often played the middleman role, from the South Asians in East Africa to the Lebanese in South America. For many years, Jews occupied that niche in inner U.S. cities, but with the Asian immigrant surge after 1965, they were gradually replaced by Korean and Chinese merchants. By the time Nak Man and Jeom Chul bought their business in Southeast Washington, Korean immigrants or their family members owned nearly half of the liquor stores in the city and controlled most of the D.C. lottery sales, even though very few of them actually lived in the District.

It was not an easy line of work. As an alien presence in a minority neighborhood, Korean storeowners often aroused enmity and mistrust and brought accusations of economic exploitation. Some of the historic tensions between Jews and African Americans stemmed from the role Jewish merchants had played in black communities, and those same tensions carried over when Korean immigrants assumed the same commercial position. If anything, the merchant-customer relationship became even more fraught with the Koreans as a consequence of the language and cultural barriers. Only a tiny percentage of the storeowners lived in the neighborhood they served, and they rarely attended community meetings or took much interest in neighborhood activities or issues beyond their own stores. With their limited English ability, the Korean merchants found it hard to make conversation with their customers or even exchange pleasantries. Nor were they likely to look their customers in the eye or count change directly into the customers' hands. In Korean culture, such gestures indicate disrespect; to the patrons, the storeowners seemed rude.

It was against a background of racial and cultural mistrust—and crime—that the Seongs opened their liquor store on Central Avenue in Southeast Washington in 1993. Not surprisingly, Nak Man and Jeom Chul—like many, perhaps most, Korean liquor store owners—kept a handgun under the counter.

In May 1995, Mark Keam graduated from Hastings College of the Law in San Francisco and returned to Los Angeles. The Korean American political scene in the aftermath of the 1992 riots had been reenergized, with local leaders launching a major campaign to get people to demand enforcement of their civil and community rights. The lead organization was the Korean American Coalition (KAC), which had been formed a decade earlier but came into its own only in response to the *Sa-ee-gu* trauma. The group pushed insurance companies and government agencies to provide support for the small Korean-owned businesses that had been destroyed during the riots. Mark Keam was a KAC member and active volunteer. After his 1988 internship with the Democratic National Committee, however, Mark had increasingly focused on the national political scene, and after taking the California bar exam in August, he loaded his possessions in a Toyota 4Runner and headed back to Washington, where he had lined up a job as a telecommunications lawyer at the Federal Communications Commission.

Not content to work on FCC policy issues alone, Mark immediately began looking around to see what was happening politically in

Korean American circles. Not much, he discovered. While Chinese, Japanese, Filipino, and Indian Americans were well represented in Washington through advocacy organizations, Korean Americans had no such voice. Despite its activism in southern California, the KAC had no representation in Washington, nor did any other Korean American group. Reaching back to his contacts in Los Angeles, he argued that the KAC needed to define a national agenda. The group's board of directors agreed and asked him to serve as an unpaid KAC representative in the nation's capital. In that capacity, he wrote action alerts and news updates highlighting political developments in Washington of concern to the Korean American community, from immigration to hate crime legislation. His overarching goal was Korean American empowerment, the importance of which he had learned as a result of the 1992 riots, though he justified the effort as supporting the corollary goal of building political alliances with other minority and special interest groups. "If you can't mobilize your own people, the others won't respect you," he explained. "You don't want to be an empty shell where you don't speak for anybody else. We have to build our own capacity, so that when we ask for a seat at the table, we can actually fill that seat, and if we're asked to mobilize 100 people for a rally, we can deliver."

A major problem for Korean American outreach efforts was the language barrier. Many groups, from the Korean American Grocers Association to the Korean American Chamber of Commerce, had been inwardly focused, with relatively little effort put into communicating Korean American concerns to non-Korean audiences. As a young lawyer fluent in both English and Korean, Mark Keam helped make up for the deficit, volunteering to speak at public meetings and writing op-ed articles for English-language publications. He also became involved in citizenship drives, training volunteers around the D.C. metropolitan area to go into the Korean community and educate newly arrived immigrants about the importance of participating in the civic life of their new country.

It was at one of those training sessions that Mark met Alex

Seong, who had recently graduated from law school at the University of Maryland. She was a reluctant participant in the citizenship drive. Ever since she was a young girl, Alex had kept a low profile in her school and social life, due partly to her own shyness, partly to Nak Man and Jeom Chul's determined efforts to shelter her. Schoolwork always had to come first, and she was not allowed to go on dates or even attend sleepovers with her girlfriends. Throughout her undergraduate years at Towson University in Maryland, she lived at home, just a few minutes from campus. Her closest friend and confidante was her mother. During and after law school, she become somewhat more independent, and she joined the Korean section of the Maryland Bar Association, but she rarely joined in group activities. She agreed to take part in the citizenship drive only after twice declining. On the third occasion, the Maryland organizers of the effort told her they had no one else to send to the training session, and she finally gave in. The workshop lasted all day, and during conversations between sessions Mark and Alex discovered how much they had in common, from the trauma in South Korea that drove their parents to emigrate to the poverty they endured during their early years in the United States and their respective experiences working their way through college and law school with part-time jobs, loans, and scholarships. At the end of the day, Mark invited Alex to go with him to a housewarming party some friends were holding that night in D.C.

"Let me ask my mom," she said. She was twenty-six years old by then and living on her own, so Mark thought she was kidding, but Alex promptly went looking for a pay phone. She did not bother to ask her father, who years earlier had told her she should find a husband as soon as possible. The guidance she sought would come from her mother, who had been forced unwillingly into marriage and had always advised Alex to put her education ahead of finding a husband. "If you can stand on your own and not depend on a man financially, you can kick him out if he doesn't treat you well," she said. "Leave marriage until later." But Jeom Chul trusted her daughter to make the right decisions, and when Alex called her that evening to say that a young Korean American man had asked her out, Jeom Chul gave her blessing. Mark Keam and Alex Seong were married about a year later.

Given the horror of racial and ethnic warfare in urban Los Angeles, minority and immigrant leaders in Washington, D.C., were determined to avoid anything remotely comparable. The 1990s brought a series of initiatives to improve relations in particular between Asians and African Americans. Mark Keam devoted much of his spare time to such work, and his marriage to the daughter of Korean storeowners working in an all-black neighborhood gave immediacy to the task. Working under the aegis of the Asian Pacific American Bar Association, he participated in a series of racial and cultural sensitivity workshops for rookie D.C. policemen, where he explained some of the Asian customs that were often misunderstood in store settings. If the police were called to the scene of some altercation in a Korean store in a black neighborhood, Mark argued, an understanding of the cultural differences would enable them to mediate between the owner and the customer more effectively. With a grant from the Community Foundation for the National Capital Region, Mark and others also launched a project called Building One Neighborhood, focused specifically on the conflict between Asian merchants and their African American customers. Volunteers were sent to survey black storeowners on their perceptions of Asian American customers and to do the same with Asian storeowners regarding their African American customers. Stereotypes had to be challenged.

13

DIVERSITY

Those immigrants like Mark Keam who knew what it had taken to eliminate national origin quotas in the United States were generally quick to salute the achievements of the civil rights movement and the trailblazing by African American leaders. Were it not for the African American triumph over racial prejudice, immigrants of color would not have found an open door in America, they knew.

The feeling was not entirely mutual, however. As Mark learned through his activism in Los Angeles and in Washington, many African Americans felt resentful of foreign-born newcomers in their neighborhoods. Not all immigrants were appreciative of the civil rights struggles that preceded their arrival, and competition in the job and housing markets aggravated immigrant-minority relations. Many American economists claim that immigration can boost, not lower, the wages of native-born workers, produce more jobs, and stimulate innovation; they say immigrant labor can make businesses more competitive, which enables them to expand. The effects are not necessarily seen across all employment categories, however. To the extent immigration increases the supply of low-skilled, low-wage labor, those low-skilled workers already in the country can be displaced or forced to work for even lower wages.

An early example in the D.C. area involved refugees from Southeast Asia. In 1983, three airlines at Washington's National Airport dropped a janitorial services contract that had previously gone to a cleaning company staffed largely by black workers and gave the contract instead to a nonunion company that employed refugees from Vietnam and Cambodia. As a result, fifty people lost their jobs. The new company paid a lower wage and did not offer the medical benefits the original company provided. Marchel Smiley, president of the local union that had been representing the janitorial workers, told *The Washington Post* that many low-paying service jobs that had previously been filled largely by blacks were going at the time to immigrant workers. "There were no whites [interested], traditionally, because they've been the most undesirable jobs," he said. "But starting basically with the Vietnam situation . . . we're seeing more and more Orientals and Asiatic-type employees." Three months earlier, the Greater Washington Research Council had warned of latent tensions between immigrants and other residents in part "because people in the established community—especially black Americans—fear that the newcomers may take jobs and housing away from them."

The National Airport case created a short-term uproar in northern Virginia and helped spur an effort to address potential conflicts between African Americans and refugees from Southeast Asia, one of the first immigrant groups to arrive in the region in the modern period. Vilay Chaleunrath, who came from Laos, and Richard Baker, a black lawyer in Fairfax County, met each other in a leadership development group in the mid-1980s and began sharing thoughts about the demographic changes taking place. They were later joined by others, including Gerald Lee, an African American judge in the Fairfax Circuit Court, and Toa Q. Do, a Vietnamese refugee who had started a computer company and was active in his community.

From their meetings, the African American–Indochinese Alliance was formed, with the mission of building ties between those communities in northern Virginia. The group organized a community dinner and forum at T. C. Williams High School in Alexandria, Virginia, where immigrants and minority families shared soul food, barbecue, egg rolls, noodles, and other dishes characteristic of their respective cultures, while airing their grievances and concerns. Judge Lee also spearheaded the Task Force on Fairness, which held a series of town meetings focused on legal and judicial issues of concern to both the minority and immigrant communities in northern Virginia. Such efforts opened channels of communication, but the deeper problem of competition over jobs and scarce public resources could not be so easily addressed.

The impact of immigration—both legal and illegal—on the African American community got recurring attention in the coming years as immigration policy became a pressing national issue. In 1995, the U.S. Commission on Immigration Reform, a panel set up by Congress under the chairmanship of former representative Barbara Jordan of Texas, took the bold step of advocating a cap on immigrant admissions at the level of 500,000 per year. As the first African American woman to be elected to Congress from the South, Jordan brought prestige and influence to the commission, and her advocacy of more restricted immigration was an attention-grabber. The commission acknowledged that immigrants "often create new businesses and other employment-generating activities," but it went on to argue that immigration also had costs. "Immigrants with relatively low education and skills may compete for jobs and public services with the most vulnerable of Americans," the commission argued, "particularly those who are unemployed or underemployed."

Many economists hastened to argue that immigration actually contributes to economic growth and even has a positive effect on wages. In truth, both generalizations were valid, depending on which workers are considered—and which immigrants. Harvard

University economists Lawrence Katz and George Borjas argued in an oft-cited 2007 paper that high school dropouts in the United States, with few marketable skills, were likely to face stiff competition from immigrants who had come to the country illegally and were willing to work for substandard wages. Moreover, to the extent racially prejudiced employers have more workers to choose from, they may hire an illegal immigrant over an African American. At the same time, the overall effect of immigration on U.S. wages and employment may well be positive, especially considering the economic activity that could shift overseas if not for low-cost immigrant labor in the United States. Moreover, some economists who acknowledge a negative effect of immigration on some U.S. workers also acknowledge that it is probably small in comparison with such influences as international trade, decline in union representation, and technological innovation. Harvard's Lawrence Katz, having called attention to a possible negative effect of immigration on wages and employment in 2007, had taken a more benign view by 2015. "I believe immigration on net has very little impact on U.S. wage inequality trends relative to other factors," Katz wrote in an email, "and [it] has huge benefits for our economy in terms of vibrancy, innovation, and diversity."

For most African American leaders, potentially divergent economic interests between black and immigrant workers were less important than their shared political interests at all levels of government and commerce. Democratic congressman John Conyers of Michigan, a founding member of the Congressional Black Caucus, was on the House Judiciary Committee in 1965 when it approved the new immigration law, and in the five decades that followed he remained a stalwart immigrant ally, as did Jesse Jackson and others. In Fairfax County, some local activists who focused on neighborhood issues complained about the effect immigrants were having on their communities, but politically active African Americans were more likely to join forces with immigrants and their advocates, at least on certain issues. The struggle for equal education opportunity in Fairfax County brought out one such leader, a black man who became a hero to immigrant parents.

For much of its history, Fairfax County had been ruled by white supremacists, but by the 1960s the D.C. metropolitan area was expanding in all directions with creeping cosmopolitan urbanism. Even as the leaders of old Fairfax fought to preserve the country's southern identity, a self-described "Jewish guy from Manhattan" named Robert E. Simon was building an entirely new town on 6,750 acres of Fairfax County farmland, calling it "Reston" after his own initials. At its inauguration he boldly announced he intended to sell his townhouses to "anyone with green money." Early newspaper advertisements for townhouses in Reston described it as an "open community" and featured black and white faces together.

No other developer in northern Virginia had dared make such a move, and it did not help sales, at least in the beginning. When potential white buyers learned they might be living next to black people, many lost interest. Nor did blacks move quickly to take advantage of the open housing, unprecedented though it was. By the time of Reston's dedication in 1966, just three of its 250 families were African American. Robert Frye, one of the early black residents, said later that he lost most of his friends when he moved from Washington to Reston, because of the stigma attached to living on the other side of the Potomac. "In our youth, you almost never went to Virginia, because it was part of the old South," he said, "and to actually move to Fairfax, there were black residents here who talked about a time when they couldn't be seen in parts of the county after sundown." By that time, African Americans made up less than 5 percent of Fairfax County's growing population, and they were isolated in all-black neighborhoods. Almost everyone else was native-born white.

An early start to the desegregation effort came there in Reston, the outpost of liberalism in the Fairfax hinterlands. The whites who settled there chose a community that by design was to be progressive, and the blacks who settled there were willing to be pioneers. Robert Frye and his wife had been open housing activists in Washington. In Reston, they helped lead an effort among the early black residents to get more African Americans to buy homes in the community, organizing a group called Reston Black Focus that would serve as the voice of the black residents and a forum for the celebration of African American culture. "We wanted to make sure the world knew there were people like us living in Reston and thriving," Frye said in an interview many years later. Many of the black residents, including the Fryes, were young, and the first focus of their community activism was the school system. A top objective was to secure the appointment of a minority representative on the all-white Fairfax County School Board.

The black parents found an early ally on the county board in Supervisor Martha Pennino, who had been a strong supporter of Simon when he launched the Reston development, which was within the boundaries of her magisterial district. During her twenty-four years on the county board, Pennino spanned the old Fairfax of the rural South and the new Fairfax of the D.C. suburbs. With her tiny frame, a beehive hairdo, and a genteel manner, the lady known as "Mother Fairfax" reassured conservative voters, even as she advocated for the Equal Rights Amendment and set up cots in her county office for homeless people who had nowhere else to sleep. It took a few years, but she eventually persuaded her fellow supervisors to set aside a minority at-large seat on the school board, a move that made it possible for Frye to play a key leadership role on behalf of black and other minority students in the county.

Frye's involvement in county school affairs stemmed originally from anger over what he saw as the dismissive treatment of his son, Robert Jr., and his daughter, Amanda, by their white teachers. Robert Jr. was not allowed to play in his middle school band, and Amanda was kept out of a reading program for gifted students, despite her proven skills. The snubs were too much for Robert Sr., whose experience as an artillery officer in the U.S. Army had given him the confidence to stand up for his interests. He met with the teachers, the school principal, and the regional superintendent and got his children properly placed. When word of his intervention reached Martha Pennino, she arranged for Robert's appointment to the county school board as the minority representative, sensing he would be an effective advocate.

Though he was the third African American appointed to the at-large seat, Robert Frye was more energetic than his predecessors in defense of minority student interests. Among his early achievements was to get the Fairfax school board to recognize the birthday of Martin Luther King, Jr., albeit with a major compromise. "The first time I suggested it," he recalled later, "you would have thought I had cursed in church. I couldn't even get a second to the motion." Fairfax schools at the time closed on what was known as "Lee-Jackson Day" in honor of the birthdays of Robert E. Lee and Stonewall Jackson, and in the end Frye managed only to get King's name attached to that holiday, resulting in the somewhat incongruously designated Lee-Jackson-King Day. He also worked to establish a new middle school in Reston, to be named in honor of the African American poet Langston Hughes. At its opening in 1980, standing alongside Supervisor Martha Pennino, Frye told the parents and students that a school in Reston named for Langston Hughes was "especially appropriate for this multi-ethnic community."

Though he was seen at the time of his appointment primarily as an advocate for black students in Fairfax County, Frye was careful from the outset to define his "minority" constituency to include immigrants, and over the next twenty-five years he never wavered in that commitment, even as interethnic tensions periodically flared. When he was appointed to the school board in 1978, Fairfax County was receiving Vietnamese refugees, Iranian and Afghan exiles, and a trickle of Hispanics. By the time his first board tenure ended in 1985, the immigrant numbers had increased dramatically, especially with Central Americans fleeing war and violence in their homelands. Many of the immigrant families lived near the poverty line, as did many African Americans in the county, and Frye pushed the school board to devote extra resources to schools where those students were concentrated, using a high level of free and reduced-price lunches as an identifier of the "special needs" schools. Another of his initiatives targeted immigrant students in particular. Teachers and administrators often complained that immigrant parents seemed to take little interest in their children's schooling. Frye arranged for the designation of "parent liaisons" in those schools with a high immigrant population, with the idea that they would reach out to the parents in their own language and encourage them to get involved in PTA activities and meet with their children's teachers. "We found that many of the immigrant parents were working two jobs and had little extra time," Frye said, "and they often came from countries where educators were highly respected. They figured if they just dressed their kids up nicely and sent them on their way, the schools would take care of them. But the schools couldn't handle that responsibility alone."

School board members in Fairfax County were appointed to their positions in those days, a carryover from the "massive resistance" era when Virginia authorities wanted to be sure that no local board would act independently to desegregate its schools. Frye was selected during a period when Democrats had a majority on the Fairfax Board of Supervisors, and within months of a Republican takeover in November 1984, he and some other appointees were dismissed from their positions. It was the first time the Republicans had political control of the county government since the Reconstruction era, and the vote indicated that some kind of broad change was under way. "It seems like the Democrats are in decline," noted Martha Pennino, the veteran supervisor, though she did not offer an explanation. The popularity of Ronald Reagan, running for a second presidential term, likely helped the Republican cause.

It was also true that Fairfax County was growing, with a rapidly increasing population and a strong economy and a diminished

association with the rural South, where Democrats had traditionally been strong. "It's becoming a more conservative county," the-
orized Thomas Davis, the Republican supervisor who represented
the Mason District. "It's a white, middle- and upper-middle class
county." But Davis was overstating his case (Democrats would re-
gain control of the board three years later), and of all the Fairfax supervisors he should have known better. While Davis himself came
from the upper-class Ravenswood neighborhood, home to many
military retirees and senior government workers, his Mason District
also included the working-class areas of Willston, Seven Corners,
Bailey's Crossroads, and Annandale, all of which had rapidly growing nonwhite immigrant populations. The changing community
makeup in those areas was already presenting Fairfax planners with
politically difficult challenges, even as Davis thought he saw white
conservatives on the ascendancy.

J. E. B. Stuart High School, on its way to becoming one of the
most diverse schools in the United States, was just a few blocks
from where Davis lived. Less than a half mile in another direction was the site of the proposed Dar Al-Hijrah mosque, which
Davis had supported. Nineteen eighty-four was also the year that
the Fairfax School Board made significant adjustments to school
boundaries, an exercise that inevitably aroused class and ethnoracial
conflict. One of the most controversial projects was the conversion
of Thomas Jefferson High School, which had served a largely white
population, into a magnet school for science and technology. Many
students as a result were shifted to Annandale High School, which
had a high share of immigrant students.

Robert Frye was in the final months of his first period of service
on the school board, and he found the boundary issue among the
most anguishing he and other board members had to face. "People
strain and pay for the best housing they can find for their family,"
he recalled later, "and they don't want what they consider to be a
lesser group having an impact on their school. The ones who live
in townhouses don't want their kids to go to school with kids who

come out of apartments. People who have detached houses don't want their kids to go to schools where the kids come from town-houses." But Frye wanted the burden of educating immigrant students to be shared across the county, a point he tried to make in the rancorous public meetings where the boundary changes were discussed. He stood out in those meetings as a bold and outspoken supporter of immigrants and challenged those parents who did not want their children going to school with foreign-born kids whose language skills and educational background may have been lacking. "These families came here through tremendous effort," he said, "and a part of their vision was to have their kids go to an American school. They didn't want an immigrant school." As the minority at-large representative on the board, Frye felt an obligation to work for maximum equity and social justice in the school system, even when those efforts exposed him and other board members to parental wrath, as they often did. Community change inevitably introduced conflict, and managing it successfully required bold and compassionate leadership.

Desperate South Koreans fleeing the Communist advance on Seoul in December 1950. Among those huddled on the top of the train were Mark Keam's mother, Nam Soo, and his grandmother, Jung Jae. *AP Images*

Representative Emanuel Celler of New York in 1924. As a new member of Congress that year, Celler opposed the establishment of national origin quotas and would spend the next forty years in Washington fighting for their abolition. *Library of Congress*

John F. Kennedy as a Democratic candidate for Congress in 1946, voting in the party primary with his grandparents, John F. "Honey Fitz" Fitzgerald and Mary Fitzgerald. Immigration policy was an issue when "Honey Fitz" served in Congress in the nineteenth century and again when Kennedy ran. *JFK Library*

Representative Michael Feighan (D-Ohio), a stalwart conservative, chaired the immigration subcommittee of the House Judiciary Committee during the 1965 debate over national origin quotas. He reluctantly came to support the proposed reforms but insisted that the goal of family unification be given higher priority in the allocation of immigrant visas. *Princeton University Library*

President Lyndon B. Johnson giving Rep. Michael Feighan the famous "Johnson treatment" aboard *Air Force One* during a presidential trip to Cleveland in 1964. LBJ put heavy pressure on Feighan to support the new immigration legislation. *Princeton University Library*

Senator Edward Kennedy (D-Mass) conferring with Senator James Eastland (D-Miss), chairman of the Senate Judiciary Committee. Though Eastland was a southern conservative, he let the young Kennedy manage the debate over the 1965 immigration reforms. *©Bettman/CORBIS*

President Johnson signing the Immigration and Nationality Act on October 3, 1965 on Liberty Island, with the New York skyline behind him. He is surrounded by key supporters. *Yoichi Okamoto/LBJ Library*

1) Rep. Phil Burton, 2) Rep. Michael Feighan, 3) Spkr. John McCormack, 4) Abraham Beame, 5) Luci Baines Johnson, 6) Rep. Ogden Reid, 7) V.P. Hubert Humphrey, 8) Sen. Phil Hart, 9) Rep. John Lindsay, 10) Lady Bird Johnson, 11) Stella Celler, 12) Rep. Emanuel Celler, 13) Sen. Mike Mansfield, 14) Muriel Humphrey, 15) Rep. Arch Moore, 16) Amb. Averell Harriman, 17) Sen. Daniel Inouye, 18) Sen. Edward M. Kennedy, 19) Sen. Robert F. Kennedy

A young Mark Keam with his political hero, the Reverend Jesse Jackson, Jr., when Jackson visited the headquarters of the Democratic National Committee during his 1988 bid for the presidency. *Keam Family Collection*

Alex Seong, with her mother Jeom Chul and father Nak Man, at her graduation from the University of Maryland School of Law. *Seong Family Collection*

Mark Keam *(front left)*, being sworn in as a freshman delegate to the Virginia General Assembly in 2010. Keam was the first Asian American immigrant elected to the Virginia legislature. *The Washington Post/Getty Images*

Dr. Esam Omeish, chief of general surgery at Alexandria Inova Hospital in Alexandria, Virginia. Omeish, who immigrated from Libya as a child, became a political activist and prominent lay leader of the U.S. Muslim community. *Omeish Family Collection*

Anwar al-Awlaki, while serving as an imam at Dar Al-Hijrah mosque in Falls Church, Virginia. Esam Omeish promoted his candidacy but was dismayed when Awlaki turned to violent extremism. Awlaki was killed in a U.S. drone strike in 2011. *Linda Spillers/New York Times/Redux*

Anwar, the daughter of Esam and Badria Omeish, joyfully greets President Obama at a Fairfax County campaign rally in 2012. Her sister Abrar, also wearing an American flag headscarf, is behind her at upper right. *Deb Cobb/www .debcobb.com*

A young Álvaro Alarcón and his mother Rhina in their apartment in the Willston complex. *Alarcón Family Collection*

Victor Alarcón, Sr., enjoying a cigar with his three sons (left to right) Álvaro, Victor, Jr., and Miguel. *Alarcón Family Collection*

Marta Quintanilla Call on the day in 2014 when she took the oath of citizenship and became a U.S. citizen. Marta, who fled El Salvador alone at the age of seventeen, was one of about five hundred immigrants from eighty-two countries naturalized that day at a high school in Fairfax County, Virginia. *Photo by Tom Gjelten*

14

MUSLIM AMERICANS

Salwa Omeish, Esam's younger sister, wore the hijab for just a few months in 1985 during her freshman year in high school and then stopped. She was the only Muslim girl at J. E. B. Stuart to cover her hair, and it exposed her to some taunting; high school was hard enough without boys making comments about the "towel" on her head or bowing before her in mock deference. Still, it was a bold move on her part. The hijab is an important symbol of modesty and piety for a Muslim woman, and Salwa's more conservative older brothers made clear they would have liked her to remain covered. So did her parents, but on this issue they allowed their fifteen-year-old daughter to make her own decision.

Not wanting to call attention to what she was doing and invite unwelcome questions, Salwa waited until the summer to make the change. Her parents were moving to Annandale, farther west in Fairfax County, and in the fall Salwa would enroll there as a new student. The family traveled back to Libya that summer to visit relatives, and during a stopover in Zurich she took it off and left it off. In Libya, where many women chose not to wear the hijab, her relatives were unlikely to take notice. As a student at Annandale that fall, Salwa could be just another white girl with a Middle Eastern name. "It wasn't fun, going to high school in a hijab and being the outcast," she said later. "I just didn't want to do it anymore." Not that she wanted to join the cheerleading squad or date a football player. Salwa's social circle was largely limited to other immigrant students, of whom there were many, both Muslim and non-Muslim. But the hijab was a step too far. She went uncovered for the rest of high school and all through college and only began wearing a headscarf again nine years later, by which time she was married and had a one-year-old daughter.

The Census Bureau in the 1980s was not tallying the U.S. population on the basis of religious affiliation, but there is little doubt that Muslims during those years were a small and fairly marginalized group, even in a cosmopolitan area like Virginia's Fairfax County. The big change was yet to come. A survey of Muslims residing in the United States as of 2011 found that more than 70 percent had arrived in the country after 1990. By then, they were a significant part of the religious landscape, and along with the other new immigrant groups that arrived after 1965, they were challenging narrow interpretations of America's cultural heritage and identity, and in unique and sometimes provocative ways.

Those Muslims who came in the early years, like the Omeish family, often had to cope with isolation. For Salwa's four older brothers, it was a less stressful experience than it was for her. Not standing out by their appearance and subject to fewer restrictions, their decisions on how observant they wanted to be could be made more privately. Mohammed and Esam were devout; the other two, Marwan and Emad, were less so.

Having organized Friday prayer services at their high school, Mohammed and Esam strengthened their commitment to Islam during their college years. Mohammed attended George Washington University, which had an active chapter of the Muslim Students Association (MSA) and during the 1980s provided a meeting place for Muslim students from across the D.C. area in cooperation with the Dar Al-Hijrah congregation across the river in Virginia. Esam was at Georgetown University, less than two miles away. After accompanying his brother to a few MSA meetings, Esam resolved to organize a chapter at Georgetown. Though it was a Jesuit institution, Georgetown had a strong international focus, and Esam found the administration receptive to his efforts to organize the Muslim students. Most had immigrant backgrounds like Esam's, but his self-confidence and leadership experience distinguished him from the rest. During his last two years at J. E. B. Stuart, he had learned how to deal with school authorities, and it carried over to his college years. By the end of Esam's first semester, Georgetown had its own MSA chapter, and he was the president. It was the beginning of what would be a succession of leadership positions for him in Muslim organizations in the United States.

The university required all freshmen to live on campus, and Esam opted to live in the International House, where foreign students were paired with U.S.-born students. Surrounded by youth from around the world, Esam found the International House a good fit generally, but it was still a dormitory, and the partying and the gender mixing sometimes bothered him in the same way the social scene at his high school had made him uncomfortable. When not ensconced in a study cubicle at the library, he often sought the companionship of other Muslim students who shared his values, and he put many hours into the organization of MSA activities. As a result of his intervention with the campus ministry, the Muslim students got a prayer room set aside for their exclusive use, and the Georgetown MSA soon became a hub of Muslim youth activity in the greater Washington area.

At the end of his freshman year, Esam moved back to his parents' house in Annandale, and for the rest of his college years he commuted to the Georgetown campus in an old Toyota that his parents purchased for him. He was one of the few Muslim students at Georgetown with a car, and as a tireless organizer of gatherings around the mid-Atlantic region, Esam was soon the designated MSA driver, and his blue Toyota the unofficial MSA vehicle. His willingness to take charge and offer his services brought him new leadership opportunities, and while still a teenager he became the head of a student group called the MSA Council of Greater Washington. Just five years after arriving in America as a Libyan boy not yet proficient in English, Esam had found a way to exercise his ambition, his values, his intellectual interests, and his organizing skills. By moving out of the International House and back in with his parents while deepening both his academic studies and his Muslim activism, he was able to narrow his college experience to those environments where he was most comfortable and productive. He was embracing American society and retreating from it at the same time. As a Georgetown student, he was engaged with his professors and classmates, even as his life outside school was demarcated by the strictures of his faith and shared almost exclusively with those who believed as he did.

Most of the Muslims living in the United States at the time were either students or professionals and other skilled workers who could take advantage of the special employment-centered visa categories created under the 1965 Immigration Act. Many of them had chosen to assimilate fully into American life, but others maintained ties to their native lands. The first Muslim Student Associations in the United States were established under the influence of the Muslim Brotherhood, the powerful but loosely organized international movement founded in Egypt in 1928. While the Brotherhood in Muslim countries advocated national governance models based on Islamic teachings, its goal in non-Muslim countries was more limited: to encourage the Muslims living in those countries to remain faithful to their roots. The Brotherhood's concern in the United States was that Muslim immigrants would forget their religion and the ongoing struggles in their homelands. Muslim Brotherhood activists spearheaded the construction of mosques in areas of the United States where large numbers of Muslim immigrants had settled, and they promoted the formation of affiliated Muslim organizations, including the Islamic Society of North America (ISNA), which served as an umbrella association for various smaller Muslim groups.

At ISNA and MSA conventions, discussions and speeches often focused on the Israeli-Palestinian conflict, the situation in Kashmir, the civil war in Afghanistan, and other global situations where Muslim interests were at stake. In the spring of Esam's freshman year at Georgetown, the United States launched air strikes in Libya in retaliation for the Qaddafi regime's role in the bombing of a discotheque in West Berlin frequented by U.S. military personnel. Though he was hardly a Qaddafi supporter, Esam was disgusted when President Reagan called him the "mad dog of the Middle East," and he and his Arab friends saw the U.S. attack as another example of American imperialism. When some Georgetown students passed out leaflets on campus calling for more bombs in Libya, Esam confronted them angrily.

Esam was not feeling alienated from his surroundings, however. Paradoxically, his admiration for America was growing, even as his Muslim identity was deepening. The diversity of the Georgetown student body and the freedom with which various groups could challenge each other in the public space, even to shout each other down, were manifestations of an open political culture that Esam appreciated. It was a Roman Catholic priest from the Georgetown Campus Ministry, Father Robert Rokusek, who had been his strongest university supporter when he set out to establish an MSA chapter on campus. Such broad-mindedness, he told his friends, would have been unthinkable in other countries. In America, an immigrant who wanted to embrace Islam could find support for that choice, just as other immigrants could freely pursue entirely different dreams. Esam's brother Emad, eleven months older than himself, was a computer whiz. His sister, Salwa, would pursue a career as a school counselor. One younger brother would become a filmmaker in Hollywood; another would become a human rights activist. Mohammed, the oldest, was the only one besides Esam who remained active in Muslim organizations such as the MSA. He also maintained close ties to the Omeish homeland, ultimately returning to serve as Libya's ambassador to Kuwait.

By the time of his graduation from Georgetown, Esam was determined to become a doctor, but he faced a major obstacle: He had not yet completed the requirements to become a permanent U.S. resident. Though he had been living in the United States legally since 1982, he had to apply for medical school as a foreign student, and his adviser warned him that his status could be a major impediment, despite his stellar grades and reputation for hard work. Three schools nevertheless admitted him, including Georgetown, his undergraduate alma mater and first choice. Of more than six thousand applicants for the fall 1989 term at Georgetown University Medical School, Esam was the only foreign student invited to enroll.

He was now twenty-two, an age when many male college grads were chasing girls, playing sports, or partying. The bars on M Street, just a few blocks from the Georgetown campus, were filled with young singles almost every night of the week, but Esam was not tempted. His interaction with girls was limited to classroom or laboratory conversations or occurred in the context of his MSA activities, which included female as well as male Muslim students. He was still living and eating at home, which saved him time and money. His medical studies and his Muslim activism left little room for other socializing or recreation. In the evenings, he attended classes at the Institute of Islamic and Arabic Sciences in Fairfax, Virginia. The school, funded and organized by the embassy of Saudi Arabia, offered classes in Islamic theology and jurisprudence and, among other missions, trained Muslim chaplains for service in the U.S. military. The education Esam received there would prepare him to serve as a volunteer imam, or worship leader, at Friday prayer services, a duty he took seriously in later years.

Esam's involvement in MSA activities elevated his profile in Muslim circles across the United States, and he became one of the best known and most effective young Muslim leaders in the country. During his years in medical school, he became head of the East Coast branch, then national vice president, and finally MSA president. His emergence as the national MSA leader came just as the U.S. Muslim population was mushrooming. Between 1990 and 2000, at least 550,000 Muslim immigrants arrived in the United States, many of them refugees or asylum seekers from such countries as Somalia, Bosnia, and Iraq. Employment opportunities, meanwhile, brought physicians and high-tech workers from India and Pakistan who in turn invited their brothers and sisters to join them. In the years that followed, Muslims constituted the fastest growing religious group in the United States. Attendance at the new Dar Al-Hijrah mosque, inaugurated in 1991, doubled and then tripled, creating traffic jams and parking problems in the neighborhood every Friday. The former university students who were the founding Dar Al-Hijrah members were soon joined at the prayer services by cab drivers, airport baggage handlers, 7-Eleven clerks, and other working-class Muslims from Africa, the Middle East, and South Asia, many of them beneficiaries of the family unification provisions of U.S. immigration law. Farther west in Fairfax County, near Dulles International Airport, an even larger mosque was built to accommodate the burgeoning Muslim population in the distant suburbs. The All Dulles Area Muslim Society (ADAMS) center was soon serving about five thousand Muslim families. Northern Virginia had become one of the principal Muslim population centers in the United States.

As the top national officer of the Muslim Students Association, Esam attended conventions and meetings around the country and found himself in the middle of vigorous debates about the Muslim agenda in America. Those individuals who had been in the United States the longest, many of them affiliated with the Muslim Brotherhood, tried to keep the focus on global Muslim causes, arguing loudly for solidarity with the Palestinian intifada and railing against the authoritarian regimes in Egypt, Jordan, and elsewhere that seemed to be more concerned with the maintenance of military ties with the United States than with the plight of their own Muslim populations. Esam did not challenge such appeals, but he and other young Muslim leaders argued that their organizations should pay more attention to the rapid growth of Muslim communities in the United States and consider how to incorporate Muslims and their institutions into American civic life in order to consolidate their position in American society and build an authentic Muslim American experience. Anti-Muslim voices in the future would lay out a conspiratorial vision of the Muslim Brotherhood trying to "infiltrate" the U.S. government and American institutions. The allegation was not entirely far-fetched. A strategy paper written by a Brotherhood member in 1991 (uncovered during a police raid in 2004) suggested that his Brotherhood colleagues "understand that their work in America is a kind of grand Jihad in eliminating and destroying the Western civilization from within and 'sabotaging' its miserable house by their hands and the hands of their believers so that . . . God's religion is made victorious over all religions." The paper was summarily rejected, however, by what remained of the Muslim Brotherhood leadership. Young Muslim leaders like Esam Omeish, a few of them with Muslim Brotherhood backgrounds, were indeed trying to position themselves and their organizations strategically in American society, but it was for the purpose of participating in American democracy, not undermining it, and it was a step in a progressive direction.

"Most of the Muslims who came early had this idea of, 'Let me get a good education, let me get know-how, and then I'll go back and help my brothers back there,'" Esam recalled later. "They were living the myth of return. Their discourse had not adjusted to reality." In Esam's view, the Muslim Brotherhood and the associated organizations, including the MSA, were focused far too narrowly on the preservation of the Muslim identity and becoming in the process largely irrelevant. "They were failing," he said. "They were not moving to the next phase and becoming part of the American mainstream." Because of such generational conflicts in the Muslim organizations, Esam focused largely on the student or youth sections, where he was more likely to find Muslims who shared his outlook. "If it hadn't been for the fact that I had gone through high school and college and had to acquire the tools and knowledge to be effective in America," he said, "I wouldn't have understood the transition we had to go through. The people I was dealing with were too comfortable in their zone. They were insular. As shopkeepers or even as diplomats, they were just living, without integrating."

Esam was at a turning point. His father, who followed the news from Libya every day and got teary when he heard the Libyan national anthem, continued to talk about returning with his family to Libya. Esam himself had considered the possibility of going back to the country of his birth to practice medicine. The more he thought about it, however, the more he realized he wanted to follow a path to U.S. citizenship. Once he had lived continuously in the United States for seven years as the son of an international civil servant, he was entitled to permanent residency status. Esam even felt that his attachment to Islam would reinforce his American identity. "Islam has a lot to do with our value system," he explained later, "and once you are able to identify and articulate those values, you see there is a stronger correlation with your experience in America than with anything you had back home. Our respect for human rights comes from Islam," he said, "but it was our American upbringing, not our Libyan upbringing, that supported it."

That pro-American outlook was not shared by everyone in the Muslim world in which Esam traveled. Virtually every national meeting of the Muslim Students Association, the Islamic Society of North America, or the Muslim Arab Youth Association (MAYA) featured speakers who took the opportunity to denounce the United States and its culture. A CNN journalist named Steven Emerson related what he encountered when he wandered into a MAYA meeting at the Oklahoma City Convention Center on Christmas Day in 1992. "I was horrified to hear a long procession of speakers,"

Emerson later wrote, "taking turns preaching violence and urging the assembly to use jihad against the Jews and the West. At times, spontaneous shouts of 'Kill the Jews' and 'Destroy the West'" could be heard." The speeches, he said, were all in Arabic but the man next to him interpreted what was allegedly being said onstage. Emerson later became a prominent investigator and critic of militant Islam, but his account of the MAYA convention was credible. The organization, composed mainly of Arab activists, was one of the more aggressive groups in its condemnation of Western foreign policy.

Esam had a top leadership role at the national conventions, but he was sometimes dismayed by the extremists who showed up. "Some of them," he said, "had left the [Muslim] Brotherhood because they thought it was too moderate, too compromising, too pro-democracy. They only subscribed to their own exclusive agenda." At another MAYA meeting in the early 1990s, Esam had an encounter with supporters of Sheikh Omar Abdel-Rahman, the spiritual leader of the underground "Islamic Group" believed to be responsible for the 1981 assassination of Egyptian president Anwar Sadat. Abdel-Rahman, who was blind, had arrived in the United States in 1990 after his release from an Egyptian prison, and he regularly delivered fiery sermons at mosques in the New York City area, calling for violent attacks on Western interests. Esam was coordinating speaker presentations at the convention when the blind sheikh, who was wheelchair-bound, showed up unexpectedly with a group of his supporters. Esam and some of his associates blocked the group from proceeding.

"I knew his radical tone," Esam recalled years later. "He would stand up and start cursing America and talk about killing people. That was not what we were about." Abdel-Rahman was more than twice Esam's age. As a venerated sheikh, he had a large and influential following, and his entourage was demanding that he be allowed to address the convention. The confrontation ended only after Esam called the hotel manager and asked that his security staff escort the group out of the ballroom. A few years later, the blind sheikh was convicted of seditious conspiracy in connection with the 1993 bombing at the World Trade Center and sentenced to life in prison.

By 1992, Esam was in his final year of medical school, still living at home. True to his faith, he had not yielded to alcohol, drugs, or intimacy with a woman. Friends were advising that it was time to consider marriage. Mulham Aldrobi, the MSA vice president in Canada, saw him at a convention and casually told him about a woman who might be a good match. Her name was Badria Kafala. She was Esam's age, an immigrant from Libya like himself, a devout Muslim, and an active member of the MSA at the University of Montreal, where she was working on a PhD in molecular biology. Her father, like Esam's father, had run afoul of the Qaddafi regime and taken his family into exile—first to Italy, then to Egypt, and finally to Morocco. Having completed her undergraduate education in Morocco, Badria wanted to attend medical school there, but it would have required her to go to the Libyan embassy in Rabat to pick up an official document. Her father, unyielding in his rejection of the Qaddafi government, would not allow anyone in his family to set foot in one of Qaddafi's embassies, and Badria ended up at graduate school in Montreal instead.

Alone in Canada, more than three thousand miles from her family, Badria had made a rare move for a young Libyan woman from a conservative family. She rented a basement apartment in the home of a French Canadian couple and focused on her laboratory work, limiting her socializing to outings with other Muslim women at the university, mostly from Libya, Algeria, Tunisia, and Morocco. Though she was far from her family and therefore able to live largely as she wished, Badria followed the conservative guidelines her parents had given her at a young age. Mulham Aldrobi had passed her telephone number to Esam and alerted her to Esam's possible marriage interest, but when Esam subsequently telephoned the house where she was staying, Badria refused to take the call. Instead, she instructed the couple with whom she lived to tell Esam that if he wanted to speak with her, he would first have to get the approval of her older brother, Abdelmonem, who lived in Pomona, California, where he owned a restaurant.

It was the traditional way in the Muslim world. An observant woman should not entertain a man's attention until a male in the family, ideally her father, gives his permission, and then only under strict rules. Esam called Abdelmonem in Pomona, who proceeded to quiz him about his background, his interests, and his future plans. Though Esam had initially tried to contact Badria directly, he was actually pleased to learn how traditional she was in her approach to a possible relationship, especially since she was far away from home and living independently in other ways. To him, it showed the conviction of her faith. His interest deepened when he found Badria's brother to be entirely cordial. "Once you take this route, it's very welcoming," Esam said later. "You're not wishy-washy [about your intentions]." Abdelmonem contacted their father in Morocco, told him about Esam, got his approval, and then told Badria she was free to speak with Esam herself.

"It was the only way I would get married," Badria said later. "When guys were around me in Morocco, I never considered talking to them about marriage." An additional consideration in Badria's case was that her father wanted her to marry a boy from Libya, thinking it would mean she would be more likely to stay close to her family. As a businessman in Libya, Badria's father had known a cousin of Esam's father, and with a little investigation he concluded that Esam came from a reputable family. In all respects, he seemed like an excellent candidate to marry his daughter. He was not only Libyan and religious and active in the Muslim community, but he was also respectful of a woman who had chosen to live alone and pursue a professional career in a distant country, an attitude other religious Muslim men might not have shared. "I felt pressure [to let the relationship proceed]," Badria recalled. "But just because my parents said yes and my brother said yes did not mean I had to say yes."

Over the next several months, Esam and Badria spoke regularly by phone, though in fairly formal ways. Esam began by asking her what she did every day and then moved gradually to such subjects as where she wanted to live and whether she was determined to go back to Morocco. As the relationship progressed, they arranged to meet in California, under the supervision of Badria's brother. They saw each other for the first time at a café in a crowded shopping mall in Pomona, custom requiring that they not meet alone. Badria had a picture of Esam but was not sure what to expect, and she approached the encounter nervously. Nor could Esam be certain of Badria. She would be wearing a hijab, and as long as they remained unmarried she would not allow him to see her without it. "It was all very formal, even in the words we used with each other," Badria explained later. "You don't talk about your feelings. You cannot say, 'I like you,' not until you have a [marriage] contract."

The proposal became official only after Esam and his father traveled to Morocco to meet Badria's parents. He and Badria were married at the Hyatt Regency Hotel in Rabat in April 1993, during Esam's final year in medical school at Georgetown University. He received his Green Card, becoming a legal permanent U.S. resident, just in time to begin his residency at a hospital in Newark, New Jersey. For his specialty, Esam chose general surgery, meaning he would have to gain the expertise necessary to operate on the human body from head to toe. A residency in general surgery is one of the longest in the medical profession; Esam was committed to five more years of training. The specialty nevertheless appeals to doctors who seek the satisfaction of making sick people better by simply cutting the disease out of their body or repairing whatever damage is causing pain or suffering. "We heal with steel," they say. As trauma specialists, they are called into action when there are shootings, stabbings, automobile accidents, and other emergency situations. For that reason, they have unpredictable work schedules, which makes it one of the less desirable specialties among doctors who rank lifestyle factors highly. Esam Omeish, however, went into medicine largely in response to a humanitarian urge, and being a surgeon satisfied it.

For the first two years of their marriage, he and Badria were separated, because she was finishing her PhD in Montreal. Esam drove up from New Jersey to see her as often as he could, though it was a seven-hour trip in each direction, and he was often sleep-deprived from long hours at the hospital. His Libyan passport meant he consistently faced long delays at the U.S.-Canadian border. "I'll be lying on this bench over here," he would tell the customs officials. "Here are my car keys. Wake me when I'm free to go." Badria joined him in New Jersey after the completion of her graduate work, and she and Esam had two daughters in quick succession, Abrar and Anwar. The city of Paterson, where they lived, was home to a large Arab population, primarily Palestinian, and one of the largest mosques in the state, the Islamic Center of Passaic County. Esam soon moved into leadership positions there, eventually becoming chairman of the mosque board of directors and president of the New Jersey chapter of the Muslim American Society, an organization established in 1993 by former members of the Muslim Brotherhood who had concluded that the Brotherhood was too isolated from American life and needed to be refashioned.

It was relatively easy, however, to advocate the integration of Muslim and non-Muslim Americans in a setting where Muslims were so well represented. Esam and Badria would soon learn what it meant to engage the broader U.S. mainstream in a far more challenging setting. Following the completion of his surgical residency in New Jersey, Esam took a position in the town of Big Stone Gap in southwest Virginia, a small community in the Appalachian mountains just east of Harlan County, Kentucky. He would be the only surgeon at the Lonesome Pine Hospital, serving a mostly poor and rural population in the heart of coal country, home to many evangelical Christians who had never encountered a Muslim.

For Badria, accustomed to living in far more cosmopolitan settings and having Muslim friends around her, it was a hard transition, especially because she was now staying at home with two little girls. Having spoken French in Montreal, she was not yet comfortable in English, and the sight of a woman in a hijab trying unsuccessfully to communicate with the cashier at the local Walmart was enough to prompt hostile glances and sharp comments like, "Why don't you go back where you came from?" As the only surgeon in town, however, Dr. Omeish soon became well known, at least among all those residents with an acquaintance or family member who needed an operation. A local Methodist minister on whom he performed surgery invited Esam to speak about Islam to his congregation, and that occasion led to similar opportunities in other churches. Esam and Badria even organized a "Know Your Muslim Neighbor" campaign, with Badria preparing posters and pamphlets for distribution in those churches willing to take them.

A moderately high salary, a low cost of living, and the rewards from serving a needy population were not by themselves sufficient to keep Esam and Badria in Big Stone Gap. After eight months, Esam found work in Fairfax County, where he had his U.S. roots. His older brother, Mohammed, had completed his PhD studies at George Washington University and was working with nonprofit organizations in the D.C. area, though he would soon move his family to Jordan. Emad, the number two son, was working at the time in Libya, though he would soon return to Washington, married to a woman he had met in Libya. Esam's sister, Salwa, by then had married Yahia Tagouri, a physician who had gone to medical school in Libya and then immigrated to the United States in 1987. They had met after Yahia's father heard that Salem Omeish had a daughter about Yahia's age and suggested that the two families meet for dinner. Yahia came with his parents and his brother and sister-in-law, and he and Salwa were sufficiently interested in each other to exchange phone numbers. Yahia had to ask Salwa's father for permission to marry her, though their courtship was not as formal as Esam and Badria's, in part because they were not so far apart. At the time they met, Salwa was an undergraduate at George Mason

University in Fairfax and living at home with her parents, while
Yahia was completing his medical residency in West Virginia, about
six hours away. They spoke often on the phone, and Yahia drove to
Fairfax every other weekend to visit her.

Two years after they married, Salwa went back to wearing a
hijab. Yahia had encouraged her to cover her head, but the decision
was Salwa's. Though she had gone nearly a decade without the scarf,
she had thought often about wearing it again. "I was ready," she later
recalled. She and Yahia had a baby girl, whom they named Noor.
"I had more confidence in handling myself," she said, "and I didn't
care so much about what other people thought." She had also been
profoundly affected by the sickness and death from cancer of Yahia's
sister, an experience that left Salwa feeling closer to God. "Seeing
her go through cancer and then having her pass away in front of me
put life into perspective for me," she said. "It was not about vanity."
In the years that followed, she grew more pious, and she and her
husband prayed daily.

Back in Fairfax, Esam's medical practice grew quickly. He was
soon named chief of general surgery at Inova Alexandria Hospital.
On weekends, he routinely filled in as the emergency trauma surgeon at a hospital in Hagerstown, Maryland, a responsibility that
took on added importance when President George W. Bush visited
Camp David, inasmuch as the Hagerstown hospital was the designated trauma center in the event of any emergency that involved
the president. As the chief general surgeon on duty, Esam had to be
vetted by the Secret Service. He was open about the leadership roles
he had played in Muslim organizations that had a record of harshly
criticizing U.S. foreign policy—and such disclosures led in Esam's
recollection to "some rolling of eyes" among the investigators—but
in the end he was cleared to perform trauma surgery on President
Bush in case it was needed.

Dar Al-Hijrah, his hometown mosque, had grown significantly
since Esam last lived in Fairfax County. He resumed his involvement in mosque activities and was soon named to the executive

committee of the board of directors. His mission, consistent with his goals in every Muslim organization he led, was to open the mosque life to the surrounding community and increase its appeal to youth and recent immigrants. He insisted that the khutba, or Friday sermon, be delivered in English, not Arabic, and when the time came to hire a new imam, Esam argued that he should be someone who could represent the mosque effectively to the local non-Muslim community. Though his hospital responsibilities took much of his time, Esam volunteered to lead the recruitment effort and began making inquiries through his vast circle of Muslim contacts around the country. Before long, he found someone who appeared to be an ideal candidate. Though he was serving at the time at a mosque in San Diego, he had been accepted in a doctoral program at George Washington University and was planning to move to the D.C. area. Just thirty years old, he had energy and magnetism and a strong sense of humor. Though he had made some strong statements about the Israeli-Palestinian conflict and some other issues, he was known as a moderate and, most importantly, had a reputation for giving highly entertaining and insightful lectures on Islam. Of Yemeni descent, he was born in the United States and a native English speaker. Esam pushed hard to hire him, and the Dar Al-Hijrah directors agreed.

The imam's name was Anwar al-Awlaki.

15

INTEGRATION

As diversity became its destiny, America was tested: Would it prove to be the exceptional nation open to all, as promised? For the communities most transformed by demographic change, the test was more practical: Could they absorb the newcomers harmoniously? Critics consistently warned that expanded immigration would bring disruptive and destabilizing changes, and Virginia's Fairfax County faced that prospect year after year—in schooling, law enforcement, and governance.

As long as the county school board was appointed, members came and went with every new party lineup on the Fairfax County Board of Supervisors. Robert Frye, the veteran African American activist from Reston, lost his seat in 1984, got it back when the Democrats regained control in 1989, but then lost it again four years later. Fairfax County was constantly evolving, becoming simultaneously more crowded, wealthier, and more diverse, and its political profile was shifting in one direction or another every year. The new chairman of the Board of Supervisors in 1993 was Thomas Davis, who as the Mason District supervisor in 1984 had claimed to see a white conservative trend in the county. With his home base in the immigrant-heavy Mason District, however, Davis in 1993 could see how rapidly the county's demographics were changing, and by then he was promising to share political power with immigrant and minority groups. As chairman he secured a second at-large "minority" seat on the school board and nominated a Vietnamese refugee, Le Chi Thao, for the position. Asian Americans at the time were the largest minority group in the Fairfax school system, and Thao said he intended "to bring in some Asian points of view." To replace Robert Frye, Davis chose another African American, Kay Coles James, a conservative activist and antiabortion crusader. Davis also promised to work for a third minority seat on the board, which he said would go to a Hispanic.

In 1995, the county switched to school board elections, and designated "minority" seats were eliminated. Immigrant and minority voters by then had more clout, however, and Robert Frye won an at-large seat on the school board, with the most votes of any candidate in the county. Never before had a black man been elected to public office in Fairfax County, and he was joined on the school board by a Korean American, Ilryong Moon, the first Asian American elected in the state of Virginia. Moon, an attorney, had come to the United States in 1974 at the age of seventeen, one year after his father immigrated to take a job with a U.S. company as a skilled electrical worker. He did not see himself as representing an Asian constituency, however. "I serve everyone," Moon said in an interview. "I do not care whether they're from Korea or Ethiopia or were born here. It doesn't matter to me."

For Moon, his Korean background was important largely for symbolic reasons. He saw himself serving immigrant interests just by being in a leadership position. "A lot of times I go to these meetings, and I am one of the very few minorities, often the only Asian," he said. "That motivates me. When students come—whether white, black, Asian, or Hispanic—and see that there's an Asian, an immigrant, on the school board, they know that anyone in the community can participate in this political process and that anyone should participate, because we are building a community. If that's a contribution I can make as the first Asian American elected official, I'm going to make it."

Moon's own story was indeed inspiring. In Korea, he and his family lived in a small housing complex with seven other families, each with a single room. There was one sink for the whole house, with no hot water, and a single shared outhouse. He started school in America without speaking any English and not understanding anything his teachers said. He soon learned to read, though not always with full comprehension. For a world civilization class, Moon literally memorized key sections of his textbook. When asked on a test to explain how World War II began, he recalled the relevant paragraph in the textbook and wrote down whatever the book had said. The big challenge was conversation. He often stayed back in his classroom during lunch hour, telling his teachers he wanted to study the Bible but actually just avoiding the pain of not being able to communicate with his classmates. He nevertheless graduated from high school with honors, went to Harvard, and obtained a law degree from the College of William and Mary.

For Moon, as for many Korean Americans, America's greatest strength was its schooling system, and his motivation for going into public service was to reinforce that tradition. When he read in the newspaper that Fairfax County was going to switch from an appointed to an elected school board, he decided on a whim that he wanted to run "for myself and my kids." He knew nothing about how the school system worked, and up to that point he had never volunteered for any school activities, but he started attending all the school board meetings. "After a while, people began noticing," Moon said. " 'There's this short Asian guy who shows up at every meeting. Who is he?' " The appointed school board members vacated their positions four months before elections were held to select a new board, and Moon persuaded the county supervisors to appoint him as an interim member, pending the elections. No one had come forward before from the Korean community, and Moon made the argument that he deserved a chance. He got the appointment, and after an energetic campaign spearheaded by Korean friends and members of his church congregation, he won the election. Beyond broad principles, however, Ilryong Moon did not stake out positions in defense of particular immigrant interests. He became known for arguing that all students in Fairfax County schools should be exposed to a foreign language and for advocating a full-day kindergarten program.

Robert Frye, on the other hand, saw his role as directly representing the county's poor and minority students, including immigrants. By the time he was freely elected in 1995, he already had eleven years of experience on the Fairfax school board as an appointed member, and he knew the challenges he faced as an advocate for the most disadvantaged segments of the county population. "My fellow school board members were some of the greatest people I ever met," he recalled years later, "but for the most part, they didn't understand. Most of them had never been poor. My family had lived in public housing, I had been poor, and a lot of my work was trying to get them to understand." Frye often advised his fellow board members to give some thought to the concerns of those parents who did not show up at meetings, either because they were working at a second job or because they didn't quite understand how the system worked. "Listen to the silence," he was famous for saying. When Ilryong Moon joined the board, Frye gained a key supporter, and Moon was instrumental in getting Frye chosen as the board chairman in 1999.

Just as the school authorities in Fairfax County were challenged by the new immigrant populations they had to serve, so was the county police department. Immigrants who lacked education or cash resources were vulnerable to exploitation by unscrupulous landlords, loan sharks, or criminals posing as immigration lawyers or businessmen, and their difficult living conditions sometimes gave rise to drug and alcohol abuse or domestic violence. Fairfax police officers, meanwhile, were no more prepared for the problems they encountered than the school board had been. The language barrier and cultural misunderstandings were major handicaps, just as they were for the police officers in Washington, D.C., who found themselves mediating between Korean storeowners and their angry African American customers.

Until 1967, the police department in Fairfax County was an all-white, all-male force. It was integrated that year with the hiring of a veteran African American officer from Richmond, Virginia, and in 1972 the first female officer was hired. By the time Suzanne Devlin joined in 1976, there were just a handful of women on the force. Her first job was patrolling thirty thousand acres of Fairfax County parkland, an assignment that involved, in her words, "a lot of walking through the woods at night, usually alone, and harassing school kids who were smoking dope." She had a radio, but in the remote stretches of the park, it rarely worked. On more than one occasion, she actually turned to campers and hikers in the park for assistance, experiences that taught her the value of public involvement in police work. In a thirty-three-year career with the Fairfax police, Devlin's community-oriented perspective would distinguish her work as a patrol officer, and she would rise to the number two position in the department.

The course of her career changed with an incident in December 1980, when she shot an African American man while on night patrol in the parkland. The man and his fourteen-year-old son were hunting raccoons for their pelts, as they did almost every night. Devlin and another officer encountered them in the moonlight. Hearing their approach, the man, who was armed with a .22 caliber pistol, whirled to face them.

"Who's that?" he yelled, fearful it was Ku Klux Klansmen, which was not an unreasonable thought in that place at that time. Devlin and the other officer, seeing the man's gun, fired immediately, hitting him in the arm and dropping him to the ground. A bone in his arm was shattered, but the officers handcuffed him and dragged him to the nearest place accessible to police and emergency vehicles, along with his son. He was seriously injured by the gunshot and never fully regained the use of his arm. From that incident, Devlin realized that her split-second decisions as a cop had life-or-death consequences. Just twenty-seven years old at the time, she resolved to remember that there may be alternatives to a physical confrontation and that good policing required effective communication skills. In the next two years, she completed a college degree in sociology at George Mason University, and she proceeded immediately into a master's program in "conflict management," a field of study that would come to define her approach to police work. "I've learned to see myself not just as an enforcer, but as a mediator," she told a reporter as she neared her graduation in 1984. "In many situations, what you need are listening skills, awareness, and sensitivity."

By the end of the 1980s, Devlin was putting her conflict management expertise to work during encounters with immigrant populations, who by then were the main focus of her police work. She was patrolling in low-income areas along the southern side of Fairfax County, where there were large concentrations of Central American immigrants, especially Salvadorans who had come straight from war zones in their country and were traumatized by what they had been through. "We had so much violence there," she recalled later. "We just kept putting cops in there, but there were knife fights every night. We knew we had to do things a little different."

A nearby refugee relocation center was assigning many of the Salvadorans to a vast complex of red-brick apartment buildings known as Springfield Gardens. More than 80 percent of the thousand or so residents in the sprawling development were Hispanic immigrants. Many were young men who held low-paying service jobs in hotels or restaurants or worked on landscaping crews, sending money home to their families. In the evenings, they often gathered on the front stoops of the apartment buildings, drinking beer or socializing. On some occasions, they got drunk or grew boisterous, and police showed up to investigate. Few of the officers spoke Spanish, and the men had trouble explaining themselves, which meant some were arrested without cause. By then, Suzanne Devlin was assistant commander of the local police station, in a position to put some of her ideas into action. She pushed patrol officers to get out of their cars and into the neighborhood, where they might get to know the people they were supposed to be protecting and have a better idea of the human and social environment in which they were working.

"We wanted cops who knew how to be aggressive in the street," Devlin said, "but who were confident being alone and comfortable enough in their own skin to be good communicators." In 1992, not yet forty years old, Devlin was already the highest-ranking female officer in the Fairfax Police Department. As part of her outreach effort in the district where she worked, she initiated Spanish language training for her officers and opened a satellite police station in a ground-floor studio apartment in the Springfield Gardens complex. The office served as a tiny government center where apartment residents could get information on all available social services, plus file reports or complaints for the attention of the police.

The immigrant residents did not necessarily appreciate the effort. Many came from countries where the public security forces were considered corrupt and associated with death squads and terror. It would not occur to a recent Salvadoran or Guatemalan immigrant to look to police officers for protection. Such encounters were to be avoided, not embraced, and the residents were not inclined to share intelligence with the police about what was going on in their buildings. What Suzanne Devlin and her officers saw as community involvement, the immigrants were more likely to see as unwelcome intrusion into their lives. The outreach effort nevertheless resulted in reduced crime rates. Devlin's performance earned her the attention of the department leadership, who promoted her again, this time to the police headquarters staff.

As an assistant to the chief of police, Devlin did not have to respond to service calls and had more time to promote her "community policing" ideas and meet with local leaders and businesspeople. Among the contacts she made was a Korean woman named Sonny who ran the salon where Devlin took her two young daughters to have their hair cut. Sonny was married to a U.S.-born Caucasian and, unlike most recent Korean immigrants, spoke decent English. Devlin found the woman to be especially friendly and eager to share her thoughts and experiences, and they began meeting regularly over lunch. Both women had something to gain from the friendship. Through Sonny, Devlin got some insight into the relatively closed Korean community. Sonny and her friends, meanwhile, sometimes needed law enforcement assistance but didn't know how to find it. Like many other Korean small business owners, Sonny had a stack of checks she had been unable to cash because the accounts had insufficient funds to cover them, and friends of hers had fallen victim to various financial fraud operations. For a time, the relationship proved productive. "She would get involved in anything we wanted her to get involved in," Devlin recalled. "She was brave in her own way."

The closer Devlin got to Sonny, however, the more awkward their relationship became. Devlin could see that Sonny's friends, though often victim of someone else's manipulation, were not necessarily engaged in entirely legal operations themselves. Many were not reporting their income for tax purposes, and some of their "investments" were in activities that Devlin considered questionable. When she had her intelligence officers check into places that Sonny wanted to take her, they cautioned her about getting in too deep. "Sonny would be, like, 'Let's go to the spa,'" Devlin recalled, "and my guys would say, 'Do not go. Do not go to the spa.'" On one occasion, while eating lunch with Sonny at a Korean restaurant, Devlin noticed a group of men sitting in the back, staring coldly at her. Afterward, she learned from her intelligence unit that the restaurant was notorious as a center of gambling activity and that the Korean owner had ties to an organized crime ring.

"I realized that just about every place she took me was probably a place I shouldn't be visiting," Devlin said. "For her, those lines were blurred. That was her life. She had to live in that world, but I could be putting myself in a dangerous situation." The turning point came when Sonny told her that she had broken up with her husband and was seeing a Korean man. Back in her office, Devlin ran a check on the man and learned he had a criminal record. She told Sonny she couldn't see her anymore. "You're traveling with people I can't travel with," Devlin said.

"In hindsight, I was being naive," Devlin said later. "As a police officer, you have to figure out where to draw the line, and you get sharper about it as you get more experienced. It's never easy. Sometimes your best contacts are in sketchy places. For a while there, it worked. I felt like we were making differences in people's lives, and you do get smarter about making emotional investments. But in the end I got rid of all of them. I just didn't get personal anymore."

The risk in a personal approach was that officers might be tempted to turn a blind eye to illegal and potentially dangerous immigrant behavior in order to gain intelligence about activities in an otherwise inaccessible immigrant community. Police encounters with Korean immigrants highlighted the dilemma. Among the criminal activities in Korean neighborhoods were cigarette smuggling, prostitution and sex trafficking, counterfeiting, and even murder-for-hire. In 2001, five of the eleven homicide victims in Fairfax County were Korean or Vietnamese. Fewer than 2 percent of the patrol officers in the county were of Asian descent, however, and none was a homicide detective. Moreover, Korean immigrants—like Salvadorans and Guatemalans—were reluctant to cooperate with police, even in the investigation of a murder, for fear of being labeled disloyal. Clearly, engagement was needed, and for years to come Fairfax authorities continued to emphasize the importance of maintaining good relations with immigrant groups. Years later, when neighboring Prince William County signed a memorandum with the federal government that committed the county police to check the immigration status of all persons arrested for violating state or county laws, Fairfax County declined to follow suit. Gaining and maintaining the trust of non-English-speaking residents was hard enough without the county authorities alienating them further by taking on a new role as enforcers of federal immigration laws.

The more diverse Fairfax County became, the more issues there were to resolve and the more conflicts developed, between immigrants and nonimmigrants and even among immigrants themselves. Alliances were made and broken and new ones emerged. Mark Keam's experience in Los Angeles and then in Washington, D.C., taught him the importance of building relationships, and when he moved to northern Virginia in the 1990s he threw himself into the immigrant political scene with enthusiasm. One entrée for him was the Korean church in Fairfax County that he joined shortly after arriving from California. He became acquainted there with a group of young Korean American professionals who were attempting to organize Korean immigrants in the area. They were also developing ties with other immigrant groups, especially Latinos, whose numbers were steadily growing. Mark was part of that effort, and he soon met Walter Tejada, a prominent immigrant activist from El Salvador. Tejada had come to the United States at the age of thirteen, three years after his mother had left to work for a family in Arizona. During the years she was gone, Tejada and his brother and sister lived with his grandmother, who made a meager living selling secondhand clothes and shoes in the central market in San Salvador. To bring in extra income, young Walter set up a shoeshine stand across the street from his grandmother's stall. By the time his mother was able to bring him and his brother and sister to America, he had learned to take care of himself. In America, he learned English quickly and emerged as a leader, and by his senior year he was captain of his high school soccer team. After finishing college, he moved to northern Virginia and immediately got involved in local politics. By the mid-1990s, he was leading the local chapter of the League of United Latin American Citizens (LULAC), the most activist of all the Latino advocacy groups in Virginia.

Tejada's friendship with Mark Keam developed from their working together to oppose an effort in the Virginia legislature to limit welfare benefits to immigrants. A 1996 welfare reform package introduced by the administration of President Bill Clinton gave states the authority to deny food stamps to immigrants who had not yet completed the process to become U.S. citizens. Asian and Hispanic immigrants alike were affected, and Keam and Tejada joined forces to lobby Virginia legislators, traveling to the state capital in Richmond to press their case for giving legal permanent residents the same rights to welfare assistance that citizens enjoyed. They were successful, and that effort was one of several that led to the formation of a Capital Area Immigrants' Rights Coalition, of which Keam and Tejada were among the founders.

For local politicians, the immigration surge put a premium on agile thinking. Fairfax County's Mason District, with the heaviest concentration of foreign-born residents, was represented in the 1980s by Thomas Davis, the Republican from the nearly all-white Ravenswood district. Though he began his political career as a conservative, he soon acquired an immigrant-friendly reputation. No one in the county had played a more important role in securing official approval for the Dar Al-Hijrah mosque, whose construction in 1993 was a seminal event in the county. Davis also sent his own children to J. E. B. Stuart High School at a time when many white parents were shunning the school because of its heavy immigrant and minority population. That disposition won him broad support among the newcomers, even as his fiscally conservative views on taxation and spending resonated with more traditional voters. His balancing of those constituencies helped get him elected to the U.S. Congress in 1994.

Beginning in 1996, Mason District was represented by Penny

Gross, a former U.S. Senate staffer who had been active in community politics for nearly twenty years before being elected supervisor. Her approach in office was to address controversial subjects head-on, with the intention of fostering dialogue and defusing tension. She convened a monthly discussion group called "Kaleidoscope," intending it as an opportunity for concerned residents, immigrant representatives, community leaders, and county officials to work through the issues that divided them. The meetings could be heated, but Gross did not hesitate to challenge her constituents with an impromptu civics lesson when she felt it necessary. "Why can't we mandate that all signs be posted in English?" wondered one citizen who was distressed by the proliferation of stores catering to immigrant customers.

"We can," Gross answered. "But first we have to repeal the First Amendment, because it guarantees freedom of speech, and that includes signs." But she also encouraged the immigrant business owners to advertise partly in English, if only to appear less secretive about what they were selling. When Korean restaurant owners complained that the county health department was shutting down their businesses because they all used a noodle machine whose operation violated a sanitary code, she worked with them, their lawyer, and county officials to find a solution. She arranged for county inspectors to explain to immigrant proprietors, with translation, why it was not a good idea to put an electrical line next to a gas line or jury-rig a plumbing connection.

One of the most polarizing issues in Fairfax County related to immigration was residential overcrowding. Many immigrants arrive in the United States with limited resources and are dependent at the beginning on relatives or friends. Victor Alarcón, coming from Bolivia, the Kim family, coming from South Korea via Argentina, and the Khan family from Pakistan via Saudi Arabia, all moved in with a brother or a sister upon their arrival. The pattern was especially pronounced for immigrants from Central America, most of whom had little education and few marketable skills. Many, like Marta

Quintanilla, the young woman from El Salvador, had made difficult journeys overland and showed up in the United States psychologically and financially exhausted. It was not uncommon for two families to share a single housing unit, just as Victor and Rhina Alarcón had to do for several months. Several single men, working as day laborers, might even squeeze into one apartment, forcing them to sleep in shifts. Suzanne Devlin, while patrolling the Springfield Garden apartments, often found people sleeping in lawn chairs and men who were renting out patio furniture for a dollar an hour.

The county zoning ordinance prohibited more than one family in a single house, and no more than four unrelated people living as a single housekeeping unit. Bedrooms had to provide at least seventy square feet for one person, one hundred square feet for two. Violations of law were widespread, with the operation of illegal boardinghouses in particular becoming a major law enforcement issue, as homes built for a single family were routinely turned into multiunit apartment houses without authorization. A strict enforcement of such regulations, however, hit immigrants hard. The Salvadoran activist Walter Tejada, who was elected in 2003 to the board of Arlington County, adjacent to Seven Corners and Bailey's Crossroads, argued from his first days in office that homeowners should be allowed to build "accessory dwelling units" on their properties for extended family members. In public meetings, he often made the argument that in the Latino community, allowing friends or family members or even strangers to be homeless was unacceptable. "It's not part of our culture," he would say.

Overcrowded neighborhoods, however, often brought congestion, noise, and parking problems, and it was politically popular to take a hard line on the issue. Leslie Byrne, a Democrat who represented Fairfax County in the Virginia State Senate, sponsored legislation that would have given Fairfax supervisors the authority to prohibit people from sleeping anywhere but in bedrooms. County code enforcers under her legislation would have had more power to go after residents who were renting out their homes to more people than they could reasonably accommodate. The Fairfax Board of Supervisors had not actually requested such authorities from the state legislature, and Byrne's bill prompted ridicule around the country before it quietly died. A year later, however, in response to the same overcrowding concerns, the Fairfax county board did enact an ordinance that prohibited residents from parking on their front lawns or paving over their lawns to create oversized driveways. The county also established a zoning enforcement "strike force" that included building inspectors, criminal investigators, and representatives from the fire department and the zoning board. The strike teams visited housing units that had been reported as having unsafe or illegal conditions, and they had the authority to refer violators for criminal or civil prosecution.

For Supervisor Penny Gross, representing a county district where two out of five residents were foreign-born, the housing issue was especially difficult. She invested much time and effort in immigration outreach efforts but also had to recognize public sentiment about overcrowding. The first time she ran for reelection as supervisor, her Republican opponent, Tina Trapnell, accused Gross of not heeding her constituents' complaints about zoning violations, and she said she would work for stronger enforcement. "I don't want to discriminate against anyone," Trapnell said, "but there are some situations, whether cultural or not, that are just against the law."

As Walter Tejada and other immigrant advocates found out, the residential zoning question was an example of where African American and immigrant interests diverged. Those suburban neighborhoods with high concentrations of African Americans, such as in the Bailey's Crossroads area, tended to have lower housing costs and thus were more attractive to new immigrants. But residents of those historically black neighborhoods had often fought hard to improve their quality of life, and many resented having to share their streets with newcomers who did not appreciate what it had taken to make the neighborhoods livable. In the Mount Vernon area of Fairfax County, where many black residents traced their lineage to

214 ★ A Nation of Nations

one of George Washington's slaves, and in the Bailey's community, founded by freed slaves after the Civil War, the local civic associations lobbied county authorities incessantly to crack down on illegal housing units.

On one occasion in 2003, Supervisor Gross arranged for one of her regular Kaleidoscope meetings to be held in the Bailey's Community Center, whose construction was itself the product of years of pressure on Fairfax County authorities by local black families. The meeting was planned as a panel discussion, featuring Toa Q. Do, the Vietnamese businessman who had helped organize the African American–Indochinese Alliance in the 1980s, as well as representatives of Arab and Latino immigrant groups. Gross had moderated similar meetings around her district previously without incident, but to her dismay the Bailey's attendees were hostile to the immigrant representatives. One resident after another stood up and berated the panelists.

"This is our community," somebody said, "and we want to keep it that way. Why don't you just go home?" Several complained that the immigrants were devaluing the neighborhood. "You guys come in here, you buy a house, and you turn the lawn into a parking lot," one audience member said. Given her extensive collaboration with the Bailey's community leaders, Gross was stunned by the tone of discussion at the meeting, and the recollection of it still bothered her years later. "The whole reason I started Kaleidoscope was to lower the tone and to pull people into their commonalities," she said, "but they weren't having any of it. It was really a shocker, to see this community I had worked with for such a long time on one side, and on the other side this newer [immigrant] community that was just trying to get its story out. Boy, there was a clash. It really saddened me, because you would think that people who had faced discrimination all their lives would understand someone else facing discrimination."

The hard feelings did not easily dissipate. One of the Bailey's seniors willing to share her sentiments ten years later was Elizabeth

Hall, who with her late husband, Edward, had played a key role in getting the community center built and was present for its inauguration in 1978. At the age of eighty-three but with the vigor and bounce of a woman twenty years younger, she was still working at the center, managing the after-school traffic and the constant stream of people wanting to use the facilities. "It's too small," she said. "We thought this was just going to be for the immediate Bailey's community. But now people are coming in from all over the county." It was a complaint Gross and other county officials heard regularly from the Bailey's residents.

Hall also thought the immigrants were getting an undue share of the subsidized housing in the area. "We've got senior citizens who have been here for years and years, and they can't get into these apartments, but these other people come into the country and they get it. It's unfair to the American citizens," she said. "Anybody who needs help should get help, but the people who have been here all their lives and are the pioneers of the community are not getting what they deserve." She also said the issue of overcrowded housing, which had dominated the Kaleidoscope meeting a decade earlier, had not been resolved. "We're still fighting about this," she said. "The problem is, you can't go in and count how many people are sleeping in each room, but you see all the cars parked out front. And we have to pay for their children's schooling!" But then she throws her head back and laughs. "I guess that's life," she says. "It's America, the land of the free, the dreamland! We just have to deal with it."

As the immigrant population in Fairfax County matured and was integrated socially, politically, and economically, generalizations about values and identity became less valid, and loyalties less predictable. County leaders like Penny Gross learned that immigrant voters were hardly of one mind. She was occasionally challenged by those who felt she paid insufficient attention to their concerns about excessive county spending and high property taxes. Twice she was opposed for reelection by candidates who were themselves immigrants, though she defeated them both. She continued to host her Kaleidoscope meetings, but attendance fell off, and the discussions were less about coping with diversity in general and more about issues like environmental regulation. The question of how to deal with the undocumented immigrant population was as contentious locally as it was on the national scene, and immigrants who had come to the United States through legal channels were not necessarily sympathetic to those who came outside the law. Having struggled hard to learn a new language and seen the rewards that came from fluency, many immigrants were convinced that government agencies at all levels should insist that immigrants learn American English.

Robert Frye's advice that school officials "listen to the silence" spurred the creation of a new advocacy organization calling itself the Coalition of the Silence, but it narrowed its focus from immigrant and minority students in general to African American and Latino students. One of the group's major complaints concerned the Thomas Jefferson High School for Science and Technology, which since its creation in 1985 had been consistently ranked as the top high school in the United States. The community concern was that some immigrants were actually overrepresented in the school, with a disproportionate number of Asian students and relatively few African Americans and Hispanics. The same pattern was reflected in a number of other math- and science-oriented secondary schools in urban areas around the United States.

Old prejudices died hard. In 2012, on the occasion of his victory in the Democratic primary race for the city council seat he had held since 2005, former Washington, D.C., mayor Marion Barry suddenly launched into an attack on Asian merchants in black neighborhoods. "We've got to do something about these Asians coming, opening up businesses, these dirty shops," Barry said. "They ought to go. I'll just say that right now. But we need African American business people to be able to take their places, too."

As mayor in the 1980s, Barry had tried to negotiate an end to a boycott of Asian shops in Washington, but at that time he was speaking to a broader constituency. By 2012 his political base had shrunk significantly. No longer citywide, much less nationwide, it was now limited largely to his own ward, where he did not need to watch his words so carefully. But other African American leaders, many of them former allies, were quick to denounce Barry's divisive comments.

Mark Keam, the Korean American leader who was thirty years Barry's junior, felt obliged to respond. In a lengthy column published in *The Washington Post*, he condemned Barry's remarks as "racist" and recalled how organizations with which he had been affiliated worked to reconcile African American and Korean American interests in order to prevent confrontations like those in Los Angeles. In the process, Keam said, he had learned how "fragile race relations can be. You never know when, where, or how any multi-racial situation could come down crumbling, with one small mistake or incident that sparks the flame of prejudice."

16

INITIATIVE

During the time it took Victor Alarcón to earn the money he needed to bring his wife, Rhina, from Bolivia to America, he worked seven days a week at the Mexican restaurant where he had first found employment. With nothing else to do and nowhere to go, Victor volunteered to open the restaurant early in the morning and close it at the end of the day. He spent almost nothing during that period, living off leftovers at the restaurant and paying only modest rent for the space in the apartment he shared with fellow workers. In just three months he had put aside enough to pay for Rhina's airplane ticket. The perseverance he showed in those months set the pattern for his approach to work in years to come, and Rhina followed suit. Like Victor, she started as a dishwasher. On her first day as a Burger King employee, the shift supervisor told her to wash some kettles that had been blackened by years on the stove. An hour later, she was still bent over the sink, scouring away, when her supervisor came by and told her there was no way she would ever be able to make the kettles shine. Assigned to clean-up duties, Rhina would routinely stay an hour past closing time, scrubbing the grease-covered floor like it had never been scrubbed before. Employers appreciated an immigrant work ethic like the one Victor and Rhina demonstrated, and they were quick to hire such newcomers to the country, not always checking to see whether their immigration papers were in order.

Victor knew that bosses would take advantage of his eagerness to succeed in America, and he knew he and Rhina would not get far on the low wages they were earning. In the years that followed their move to northern Virginia, Victor dabbled restlessly in ventures that appealed to his curiosity and ambition, always looking for a way to get ahead. Though he had no experience back in Bolivia as an auto mechanic, fixing and reselling cars became an early interest. His first project was a Ford Escort with an oil leak that Rhina's sister Marilu had driven into the ground, going too long without checking the oil level. With the engine damaged beyond repair, the car wasn't worth much, but the body was in near perfect condition, and Victor agreed to buy it from her. With no idea how to replace the engine, Victor went to the local library one evening to review some books on auto repair. It was his first library visit, and he did not realize he could actually check books out and take them home, so for three nights straight he sat at a table reading about car engines with a Spanish-English dictionary at his side.

When he was ready to try the repair, he went to a junkyard with a friend, found an engine for a Ford Escort, and hauled it back to the parking lot of his apartment building. Next, they removed some bolts that fastened the damaged engine to the Escort frame, tied a heavy rope around the engine, and looped it over a tree branch that hung over the parking lot. With other men from the neighborhood helping, they attempted to hoist the engine out of the car, but when they pulled on the rope, the entire car lifted off the ground. After several unsuccessful attempts to remove the engine, Victor gave up and sent his friends home. The next night, he returned to the library to consult his auto books. After a few more hours studying engine diagrams, Victor realized the engine block was attached to the transmission assembly with twelve bolts he had not previously noticed. With those removed, the old engine came out easily, and Victor and his friends dropped the new one in its place. Victor had completed his first major car repair, thanks to the books he found in the Fairfax County Public Library.

Immigrating can be seen as an entrepreneurial act, a gamble taken with the expectation of a return to justify the investment, the promise of a future reward for the up-front risk. Among the men of his age and education in La Paz, Victor Alarcón was not typical. He had a job and a decent life with his family, but he chose to go alone to the United States. He did not speak the language and had no contacts other than his sister-in-law, but he believed there were opportunities in America that he did not have in Bolivia. To pursue them, he had to explore and experiment and take the initiative, and over the next two decades he would try different careers and start businesses of his own. He was not necessarily successful, but he and his family managed every year to move ahead. Victor probably would have had that same attitude if he had been born in America; some people by nature are more enterprising. But that also explains why some people emigrate while others do not. As a class, emigrants are the ones with the courage and the confidence to take that initial step, and that disposition may portend a more entrepreneurial inclination. Across all ethnic groups, U.S. census data show much higher self-employment rates among first-generation immigrants—those who are born outside the United States—than for the second and subsequent generations, who may be less driven to make a risky move.

Like Victor Alarcón, Sang Sook Kim and her husband, Miyung Jun, who immigrated from South Korea to the United States via Argentina, taught themselves a new business in a foreign country. Indeed, they did it twice, first in Argentina and then in the United States, though in their case they were able to build on a history of entrepreneurial activity. Back in South Korea, in Inchon, they had a small restaurant that catered to taxi and delivery drivers in need of a place to grab a quick lunch. In addition, Miyung Jun had a small business selling charcoal briquettes, widely used by Koreans for heating their homes. They decided to emigrate rather suddenly, in 1982, after they discovered that their infant daughter, Un Joung, had cerebral palsy. Though there was no cure, an injection of fetal stem cells directly into her spinal column through a lumbar puncture might bring an improvement. But no such treatment was available in South Korea. Because Sang Sook's brother was a U.S. citizen, living in Annandale, she and her immediate family members were entitled to permanent U.S. resident visas, but there was an application backlog, and they faced a wait of several years before their admission could be processed. Determined to leave South Korea, they headed in the meantime to Argentina, which accepted Korean immigrants more readily and where they could get some initial medical attention for Un Joung.

In Buenos Aires, Sang Sook, Miyung Jun, their infant daughter, and their two sons, ages seven and five, settled into a small apartment in an all-Korean neighborhood. More than twenty thousand Korean immigrants were already living in Argentina, but for Sang Sook and Miyung Jun, it was still an alien culture. Their savings would soon be exhausted, and they would have to start new careers from scratch. Realizing that she and her husband would both need to work full-time to cover their expenses, Sang Sook asked her mother to join them to care for their sick girl. She arrived five months later, enabling Sang Sook to seek employment.

The Koreans in Buenos Aires were associated primarily with the garment industry, and Sang Sook initially took a job as a seamstress. With their business backgrounds, however, she and her husband had ambitions to work for themselves, and once Un Joung was secure in Grandmother's care, they found a large house to rent and opened a small clothing factory of their own on the premises. Their specialty was the manufacture of clothing patterned after designer lines but produced much more cheaply. A brand-name suit, coat, or skirt, could be carefully taken apart along the seams and then reproduced. Sang Sook and Miyung Jun purchased thirty machines, all designed for particular sewing tasks, and employed workers to operate them. Sang Sook oversaw the sewing, while Miyung Jun was in charge of finding and purchasing the fabric and selling the clothing to discount retailers. The garment workers were given meals and housed in bunk rooms in exchange for their labor. Such small live-in factories were common in the Korean district of Buenos Aires at the time and provided employment to low-income immigrants from other South American countries. Sang Sook and Miyung Jun brought business acumen to their operation, and they ran it successfully as long as they remained in Buenos Aires.

The lumbar puncture done by Argentine doctors gradually brought some improvement to little Un Joung's condition. Her fist, which had been clenched tight since a few months after she was born, began to loosen, though the right side of her body remained stiff. With Sang Sook working twelve hours a day or more, Un Joung was nurtured by her grandmother, for whom it was a life mission. A devout Buddhist, Grandmother chanted for hours each day, in the belief the incantation would further the girl's healing. The phrase she repeated, "Nam-Myoho-Renge-Kyo," dates from thirteenth-century Japan and literally means, "I devote myself to the Lotus Sutra." The practice of chanting was intended to bring a person into harmony with Dharma, the law of life, and it had a calming effect on Un Joung. The girl learned to read and write Korean with Grandmother's guidance, and it was Grandmother who made sure she knew what it meant to be Korean. She taught Un Joung to show deference to anyone older than she, even by just a year, to use both hands (as best she could) when giving or taking something, and to keep quiet in the midst of company. Though she would remain handicapped, Un Joung was eventually able to walk and play, first with leg braces and later without. A bright and inquisitive child, she learned Spanish quickly once she began mixing with other children, and in school she had many more Argentine than Korean friends.

After ten years in Buenos Aires, the Kims' turn to immigrate to the United States finally came in 1992. Sang Sook's brother had prepared a three-room apartment for the Kim family in the basement of his house in Annandale, the Fairfax County community known locally as Koreatown for its heavy concentration of businesses catering to Korean immigrants. With no ability in English, Sang Sook and Miyung Jun first sought work in the tight-knit Korean community, where family ties and informal networks counted for everything. Sang Sook found employment for a time at an upholstery shop, but her husband resisted the idea of working for someone else. Like many Koreans, he preferred a situation where he could be his own boss, where his willingness to put in long hours and extra effort could bring rewards. He and Sang Sook finally decided to set up a garment factory like the one they had run in Argentina.

With money saved in Argentina they rented a small building, and Miyung Jun went looking for clients who would buy cheaply made clothes and fabric suppliers who could provide the necessary material at discount prices. The Kims quickly discovered, however, that U.S. employment laws were far more restrictive than Argentina's. They could not compensate their employees with food and shelter, as they had done in Buenos Aires. In the United States, they had to pay cash. Health and environmental regulations were also more stringent. Between the higher labor costs and the travel expenses involved in dealing with clients and suppliers, the Kims soon ran into financial trouble. For two years they struggled mightily to keep their factory open, but it was losing money, and in the end they were forced to shut it down and look for something else.

Sang Sook had just one marketable skill—sewing—but it was one for which there was abundant demand and one where limited English ability was not a serious liability. Virtually every small dry cleaning establishment in the Washington area offered alteration services, and the vast majority of the stores were owned by Koreans.

With her skill and experience, Sang Sook had no trouble finding shops that needed her sewing services to supplement their own. She did some of the alteration work at home, with Miyung Jun picking up clothes at the stores and returning them when finished. At first, there was not much else for him to do but drive around in his old black Lincoln, but in the process of visiting dry cleaning shops on Sang Sook's behalf, he learned that many of the proprietors had no one to service their sewing machines. Miyung Jun was no sewing expert himself, but he did know the machines and how to repair them. Recognizing a business opportunity, he bought a tool kit at his local Home Depot for twenty dollars and stocked it with the few things he would need to fix a broken machine. Before long, he had all the repair work he needed, and he and Sang Sook were familiar with many of the Korean cleaners across the D.C. area.

Sang Sook connected with one proprietor in particular, Hung Ceng, the owner of Custom Cleaners on Connecticut Avenue in the upscale Woodley Park neighborhood of Northwest Washington. Sang Sook was the best seamstress Ceng had ever worked with, and she impressed him with her diligence and responsibility. An especially hard worker, she also showed the confidence and managerial aptitude that came from years of running her own business, experience that Ceng's other employees did not have. Ceng was thinking of getting out of the dry cleaning business and looking for someone to take over his store, and Sang Sook struck him as an ideal candidate. At first, she deferred, saying she and her husband could not afford to buy the store and had no experience running a dry cleaning operation, but Ceng offered to sell the establishment to them on an installment plan and promised to teach her what she needed to know about the business. She agreed to buy the shop, and by 2000 the Kims were back in business for themselves, trying their hand at a whole new enterprise.

Their unfamiliarity with the dry cleaning and laundry business was not much of an obstacle. At the time, almost all the dry cleaning establishments in the area were run by Koreans, and many of them had started on the same basis as Sang Sook and her husband. Dry cleaning was not a trade Koreans brought to America as immigrants the way Jews brought expertise in the diamond industry, or Portuguese in stonework, or the French in baking. The Korean association with the dry cleaning business developed indigenously in the United States as the product of several factors. One was the desire of many Koreans to work for themselves, an inclination some attributed to the discrimination they encountered in traditional workplaces. Sang Sook, explaining her decision to start a business of her own, said it was "uncomfortable" to work as an employee in a factory or office. "They always look at you, and if you do one thing wrong, they'll pick on you," she said. "Even though someone works really hard, no one will recognize it," she said, "unless you yourself are the owner."

Self-employment opportunities in the United States were limited for Koreans, however. Many first-generation immigrants, because of their inclination to live and work close to other Koreans, had limited English ability. In dry cleaning establishments (and in mom-and-pop groceries, another Korean specialty), transactions with customers were fairly routine and redundant and didn't require much fluency in English. Most such businesses required only a modest capital investment, and the hours were fixed and predictable, with Sundays free. In addition, the tendency of Koreans to work through social networks facilitated a collective move into the dry cleaning business, as one proprietor typically helped others get started in the same line. Many Koreans raised capital for their business investments through money clubs, the members of which pooled their savings and made monthly disbursements to one person at a time, enabling the recipient to make a down payment on a house or small business. As a result, once a critical mass of Korean entrepreneurs was established in the dry cleaning world, it expanded under its own momentum. Sang Sook was able to pick up the basic knowledge necessary to operate her new business—from steaming and pressing to the use of chemical solvents—by learning from Hung Ceng and other Korean shop owners she knew.

The willingness to put in long hours and use family members as workers, key features of Korean businesses in the United States, was a natural outgrowth of the Confucian influence in Korean culture, which remained important even after Confucianism as a separate religion faded in importance relative to Christianity and Buddhism. Confucius emphasized family relationships and respect for elders and ancestors, which meant that children were expected to assist and support their parents throughout their lives and bring pride to the family name. Grandmother made sure Un Joung understood those obligations and values, and she reinforced her teaching with practiced rituals. Each day, Un Joung knelt at Grandmother's side before the Buddhist shrine in their house and polished the bronze mirror in the middle of the shrine, because one's inner life, like a mirror, becomes tarnished if not kept shiny.

Having overcome so many obstacles, however, Un Joung grew up with a determination to be independent and meet challenges head-on. As a girl in Argentina, she lost count of the number of times she tripped and fell while trying to keep up with her brothers and her friends in outdoor games. Wanting desperately to be "normal," she refused to be carried, and she gave up her leg braces as soon as she could manage without them. She married a Korean boy she met in college, but divorced him just six months later because she couldn't put up with his insistence on a traditional Korean marriage, with the wife subservient to her husband. Grandmother had told her of the traditional Confucian teaching, "Man is the sky and woman is the ground," but that was one principle she emphatically rejected.

Nevertheless, it was Un Joung, more than her brothers, who took filial duties most seriously and who proved most helpful to her parents in their dry cleaning business. She was keenly aware of how much they had sacrificed in order to provide her medical care, and she felt a need to repay them in some fashion. After three years in college, she dropped out to be of greater assistance to them in their business. Even when she took a separate job as a property manager for a real estate company, Un Joung was looking for ways to help her parents. In one of the apartment buildings she managed, she noticed that no dry cleaner was providing a pickup and delivery service, and she worked out an arrangement with the clerk at the front desk. The tenants appreciated the service, so Un Joung began contacting other buildings to offer similar service. Before long, she had worked out exclusive dry cleaning and laundry services with the front desk attendants at more than twenty buildings in the Washington area, and it became one of the most successful aspects of the Kim family business. Still, Un Joung was not ready to promise her parents that she would take over their operations when they retired. They had to take in and clean at least four hundred items per day in order to make ends meet, and there was no letup in the work. Sang Sook had four scars on her arm from burns she received on the steaming machine, and Un Joung was not resigned to working the rest of her life as her parents had.

The management philosophy Sang Sook Kim and her husband, Miyung Jun, followed in their dry cleaning shops was the same one the Seongs employed in their convenience store and their lounge in Maryland and then their liquor store in Washington: work long hours, keep the enterprise simple, make use of family members, and save as much money as possible. For the Seongs, the paramount goal from the day they set foot in the United States was to make sure their children got the best schooling possible. For the Kims, it was to finance the treatment of their daughter's cerebral palsy and to provide a comfortable life for Sang Sook's elderly mother. Each story followed classic Korean scripts, both in the way the enterprises developed and in the motivation to keep them going. Among all immigrant groups, Koreans have one of the highest entrepreneurial scores, with more than one out of four economically active Korean immigrants working independently as of 2010. Over the past twenty years, Koreans have trailed only Greek immigrants in their rate of self-employment, and in absolute numbers of entrepreneurs, no other immigrant group comes close. Compared to native-born American workers, Korean immigrants are three times more likely to be self-employed.

On the surface, therefore, the Korean example supports an argument that the arrival of large numbers of non-European immigrants during the last fifty years has boosted the entrepreneurial spirit in the United States. Indeed, the groups that have benefited most from the more open immigration policies since 1965—the East Asians and South Asians—are among those that rank especially high in entrepreneurship. It is important to look closely at these entrepreneurship experiences, however, because generalizations can be flawed. Experts distinguish entrepreneurial activity born of necessity from that which springs from the pursuit of opportunity, with the latter far more associated with innovation and job creation. Many Korean immigrant entrepreneurs have felt compelled by life circumstances to start their own businesses. Even for those with a strong educational or professional background, employment possibilities for a Korean immigrant with minimal English are limited, and running a small retail business may be the best way to get ahead. Another practical motivation for Korean entrepreneurship in America is the relative ease with which an immigrant can get started. A joke in the Korean community is that the business new Korean immigrants select as their own will be determined by who picks them up at the airport. Those same networks also provide opportunities for small business financing that might otherwise be hard to arrange. By 2012, nine out of ten dry cleaning establishments in the Washington, D.C., metropolitan area were owned and operated by Korean immigrants or their family members.

Taken as a whole, the profile of Korean immigrant entrepreneurship in the United States is one of investing in relatively low-risk ventures that do not require a large amount of start-up capital and offer the prospect of a reliable, if modest, cash flow. They are distinguished among other enterprises more by their conformity to an established pattern than by their creativity, which raises the question: Do such cases really show that immigration in America has energized entrepreneurial activity in the country? One noteworthy point in the Korean example is that entrepreneurship is not necessarily esteemed in Korean culture. A teacher or a government servant ranks higher than a merchant, and it is preferable to be employed in a large firm than to work on one's own. Confucius is alleged to have said that "those who work with their heads will rule, while those who work with their hands will serve," and fewer Confucian principles are taken more seriously in the Korean immigrants' world.

The sociologist Pyong Gap Min, who has written extensively on Korean entrepreneurship, has pointed to the importance Koreans put on discipline, family welfare, and upward social mobility, all values that he says "are partly inherited from the Confucian tradition." From this perspective, self-employment in the Korean community is largely a means to an end rather than something with intrinsic merit.

For immigrants in general, the data on entrepreneurship do not lend themselves to easy analysis. As of 2009, foreign-born workers were slightly more likely to be self-employed, in either incorporated or unincorporated enterprises, than U.S.-born workers, but the difference—11.2 percent versus 10.9 percent—was so small as to be insignificant, and the margin had been shrinking in the previous decades. The Center for Immigration Studies, whose research agenda supports more restrictive immigration policies, argues that these data undercut the notion that immigrants are an especially entrepreneurial group, composed of a self-selecting group of adventurous risk takers. A more careful look at the data, however, produces stronger evidence that immigrants are indeed especially enterprising. Self-employment, after all, is not the only measure of entrepreneurship. Data from the 2007 Survey of Business Owners show that immigrants have a significantly higher business formation rate, meaning that on a month-to-month basis, immigrants are more likely than nonimmigrants to start a new business. Research also makes clear that entrepreneurial initiative depends on educational background and financial resources, and when those factors are controlled, the difference between immigrant and U.S.-born workers is more significant. A decline in immigrant self-employment rates in recent years may be due in part to an increase in the number of immigrants arriving in the United States with low educational attainment and fewer financial resources. The most highly educated group, immigrants from India, have impressive rates of entrepreneurship. One survey of engineering and technology companies launched in the United States between 2006 and 2012 found that about one in four had at least one key founder who was foreign-born, and of those companies, fully a third were started or cofounded by an immigrant from India.

Finally, the contribution immigrants make to American economic culture should not be measured narrowly in whether they go into business on their own. Their enterprising character may come out in how diligent they are in seeking employment opportunities, how creatively they think about their prospects, and how energetically they develop their own skills and knowledge. Given the linguistic, educational, social, and financial barriers immigrants routinely face, their self-reliance and their work ethic consistently set them apart from the general population. This goes even for the undocumented immigrants who sneak across the U.S. border in search of an opportunity to make some money. They may stand in a parking lot with other day laborers waiting for someone to hire them for a few hours, but they are not likely to be found at a stoplight with a hand-lettered cardboard sign asking for a handout. They look for work instead.

After finding his car repair answers in self-help books, Victor Alarcón turned to the library for guidance on nearly every technical

challenge he and his family faced and for instruction in every subject that piqued his interest. Noticing that he was often consulting
the same books night after night, a librarian asked why he didn't
just check the books out; only then did Victor realize he could
take the books home. He was not yet conversationally proficient in
English, but with enough time and with the help of his dictionary
he could comprehend what he read. "It's the one thing I always
told my friends," Victor later recalled. "Your best friends are books.
Nobody will teach you better." From reading books or technical
manuals, he figured out how to fix the family TV set, the stereo,
and the dishwasher. He refreshed his grasp of accounting, a field
in which he had worked back in Bolivia. He and Rhina checked
out books on English grammar and American history in preparation for their U.S. citizenship tests. When his sons, Victor Jr. and
Álvaro, expressed interest in something, Victor dragged them to the
library as well. "Get a book and read about it," he would tell them.
"Then you can do it." The boys learned to do magic tricks and even
some karate moves by reading books. The Fairfax librarians loved
the Alarcóns, even when they checked out several dozen books at a
time, as they often did.

Victor would never become a millionaire entrepreneur, but his
broad interests and his determination to teach himself whatever he
needed to know led him to take on new projects and impressed his
employers. When the Vietnamese owner of the second restaurant
where Victor was employed learned how good he was with numbers, he asked Victor to inspect the books at four other establishments he owned. The proprietor was worried that his employees
might be embezzling from him and wanted Victor to investigate.
Such experiences set him up for a cashier position at a 7-Eleven,
where in short order he was promoted to assistant manager and
then to general manager, responsible for overseeing employees and
handling inventory and finances.

With his thick silver hair combed neatly back and his engaging
smile, Victor was a friendly presence behind the 7-Eleven counter,

and he enjoyed dealing with the stream of customers that came through his store. Still, he kept looking for other business opportunities. Car repair appealed to him in particular. He took out ads in Spanish-language newspapers, offering to make house calls and work on people's cars in their own driveways. As he found more customers, he decided to open his own shop and put money down on an old garage on a busy street in downtown Annandale. It was not far from his store, and Victor headed to the garage each day after finishing his shift at the 7-Eleven. The garage and lot outside were soon filled with junked cars that Victor bought to rebuild and resell, or salvage. Rhina would drop Victor Jr. and Álvaro off at the garage every day after school, and they would play in the cars or hang by their dad as he patiently showed them how engines work, piece by piece. They would invariably come home filthy, but for the boys the garage was like Disneyland, a place of wonder and exploration.

Eventually, Victor decided the garage wasn't worth the expense. He used his earnings to make a down payment on a small house in the city of Fairfax, thus achieving a key element of the immigrant dream. The house sat on a large corner lot, and Victor's plan was to continue to buy old cars and work on them in his backyard. He had accumulated ten cars before the Fairfax city authorities notified him that each car he parked in his yard had to be registered and insured, regardless of whether it was running. He was not prepared for that expense and had to scale back his repair work, though for years to come he would keep three or four cars in his yard, in various stages of repair. He rebuilt a Jeep Cherokee three times, repaired and re-painted a 1957 Chevrolet Camaro, and got a Land Rover with more than a hundred thousand miles on it in near perfect running condition.

Though he had given up on his garage and was frustrated by the city regulations that made it difficult to work on cars in his back-yard, Victor had not yet abandoned all thought of establishing a business of his own. He was friendly with the managers of an Exxon gas station around the corner from the 7-Eleven he managed, and when the owner was ready to sell, he encouraged Victor to buy it. The station would give him the opportunity to devote full-time to car repair. Once again, however, he was frustrated in his business planning, this time by the complications that owning a franchised gas station would bring, either from the government or the parent oil company. Victor learned that Exxon would still maintain much control over the operation and could veto his own decisions, such as whether to have one repair stall or two and whether to include an emission inspection unit in the operation. "You give them all your money," Victor said, "but they still control it. Plus, there were too many regulations. I finally said, Forget it."

An enterprising spirit, ingenuity, and a willingness to work is not always enough to produce an entrepreneur. The story of Victor's efforts reveals some of the obstacles faced by immigrants as they struggle to understand what it takes to succeed in an unfamiliar country. When he arrived in the United States, Victor did not fully comprehend the requirements for working legally in the country. He and his wife did not know their boys could ride buses to school. He did not realize he could not keep junked cars in his yard or how much power the government or oil companies had over the operation of franchised gas stations. One lesson he and Rhina took from their first twenty years in America was that it was a country of laws and regulations. Coming from a country where the legal system was not so well established, where bribery of government officials was routine and following the rules was not always rewarded, they were impressed by the integrity of the U.S. system. Though often frustrated by the bureaucracy, they were not discouraged. After her initial stint at Burger King, Rhina was hired as an aide at a nursing home in northern Virginia, and she stayed there for more than twenty-five years, with regular promotions. After his 7-Eleven jobs, Victor moved to a Kinko's store in Springfield, on the south side of Fairfax County, where he was better able to make use of his mechanical skills. "Everybody is good at something, and I think I'm good with my hands," he would say. "You give me one or two days, I can fix anything."

It was an aptitude he passed on to his sons, Victor Jr. and Álvaro, along with the positive life lesson that went with it: When confronted by a problem, just find the solution.

From the moment she was released from immigration detention in Texas, Marta Quintanilla was in the United States legally, with official permission to work. The problems that burdened her in America did not derive from her immigration status; they were ones she carried on her own. She was only marginally literate, she had no particular job skills, and she had been manipulated and exploited by the men who came into her life. She was just seventeen when she moved in with Mauricio, the distant cousin in Virginia who sponsored her move to the United States. For the first few months, ignorant of her options in this unfamiliar country, Marta was lost, and the man on whom she depended for everything in her life did little to help her get oriented. Her first break came with a chance encounter at a McDonald's, where she met a man from Peru who was looking for someone to help him clean houses. She worked six months for him, until the pregnancy with her son Jonis forced her to quit. Three months later, ready to work again, she found a job cleaning rooms at a Days Inn where the housekeeping manager was a woman who had befriended her. Marta stayed there for three years, then left to take a job with MetroClean, a housecleaning company that employed her for the next four years. It was while working at MetroClean that she began to imagine the future that she wanted: Someday, she would have a cleaning company of her own and employ Hispanic immigrant women like herself who had demonstrated the courage and discipline that coming to the United States required. She carefully took note of the licenses and permits that the MetroClean proprietor had acquired, and she resolved to follow his example.

Marta realized, however, that there was no way she could establish a business of her own unless she learned to speak English, so she enrolled in weekly English classes through an adult learning program. In the meantime, she found secure employment as a cashier at a store on the Fort Myer military base in Arlington, Virginia, working for the Army and Air Force Exchange Service. Two years later, finally feeling confident, she divorced her husband, and settled into life as a single mother. Three years after that, she married Troy Call, the soldier she met at Fort Myer, with whom she had two more children. It was only in 2012, after leaving employment with the U.S. military, that Marta was able to take some tentative steps in the direction of her dream to have an independent business. One by one, she began acquiring her own housecleaning jobs.

Determined to work legally, she went to the Fairfax County authorities for information on what she needed to do to start her own company. An officer told her that she needed a business license, which cost her nothing, and that she should keep a careful tally of what she earned. At the end of the year, she dutifully filed a tax return, reporting all the income she had earned over the previous twelve months cleaning houses. It was less than $10,000, the threshold above which she had to pay a business tax, but it was a start. She did not yet have enough business to necessitate finding someone to help her, but she got a small business manual and studied what she would have to do when the time came to hire an employee. Thinking as ambitiously as she dared, she prepared a listing for the Thumbtack website, designed to connect potential customers with independent service providers. Calling herself "Marta Call Cleaning," she advertised her services in the best English she could manage: "I do everything that brings satisfaction to the home. I clean bathrooms and cabinets, vacuum carpets and floors, and clean windows too."

Two years later, Marta still did not have enough housecleaning jobs of her own to keep her busy full-time, much less to justify hiring an employee or even to trigger the business tax she was eager to owe. She had gone back to work two days a week at the Days Inn where she had been employed as a housekeeper off and on for more than twenty years. Her hope of becoming an independent businesswoman was nevertheless still alive. Because it was only a dream, it was not yet reflected in the data on immigrant entrepreneurship; nor was there any way to quantify the willingness to work that Marta Quintanilla Call and other newcomers brought to their lives in this country. As long as America was still seen as a land of possibility, however, it would attract people with energy and determination, and that would arguably be its greatest strength.

PART FOUR

17

BACKLASH

The immigration debate of 1965 framed the question of "whom we shall welcome" as an issue of civil rights. At a time when the country was dealing with an ugly history of segregation and discrimination, this was a game-changing development. The nationality of visa candidates could no longer be held against them. In the immediate aftermath, if any concerns were to be raised about immigrants, it would have to be done without any suggestion of racial or ethnic prejudice. The use of national origin quotas had discredited such thinking, at least for the moment.

A large influx of foreigners was inevitably an unsettling prospect, however, and the immigration question soon returned to the national agenda, where it would remain for the next half century, albeit with changing arguments. One new issue after 1965 was a surge in the number of undocumented workers, largely Mexican, coming across the border to take low-wage jobs in the United States. The development, unrelated to the 1965 legislation, was prompted by the elimination in 1964 of the bracero program. Laborers who were previously permitted to work temporarily in the United States were now reclassified as illegal immigrants if they tried to return to their former places of employment. The hiring of these workers at substandard wages, and not just in agriculture, prompted vigorous protests by labor union leaders and their backers in Congress, including Peter Rodino, the New Jersey Democrat who took over chairmanship of the House immigration subcommittee in 1971. Rodino had been one of the most outspoken supporters of the 1965 amendments, but he convened a series of hearings addressing the effects of illegal immigration on employment and wage rates, and he offered legislation that would impose heavy fines on employers who hired undocumented foreign workers. The Rodino legislation, which died in the Senate, did not mean he or others had second thoughts about the wisdom of the 1965 reforms—the issue this time was immigration occurring outside the law—but the hearings reframed the immigration debate by focusing on the impact on U.S. workers, a concern that would only grow as the number of immigrants steadily increased in the years ahead.

More surprising was the emergence of immigration as a potential *environmental* concern. It began with an argument that population growth was straining the earth's resources, a notion that gained broad attention with the publication in 1968 of a somewhat alarmist book called *The Population Bomb* by Stanford University biologist Paul Ehrlich and his wife, Anne. The Ehrlichs predicted that overpopulation, if unchecked, would bring environmental destruction and mass starvation. Along with a Cornell University ecologist named Thomas Eisner, they founded the organization Zero Population Growth (ZPG), dedicated to the goal of reducing the number of births around the world for the good of the planet and the human race.

The Ehrlichs were not initially concerned about immigration, because they had a global perspective on population; the movement of people from one country to another had no meaning for overall population levels. Those ZPG activists and other environmentalists who had a country-by-country perspective on ecosystems, however, did see a connection between overpopulation and immigration. Any success a country like the United States had in bringing population growth down to a level where it no longer threatened environmental sustainability could be negated if a flood of immigrants were allowed into the territory. Their argument got a small boost in 1972 when the U.S. Commission on Population Growth and the American Future, appointed by President Richard Nixon and chaired by John D. Rockefeller III, concluded with respect to the United States that "the gradual stabilization of our population through voluntary means would contribute significantly to the nation's ability to solve its problems." In pursuit of that goal it recommended limits on immigration.

The Rockefeller Commission's linkage of the immigration and population issues caught the attention of a young physician, conservationist, and population activist in northern Michigan named John Tanton. Already a critic of mass immigration, Tanton seized on the commission's recommendation and proceeded in the coming years to establish several organizations devoted to the cause of closing America's doors to most foreigners. Though he had a full-time ophthalmology practice in rural Michigan and worked largely behind the scenes, Tanton would play an unrivaled leadership role over the next three decades in the campaign to restrict immigration; in fact, no one in America was more influential in moving the immigration issue back into the political mainstream after it was effectively neutralized in 1965. As the overpopulation issue diminished in importance, the environmental consequences of immigration became less worrisome, but Tanton and his groups shifted to other arguments, beginning with the complaint that immigrants took away jobs from U.S.-born workers. Eventually, Tanton and many of those who followed him were drawn back to the same argument that animated supporters of the old national origin quotas—that the new immigrants were less likely to become good Americans. With Asians, Latinos, Africans, and Arabs constituting a much larger share of the population, the temptation to make that cultural argument proved irresistible. The definition of a unique American nationality was indeed becoming more complicated, and immigration critics charged that the institutions set up to facilitate the assimilation of these new groups were failing in that task.

The cause of limiting immigration brought together strange bedfellows, from white nationalists to environmental activists. Tanton was a beekeeper and avid outdoorsman, and his civic involvement began with leadership positions in local chapters of the Audubon Society and the Sierra Club. But he had always seen people and their activities as a potential threat to nature, and his private passion within the environmental movement was population stabilization. As part of his medical internship, Tanton worked at a birth control clinic at a hospital in Denver, and in Michigan he and his wife helped open a Planned Parenthood clinic, a venture he later described as "an expression of our interest in the population problem." Most of the women they served merely wanted to avoid unwanted pregnancies, but Tanton saw himself as something of a proselytizer. "There were women," he said, "who already had large families and who perhaps still wanted more children, but who could be convinced that two or three or four were enough, rather than five or six."

With such proactive advocacy, Tanton was heading into delicate territory. In the past, some of the most vigorous proponents of birth control as a way to limit population growth were associated with unsavory social movements. Among those who opposed the immigration of southern and eastern Europeans in the 1920s for fear of tainting the Anglo-Saxon "stock" were several birth control zealots. Margaret Sanger, the founder of the modern birth control movement, was herself a eugenicist, believing that the scientific principles of "stockbreeding" should be applied in the control of the human population. "More children from the fit, less from the unfit—that is the chief issue of birth control," she said. The "unfit" in her judgment included many immigrants from southern and eastern Europe, whom she regarded as ignorant when it came to hygiene and modern sanitation practices.

By the 1960s, such sentiments could no longer be expressed so candidly, but they lay not far below the surface. Among John Tanton's "heroes" by his own admission was Garrett Hardin, an ecologist at the University of California, Santa Barbara, and a fellow member of the Sierra Club. Hardin repeatedly called attention to the dangers he foresaw as coming from too many people crowding the planet, but he went on to criticize the Zero Population Growth movement for focusing too narrowly on numbers and not paying sufficient attention to the *quality* of the populations that were growing most rapidly. "To put it bluntly," Hardin argued, "it would be better to encourage the breeding of more intelligent people rather than the less intelligent." Without explaining exactly what he had in mind, Hardin called for "breeding controls" to be imposed on some populations. "If the world is one great commons, in which all food is shared equally, then we are lost," Hardin wrote in a 1971 editorial in *Science* magazine. "Those who breed faster will replace the rest." Not surprisingly, he was a harsh critic of immigration, arguing that if people from poor and underdeveloped countries were allowed to move freely to prosperous countries, the receiving country would inevitably suffer, in the same way that too many people crowding into a lifeboat raise the risk of the lifeboat sinking. John Tanton met Hardin at an environmental conference in Chicago in 1970 and immediately reached out to him as a potential collaborator on immigration matters.

Reflecting in 1989 on his history as an immigration restrictionist, Tanton said his interest in the issue dated from the late 1960s, when he discovered that immigrants were accounting for 10 to 15 percent of U.S. population growth. At the time, he was rising in the ranks of the Sierra Club, where his concerns about overpopulation and immigration were shared by the group's executive director, David Brower. Tanton was also lobbying Zero Population Growth, and as a national board member of the organization in 1973, he was invited to chair an immigration study committee, though the move into immigration issues aroused considerable unease within the organization. Two years later, he became the national president and pushed his fellow board members to make immigration reform a ZPG priority agenda item. This time, he was firmly opposed by ZPG staff members and officers who did not want the organization associated with any movement that even hinted at anti-foreigner sentiment. With the ZPG board refusing to follow his advice, Tanton moved on his own to establish a new organization that would tackle immigration.

For the remainder of his active days, resisting mass immigration would be Tanton's number one cause, and he brought an almost messianic devotion to the task, leaving work on broader environmental and population issues to others. "Most people hadn't even noticed the [immigration] phenomenon," he said later, and he was determined to change that. Though opposition to immigration eventually became a popular cause, this ophthalmologist from Petoskey, Michigan, would be credited with turning it into an organized movement, and he did it almost entirely in his spare time and on a meager budget. Beginning with a single grant from a ZPG supporter, Tanton hired a thirty-two-year-old environmental lawyer named Roger Conner with whom he had worked in Michigan and sent him to Washington to find cheap office space and set up a small lobbying effort. Tanton had come up with an acronym for the new organization that summarized the immigration reform message he hoped to convey—FAIR—but it took a while longer to figure out what the letters might actually stand for. After experimenting with various possibilities, he and Conner settled on Federation for American Immigration Reform.

Conner would be the executive director. Though he had been involved with Tanton in ZPG work for several years, Conner later acknowledged that he didn't entirely understand the connection between immigration, population growth, and environmental concerns, and he was rebuffed in some of his early encounters with fellow liberals in Washington. One old friend told him he should go after greedy capitalists if he wanted to get at the root of environmental problems. Another said he should focus on America's consumption culture. "Don't take it out on these poor immigrants," she told him. "They haven't done anything." Conner had a hard time responding to their scolds. He said later he felt like a soldier in combat who was uncertain of his mission. The case for a more restrictive immigration policy was not an easy one to make. The foreign-born share of the U.S. population was still relatively low in historical terms. The ethnic profile of the new immigrants was different, with more Asians and Africans and fewer Europeans, but in the aftermath of the civil rights movement, Conner was determined not to make that an issue. He and Tanton decided they should focus first on unlawful immigration from Mexico, a more widely recognized concern.

Key intellectual leadership for the FAIR effort came from a young history professor named Otis Graham at the University of California, Santa Barbara, the institution where Garrett Hardin was a professor of human ecology. In a 1979 article for *Center Magazine,* a publication of the Center for the Study of Democratic Institutions, Graham argued that the new immigration should be countered by a "new restrictionism" movement, one that was free of the racism that tainted the 1920s movement. Like Tanton, Graham was an environmentalist, having been provoked to activism by a disastrous oil spill off the Santa Barbara coast in 1969. Like Conner, he was a liberal, having served as faculty adviser to students working for Robert Kennedy's presidential campaign in 1968. In the years since, however, Graham had developed strong feelings about the need to limit immigration, and in his *Center Magazine* article he offered two arguments: First, a reduction in the number of immigrants entering the country would relieve the strain on the country's resources; second, reduced immigration would limit the pool of exploitable labor at the bottom of the labor market and thereby force employers to pay higher wages to native-born workers.

246 ★ A Nation of Nations

Tanton and Conner both saw Graham's article and invited him to join them and others for an inaugural meeting in 1979 of the FAIR organization in Washington. At the end of those discussions, Graham drafted a three-page memo, outlining what he understood the FAIR perspective to be regarding the growing immigration challenge in the United States. The problem to be highlighted, he said, was "not race or ethnicity but numbers." Graham expanded that argument in a 1980 paper published by FAIR, "Illegal Immigration and the New Reform Movement," taking pains to differentiate the organization from the "nativist right" groups that advocated curbs on immigration in the 1920s. "True, there are still with us those who urge restriction out of what may appear to be motives of ethnic, racial, and class dislike, or feelings of cultural superiority," he acknowledged. "Yet these sentiments are quite muted, for the country is far, far from the openly racist operating assumptions of the 1920s and before."

Tanton recruited an eclectic group of advisers for FAIR, including Cornell University labor economist Vernon Briggs, Jr., Planned Parenthood activist Sharon Barnes, ecologist Garrett Hardin, former Gulf Oil president Sidney Swensrud, and agronomist William Paddock, who had been one of Tanton's allies at ZPG. Most of the organizational planning and strategizing, however, was done by Tanton, Otis Graham, and Roger Conner. The three of them drafted a FAIR manifesto, laying out the principles they thought should govern U.S. immigration policy. In their eagerness to appear moderate, they barely challenged the status quo, daring only to say that immigration outside the law was "unacceptable." Notably, they affirmed the "wisdom" of the 1965 Immigration Act's elimination of racial and ethnic criteria in the allocation of visas. The only hint of dissent from the 1965 legislation was their suggestion that immigration preference should be given only to immediate family members of U.S. citizens, as opposed to the adult brothers and sisters who had an elevated standing under the law thanks to Ohio congressman Michael Feighan.

To the dismay of the FAIR leadership, the campaign got off to a slow start. The argument that a growing immigrant population was an environmental burden did not prove especially compelling, and the allegation that undocumented laborers from Mexico were taking jobs away from working-class Americans was not exactly newsworthy. Especially disappointing was the position that Paul and Anne Ehrlich, the ZPG founders, took on the immigration issue. Writing in the January/February 1980 issue of the bimonthly magazine *Mother Earth News,* the Ehrlichs disputed whether "illegals" were really taking jobs away from American workers and burdening the welfare system. "Our studies—as well as those of other students of the problem—indicate that neither of these claims has much basis in fact," the Ehrlichs wrote. They expressed concern that people coming to the United States illicitly "are particularly vulnerable to exploitation and abuse," and they worried that "public hysteria" over illegal immigration could push the U.S. Immigration and Naturalization Service into "a witch hunt."

John Tanton had worked closely with Paul Ehrlich on the ZPG board, and the criticism stung. Roger Conner, as the FAIR executive director, wrote the Ehrlichs a three-page letter, objecting to their commentary. "People with unsullied liberal credentials, like [U.S. secretary of labor] Ray Marshall and Otis Graham, believe that illegal immigration is hurting American workers," Conner said. "A casual reading of your paper lumps them with those contributing to 'public hysteria' and 'witch hunts,' mindlessly advocating discrimination or repression. I hope I am not speaking out of turn to say that we need for people of your stature to spend more time insisting on the legitimacy of a full debate on the implications of the [immigration] numbers and less time seconding motions for cloture!" Obviously, the arguments for curbing immigration would have to be made very carefully.

By 1981, Tanton was complaining that FAIR's narrow focus on the environmental and economic coasts of mass immigration was not producing the results necessary for an effective national movement. The time had come, he argued, to draw attention to the cultural differences between the prior immigrants who came from Europe and the groups coming to the United States in the current period, whether legally or illegally. According to Graham, "John had become convinced from years of conversations with ordinary people about large-scale immigration that the rawest nerve was not job competition or social welfare costs, [and] certainly not population growth or environmental impacts, but social assimilation and national identity." In Tanton's view, the issue to be highlighted was whether the new immigrants were prepared to become Americans.

That same question was being raised at the time by Senator Alan Simpson of Wyoming, one of two Republicans appointed to President Jimmy Carter's Select Commission on Immigration and Refugee Policy, chaired by Father Theodore Hesburgh, president of Notre Dame University. The Hesburgh Commission's 1981 report set the agenda for immigration legislation over the next decade, recommending measures to reduce illegal entry while opening the door to more legal immigration. Simpson argued in vain that the commission should take a tougher stand. In a dissenting note to the final report, he raised doubts about "the degree to which immigrants and their descendants assimilate to fundamental American public values and institutions." He warned that "if linguistic and cultural separatism rise above a certain level, the unity and political stability of the nation will in time be seriously eroded." His thinking was strongly influenced by his chief of staff on the commission, Leon Bouvier, a demographer at the U.S. Census Bureau who had been detailed to the Hesburgh Commission and who brought to his work considerable skepticism about the value of immigration, both legal and illegal. Bouvier's views caught Tanton's attention, and he recruited him to serve as a FAIR adviser.

Energized by the debate around the Hesburgh Commission report, Tanton tried to convince his board members that FAIR could mobilize more popular opposition to immigrants if it highlighted their apparent unwillingness to learn English or study U.S. history. He proposed that FAIR launch a new initiative with the aim of focusing popular concern on the danger that English could lose its place as the dominant and unifying language of the country. Several FAIR board members opposed the idea, however, fearing it would open the organization to charges of being unfriendly to foreigners. Roger Conner, the young executive director, was especially wary of a political strategy that would challenge the pro-immigration forces in the country by appealing to anti-immigrant sentiment. "If the only way to beat them was to turn to animosity toward the ethnically and racially different immigrants," he later recalled, "I wasn't willing to do that. I thought that was the one thing that would do more harm to America than the continuing immigration." Conner argued in favor of keeping the FAIR focus on the negative effect that mass immigration might have on the employment of U.S.-born workers, particularly those on the low end of the skills ladder.

In November 1983, Conner arranged for FAIR to cosponsor a seminar on "Immigration Policies and Black America" at the historically black Howard University in Washington, D.C. Speaking at the conference, Conner charged that the rising number of immigrants was creating "a new excuse for job discrimination" against native-born American workers. Employers, he said, were claiming that immigrants only took those jobs that American workers were too lazy to take. His counterclaim was that employers took advantage of the presence of immigrants in the U.S. labor market and offered jobs with "desperation wages and desperation working conditions" that no worker should be obliged to accept. The conference was held just a few months after African American workers at Washington's National Airport had been displaced by immigrants from Southeast Asia, and the arguments made at the conference were well received by several of the Howard University academics. Sociologist John Reid said the gains African Americans had made in recent years were being threatened in part by "the current flood of immigrants into the U.S. who compete directly for the low level jobs on which many blacks still rely."

At the time, black political leaders were building alliances with Hispanic and other immigrant groups and did not want to be seen as anti-immigrant, but at the local level concerns about job competition were growing. Another Howard sociologist at the FAIR conference, Jacquelyne Jackson, argued that "the majority of blacks and Hispanic citizens in the United States want something done about immigration. They regard it as a very important problem, and they're not likely to be mollified by efforts of leaders who go against them." After the conference, Conner invited Jackson to join FAIR, and she subsequently became a regular at FAIR meetings.

John Tanton was supportive of outreach efforts to the African American and Hispanic communities, but he was heading in a different direction. His political instincts about the mobilizing potential of an appeal to Americans' suspicions of culturally different immigrants would soon prove well founded. When the FAIR board declined to establish an organization in defense of English as America's official language, Tanton did it on his own, setting up a group he called U.S. English. He had correctly recognized a developing anti-immigrant backlash and was ready to take advantage. An initial direct mail solicitation in June 1983 brought a flood of donations to U.S. English, and within a year Tanton's new organization had 300,000 members, leaving FAIR far behind. Conner and the dissenting FAIR board members remained friendly and cooperative with Tanton, but their tactical disagreement over whether to emphasize economic or cultural issues in the fight against mass immigration would persist for years to come.

With donations flowing in and with grants from conservative groups, Tanton was able to build a network of organizations, all devoted to curbing immigration growth and all tied to Tanton's office in Petoskey, Michigan. In 1985, he and other FAIR leaders set up the Center for Immigration Studies, based in Washington, D.C., to serve as a think tank for the immigration restriction movement. In the years that followed, the center would provide serious research and empirical arguments to support FAIR positions on immigration policy issues. Later years brought the establishment of the Immigration Reform Law Institute, specializing in litigation on behalf of U.S. citizens who claimed to have been damaged by illegal immigration, and NumbersUSA, an organization focusing on the economic impact of immigration with less regard for its cultural ramifications.

Tanton, however, was personally focused on the threat he believed foreigners posed to America's national identity, a problem he repeatedly brought to the attention of an exclusive circle of intellectuals, activists, academics, and politicians he convened regularly to discuss the immigration challenge. In preparation for one such session in 1986, Tanton sent the attendees a study of population trends in California by Leon Bouvier, the demographer who had advised Senator Simpson on immigration policy. Bouvier had concluded that by 2010, "Anglos" (excluding Hispanics) would be in the minority in California and that by 2030 the Hispanic population would equal the Anglo population. In an accompanying memo, he said the time had come to consider "the non-economic consequences of immigration."

Tanton even wondered about the implications of a declining white population on the conservation movement. In an oral history interview he provided later for the FAIR archives, he explained that he was worried the new immigrants would not take care of the environment, because the "conservation ethos" in the United States reflected "values that are characteristic of American society. We could probably trace their roots back through Western civilization. If we look at the conservation ethic of some of the countries from which large numbers of immigrants are coming, we don't find the same sort of respect for the land and our fellow creatures that has developed here. We certainly don't see this in many of the southeastern Asian cultures or in Latin America."

With such comments, Tanton was veering dangerously close to

252 ★ A Nation of Nations

an anti-immigrant argument based on "feelings of cultural superiority," precisely the approach Otis Graham and others had promised FAIR would never embrace. At the same time, Tanton began working with John Trevor, Jr., whose father, John Trevor, Sr., had played a key role in drafting and passing the infamous 1924 Immigration Act, which judged the suitability of visa candidates on the basis of their national origins. The senior Trevor had been a close associate of eugenicists who believed in the superiority of the white race and argued on that basis for the exclusion from the United States of supposedly lesser races and ethnicities. He was a founder of the American Coalition of Patriotic Societies, the major nativist group of the era. Trevor Jr. took over leadership of the group upon his father's death and used it to organize a defense of the national origins quota system during the debate over the 1965 immigration amendments. The junior Trevor, through his direction of the Pioneer Fund, was also sponsoring research on racial differences in intelligence. Partly due to Tanton's friendship with Trevor, the Pioneer Fund for a time was a major source of support for FAIR and other Tanton organizations.

Over the next decade, FAIR and its affiliated groups in the movement to limit immigration continued to evolve in two directions, with the more moderate elements focusing on the impact of immigration on working-class Americans and on government spending and infrastructure. John Tanton, the movement's founder, concentrated instead on what he saw as the threat to America's traditional European character. His preoccupations, often candidly expressed, increasingly created problems for his FAIR colleagues. Several members of the board of U.S. English quit, and Tanton himself resigned as chairman. He continued to host his regular discussion retreat, sometimes at his home in Petoskey, but referred to it from then on as a "Writers' Workshop." The invitees included several with clear white nationalist views. One was Samuel Francis, an editorial writer at the *Washington Times* who lamented what he called "the war against the white race" and called on white Americans to "reassert our identity and our solidarity . . . in explicitly racial terms." Another was Lawrence Auster, who in 1989 wrote *The Path to National Suicide*, an anti-immigrant tract in which he suggested that the growing number of non-Europeans in America was obligating white Americans to abandon their cultural tradition. "Is it not an inescapable conclusion," Auster asked, "that the white majority in this country, if it wishes to preserve that tradition, must place a rational limit on the number of immigrants?"

Such sentiments horrified some of Tanton's FAIR colleagues. No one was more upset than Roger Conner, the environmental lawyer whom Tanton had personally recruited to lead FAIR in 1979. "I used to go to those meetings and see those people, and I'd just want to take a shower when I got home," he said years later. He left FAIR in 1989. In the wake of his departure, Tanton moved further to the right. In 1990, he founded a journal he called *The Social Contract*, focused on the idea of "national unity." In the coming years, it would provide a forum for Francis, Auster, and other white nationalist writers, including Wayne Lutton, a right-wing historian who was a regular speaker for the Council of Conservative Citizens, a group with roots in white supremacy movements.

Nineteen ninety was the twenty-fifth anniversary of the 1965 Immigration Act, and the occasion brought a new round of reflection on the significance of that legislation. FAIR had long criticized the legislation's establishment of a visa category for brothers and sisters of U.S. citizens, a preference the organization said created "a geometrically expanding chain of people who qualify for special treatment," but by 1990 the criticism was broader. Though Tanton and his FAIR colleagues had initially praised the "wisdom" of the decision to eliminate national origin quotas, several of his associates argued that the move had proved to be a mistake, precisely because it had brought an end to the pro-European tilt in U.S. immigration policy. Lawrence Auster criticized the authors of the 1965 Act for failing to include provisions for "reasonable discrimination" in the mandated visa selection process. Otis Graham, writing for the FAIR-affiliated Center for Immigration Studies, claimed that the sponsors of the 1965 Act had as one of their aims "the alteration of our demographic future." He extended that argument in a column he wrote four years later for *The Christian Science Monitor*, titled "Tracing Liberal Woes to '65 Immigration Act." In retrospect, Graham wrote, the 1965 Act could be considered "perhaps the single most nation-changing measure of the [Great Society] era." The sharp increase in the size and composition of the immigrant population over the previous thirty years were "momentous changes," he wrote, that brought about "the demographic transformation of America."

Obviously, the 1965 changes in U.S. immigration policy did not account for the growing number of people entering the country illegally. Legal immigration, however, was clearly boosted as a direct consequence of the 1965 legislation. By 1995, two thirds of all immigrants acquiring legal resident status in the United States were doing so under the family unification provisions of the 1965 law. In his newspaper column, Graham claimed that liberals had "engineered" the immigration policy shift as "a cheap way to please special interests," but that the move had cost them politically, given how the costs of increased immigration were being borne disproportionately by the Democrats' working-class base. He said the demographic changes resulting from the 1965 Act "are now deeply and widely unpopular," and he speculated that the legislation "will take its place as the leading example in the second half of the 20th century of elite arrogance and disconnect from either the sentiments or the interests of the broad public."

Graham's assignment of responsibility for the immigration changes to "liberals" was off the mark, however, because the prioritization of family unification over employment criteria in visa considerations and the creation of a special category for brothers and sisters of U.S. citizens were the work of Congressman Feighan, a conservative Democrat who was allied politically with the right-wing American Coalition of Patriotic Societies. Graham was correct, however, in his assessment that immigration was becoming a hot political issue in the United States, a fact demonstrated in California in 1994 by the passage by a wide margin of Proposition 187, a ballot initiative that established a state-run citizenship screening system and prohibited undocumented immigrants from using public education, health care, and other social services. (The law was later declared unconstitutional and was never implemented.)

Advocates of new curbs on immigration got a boost with the work of the U.S. Commission on Immigration Reform, the congressionally mandated panel chaired by Barbara Jordan. The commission under Jordan's leadership did acknowledge that immigration "promotes family values and ties . . . [and] can demonstrate to other countries that religious and ethnic diversity are compatible with national civic unity in a democratic and free society," but it called for increased regulation. A prominent recommendation was that family unification visas be restricted to immediate family members of U.S. citizens and permanent residents, effectively disqualifying the adult sons and daughters and the brothers and sisters of citizens. Such a change, the commission calculated, would mean an immigration policy based on a "compelling national interest" rather than the desires of individual immigrants and their family members. Aside from accommodating the unification of nuclear families, immigrants were to be chosen "on the basis of the skills they contribute to the U.S. economy."

In a memo to his board of directors, FAIR President Dan Stein (who had replaced Roger Conner) said the commission's report came as "a big surprise." If implemented, Stein said, the proposed changes would "break the back of chain migration." With President Clinton publicly endorsing the commission recommendations, Stein predicted they would be incorporated in congressional legislation during the next year. Jordan's leadership on the immigration issue helped remove the stigma of racial and ethnic prejudice that had been hanging over the immigration restriction movement in recent years. There was not a trace of concern in the commission report about the erosion of European values by Asian or African immigrants or of any threat immigrants might pose to the "conservation ethos" in the United States. For a time at least, the Jordan Commission arguments advantaged the FAIR moderates over John Tanton and his white nationalist friends. Roy Beck, a longtime Tanton associate, began to distance himself from his mentor, forming the separate NumbersUSA organization in 1996. "The chief difficulties that America faces because of current immigration," Beck wrote, "are not triggered by who the immigrants are, but by how many they are."

By arguing that that U.S. immigration policy should serve the national interest, Barbara Jordan and her colleagues effectively relegated the human interest of the immigrants themselves to a secondary status. The alternative view was that all people are of equal worth and have an inalienable right as individuals to pursue a better life, regardless of their place of birth. After all, migration from one place to another has been a fact of human life throughout history, governed by forces and circumstances beyond the control of the migrants. The right to migrate was supported by those who believe that someone should not be consigned to a life of misery because of the unequal global distribution of wealth and power. The rise of the nation-state brought limits on migration; from then on, the right of the nation-state to determine its own membership trumped the right of individual people to flee or find opportunity.

The debate over those competing ideas was not overtly partisan. As a progressive, Barbara Jordan was joined in her restrictionist perspective by former senator Eugene McCarthy, the liberal Minnesota Democrat who argued in his 1992 book, *A Colony of the World*, that the United States was losing control of its borders and needed to assert sovereignty over its own territory, in order to defend the interests of its citizenry. The imposition of a strict new cap on legal immigration, however, would challenge some key political constituencies. An immigration reform bill sponsored by Republican congressman Lamar Smith of Texas and incorporating several of the Jordan Commission's proposals encountered immediate opposition from Asian American and Hispanic groups, from organizations working on behalf of immigrant rights, and from business and trade interests. Despite Barbara Jordan's standing as a leader of the Democratic Party, most liberals in Congress came out against the proposed elimination of visas for extended family members. The Clinton administration, having initially supported the Jordan Commission recommendations, reversed course and said it would back only a crackdown on illegal immigration. Republicans were sharply divided on the measure, with several key conservatives saying they could not support new curbs on legal immigration. The bill that was finally approved was stripped of those provisions, focusing only on illegal immigration. Stein, the FAIR president, called the compromise bill "a shell of reform" and blamed both political parties for the setback. "I fear for the future of this debate and the future of politics," he said.

Over the years, the one approach that had proved powerful in mobilizing popular sentiment against mass immigration was the appeal to Americans' fear that they were being overrun by culturally alien foreigners. In 1995, a British-born writer who had moved to America, Peter Brimelow, published *Alien Nation: Common Sense About America's Immigration Disaster*. The book was an anti-immigration best-seller, with none of the nuance and cautious argument that Barbara Jordan and her commissioners had made. Its message was not that immigrants were crowding working-class Americans out of their low-skill jobs but rather that they were turning America into a nation alien unto itself.

"The racial and ethnic balance of America is being radically altered through public policy," Brimelow wrote. "This can only have the most profound effects. *Is it what Americans want?*" (emphasis in original). American society by then had become far more diverse, but Brimelow's message to white Americans was that they could not get along with people unlike themselves. Conflicts or tensions emerging in the United States, he argued, were in part the consequence of having admitted so many non-Europeans. "The culture of a country, exactly like its ecology, turns out to be a living thing, sensitive and even fragile," he wrote. "Neither can easily be intruded upon without consequences." He placed the blame for this alien intrusion squarely on the 1965 Act and its reckless elimination of the European bias in immigration policy. Following the publication of his book, Brimelow went on to found VDARE.com, named for Virginia Dare, the first white child born during the colonial period in what would become the United States. His website in the coming years would feature essays and commentaries from a variety of writers, almost all of them lamenting multiculturalism and the attendant threat to America's European heritage.

In Petoskey, John Tanton turned the editorship of *The Social Contract* over to Wayne Lutton, whom Tanton had hired in 1992 as an associate editor. Under this direction, the journal became increasingly an outlet for white nationalist views that recalled the nativism of the 1920s. The theme of the summer 1998 issue, the most inflammatory in the journal's history, was "Europhobia: the hostility toward European-descended Americans." In an editorial, Tanton projected that "U.S. immigration policy, coupled with high immigrant fertility, will reduce the historic white, European-descended majority in the country to minority status. Whether the current majority group will acquiesce in its disenfranchisement . . . will be one of the chief problems of the twenty-first century."

One of the most effective ways to highlight the threat that immigrants might present to traditional America was to link them to terrorists. In 1999, FAIR ran a newspaper ad against Republican senator Spencer Abraham of Michigan, who at the time was chairman of the Senate immigration subcommittee. The ad asked, "Why Is a U.S. Senator Trying to Make It Easy for Osama bin Laden to Export Terrorism to the U.S.?" and showed a picture of Abraham, a Lebanese American, alongside one of bin Laden. The ad accused

Abraham of trying to kill a provision of immigration law that would have required the Immigration and Naturalization Service to be notified whenever foreign visitors overstayed their visas. The ad made no mention of Abraham's background, but critics of the ad noted that the only tie between him and bin Laden was their Arab ethnicity. In response to the FAIR ad, sixteen Republican senators charged FAIR with "engaging in a smear campaign against immigrants in general and one of our colleagues in particular." Wyoming's Alan Simpson, who had been serving on the FAIR board, resigned in protest over the ad.

The advocates of a more restrictive immigration policy were at a turning point. Many of their arguments resonated with the American public, and their movement was finding a place within the political mainstream, but they were still in danger of marginalizing themselves. FAIR's association with unsavory characters and offensive ideas was a significant problem. John Tanton's flirtation with an organization that sponsored research into racial differences had already angered Jacquelyne Jackson, one of FAIR's early African American supporters. In 2007, the Southern Poverty Law Center placed the "hate group" label on FAIR (unjustly, FAIR said), citing the group's indirect ties to bigots. When *New York Times* reporter Jason DeParle profiled Tanton and his questionable friends in 2011, Jerry Kammer of the FAIR-affiliated Center for Immigration Studies denounced the story as "lopsided" in its critical assessment of Tanton's legacy, but Kammer himself found it hard to defend the FAIR founder. "Tanton, who did more than anyone else to establish the modern movement to restrict immigration," Kammer said, "has indeed done more than anyone else to undermine that movement."

By not breaking earlier and more cleanly with the white nationalists and racists in their ranks and by failing to project a more compassionate attitude toward people who came to America seeking freedom, opportunity, or refuge, the advocates of restricted immigration made it awkward to explore the issues of national identity that they justifiably posed. Arthur Schlesinger, Jr., the JFK liberal and historian, was among those intellectuals who felt multicultural-ism sometimes got too much attention, but he told Otis Graham in 1991 that he nevertheless felt a certain "queasiness" in approaching the immigration issue.

The writer Michael Lind, reviewing Peter Brimelow's *Alien Nation* for *The New Yorker* magazine, faulted him for missing the op-portunity to make a more interesting argument. "The questions that Brimelow raises about the effect of immigration on national culture are not in themselves illegitimate," Lind wrote, before adding that Brimelow's own answers to those questions reflected "a profound misunderstanding of American society." Brimelow wrote that the racial and ethnic transformation of America brought about by the 1965 Immigration Act was "an astonishing social experiment." In-deed it was, and it was perfectly natural to wonder what would hap-pen in the country as a result. Brimelow said the consequence would be the decline of Western values and the onset of tribal conflict because he lacked faith in the resilience of the American nation and had such evident distaste for the newcomers.

The failure to think carefully and creatively about what was at stake in America's changing character was of long standing. John Higham, whose 1955 book *Strangers in the Land* was a definitive history of the nativist movements of the late nineteenth and early twentieth centuries, wrote an epilogue in 2002 in which he regretted having been so disgusted by the racism of the early period that he had not paid enough attention in his book to the possibility of "an alternative form of nationalism . . . that stressed the diversity of the nation's origins, the egalitarian dimension of its self-image, and the universality of its founding principles." The unprecedented mixture of ethnicities in the post-1965 immigrant population did not rule out the possibility of the United States still having a sense of ex-ceptional national purpose, but articulating it would be a challenge. It would require settling on a common creed that was sufficiently substantive to mean something but not expressed in such explicitly

Anglo-Saxon terms as to exclude some people almost by definition. The rise of groups that did not fit a U.S. stereotype—devout Muslims might be one example—would force a more granular definition of Americanness. And if the discussion were to be faithful to America's principles, it would have to unfold in an atmosphere of tolerance and respect.

18

AFTER 9/11

Muslims in the United States, like other Americans, would never forget where they were on September 11, although the memory in their case was more likely linked to how that day altered their lives. That was certainly the case at the Dar Al-Hijrah mosque, where the leaders closed their doors when they heard about the attacks on the World Trade Center and the Pentagon. Terrorism was already synonymous with Islamist extremism in the minds of many Americans, and the mosque leaders feared from the first moment that they would be a target of angry protests.

The mosque's executive director, Samir Abo-Issa, who had immigrated to America twenty years earlier from Lebanon, was at his home in Annandale drinking coffee with his wife when one of youth leaders from the mosque telephoned him.

"Have you seen the news?" he asked. Abo-Issa didn't know what he was talking about.

"Turn on the TV."

The towers in New York were both aflame, with clouds of black smoke billowing over the Manhattan skyline, and the network anchors were reporting that people on the top floors were jumping to their deaths rather than be burned alive. Footage of a plane flying straight into the second World Trade Center tower was played over and over. Abo-Issa shuddered as he watched, contemplating the loss of life and anticipating what it might mean for his mosque, his congregation, and his family. He quickly dressed, got in his car, and headed for Dar Al-Hijrah. Normally the drive would take fifteen minutes or less, but with the emergency vehicles racing up and down the streets that day, it took an hour. He remembered later that he kept thinking of a movie he had seen about how the world would end.

After consulting with other mosque leaders, Abo-Issa decided that prayers at the mosque should go on as scheduled, but worshippers would have to ring the bell and ask to be let in. Later that day, a neighbor came to the door, a non-Muslim, and told Abo-Issa that the mosque should be open. "We know you had nothing to do with what happened," she said. But Abo-Issa and the others were still worried about a mob showing up outside, and they began making arrangements for extra security around the mosque. Late that afternoon, Abo-Issa and the mosque's outreach director, Hossein Goal, contacted the Fairfax County supervisor for the Mason District, Penny Gross, and asked if they could meet with her. The mosque leaders had a long relationship with Gross, having been regular participants in her Kaleidoscope meetings and having hosted her on several occasions at the mosque. Now it was time to ask a favor. Abo-Issa and Goal almost begged her to stand with them.

"Please, you have to go on television and tell people that it was not us who did this," they told her. "Our wives and children are behind locked doors. We're afraid to go out."

Gross's own daughter had been near the World Trade Center at the time of the attacks, and forty-five frightening minutes had passed before she got the news that her daughter was safe. She was still rattled when the Dar Al-Hijrah delegation showed up at her office, pleading for support. "Nobody is going to put a little old county supervisor on television at a time like this," she told them. "The president of the United States is the one who will be talking. But in situations like this in America, we often turn to prayer. I suggest you have a prayer service at the mosque and invite people in the community to come." They followed her advice and the next day hosted a candlelight vigil with local Christian ministers, sympathetic neighbors, and elected local officials, including Gross. For a few days, intercommunal solidarity was the rule. At the headquarters of the American Red Cross in downtown Washington, Muslims were prominent among those who stood in line for hours to donate blood for victims of the attacks.

Dr. Esam Omeish was at the Virginia DMV office helping his wife, Badria, get her first U.S. driver's license when the Pentagon was hit. He was the general surgeon on call that day at Inova Alexandria Hospital, and when his pager went off, he tried to call the hospital, only to find that his cell phone was no longer working. He did not know what had happened until he dropped Badria off at their home near the hospital and turned on the television. He went immediately to the hospital just as the first victims were arriving by ambulance. As a general surgeon, it would be up to Omeish to oversee the treatment of internal injuries, shrapnel wounds, and other emergency trauma cases. Sadly, however, the Pentagon attack left few survivors, and he had no one to treat. A few victims were brought to the hospital for burns and inhalation injury, but the emergency room and critical care physicians handled them all. After a few hours, Omeish went home to be with his family.

When Dar Al-Hijrah reopened on the Friday following the attacks, the sermon was given by Anwar al-Awlaki, the thirty-year-old imam whom Omeish had promoted as someone who could represent the mosque effectively to a non-Muslim audience. On Tuesday morning, September 11, Awlaki was en route back to Washington from San Diego, where he had attended a fundraiser for Jamil al-Amin, the African American militant previously known as H. Rap Brown, who was facing trial on charges of killing a policeman. Awlaki arrived at the mosque late that morning, just as the mosque was closing. In his sermon three days later, Awlaki said the New York and Pentagon attacks were "heinous," and he read an edict from a prominent Muslim scholar in the Middle East who had called the attacks un-Islamic. "We came here to build, not to destroy," Awlaki said. "We are the bridge between America and one billion Muslims worldwide." The local authorities, meanwhile, were proceeding cautiously. The Fairfax County chief of police, Thomas Manger, told a Dar Al-Hijrah delegation that his force would "do what we can" to protect the mosque and ensure the safety of worshippers there.

On the following Monday, President George W. Bush visited the Islamic Center in Washington and quoted from the Quran to emphasize its rejection of evil. "The face of terror is not the true faith of Islam," he said. "Islam is peace." Speaking of the Muslim leaders with whom he had met, he said, "They love America just as much as I do." He was clearly hoping to forestall some hateful backlash against Arabs or Muslims in the country. September 11 would nevertheless be seen as a watershed day for Muslim Americans, marking the moment they came under suspicion because of their religion or foreign origin. After that, many faced repeated tests of their loyalty and patriotism. The hijackers who commandeered the United and American Airlines jets and flew them into buildings, mostly Saudis, had entered the country legally and had not aroused great suspicion. After the terror attacks, Americans inevitably wondered whether it made sense to be more wary of strangers, especially Muslims, and the post-1965 ideal of a culturally diverse American citizenry was put to its most severe test. In Fairfax County, with one of the largest Muslim concentrations in America, rumors of plots and terrorist conspiracies swirled for months, and even law-abiding Muslim Americans found themselves monitored or followed. Within days of the attacks, the FBI concluded that the attacks had been an al Qaeda operation and that several of the hijackers had resided at least temporarily in northern Virginia and

obtained Virginia driver's licenses. At least two had worshipped at
Dar Al-Hijrah and come into contact with Awlaki.

Two FBI agents showed up at the Dar Al-Hijrah mosque on Thursday, September 13, with a picture of one of the hijackers and asked whether anyone at the mosque recognized him. They were especially eager to interview Awlaki, but he was not at the mosque when they arrived. Two days later, the agents found him at his home, a 1950s-era brick split-level house about a mile from the mosque. Over the next four days, the FBI agents interviewed him three more times. By then, the FBI and other law enforcement agencies knew the identities of all the hijackers and had determined that two of them, Nawaf al-Hazmi and Khalid al-Midhar, were regular worshippers at the Al-Ribat mosque in San Diego during the time Awlaki was the head imam there. Awalki acknowledged having met Hazmi at the San Diego mosque but he said he did not remember meeting Midhar, and he denied having seen Hazmi again after he left the Al-Ribat mosque in June 2000. A week later, the FBI put Awlaki under surveillance, having concluded that their preliminary investigations suggested "a more pervasive connection" with Hazmi "than what he admitted to during his interview."

This wasn't Awlaki's first time on the bureau's radar. In 1999 information surfaced that one of Osama bin Laden's agents may have contacted him. During that investigation, the FBI also learned that Awlaki was in contact with individuals who had been raising money for Hamas, the Palestinian group that the U.S. government had identified as a terrorist organization. In the weeks after 9/11, the FBI's suspicion of Awlaki deepened. An informant in California reported that Awlaki had been a spiritual adviser to Hazmi and Midhar in San Diego and met with them "consistently and privately." In March 2001, Hazmi and Hani Hanjour, another 9/11 hijacker who had arrived in San Diego, drove across the county to the D.C. area. They settled in Falls Church, Virginia, and immediately began attending services at Dar Al-Hijrah. Despite Awlaki's insistence that he had not seen Nawaf al-Hazmi since their days in San Diego, an informant subsequently reported that he had witnessed Awlaki meeting with Hanjour and Hazmi at the mosque. The 9/11 Commission concluded that Hazmi's appearance at Dar Al-Hijrah when Awlaki was the imam there "may not have been coincidental," given the history of their relations in San Diego, but that it was unable to reach any definitive conclusion about their relationship, nor whether Awlaki had any idea about Hazmi's plans.

Awlaki was a complicated personality. Born in the United States to immigrants from Yemen, he was well educated and worldly. There was enough in his biography and public statements to support the belief that he was a moderate and articulate Muslim, well suited to represent his religion and his mosque to a non-Muslim audience. His condemnation of the 9/11 attacks, before non-Muslim and Muslim audiences alike, seemed genuine. On the second Friday after the attacks, Awlaki emphasized the support the mosque was receiving from local Christian churches, and he pointed out that among those who died at the World Trade Center was the niece of a Dar Al-Hijrah worshipper and her husband. In an interview with *The New York Times,* Awlaki said he and other Muslim leaders had often dismissed inflammatory statements by militant Muslims as "just talk." After 9/11, Awlaki said, "we realized that talk can be taken seriously and acted upon in a violent radical way." This was the side of Awlaki that Esam Omeish had expected to see when he urged Dar Al-Hijrah directors to hire him, and the FBI's insistence on questioning Awlaki surprised and troubled Omeish.

In fact, Awlaki had long been an outspoken critic of the United States, and in his second sermon after the attacks, he suggested that the 9/11 attacks were, if not acceptable, at least understandable. "We were told this was an attack on American civilization. We were told this was an attack on American freedom, on the American way of life," he said. "This wasn't an attack on any of this. This was an attack on U.S. foreign policy." Moreover, Awlaki had a personal weakness that severely compromised his ability to be a moral or religious leader. Unbeknownst to his Dar Al-Hijrah associates, he had been charged several times in California with soliciting prostitutes, and he kept up the activity after moving to the Washington area. With the FBI monitoring his movements, it was not long before they followed him to several encounters with prostitutes and then confirmed the encounters by interviewing the prostitutes afterward.

In February 2002, the FBI agents who had been following Awlaki reported that they believed he knew he was under surveillance. A month later, he suddenly left the United States for Britain, without his family. Some former associates later speculated that Awlaki found out that the FBI had evidence of his association with prostitutes and that he had disappeared rather than face the shame. The agents who investigated him fretted that they never got the opportunity to question him fully about his relationship with the hijackers. Awlaki returned to the United States briefly in October to wrap up his affairs, but the State Department told immigration officials that he not be detained, apparently out of deference to Saudi authorities, who had taken an interest in him. He went on to Yemen, where his Islamist activism took a radical and far more violent turn.

Senior counterterrorism officials eventually reached a consensus that Awlaki probably did not know about the 9/11 attacks in advance, and they were soon satisfied there were no 9/11 accomplices or plotters still at large in the United States. Still, they wanted to determine whether any of the money for the attacks came from within the country. If there was a U.S. connection to the global terrorist network, it might be uncovered by following money transfers to and from countries in the Middle East, especially Saudi Arabia. Islamic charities, which often funded relief operations and social programs in regions where terrorist attacks were presumably planned, came under particular suspicion, in part because the charities' nonprofit aims meant they had faced less scrutiny from the Internal Revenue Service and other U.S. government agencies. The U.S. Treasury

Department organized an interagency counterterrorism task force and gave it the mission of finding and blocking the flow of money to terrorist organizations. It was this investigation that caused an uproar in Muslim American communities.

On the morning of March 20, 2002, about 150 federal agents from the task force launched a series of raids, targeting more than twenty Muslim organizations and charities. All but one of them were based in northern Virginia. Among them were the U.S. offices of the Muslim World League and its offshoot International Islamic Relief Organization (IIRO), along with the American Muslim Foundation (AMF), the Success Foundation, the International Institute of Islamic Thought, and the Graduate School of Islamic and Social Sciences. Virtually every Muslim organization in the area was hit, including many known for their moderation and their commitment to nonviolence. The director of the Graduate School of Islamic and Social Sciences, for example, had recently issued a fatwa decreeing that Muslim American soldiers were obligated to defend the United States against terrorist attacks.

Muslim leaders were uniformly outraged. The executive director of the Islamic Institute, Abdulwahab Alkebsi, told a reporter it seemed to him "like the government is declaring open season on Muslim American groups." The task force was indeed casting a wide net, hoping to snare any organizations or individuals who were funneling cash into al Qaeda coffers, even as inadvertent third parties, by sending money to organizations that gave material support to people or groups linked to the terrorist network. Esam Omeish was not himself affected by the raids, but his older brother Mohammed was among those indirectly targeted, and Esam rushed to his defense. Mohammed had been an important influence on Esam during high school and in their days as fellow leaders of the Muslim Students Association, when Mohammed was at George Washington University and Esam at Georgetown. After completing his PhD in education administration at George Washington, Mohammed had worked with various nonprofit Muslim organizations in northern

Virginia, holding leadership positions in the IIRO, the American Muslim Foundation, and the Success Foundation. There was never any indication that he had any knowledge of money going from his organizations to al Qaeda, but five months after the raid, his close association with the targeted groups was enough to get him listed as a defendant in a trillion-dollar civil lawsuit filed by relatives of 9/11 victims against what they alleged were the "financial supporters of terror." The accusation infuriated Mohammed, and he soon left for Jordan, where he and his wife had long planned to raise their children. Unlike Esam, he had never sought U.S. citizenship.

A search of the computers in the Alexandria, Virginia, office of the AMF and the Success Foundation produced intriguing information about the overseas financial transactions of the AMF president, Abdurahman Alamoudi, the son of a wealthy Saudi family. Alamoudi was handling tens of thousands of dollars in transfers to and from Saudi Arabia, Syria, and Libya, and he had repeated dealings with Libyan president Muammar Qaddafi. In August 2003, Alamoudi was stopped at Heathrow Airport, en route to Syria, after customs officials found he was carrying $340,000 in cash that he had not declared, including $20,000 that he had hidden on his body and that was discovered only during a pat-down. Unable to satisfy the British officials with his explanations of where he got the cash and what he intended to do with it, Alamoudi was detained, and a month later he was extradited to the United States, where he was charged with tax offenses and illegal transactions with the Libyan government.

The investigation of Alamoudi quickly led to Mohammed Omeish, his fellow AMF officer. Esam had supported Mohammed's decision to move his family to Jordan, but his departure left Esam in the uncomfortable position of having to serve as an intermediary between his brother and the government. Mohammed had always said he would cooperate with federal agents in the Alamoudi investigation, but he objected to a meeting in the United States. "He was already outside," Esam later recalled, "and he said, 'Heck, I'm

not coming back.' He just didn't want to go through the headache."
Eventually Mohammed met with federal agents in Malta.

Alamoudi pled guilty in July 2004 to various charges involving
terrorism financing and was sentenced to twenty-three years in jail.
A year later, the Treasury Department went even further in characterizing his financial activities. In a July 2005 press release, it alleged that Alamoudi had "a close relationship with al Qaida and had
raised money for al Qaida in the United States," although it offered
no evidence for that claim. The news shocked many in Washington
who had known Alamoudi as a moderate and influential voice for
Muslim Americans and a liaison between the Muslim community
and the U.S. government. As the founder of the American Muslim
Council (affiliated with the AMF), he advised Presidents Bill Clinton and George W. Bush, and the Bush White House invited him
to speak at a prayer service at Washington's National Cathedral in
honor of the victims of the 9/11 attacks. Alamoudi's friends and
associates, while acknowledging that he had been sloppy and reckless in his dealings with Qaddafi, nevertheless remained skeptical
of the government's case against him. Through his attorneys Alamoudi vigorously denied ever supporting al Qaeda or financing their
operations in any way.

While the extensive counterterrorism investigations in the years
after 9/11 did not reveal much of a terrorist network in northern Virginia, they did reveal that there was substantial support in Muslim
circles for Hamas, the Palestinian organization that governed the
Gaza Strip. Hamas did not have global reach, had no connection to
the 9/11 attacks, and it was not exactly al Qaeda, but the organization held the attention of counterterrorism investigators for several
years. Unlike the Palestinian Authority, its West Bank rival, Hamas
governed with an Islamist orientation, meaning it was guided by
Islamic teachings, and it had the support of Muslims around the
world who held Islamist views. The military wing of Hamas carried
out terrorist attacks, though exclusively against Israeli targets. Its
political wing ran schools and administered other public services,

and raised funds abroad, including in the United States, to support its programs. The U.S. government listed it as a terrorist group, and an executive order issued by President Clinton in 1995 barred all financial transactions with Hamas, without distinguishing between its political and military operations.

For those investigators who were looking to uncover a terrorism financing network, the Hamas case was irresistible. At the center was Mousa Mohammed Abu Marzook, the leader of the political wing of Hamas and a prolific fund-raiser for Hamas in the United States. Marzook, who did his university study in the United States, was one of the founders of the Holy Land Foundation, the largest Islamic charity in the United States and a major supporter of re-lief operations and social programs in the West Bank and Gaza. In 1997, under pressure from the Israeli government, U.S. authorities deported Marzook to Jordan. It was not until December 2001, how-ever, that the U.S. government declared the Holy Land Foundation itself a terrorist organization and froze its assets, claiming that it had provided millions of dollars to Hamas-affiliated organizations and individuals. A year later, a grand jury in Texas indicted Mar-zook, saying he had been engaged in terrorism finance, and in 2004 the Holy Land Foundation was indicted on similar charges.

The prosecution of the Holy Land Foundation and of Mar-zook (in absentia) reverberated throughout Muslim activist circles, especially in northern Virginia. Marzook had spent considerable time in the area, frequently speaking at the Dar Al-Hijrah mosque, and many of the Islamic organizations in northern Virginia had ties either to Marzook or the Holy Land Foundation or both, dating from the time when their fund-raising and charitable activities were entirely legal. Prosecutors in the two cases identified hundreds of unindicted co-conspirators, including some prominent Islamic or-ganizations and Muslim leaders in the D.C. area. Among them was Ismail Elbarasse, one of the founders of the Dar Al-Hijrah mosque and a friend and former business partner of Marzook. Elbarasse had long been linked to Hamas through Marzook and had spent eight months in prison in 1998 for refusing to testify in a Hamas-related case in New York. He lived in Annandale, in Fairfax County, and was close to many of the Dar Al-Hijrah leaders, including Esam Omeish.

In August 2004, while returning with his family from a two-day vacation to the Eastern Shore of Maryland, Elbarasse was stopped by a Baltimore County police officer after crossing the Bay Bridge, which spans the Chesapeake Bay. The incident involved a near farcical series of events that exemplified the racial profiling that enraged many Muslims in the aftermath of 9/11. The police officer noticed Elbarasse's wife, whom he described as "a female of foreign origin," videotaping out the passenger-side window of the car, and he grew suspicious. In a witness statement, he claimed that when the woman saw he was watching her, she lowered the camera "in a hurried motion to avoid detection." He immediately called for backup from the bridge police, and the family was detained.

When the police reviewed the tape in the camera, they found what in normal circumstances would have seemed to be innocent. The bridge occupied just the last three minutes of a twenty-seven-minute tape, which included footage of the family at their beach condo. "We had taped our whole vacation," Elbarasse's twenty-year-old daughter, Dua'a, later told *The Washington Post*, "and we thought the bay looked really nice off the bridge." The investigating officer nevertheless titled his report, "Suspected Terrorist Activity" and noted that the bridge footage included shots of the cables and span, as if to suggest that the Elbarasse family was casing the bridge for a possible attack.

The bridge police ran Elbarasse's name through a database maintained by the National Crime Information Center and discovered, according to the report, that he was "a person of interest from the FBI, as having possible ties with terrorism." The reference was to Elbarasse's identification as an unindicted co-conspirator in the 1998 Marzook case. He was immediately arrested and held as a material witness in that case, even though he had not yet been called to testify. The Maryland authorities ordered that he remain in detention, with bond set at one million dollars. Elbarasse's friends and associates, including Esam Omeish, were outraged at his arrest and among them came up with the money to bail him out, even putting up their own homes as collateral. Not surprisingly, the authorities concluded that the videotaping was innocent. No charges were filed, and with no date set for his testimony in the Marzook case, Elbarasse was released and the bond money returned. During the time he was in custody, however, federal agents raided his home and hauled off a huge trove of documents dating from the years he was involved with Marzook and other Muslim leaders in America.

During the 1990s, Suzanne Devlin was deputy chief of police for administration in the Fairfax County Police Department, which was the post she held on 9/11. The September 11 attacks would prompt an abrupt and far-reaching shift in Devlin's police world. For her and other Fairfax County officers, bike patrols, Spanish immersion classes, and other community policing activities were out. Counterterrorism was in. No priority ranked higher. Prior to 9/11, the counterterrorism mission was largely seen as taking place somewhere else, but the attacks on the World Trade Center and the Pentagon came from within and brought a new fear of terrorists living undetected in our own neighborhoods. Finding them was largely the work of local police departments, cooperating with other law enforcement agencies and the federal government.

In the year that followed the 9/11 attacks, Devlin tallied as many as fifty counterterrorism leads a week, each of which had to be investigated. Some were based on flimsy evidence or mere hunches, while others were potentially alarming and had to be taken seriously. In her twenty-five years as a Fairfax police officer, Devlin had focused largely on crime prevention, conflict resolution, and community relations. The hunt for terrorists or potential terrorists required an entirely different orientation, with more focus on investigations and a much greater need for secrecy. For a police officer like Devlin, who considered herself a "people person," it was a troubling change. For Fairfax County's Muslim community, with their mosques and Islamic organizations subjected to surveillance and undercover operations, the new policing focus was far more upsetting.

U.S. government officials insisted the "war on terror" was not a war on Islam or against Muslims, but it sometimes felt like that to the Muslims themselves, especially in northern Virginia. "People were intimidated," said Esam Omeish. "They were upset by the FBI putting informants in the mosques." Muslim leaders had a variety of reactions to the unwelcome attention they received. A very few—Anwar al-Awlaki for example—became more extreme in their rhetoric. Most took more constructive lessons from the experience. Mukit Hossain, a Bangladeshi immigrant who was active in the ADAMS mosque in Sterling, Virginia, gave up his telecommunications business after 9/11 to organize a new political action committee for Muslims, the Platform for Active Civic Empowerment, with the intent that it create a "Muslim powerhouse" in northern Virginia, strong enough to influence local and state elections. "If we really want to have a voice in the government, we need to actively participate or else we will be pushed into a corner and end up in concentration camps much like what happened to the Japanese during the Second World War," he told *The Washington Post* in June 2003.

Esam Omeish, on the other hand, argued that American Muslims needed to take a more self-critical lesson from the 9/11 experience. "Most Muslim immigrants who came here chose to be insular," he said. "They were threatened by big change, so they concentrated on building their own institutions." As a result, they found themselves isolated in American society at their moment of greatest crisis. Omeish in 2001 was already serving on the board of trustees of the Muslim American Society, and he and MAS president Souheil Ghannouchi were determined to transform the group from an association of exiled Muslims who were focused on struggles overseas to a group of Muslim Americans who were integrated into U.S. society and helping to shape the national debate. MAS's efforts included voter registration drives, consistent with Mukit Hossain's campaign to get Muslims more politically involved on their own, but much of the campaign was devoted to building relationships outside the Muslim community. "We are stepping up our civic participation and outreach efforts to make up for years of isolation that put us in a vulnerable position: being a largely unknown community and therefore easy target of stereotyping," Ghannouchi wrote in an online chat quoted in *The Washington Post*.

In June 2004, Esam and other Dar Al-Hijrah leaders invited a team of eight FBI agents to come to the mosque and respond to Muslim concerns. The delegation was led by Michael Mason, who was in charge of the bureau's Washington Field Office. The agents were served a dinner of lamb and rice, but the subsequent assembly in the mosque's main prayer room quickly grew heated. Esam sat at the head table with Mason and the other agents and tried to moderate, but it was soon clear the attendees had a lot of anger to get off their chests and no trust in the FBI to protect their interests. "Sometimes you would go to mosques where people were overly polite because you're the FBI. That wasn't the case there," Mason told *The Washington Post*. When one attendee told Mason he didn't believe anything the FBI agent said, Mason, who is African American, was offended. "I didn't come here to be spoken to like that," Mason snapped. The man came up after the meeting to apologize, and Mason reassured him he was sympathetic to the community's concerns. "I'm a black man," Mason said. "I know something about being treated for what you are rather than who you are."

The leadership role that Omeish took in the early years after 9/11 impressed his fellow MAS trustees, and in 2004 they elected him as the organization's new president, with Souheil Ghannouchi staying on as executive director. It was a time of challenge. Mistrust of Muslim motives and intentions remained high in the broader society, and even good-faith outreach efforts on the part of Muslim leaders were often met with suspicion. When Mukit Hossain, the telecom-entrepreneur-turned-Muslim-activist, launched his political action committee's website, aiming "to portray Islam in its true nature as a complete religion" and "to boost the political participation and empowerment of Muslim Americans," he was accused by an anti-Islam weblog of "furthering his Islamist agenda."

For Muslim American leaders like Hossain and Omeish, the political atmosphere was growing constantly more hostile. In September 2004, *The Washington Post* and the *Chicago Tribune* both published lengthy articles about the Muslim Brotherhood. The *Tribune* called the Brotherhood "the world's most influential Islamic fundamentalist group" and alleged that it hoped "someday" to create a Muslim state in America. "Because of its hard-line beliefs," the *Tribune* reporters wrote, "the U.S. Brotherhood has been an increasingly divisive force within Islam in America," and it declared that the Brotherhood had operated in the United States since 1993 "under the name Muslim American Society." The *Post* article was more nuanced, noting that the Brotherhood included moderate wings that rejected violence and terrorism, and pointing out that "some U.S. diplomats and intelligence officials believe its influence offers an opportunity for political engagement that could help isolate violent jihadists," though it quoted another U.S. counterterrorism expert saying that the Brotherhood's ultimate objectives were "radical Islamist goals that in many ways are antithetical to our interests."

Esam Omeish, in his capacity as MAS president, responded to the *Post* article with a letter to the editor, saying it "falls short in many respects, contains many inaccuracies and confuses some issues." In the letter, which the *Post* declined to publish, Omeish described what he said was "the moderate school of thought prevalent in the Muslim Brotherhood." He did not deny claims in the two newspaper articles that Brotherhood leaders in the United States were key founders of both the MAS and Muslim Students Association. Omeish said the MAS was now independent, but he acknowledged it had reflected Muslim Brotherhood doctrine "as it applies to our American identity and relevance for our American reality." The Brotherhood influence, he wrote, "has been instrumental in defining our worldviews of justice and human rights; of terrorism, its scourge and its rejection in Islam; and of differentiating between terrorism and legitimate struggles against tyranny, dictatorships, and occupations." He defended Islam, saying the Muslim American Society advocated "Islam's values and its solutions to society's problems," but he insisted the MAS as an organization subscribed to "the values and ideals of our country, its Founding Fathers and the Constitution of the Land."

A year later, Omeish made a direct pitch to U.S. secretary of state Condoleezza Rice, submitting a paper to her in which he suggested that the U.S. government engage with the Muslim Brotherhood, arguing it was in the "strategic national interest" to do so. In the paper, Omeish acknowledged that the U.S. government and the Brotherhood were unlikely to be "friends" given their sharp disagreement over Israel, but he said they could be "partners" in an effort to promote democratic reform and isolate the Muslim radicals who were the foundation of al Qaeda's support in the Muslim world. While generally focused on Muslim issues in the U.S. context, no leader of his community could avoid talking about Muslim struggles abroad, particularly the plight of the Palestinians. Like virtually all Muslims, Omeish was strongly opposed to Israel's occupation of Palestinian territories. "I think it's abhorrent and has to be resisted," he said in a 2013 interview. In his view, it was unfair to label Hamas simply as a terrorist organization, given the importance of its political wing. "Hamas is an institution," he said. "They rule a million and a half people. They are a government." He likened the separate wings of Hamas to the Irish Republican Army (IRA) and its political counterpart, Sinn Féin, and pointed out that the United States dealt with Sinn Féin even while rejecting the bomb-throwing IRA.

Omeish came close to endorsing Hamas during a speech in Kansas in 2004, when he decried the Israeli gunship attack in Gaza that killed "our beloved brother Sheikh Ahmed Yassin," the founder and spiritual leader of the Hamas organization. In most of his speeches, however, Esam generally avoided all mention of the group. "The U.S. position is very clear on Hamas," he said. "We are law-abiding citizens, so the fact that it's listed as terrorist, that becomes the law of the land, for us as well."

Terrorism and the government's counterterrorism efforts were the driving MAS concerns. In July 2005, in the immediate aftermath of the suicide bombings in London that killed more than fifty people and injured over seven hundred, Omeish organized a press conference in Washington to emphasize his group's commitment to use "balanced mainstream advocacy of Islamic principles" to combat extremism and "deny terrorists any religious, ideological, or political legitimacy." It would help, he argued, if the U.S. media and the U.S. government took stronger stands in opposition to the anti-Muslim "backlash" in the country. In an interview later, he said he wanted people "to come away with the feeling that Muslims are at the forefront of what is going on with this fight against terrorism and not be on the receiving end of what goes on in the fight against terrorism."

As part of his effort to defuse the tensions that continued to flare between Muslims and law enforcement agencies, Omeish in 2006 asked for a meeting with Arthur Cummings, the chief of the FBI's counterterrorism division in the Washington Field Office. Cummings was a former Navy SEAL who had been working in counterterrorism since 1996. He helped reorganize the bureau's counterterrorism program after 9/11, headed up the FBI portion of the team pursuing Osama bin Laden in Afghanistan, and then served as deputy head of the National Counterterrorism Center. As head of the FBI's counterterrorism effort in the Washington area at the time, Cummings was trying to determine how much support there was for extremism in the local Arab and Muslim communities. For his part, Omeish wanted to clear up any misunderstandings or suspicions hanging over him and the Muslim American Society.

He was accompanied in his meetings with Cummings by Souheil Ghannouchi, the MAS executive director and former president. "We went to him and said, 'What's the problem? Whatever you have against us, I want to take it on,'" Esam later recalled.

"Well, you guys are about ten years too late," Cummings said. "But I guess, better late than never." He had been frustrated with the lack of cooperation his agents were getting from Arab and Muslim leaders and their organizations.

Omeish and Ghannouchi voluntarily brought all their MAS files to show Cummings, and they laid out the history of their organization and their connections to the Brotherhood, something they had not previously done.

Cummings's concern about the Muslim Brotherhood's influence in America probably stemmed in part from the 1991 document proposing that the Brotherhood's mission in America was "a kind of grand Jihad in eliminating and destroy the Western civilization from within." The document was seized during the raid on Ismail Elbarasse's house in 2004 but only made public in 2007 during the Holy Land Foundation trial. Omeish was the MAS president at the time the document was made public, and he immediately wrote an email to all the MAS chapter heads and board members explaining the significance of the document. "While some of these ideas were part of the debate that preceded MAS, what MAS emerged with was a new framework and an intellectual paradigm that negates some of these advocated positions and ideas." Omeish told his MAS colleagues that their organization "does not offer its Islamic program as an alternative to Western civilization. . . . We find these to be abhorrent statements and are in direct conflict with the very principles of Islam."

Omeish shared such communications with Cummings and other investigators on his team and with Cummings's successor at the FBI over two years of regular meetings. "It was hard work," Esam said. "I mean, these guys are not easy to deal with. But it was very straightforward. I said, 'I don't care. Cameras in my house? Feel free. If you've got a grand jury, if you've got questions, do what you have to. That's your job, just do it right."

Hard as it was for Muslim leaders to deal with the aftermath of 9/11, it was not much easier for law enforcement agents and other government officials. They were under enormous pressure from their superiors, from politicians, and from the American public to make sure there were no more terrorist attacks, and their interactions with Arab and Muslim communities were not always reassuring. The meetings with Arthur Cummings initiated by Esam Omeish and Souheil Ghannouchi were exceptions to the general pattern. Many community leaders told government investigators they did not support terrorism, but they would then hint that they sympathized with the attackers or understood what motivated them, and the investigators were left wondering how much cooperation they could expect. In case after case, police officers and FBI agents were uncertain whom they could entirely trust. Some spokesmen for the Muslim community, it seemed, could be disingenuous in their public utterances denouncing violence.

The best example was Anwar al-Awlaki. In the months after 9/11, he was widely quoted expressing disgust over the attacks and sympathy for the victims, but by 2008 he was counseling U.S. Army Major Nidal Hasan from Yemen via the Internet, and when Hasan shot and killed thirteen people at Fort Hood, Texas, Awlaki pronounced it a "heroic act" and said other Muslim soldiers should "follow the footsteps of men like Nidal." Was Awlaki radicalized in response to U.S. counterterrorism actions, or during the eighteen months he spent in a Yemeni prison, or did he have violent tendencies all along and was merely hiding them? Even his friends and associates weren't entirely sure.

Tensions were felt most keenly in local police departments, especially among those officers who had always taken pride in their knowledge of their community and who had worked to build trusting relationships. By 2004, Suzanne Devlin was Fairfax County's lead liaison with the FBI and other federal intelligence and law enforcement agencies. She was directly responsible for the National Capital Regional Intelligence Center, one of the "fusion centers" set up in the aftermath of the 9/11 attacks to gather and analyze "threat-related information" and share it with other agencies. Given that Fairfax was the locus of so much of the alleged terrorism activity on the East Coast, Devlin occupied a key position, but in the years after her 2009 retirement, it was her earlier days in community policing that she recalled most fondly. "I loved it," she said, "because I've always been a dreamer about this perfect democracy, and I thought Fairfax was the closest thing I could imagine to having one. We had all the resources and talent. I mean, call me a social worker, but you're always going to get the bad guys. If you don't spend time moving people away from the dark side, you give them to the dark side." For Devlin, however, the post-9/11 environment in the county left little room for idealism. Terrorism financing was the new concern, with "follow the money" as the mantra. She and other officers did not feel that trust was an option in dealing with the Muslim community.

"Suspicious cases were everywhere," Devlin said. "All of a sudden, you had a completely different feeling about the country and who was really here and how much duplicity might be going on underneath your nose," she recalled. She had several Muslim friends, but she found herself wondering if she really knew them. "I didn't have the confidence that I was not being manipulated," she said, "because by then I had gotten cynical. I figured, I'm being genuine with them, but maybe they can't be genuine with me. Maybe they have divided loyalties. I never looked at people the same way after that."

In 2007, the Virginia General Assembly created a twenty-member commission to advise the legislature and the governor on immigration issues. The panel's assignment was to assess the costs and benefits of immigration and to review the effects on the state of federal immigration policies. The governor at the time, Democrat Tim Kaine, was able to name ten of the members, and among those he invited to serve was Esam Omeish, in his capacity as president of the Muslim American Society. Esam's experience as an immigrant was a core part of his identity, and he had thought deeply about what it meant to him and how it had changed him. "That's exactly what I'm about," Omeish said when the governor's office called him, "and I'd be happy to serve."

There were two points he was eager to make as a commission member, points he had often emphasized in his public presentations. One was that immigrants developed resilience. "It's something you can't learn anywhere else," he said. "You learn not to be limited by what others might think of you. It's the knowledge that you can go further if you constantly work at it." The other point was more cautionary. "If for whatever reason you're not in position to take that high road, it can be very hard to have a healthy experience as an immigrant, because so much depends on the opportunities that come your way." He often thought about his fellow Middle Eastern immigrants who ended up as baggage handlers at Dulles Airport or got stuck in other low-end positions. Serving on the Virginia Commission on Immigration would enable Omeish to address a much broader audience than he had faced as a speaker in his mosque or as the MAS president.

The appointment of a prominent Muslim, however, was bound to be scrutinized. A Republican legislator and fellow immigration commission member, C. Todd Gilbert, with considerable hyperbole, claimed that Omeish was president of "a dangerous international organization that seeks to bring about worldwide Islamic government." A day later, the investigative journalist Steven Emerson, who founded a website dedicated to reporting on "radical Islamic terrorist groups," posted online a video of a speech Esam had given in front of the White House at a Jerusalem Day rally in 2000. In the speech,

Esam's message for "our brothers and sisters in Filastin [Palestine]" was that "you have known that the jihad way is the way to liberate your land. And we . . . are with you and we are supporting you, and we will do everything that we can, Insh'Allah, to help your cause."

The word "jihad" in that context, Esam later explained, was not an endorsement of suicide bombings or terrorism and only indicated his support for the Palestinian uprising or intifada more broadly, which he insisted was legal under international law. The damage was done, however. Governor Kaine learned of the video when a caller to a talk radio show incorrectly told him on the air that Omeish had called "for the destruction of Israel" in his Jerusalem Day speech.

"That is news to me, what you say," Kaine told the caller, "and it's something we will check out." By the end of the day, Esam was forced to resign from the commission. In a statement, Kaine said, "I have been made aware of certain statements he has made which concern me. Dr. Omeish indicated that he did not want this controversy to distract from the important work of the Commission." Emerson's organization, the Investigative Project on Terrorism, crowed about its achievement in an online posting. "IPT Footage Takes Down Omeish."

Omeish was furious. "The controversy that erupted around my appointment . . . highlights the very issues we need to address in America," he wrote in an op-ed column published in *The Washington Post*. "I still believe that I am highly qualified to serve on the commission. I am an immigrant, as well as an accomplished surgeon, a community leader, a person of faith, a passionate activist and a good representative of America's growing community of Muslims. I am disappointed that I was unable to defeat propaganda and partisan politics." In a press conference on the day following his resignation, Omeish said he had been the victim of "a smear campaign." He emphasized, as he had before, that "jihad" as he used it means "struggle" broadly, that his Jerusalem Day speech "was not a call for violence," and that his message was one of "support to people who are under occupation and who are under severe conditions of repression."

The 9/11 attacks put Arab and Muslim immigrants in a special category. When the FBI's Arthur Cummings met with representatives of the American-Arab Anti-Discrimination Committee to respond to their concerns about U.S. counterterrorism policy, he asked them, "Are you American, or are you Arab?" The question would not likely be asked of other ethnicities, but under the circumstances it was not unreasonable. Esam Omeish routinely challenged his fellow Muslims to affirm their American identities, even as he sought to ground them in the principles of Islam. "You have people in your community who are nowhere near understanding what America is or loving it and who are still living in the village, in Mogadishu, or in Gaza," he once complained, speaking of his own community.

America had come under attack from terrorists who were Muslim and Arab, and the attacks inevitably raised questions of loyalty, just as happened in other eras with other ethnic groups. For the anti-immigrant activists, the story of subversive Muslims in America beautifully reinforced their nativist inclinations. At *The Social Contract*, the journal founded by John Tanton, the father of the modern immigration restriction movement, the first issue after the 9/11 attacks was organized around the theme "The Terrorists Among Us." The Fall 2010 issue was devoted to "The Menace of Islam." By then, Tanton and his associates, at least those who worked with him in Michigan, had finally decided that potential immigrants to the United States could be barred on the basis of their religion, if not their race or nationality. "It seems clear to us," the editor wrote, "that it is (past) time to halt Muslim immigration to the United States."

Their conclusion amounted to a decisive rejection of the non-discriminatory premise of the 1965 Immigration Act, a law whose essential "wisdom" Tanton and his colleagues had once saluted, even while criticizing some provisions as overly generous. It had taken forty-five years, but the turn was not surprising. Muslims seemed just different enough, just dangerous enough, to present the biggest challenge to America's welcoming attitude since the 1920s and a fundamental test of the 1965 promise of a bias-free immigration policy.

19

THE SECOND GENERATION

The grassy spaces between the red-brick apartment buildings offered a decent place to play soccer, and Álvaro Alarcón and the other boys in the Willston complex gathered there every afternoon. Almost all of them were Latino immigrants, for whom soccer was a passion. Álvaro was helped by having a father who played well himself, and with Victor's coaching Álvaro improved year by year, eventually playing soccer all across northern Virginia. After the shooting incident in the parking lot and the burglary in their apartment, Victor moved his family to a new apartment farther west in the county, and Álvaro enrolled at Fairfax High School. He made the varsity soccer team in his freshman year, which thrilled him. A successful high school career in soccer, Álvaro figured, might actually help get him into college somewhere.

It did not happen. The soccer coach never warmed to Álvaro. "I had really good tryouts, and I did really well with the team and in practice," he recalled, "but for some reason I just could not get on his good side, no matter what I did." For the first time in his life, it occurred to Álvaro that he was experiencing some ethnic prejudice.

Although most of the boys in the soccer tryouts with Álvaro were Latinos, the coach selected an almost entirely white squad, and the coach's dismissive attitude toward him convinced Álvaro that he would never have a chance to be a high school star. As a sophomore, he did not even bother to go out for the varsity team, choosing to play instead on travel and club squads in the area. The varsity coach made no effort to persuade him to stay.

Álvaro's hopes of going to college took a further hit when he got the idea from his high school teachers and counselors that they did not consider him college material. Those who gave him any guidance suggested he go to trade school. The counsel deflated him. "My attitude was, 'Oh well, if I'm not going to college, what's the point?'" He figured he could educate himself if necessary, as his father had successfully done. It did not occur to Álvaro to push back against what his teachers were saying. "I was an impressionable teenager," he said. "I was thinking, 'You're probably right. You're an adult, you've been to college, you know better.' I didn't know anything. You just believe what they tell you." He was well into his senior year at Fairfax before he reconsidered their advice, and then it was only because his dad kept badgering him about his post–high school plans.

"I really don't know," Álvaro finally told him. "I have no idea. College is apparently not an option for me."

"What!" his father said. "Whoever told you that?"

"That's what they said at school."

It was the first that Victor had heard what the high school teachers and counselors were telling Álvaro, and he was furious. He had always been quick to get riled up, especially over how his kids were treated in school, and the next day he marched into the high school offices and demanded a meeting with Álvaro's teachers, his counselors, and the administration. Álvaro's academic record was not stellar—he had a C+ average and an SAT score of about 1150—but it was not disqualifying for college, and he had participated in extracurricular activities. Victor demanded that the high school staff give Álvaro some advice and encouragement about his college options.

"Everybody was offering excuses," Victor recalled later, "and I got really upset. I said, 'You guys aren't doing your job! And I know why: It's because Álvaro speaks Spanish, and he's quiet.'" The school staff belatedly agreed to do more to help him. It was already late in the application cycle, but there were a few schools that were still open for admissions. Álvaro applied and was accepted at a small liberal arts institution in rural Virginia. It was four hours south of Fairfax, but that did not bother Álvaro, who had spent his whole life in close quarters with his family and was eager to be on his own. What he and his family did not realize was how little experience the school had with nonwhite students. Álvaro was attending an orientation session on his first day when he noticed another boy who appeared to be Hispanic sitting in the row ahead of him. At some point, the boy turned around and saw Álvaro, with his brown skin, straight black hair, and vaguely indigenous features, clearly a fellow Latino. The boy's name was Danny Pérez, and he was from suburban Maryland.

"Hey," he whispered. "It's kind of weird here. I think you're the only other Spanish kid." Within a few hours, Danny and Álvaro learned not only that they were indeed the only two Latino boys in the freshman class, but that the college housing staff had assigned them as roommates, perhaps thinking that they would want to be together or that it might be risky to match either of them with a non-Hispanic white student. For Álvaro, it did not make for a good first impression. Few of the students he met that year had ever known a Latino, and many were shocked that Álvaro spoke English as well as they did. He finished his freshman year but then transferred to Northern Virginia Community College, a school closer to home and much more accustomed to a diverse student population.

The somewhat unwelcoming experiences that Álvaro had both at Fairfax High School and at college might have alienated him from mainstream America and inclined him to identify more with other Hispanics. Sociologists Alejandro Portes and Rubén Rumbaut, who studied second-generation immigrants over many years, found that many children of immigrants shift toward "a more militant reffirmation" of their own ethnic backgrounds during adolescence. Those who identified themselves as Americans during their early teenage years were less likely to do so by the time of their high school graduation, seeing themselves instead as Mexicans or Koreans or Filipinos or, more broadly, as Hispanics or Asians. One factor driving those identity shifts, Portes and Rumbaut concluded, was the experience of ethnic prejudice. "Groups subjected to extreme discrimination and derogation of their national origins are likely to embrace them ever more fiercely," they wrote.

Sociologists such as Portes and Rumbaut focused primarily on identity shifts in the second immigrant generation because first-generation immigrants were seen as preoccupied with the struggle to survive, adapt, and provide for their families in the new land. They still had ties to the countries they had left and were less likely to be fluent in English, so it would not be surprising if their American identity was not yet fully formed. Nativists had raised the identity question with their suggestion that the post-1965 surge of "new seed" immigrants from Asia, Africa, or other distant lands might not make good American citizens, given their cultural background, their political profile, or even their allegedly inferior ethnic "stock." With so many colored differently and practicing different religions, the chances of their alienation from the American mainstream were probably greater than for earlier immigrants. The "assimilability" question became even more pressing as their children came of age. As Portes wrote in 1996, "The adaptation of the second generation will be decisive in establishing the long-term outlook for contemporary immigration. It is indeed among the second generation, not the first, where such issues as the continuing dominance of English, the growth of a welfare-dependent population, the resilience of culturally distinct urban enclaves, and the decline of ethnic inter-marriages will be decided permanently."

Álvaro Alarcón was not one of those who reacted to prejudice by embracing their own national origins more fiercely. The experience more often left him confused, uncertain where he belonged. He had come to the United States from Bolivia at the age of five, and by the time he was a young adult he had largely forgotten his Bolivian roots. He returned to the country just once, at the age of nine, for a month, and he was miserable the whole time. Arriving in La Paz at an elevation of nearly twelve thousand feet, Álvaro immediately developed altitude sickness, as visitors often did, and his grandmother put him to bed. A short time after that, he came down with chicken pox, followed by the flu. Though he had left just four years earlier, he no longer had friends in Bolivia and did not feel at home there. Upon his return to the United States, he said he never wanted to go back.

In the United States, the Alarcón family celebrated Thanksgiving and Christmas in the American style, with turkey, mashed potatoes, macaroni, and cranberries, not with traditional Bolivian food. Álvaro did not follow the news from Bolivia and cared little about developments there. He had spent several years in a neighborhood with immigrants from Central America and spoke their language, but he did not have enough in common with them to fully share their Hispanic identity. By the time he graduated from high school, he considered English his first language, speaking it with his father and his brothers, and using Spanish only with his mother and grandmother. On the other hand, every time people asked him where he was from, Álvaro interpreted the question as meaning they didn't see him as genuinely American. "I feel like I'm in limbo," he said. "I can't say I'm Bolivian, because I don't know anything about the place, but I can't say I'm American, because I wasn't born here. So when people ask me where I'm from, I can't give a straight answer."

Uncertainty about a national identity was a feeling Álvaro shared with other immigrants who had come to the United States at a young age, and the Fairfax County schools were full of them. Álvaro grew up alongside Vietnamese, Korean, African, Middle Eastern, and South Asian youth. While in middle school, he became friends with Fasih Khan, the son of Abdul Shaheed Khan, who had come to America from Pakistan by way of Saudi Arabia. "Al" and "Fas" remained buddies through high school and into their college years, when they teamed up with Ho-Kwon Chun, an outgoing and talkative kid they met through a mutual Vietnamese friend. Ho-Kwon, who called himself Brian, had immigrated from South Korea with his parents and his sister when he was seven years old and had gone to work with them at the family dry cleaning plant when he was just ten. All three boys—Álvaro, Fasih, and Ho-Kwon—had arrived in the United States at about the same time, at the same age. They had all lived with friends or relatives during their early years in the country, and each knew what it meant to be poor in America. All three had spent time in ESL classes and had to work to reach their grade level, but all did so successfully. They came to the United States from distant corners of the world, with Spanish, Urdu, and Korean as their mother tongues, but they found they had more in common with each other than they did with their native-born white schoolmates. No longer Bolivian, Pakistani, or Korean, but not yet feeling entirely accepted as American, their shared experience as immigrant youth was so central to their identity that it bonded them in a way that ethnic kinship could not.

"We used to get a kick out of thinking how strange we probably seemed to people," Ho-Kwon said. "I mean, people would look at us and see a 'Chinese' guy, a 'Spanish' guy, and a 'Middle Eastern' guy coming into a store together. How often did people see that? We joked about that all the time." Though they were young men emerging from the margins of society, they had the grandiose dreams that often spring from the immigrant experience. "We were all trying to find what we could do, trying to find that opportunity, wanting to do something big," Ho-Kwon recalled. "But it was very amateurish, all amateur ideas." Ho-Kwon had lots of energy and made friends easily, and for a time the boys' entrepreneurial scheming revolved around White Pearl Cleaners, the Chun family's dry cleaning business. For lack of a better employment opportunity, Álvaro had been working at the front counter of another dry cleaning establishment, and Ho-Kwon offered him a job at White Pearl, with the idea of bringing him into the family business. He and Álvaro devised a grand plan for taking over the operation and expanding it with new locations and innovative approaches, reaching out to hotels and other large-volume customers and incorporating a drive-thru option. Their friend Fasih Khan had another job at the time, but he joined the brainstorming, suggesting they develop a White Pearl website, so that customers could go online and request a pickup or delivery.

None of their ideas for revamping White Pearl Cleaners worked out, largely because of opposition from Ho-Kwon's father, a stern and highly traditional Korean male. Like many Koreans of his generation, Yeop Chun had grown up desperately poor in the postwar 1950s, when Seoul was a devastated city. He had minimal contact with his own father, and his mother worked long days as a maid, earning barely enough to feed her children. At the age of fourteen, for lack of an alternative, Yeop had enlisted in the South Korean military, lying about his age. He spent twenty years in the military, but did not qualify for a pension adequate to support his family, and upon his retirement he had to look for other work. His brother lived in the United States, and the sibling unification provisions of the 1965 Immigration Act offered Yeop and his family the opportunity to relocate to America in 1988. He had been a judo master in the Korean military, and before he opened his dry cleaning business he had a job teaching martial arts in a studio run by his brother, a ninth-degree karate grand master.

Whether because of his own childhood experience or because of his years in the military, Yeop Chun could be severe as a father. "I heard his story all the time growing up," Ho-Kwon said, "how nobody ever gave him anything, never patted him on the head or said, 'Good job, son.' He relayed all that to me. He always said, 'Nothing comes free. Don't expect anything from anyone. You'll have to go get it yourself.'" It was, Ho-Kwon said with some sadness, "a different kind of fatherhood. He would say, 'A man does this. A man does that. Don't talk too much. Don't do this. Walk this way. Eat this way. Sit this way.' He went overboard." Yeop, who took the name Steve in America, insisted that his son address him always as *Abeoji*, meaning "Father," not *Appa*, meaning "Dad." Not surprisingly, Ho-Kwon did not feel comfortable turning to him for support or counsel. "I missed being able to say, 'Hey, Dad, I have an issue here. Can I talk to you?' His attitude was, Men don't succumb to pressure."

At one point, when Ho-Kwon's mother was ill and returned to South Korea for medical treatment, his father asked him to commit to the family business. "We need to get together," he told Ho-Kwon. "I need you. But I know you want to go out and do your own thing, so make your decision." Ho-Kwon, a loyal Korean son, did not hesitate, but it meant putting his personal interests and ambitions indefinitely on hold. He had to work six days a week, every week, year after year, passing up all opportunities to travel or take vacations, even for a weekend. He became the public face of White Pearl Cleaners, known to his customers as Brian, and earned a reputation for being friendly and solicitous. The business had dozens of five-star ratings on Yelp, the online customer review site, and with a prime location on Wilson Boulevard in Arlington, it was profitable year after year.

Ho-Kwon's friendship with Álvaro and Fasih gave him a welcome break from the long hours at his business, and their late night discussions about what could be done with White Pearl always excited him and left him full of optimism. In the end, however, there was no way around his father's refusal to tamper with a proven model, his aversion to risk, or his opposition to anyone outside the immediate family taking a management role in the business. Álvaro saw no future for himself working with Ho-Kwon, at least in the short term, and he left the enterprise. There was no bitterness, and their friendship was unaffected.

One of the things that united the three boys and other immigrant youth was the sense of obligation they had to their parents. A common theme of the immigrant narrative in America was parental sacrifice for the sake of their children's future. Álvaro, Fasih, and Ho-Kwon were all keenly aware of the struggles their parents had endured in order to start new lives in America and make possible a better life for their children, and they were determined to repay them. All three of them were still living at home at an age when many of their American peers had moved out, less because of their dependence on their parents than because of their parents' dependence on them. When Ho-Kwon left home at the age of twenty-six, he had to deal with his father's anger. "What do you think you're doing?" he said. "Why would you do this?" Fasih Khan and his brother Muzammil not only lived at home but also helped with their parents' housing expenses, paying a portion of the mortgage. Both had well-paying jobs and could easily have afforded to live on their own, but chose to stay out of duty. When asked by their friends why they still lived with their parents, they would explain it as a case instead of their parents living with them. Álvaro Alarcón stayed at home through most of his twenties. He did live for a time in Washington and New York City, but he went back to living with his parents when his mother, Rhina, had a bout with cancer and help was needed around the house.

From the time he chose to drop out of college rather than rack up a big student loan debt, Álvaro followed his father's career example, working at a succession of jobs and developing a variety of practical skills. Over the next decade, his moves from one job to another did not reflect trouble adjusting to a work setting as much as his interest in exploring different occupations. Like his father, he had entrepreneurial instincts and curiosity about what was required to succeed in one field or another. He worked in restaurants for a time and learned to cook, eventually rising to a sous chef position at a Le Pain Quotidien café in Washington, D.C. He would have stayed in the industry but was put off by the amount of time that went into cleaning. "Half of your time is taken up with those chores," he said. "They never tell you that." Still, Álvaro became comfortable in the kitchen and often cooked at home for friends and family. His experience in dry cleaning shops set him up for a management position in that business had it not been for the difficulty of breaking into a world that in the D.C. area was predominantly Korean. Through his dad, Álvaro got a job at Kinko's, where he became proficient at graphic design. And then there was social work, a field to which he was intermittently drawn between other jobs.

One of his first work experiences after his stint in college was at Northern Virginia Family Services, a nonprofit agency that provided a variety of social services to families in need. Álvaro worked as a counselor, almost entirely with immigrant youth, and it suited him well. Coming from a solid family background, with loving and supportive parents, he had the self-assurance required of someone dealing with youth in the midst of personal crises; he also knew firsthand the hardship of growing up poor in an often unfriendly world. His parents frequently had to work night shifts, and he and Victor Jr. were left in charge of their younger brother, an experience that gave them maturity beyond their years. Counseling other immigrant youth came naturally to Álvaro, and although he needed regular breaks from the stress and long hours associated with social work, he returned again and again to the field. Over the years, following his initial experience at Northern Virginia Family Services, he counseled foster children, worked at a Latin American youth center in Washington, and coordinated education programs for a nonprofit group in New York City, where he lived for a time with his brother.

After his New York experience, Álvaro returned to northern

Virginia to help his friend Fasih Khan launch a business in sales outsourcing. Álvaro was often torn between his interest in social work and his passion for business, and he regularly went back and forth between the two fields. He and Fasih were both determined to become successful entrepreneurs, and when one venture proved unsuccessful, they explored another. After their experimentation with third party sales, they formed a company they called Sagan Entertainment, providing a variety of party services, from photo booth rental to videography and custom cakes, made by Álvaro's aunt Gloria. They promoted the business through the online consumer service Thumbtack, sought Internet marketing support through a Meetup group, and before long were busy with events every weekend. But Álvaro was not yet ready to leave social work, even while launching new businesses. After being away from the organization for several years, he returned to Northern Virginia Family Services in 2013, working largely around gang prevention.

About three fourths of the NVFS clients by then were from immigrant families, and the agency's work largely involved the negative side of the immigration experience. After a few months on the job, drawing on recollections from his own childhood and his prior work with Latino youth, Álvaro could list the characteristic situations that accounted for the vast majority of his cases. Those immigrants who came illegally or without marketable skills or literacy in any language frequently fell into deep poverty, with few prospects for moving up. To the extent their children became more integrated culturally in America, it was often by becoming part of a vast underclass, composed of immigrants and nonimmigrants alike. They exemplified the "segmented acculturation" phenomenon, meaning an acculturation experience that transcends ethnic lines but is limited by rigid class distinctions. "A ton of kids fall through the cracks," Álvaro said, and when they did, they often dropped out of school and slipped into gang activity or other criminal behavior.

Family dysfunction was a major problem area. One of the most frequent patterns arose when adult immigrants had to wait several years before they were able to bring their children to join them in America. In the meantime, the children had adjusted to life in the old country on their own, or with permissive grandparents or other relatives, and when they were reunited in America with parents who wanted to reestablish their authority, they often rebelled. "It's a whole new family dynamic," Álvaro said, "and the parents aren't prepared for it." As a case worker, Álvaro would often be asked to intervene in such situations, and generally he had strong words for the immigrant parents. "He won't listen to me!" they would complain. "Why should he?" Álvaro would say. "He doesn't know you!"

Álvaro would probe a boy for the stories he had never shared with his parents, stories that helped explain why the son could not relate to these people he barely knew. A boy coming from El Salvador or Guatemala may well have been beaten up by criminal gangs during his childhood. He may have been threatened. The house where he was living may have been robbed. He may have been homeless for a time or gone without eating. "In that case," Álvaro said, "I will tell the kid, 'How can you expect them to help you if they don't even know what took place? I know this is a new relationship with your parents, but at some point you have to feel comfortable enough to share these things, so they can be more aware of what's going on with you and more respectful of your situation.'" Such problems were compounded when the immigrant parents had had a new child in the intervening years, or had gotten divorced and remarried, with new stepchildren added to the family. In such cases, the son or daughter who "parachuted" into the household from another country after a long separation had to deal with a new sibling with a far more secure place in the family.

Some immigrant parents dealt more successfully with these challenges than others. Marta Quintanilla left her two young sons behind in El Salvador when she emigrated at the age of seventeen. Erick was three years old and René was just an infant. She spoke to them often by telephone as they were growing up, but almost twenty years passed before she was able to bring them both to the United States, and they were virtual strangers when they finally joined her. Inevitably, it was hard. The boys accused her of having abandoned them and repeatedly asked why she had left. They dismissed her explanation that she had to become a permanent resident before she could bring them to the country legally and that there was no way she would allow them to make an overland journey without papers, which had become even more dangerous than when she made the trip in 1992. Her husband, Troy, scolded the boys for not acknowledging how hard their mother had worked to bring them to America, but it was no use. Erick and René were especially jealous of their half brother, Jonis, who was born in the United States a year after Marta arrived in the country and whom they thought was favored. They found their own housing as soon as they were able and often shunned family gatherings. Theirs was precisely the situation that often led to family crises and required the intervention of social workers like Álvaro Alarcón, but Marta dealt with her boys sympathetically and continued to support them, ignoring any abuse they directed toward her. Her patience paid off. Within two years of their arrival in America, both boys had jobs and were supporting themselves, had avoided trouble, and were slowly mending fences with Marta, their stepdad, and their half brother, Jonis.

As an NVFS case worker, Álvaro routinely dealt with similar situations and some that were far more challenging. One day in October 2013, he got a call from a local high school counselor, asking for his help. A student I will call Julio, the son of Salvadoran immigrants, had been suspended from school for carrying a weapon and was facing possible criminal charges. He lived in a low-income neighborhood where MS-13, the Salvadoran gang, was active, and he had encountered some wannabe gangsters on the street. Julio himself was born in the United States, spoke English fluently, and tended to be a bit cocky. The young thugs, some of whom attended Julio's high school, were relatively recent arrivals from El Salvador and most of them were undocumented. Apparently wanting to put Julio in his place, they jumped him. After Julio identified the thugs in a meeting with the school's gang task force coordinator, the same crew jumped a close friend of Julio's and hacked him with a machete, sending the boy to the hospital. Julio figured the attackers were sending him a message, and he began carrying a pocketknife for his own defense. The school's gang specialist learned of the attack and during a meeting with Julio asked whether he was carrying a weapon. Julio admitted that he had a knife and laid it on the table. Under the school's zero tolerance policy on weapons, he was immediately suspended, but the counselor wanted Álvaro to meet with Julio and his family, prepare him for his court appearance, and emphasize what he needed to do to avoid another school suspension.

Over the next three months, Álvaro learned that Julio lived with his parents and siblings in a small apartment. He often slept on the couch. His mother did occasional housecleaning, but Julio's father was unemployed. Julio had almost no relationship with his parents and wanted nothing to do with them. As was often the case in such situations, Álvaro had to mediate between Julio and his parents and reestablish some family communication. Álvaro had only a community college degree, but with his own cultural background, his firsthand knowledge of life on the streets, his extensive counseling experience, and his calm manner, he could get people to share feelings they had not previously expressed. He got the family to sit down together around the dinner table, something they never did, and Álvaro had Julio tell his parents the whole story of his encounters with the gangsters, which they had never before heard in detail.

"You think this only happened to you, that you were the only one that got hurt," Álvaro told him, "but you don't see that your parents are hurt as well. Just ask your dad." When he did, Julio's father could not hold back his tears.

It was only a start. Over the next three months, Julio suffered more staggering blows, including the death of a close friend, and he sank into a deep depression. He found out his girlfriend was pregnant, and he stopped going to classes. Álvaro stayed constantly in touch with him, making himself available 24/7. "We take small steps," he said.

The factors that go into differentiating a good immigration experience from a bad one are not hard to identify. The family situation is especially important. When parents and children are separated and reunited only later, problems ensue. When families go through a migration together and maintain bonds of support, the adaptation to the new life is much smoother. The resources available to the immigrants matter; poverty makes everything more difficult. A high priority on educational advancement provides a focus and a goal for the acculturation effort and brings its own rewards. Álvaro Alarcón, Fasih Khan, and Ho-Kwon Chun all had a solid family foundation and strong parental guidance and support (even if unnecessarily strict on occasion). They enjoyed few material comforts, especially in the early years, but they were well fed and housed, and they were raised in secure surroundings. Their parents uniformly valued education and insisted that their children improve themselves. Fasih's father, Abdul Shaheed Khan, took a significant pay cut when he moved his family from Saudi Arabia to the United States; the opportunity for his children to get a good education was the benefit that mattered most to him.

One lesson in the acculturation experience of these Fairfax families is that it is inherently liberalizing when it works. As these children of immigrants became integrated into American life and society, they were more likely to become broad-minded, respectful of cultural differences, and universal in outlook, perhaps even to a greater extent than their parents may have expected or wanted. Once a young person is turned relatively loose in America, the effects of an exposure to a broader culture cannot easily be contained.

Abdul Shaheed Khan and his wife were themselves religious and hoped that their sons and daughters would remain devout Muslims as well, but they were also determined that they get the best education possible in the United States, and the schooling had some unpredictable effects. This was especially true in the case of their sons, Fasih and his brother, Muzammil, both of whom were eager learners and curious about the world outside the boundaries set by their religion. The younger, U.S.-born Muzammil, having attained a master's degree in cybersecurity by the age of twenty-three, articulated his views in conversations with his parents, with whom he remained close.

"You came over here for a reason," he would tell them. "You wanted your kids to get an education, and we're getting it. I got my undergraduate degree. I got my master's degree. I'm going to do all these certifications. I'm going to try to become successful, not only so that you can be proud and feel like coming here achieved something, but also to open the eyes of my whole extended family." He told them he realized he was probably not as religious as they would like him to be and that he understood they were not happy about that. "But then," he said, "I reminded them of all the other things they came to America for, and I said you can't have all the good things and not have some bad." He could not understand immigrants who worked hard to come to America but did not take advantage of the opportunities that the country offered. "Some of the people I've grown up with are focused just on staying happy in their little cultural bubble," he said, "not really exploring outside of it. I've started exploring. I've opened up my eyes."

In his case, it meant challenging some of the strictures associated with Islam. "The way I grew up," he said, "I learned that some things are right but not others. Talking to girls is bad. It's *haram* [sinful]. When you believe those things and then you grow up and try to become better, you get stuck. You can only go so high. You have to branch out and start talking to other people and realize, okay, it's all right to talk to women and even shake their hand. It's not disrespectful. If I had spent all my time trying to be an extremely good Muslim, I wouldn't have been able to get such a good education, to make so many friends, or to have such a good job." Muzammil by then was working as a cybersecurity auditor, assessing the vulnerability of highly classified government data networks against attacks from a cyber adversary. "I wanted to help my country," he said. "but I wasn't designed for the military, so I do something else. This is really cool. I may be able to help get some bad guys."

His older brother, Fasih, had served as a role model for Muzammil. The two of them shared an interest in technology, and as boys they built a computer tower piece by piece and worked on cars together. Fasih, who had many non-Muslim friends besides Álvaro and Ho-Kwon, had also led the way in showing how a good Muslim boy could explore the secular world and still be true to his family. He was not impressed by the Pakistani boys they knew who drank and partied and went out with girls, only to announce in their mid-twenties that they were determined to marry a devout Muslim girl who stayed home and kept herself covered, even if it meant going back to Pakistan to find one who didn't know the young man's history. Fasih was respectful of the traditions of his faith and was open to finding a Muslim mate in the customary way. At the suggestion of a friend of his sister, he had reached out to a girl from a religious family in California and even flew there to meet her, but the relationship did not click. One of his close cousins had married a Christian girl who subsequently converted to Islam. Fasih himself was open to marrying a non-Muslim girl, though he acknowledged being occasionally "confused" about how far he should go in that direction.

If it was difficult for a Muslim boy, it was far more challenging for Muslim girls, who had to decide on how they should dress in addition to setting limits (or not) on their socialization. While it is generally acceptable for a Muslim man to marry a non-Muslim woman if she converts to Islam, the option does not apply the other way around. Fasih and Muzammil had two sisters, Hiba and Nida, both born in Pakistan, who chose to wear both the hijab and the abaya, the full-length robe-like dress, and who both married Muslim men from Pakistan. For them to have done otherwise would have been controversial. Still, they had the freedom to make decisions of their own. Some of the Khan women, first cousins of Hiba and Nida, had chosen not to cover themselves.

No immigrant youth growing up in Fairfax County, Virginia, and attending public schools there could avoid the influence of other cultures. One consequence of this intermingling of populations was that acculturation worked more rapidly and thoroughly than it would have in more tightly bounded immigrant enclaves, with more relationships that crossed ethnic lines. Un Joung Kim lived with a man from Peru after she divorced her Korean husband. The daughters of Esam and Badria Omeish, Abrar and Anwar, were religious Muslim girls but they had only a few Arab friends, and both of them were active in organizations that promoted social and economic justice for all people of color. Fasih Khan, rummaging in Rhina Alarcón's kitchen, was surprised to open a cupboard one day and find a box of Shan Masala, a spice mix used in South Asian dishes. "You guys eat this?" he said. Álvaro had tasted it at the Khan house, and it was thereafter a staple of Alarcón cuisine. Álvaro himself married a girl from Jamaica.

Anti-immigrant activists who questioned whether foreigners from other cultures could become truly American could have taken a cue from the immigrant youth of Fairfax County. They built inter-ethnic bonds more naturally than many of their white Anglo classmates, who were less inclined to develop friendships that crossed racial or ethnic lines. Álvaro found that many of the people he met during his one year at college in southern Virginia expected him to be self-conscious about his Hispanic immigrant heritage, assuming that it somehow made him different. He was tempted to challenge them, saying, "I'm not the one who should feel awkward. You are. You guys live in this tiny bubble. You don't even know how out of touch you are with society." But he never said that, because he was too polite.

It is possible that Fairfax County was an outlier, with unique conditions that had little relevance elsewhere. One noteworthy fact about the county was that it was as wealthy as it was diverse, consistently ranking in the top three or four counties in the nation by per capita income, even with a quarter of its population born outside the United States. By incorporating a large immigrant population without developing immigrant enclaves, however, the county was an example of generally successful assimilation. Demographers Audrey Singer and Marie Price, after studying how immigrants had settled in Fairfax County and nearby areas, suggested in a 2008 study that a new pattern was being established, "one in which clusters of immigrants are not easily organized into distinct ethnic communities, but live in a more multiethnic context. This pattern," they wrote, "may have important implications for the long-term process of integration in American society. . . . Suburbs should be the key location in which to understand how a multiethnic society will function in the twenty-first century." The immigrant youth of Fairfax County could actually be leading the way, as America's population continues to grow more diverse.

20

POLITICS

Barack Obama's campaign for the presidency in 2008 excited non-white immigrant voters as no such contest ever had. Here was a candidate whose father was born a Muslim in Kenya, whose middle name was Hussein, and who had spent four years of his youth living in Indonesia with his white mother and Indonesian stepfather. He had both African and Asian half siblings, four on the Kenya side and one on the Indonesian side, whose husband was of Chinese ancestry.

"I learned to slip back and forth between my black and white worlds," Obama wrote in his 1995 autobiography, "understanding that each possessed its own language and customs and structures of meaning, convinced that with a bit of translation on my part the two worlds would eventually cohere." Bringing identities from different worlds into a coherent whole is a life challenge for virtually every American born outside the United States or even to immigrant parents. Barack Obama's story resonated among all those who had grown up on the margins of the U.S. experience. Whatever his politics, the idea that someone with his background could actually become president affirmed the American promise and gave immigrant Americans new reasons to engage in civic life and help build a nation where such achievements would become routine.

Among the earliest Washington insiders who signed up to work on the Obama campaign was Mark Keam, the immigrant from Korea who twenty years earlier had been inspired by the Reverend Jesse Jackson. Following law school, he had worked for the Federal Communications Commission and the Small Business Administration and then moved to Capitol Hill, where he was chief counsel to Democratic senator Dick Durbin of Illinois. As a state senator and then as the junior U.S. senator from Illinois, Obama knew Durbin well, and as a Durbin aide Keam had met Obama frequently, even volunteering for his first Senate campaign in 2004. He also felt a kinship with Obama based on their both having lived as children in unfamiliar Asian lands, Keam in Vietnam and Obama in Indonesia. In October 2006, when Obama announced on *Meet the Press* that he was considering a run for president, Keam was already thinking about leaving Capitol Hill, and a few weeks later he told Durbin he wanted to help organize support for an Obama candidacy. He had a government relations job waiting for him at Verizon, and Durbin suggested he use that position to work "downtown" for Obama, meaning in the world of lobbyists and their corporate clients on K Street. He started at Verizon the same week Obama announced his candidacy.

As an experienced congressional operative with extensive contacts in the Democratic Party, Keam was first assigned to help line up support for Obama among the unpledged "superdelegates" who had a guaranteed vote at the Democratic National Convention based on their party leadership positions. Later, he joined forces with Konrad Ng, the husband of Obama's half-sister, Maya, to establish Asian Americans for Obama. By the end of 2007 he was organizing Fairfax County, where he lived with his wife, Alex, and their two children. Despite the strong support of Governor Tim

Kaine, one of Obama's national campaign cochairs, Virginia was not yet considered fertile ground for an African American candidate. Keam and others, however, were convinced that Obama could run competitively there, both against Hillary Clinton in the primary and in the general election in the fall. The state had gone Republican in every presidential election since 1964, but a big effort in northern Virginia, with its diverse and growing population, might turn that around.

In February 2007, in his first public appearance after announcing the formation of his campaign exploratory committee, Obama had been greeted by an overflow crowd of screaming students at George Mason University in Fairfax, many of them shouting, "I love you!" Not since the GMU men's basketball team had reached the Final Four in the NCAA tournament two years earlier had a rally so rocked the school, a commuter campus where most of the students came from northern Virginia.

"This is unbelievable!" Obama had shouted that day, looking up at the students lining the balconies around the three-level atrium where he was speaking. "Settle down, you all!" he said. "Settle down! You're too fired up!" He was beaming.

Those students and others like them were an army waiting to be mobilized, and by the time Mark Keam began organizing Fairfax County for Obama in late 2007, he had more volunteers than he could handle. Within weeks, Keam had set up offices across the county and was running phone banks and canvassing operations. By the time the Obama campaign sent its first paid staffer to northern Virginia, just a few days before the February 12 primary, much of the work of identifying committed voters was already done. Obama defeated Clinton decisively in the primary, helped by a big turnout in northern Virginia. In Fairfax County, Obama triumphed in each of the nine magisterial districts, winning 59 percent of the vote countywide. The extent of his victory raised hopes that he might actually win Virginia in the general election if he secured the Democratic nomination. The statewide turnout in the Democratic primary was double the Republican turnout, and exit polls showed that a third of the voters in the Democratic race had never voted in a primary election before. Obama won 90 percent of the black vote, a majority of the Latino vote, and twice as many independents as Clinton did.

In the general election nine months later, Obama broke the modern pattern in Virginia by carrying the state, defeating John McCain by a margin of more than 6 percentage points. America's changing demography was clearly a factor, though it probably took a candidate of color like Obama to mobilize the new voter groups. In Fairfax County alone, Obama campaign workers on the eve of the presidential election claimed to be registering four to five hundred new voters each week, many of them immigrants. Across the United States, voting rates for Hispanics and Asian Americans rose significantly in 2008 from the 2004 levels, and in Virginia especially those immigrant groups were fast becoming much more important. The 2010 census would show the Hispanic share of Virginia's population increasing from 4.7 percent to 7.9 percent over the 2000 figure, while the Asian American share grew from 3.7 percent to 5.5 percent. Obama won both those groups in 2008 by large margins.

The U.S. electorate had been growing steadily more diverse for years. The number of Asian Americans registered to vote increased by 88 percent between 1996 and 2008, while the registration of Hispanic voters increased by 77 percent during that period. It was only with Obama's candidacy, however, that this new electorate had a dramatic political impact. According to exit polls, Asian Americans supported Obama over McCain by a margin of 62–35, while Latinos voted two to one for Obama. Both results represented a drop in support for the Republican candidate from the 2004 results. The shift among Asian American voters in particular was stunning. They had split 56–43 for John Kerry over George W. Bush in 2004, but in both the 1992 and 1996 elections, Asian voters had favored the Republican nominees, George H. W. Bush and Bob Dole. With both immigrant groups taking a bigger share of the electorate, the shift in their preference proved decisive.

Voters with a Muslim background switched their political allegiances even more dramatically, though in their case the shift came earlier. Many of the Muslims who moved to the United States in the years after the 1965 Immigration Act were professionals, scientists, and others of "exceptional ability," categories that were preferenced under the legislation. A large number of them were drawn to the Republican Party. Those who came later were less educated, but many were devout and tended to agree with conservative Republican positions on such issues as sex education, abortion, and same-sex marriage. A survey team from the Muslims in the American Public Square (MAPS) project at Georgetown University concluded that a plurality of Muslim voters chose George Bush over Al Gore in the 2000 election, 48 percent to 36 percent, and a survey by the Council on American-Islamic Relations showed an even sharper tilt to Bush. In response to the invasion of Iraq and the Bush administration's counterterrorism policies, however, the Muslim vote had turned decidedly in the Democrats' favor. The MAPS team found that Bush took only 7 percent of the Muslim vote in 2004, with John Kerry getting 82 percent and Ralph Nader 10 percent.

Obama's 2008 campaign energized Muslim Americans, just as it did Asian and Hispanic voters. The ADAMS mosque in Sterling, Virginia, and Dar Al-Hijrah in Falls Church both hosted more political candidates in 2008 than they ever had before. Mukit Hossain, the D.C. telecom entrepreneur who became a political activist after 9/11, could take credit for some of the Muslim mobilization. A frequent speaker at the ADAMS mosque, he emphasized the importance of political involvement, organized voter registration drives, and even arranged for taxi drivers to give people a ride to the polls. "Many of the Muslims who came to this country came from countries where voting was a dangerous and dirty thing to do," he told *The Washington Post* on the eve of the 2008 election. "We have to convince them that voting is not only safe and clean but a civic responsibility." Hossain had relaunched his political action group, making its purpose more explicit under a new name, the Virginia Muslim Political Action Committee or VMPAC.

Officially, the committee was nonpartisan, reflecting the fact that Muslims had previously supported Republican as well as Democratic candidates. In 2008, with George Bush out of the picture, anti-Republican sentiment among Muslim voters may have lessened somewhat. The McCain campaign had a committee devoted to Arab Americans and Muslim Americans, and his campaign staff met with a group of Muslim voters at the ADAMS mosque in September. Enthusiasm for Obama, however, based in part on his minority background, made up for any gains that McCain might otherwise have made with the Muslim electorate. With some right-wing activists spreading untruths about Obama being a Muslim, they rallied indignantly to his defense, and he won more than 80 percent of their vote nationwide, according to telephone polls. The tally might have been even higher, but some Muslims were disappointed that Obama did not distance himself more clearly from Bush's "war on terror." Some were further upset that he had not defended Islam on those occasions when he was accused of being a Muslim, rather than simply denying the charge and emphasizing his Christian faith.

Like others who had been associated with the campaign, Mark Keam was so energized by Obama's election that he decided he wanted to run for office himself. Actually, he had been thinking about it for years. He had always been politically ambitious, and the Obama campaign experience sealed it, convincing him that a run for office would be good not just for himself but for the Korean American community as a whole. His main political heroes were Asian American congressmen like Norman Mineta and Bob

Matsui, both of whom had been sent with other Japanese Americans to internment camps during World War II, and Daniel Inouye of Hawaii, who fought heroically in World War II as a member of an all-Japanese American unit of the U.S. Army and then went on to serve for nearly fifty years in the U.S. Congress. In connection with those examples of public service, Keam often recalled a conversation he had had with his father-in-law, when he and Alex visited her parents for lunch one day shortly after Mark had gone to work for Senator Durbin. Nak Man Seong was a man of few words, and until that day Mark could barely recall him sharing many deep thoughts.

Mark was talking that day about his work on Capitol Hill, when his father-in-law turned to him and said, "You know, my dream is that you become a congressman yourself someday." Mark and Alex were both a bit taken aback by his sudden comment, but Nak Man continued. He said that he and Alex's mother had been playing the lottery at their D.C. liquor store. "If we ever win," he said, "we'll give the money to you so you can use it for an election." He said something about how he had left Korea for America in order to give his children a chance to do things they couldn't do in Korea, and that now it was time for them to become part of the American system. It would be good if Mark could become a successful politician, he said.

A few years later, Mark brought up the conversation with Alex, though at an inopportune time. It was their wedding anniversary, and Alex was expecting a romantic date, but Mark had politics on his mind, as he so often did. They were talking about their young children, Tyler and his little sister, Brenna, and their thoughts about them and their future.

"You know, I've been thinking about running for office," Mark abruptly said. "I've done everything else. I've been in the executive branch and worked on Capitol Hill and in campaigns. The only thing left is running for office myself." Alex said nothing. "I lecture young people all the time about how they should get involved in politics, and I need to walk the walk, not just talk the talk. Whether I win or lose, it would teach our kids something, maybe give them some confidence and show them how we're part of this country and that there's no barrier that can't be overcome." Alex was staring at him blankly, but Mark kept talking. "Becoming a legislator or congressman or governor, I could show that we as Korean immigrants can do anything we want in this country."

"What in the world are you saying?" Alex finally said. "Are you crazy?" She knew what Mark launching some campaign might mean for herself, for their marriage, and for their family, and she did not like the idea at all. He reminded her what her father had said a few years earlier, but it made no difference. It was not what she wanted to hear, especially on their anniversary.

"She freaked out," Mark acknowledged, recalling the moment years later.

"He ruined our whole lunch," Alex said in her own recollection. "For the rest of the meal, I couldn't enjoy it. It was awful. I told him he should never bring up a touchy subject like that at such an important time."

Mark dropped it, but the idea of running for elective office never left him, and after Mark saw how transformative Obama's election had been for so many people, his resolve returned. This time, Alex gave her consent. She had all her old reservations, but it was hard to argue with the energy and passion that Obama had produced in Mark and everyone associated with his campaign. Besides, a once-in-a-lifetime opportunity had just presented itself. Just prior to the presidential election, the Keams's local representative in the Virginia House of Delegates, Steve Shannon, announced he would not seek reelection in 2009, planning instead to run for Virginia attorney general, and he told Mark that he should compete for the open seat. The 35th District, entirely within Fairfax County, included the Tysons Corner shopping district, parts of the wealthy suburb of McLean, and the communities of Oakton and Vienna, where Mark and Alex lived. Mark knew virtually every square inch of the territory, having just organized it for Obama. His employers at Verizon agreed to give Mark an unpaid leave of absence so he could devote full time to a campaign.

It would be a tough contest. He would first have to win the Democratic primary in June. Obama's decisive victory across Fairfax County showed the Democrats' strength there; the 35th District would be alluring for any possible Democratic candidate. Before long, Mark had three competitors for the nomination. John Carroll, a former Fairfax County prosecutor, was running. So was Roy Baldwin, another lawyer, endorsed by the Sierra Club. The third candidate was a political novice, a physician, and an immigrant like Keam, with his own inspiring story. He was born in Libya, and he was a Muslim. His name was Esam Omeish.

Mukit Hossain was constantly looking for Muslims who would be good political candidates and places where they could run with a chance of winning. Steve Shannon's decision not to seek reelection offered one of the most promising opportunities in years. As soon as he heard of the opening, he contacted Omeish, with whom he had worked often over the years, and urged him to consider running. Omeish took an immediate interest. Months earlier, he had resigned his leadership positions in both the Muslim American Society and the Dar Al-Hijrah mosque. In part, he was frustrated that he had not been able to move his Muslim community beyond its status quo positions; he also wanted to develop his profile and influence outside the Muslim community. His forced resignation from the governor's immigration commission a year earlier had left him wanting to develop a wider reputation and leadership role in American society. "I don't want to be labeled through the 9/11 lens," he said. Omeish established an exploratory committee and gave Hossain a $5,000 per month contract to begin organizing a campaign. In January he formally announced he was running for the 35th District seat in the Virginia House of Delegates.

With four candidates in the mix, it might be hard to get a lot of attention, but the competition between Omeish and Keam would be the most compelling story in the race. If either won the primary and then the general election, history would be made. Neither an Asian American immigrant nor an immigrant who was a religious Muslim had ever been elected to the state legislature. An Arab American born in Lebanon to a Muslim family was serving in the House of Delegates, but he was no longer active in his faith. Keam and Omeish both carried a burden of immigrant expectations on their shoulders.

For Omeish in particular, however, it would be an uphill battle. The "jihad" comments that ended his immigration commission appointment were certain to come back. He had no experience in politics and no professional staff apart from his adviser Hossain. He could not afford to take time off from his hospital duties. Mark Keam had a six-month leave of absence from his Verizon job, and he had just spent nearly a year organizing a campaign in the very communities where he would now be running. He knew his way around, and in the months before the primary he would be able to knock on virtually every door in the district. For Omeish, daily campaigning had to wait until he finished at the hospital, and when he was on call he had to be prepared to drop whatever he was doing and go back to surgery. On evenings when he was free, Badria would meet him in the driveway with some food as soon as he came home, and he would head off immediately to make phone calls or go door-to-door. His one asset was Mukit Hossain, who had raised some funds through the Virginia Muslim Political Action Committee. Hossain knew his way around the state capital, where many legislators knew him by his first name, and he introduced several of them to Omeish. He organized materials and briefings for Omeish on policy issues in such areas as transportation and education, and he helped prepare him for debates and candidate forums.

One area where Omeish and Keam were relatively competitive with each other was in fund-raising. Both had access to donors who had a special interest in their candidacies by virtue of their immigrant backgrounds. Keam had extensive contacts in the Korean American community in Los Angeles, while Omeish had financial support from Dearborn, Michigan, long a center of Arab American influence and money. In addition, both candidates relied on their own professional networks, Keam in telecommunications and Omeish in medicine. In the six months leading up to the June 2009 primary, Keam raised $194,000, more than half of it from outside Virginia, and Omeish raised $144,000, with about $27,000 raised out of state. In addition, Omeish contributed $52,000 of his own money. Those fund-raising totals put them in the top four of all candidates running in Virginia delegate races, but the money was necessary. Running for office in Fairfax County, where voters were relatively wealthy and well educated and where advertising rates were higher, was far more expensive than elsewhere in the state, especially on a per vote basis. Party primary elections in an off-year, when only a few elective offices are contested, typically draw only a few thousand voters. The other two candidates in the 35th District race, John Carroll and Roy Baldwin, both trailed Keam and Omeish significantly in money totals.

The Keam and Omeish platforms featured generic Democratic ideas. Keam focused more on transportation, Omeish on health care, but otherwise there was little to distinguish them. In his general campaign strategy, however, Keam gave more emphasis to his immigrant story. He hired a political consultant, Anil Mammen, whose firm produced separate mailings to Korean, Vietnamese, and Chinese voters, all in their own languages. "I am proud of my Korean heritage," Keam told Korean voters, and the mailing was headlined

"A Korean American Success Story." In his Vietnamese mailing, he noted that his family had moved to Saigon when he was a boy and that his father, a Presbyterian minister, had been imprisoned for a year by the Vietnamese Communists. The mailing featured the flag of South Vietnam, which was abandoned after the country fell under Communist rule. His "special message to Chinese Americans" highlighted his appointment to the Asian American Advisory Board of Virginia and his role as an advocate for the civil rights of Asian Americans. Each of the groups was relatively small, but in a primary race, with a tiny turnout, mobilizing small groups can be an effective strategy.

In fact, there were few places anywhere in the United States where it made more sense for an Asian American to run for public office than in Fairfax County. At the time, people of Asian ancestry made up about 16 percent of the county population, higher than the Asian percentage in New York City or California, and their share was steadily growing. No other nonwhite racial or ethnic group in the county came close. Nearly a quarter of the Asian Americans in Fairfax County were from a Korean background. As a member of the House of Delegates, Keam would have an opportunity to play a key leadership role on behalf of Asian Americans in northern Virginia and even statewide, and it was a message that his campaign highlighted.

Esam Omeish, on the other hand, barely mentioned his immigrant story in his public appearances, nor did he talk much about what it was like to be a Muslim in northern Virginia after 9/11. If elected, he would have been one of the few doctors in the Virginia legislature, and he highlighted his selection in 2007 as the Inova Alexandria Hospital's "Outstanding Physician of the Year." When asked by a suburban newspaper what piece of legislation he would most like to pass as a member of the House of Delegates, his answer was "a bill that will increase access to health care in Virginia." There was nevertheless little doubt that his fellow Muslims were his core constituency, as was evident from the number of women in headscarves at his campaign kickoff rally at a fire station in Vienna. He made no effort to hide his Muslim background, but he did not feature it the way Mark Keam stressed his Asian American heritage. Omeish always wore an American flag pin in his lapel, and on Memorial Day he released a message honoring veterans, saying, "Our brave, selfless, and devoted men and women have fought and died to protect the rights and freedoms we all enjoy every day." He told a reporter that his resignation under pressure from the immigration commission two years earlier was the result of "a campaign to project me as extremist. I am a staunch American patriot," he said, "and I love this land."

It was not enough. *The Washington Post*'s Marc Fisher, writing in his "Raw Fisher" blog in April 2009, said Omeish's reference to "the jihad way" in his Jerusalem Day speech in 2000 showed he was a "Muslim fundamentalist rabble-rouser," while a reporter for *Washington Jewish Week* brought the Omeish speech to the attention of several Democratic leaders and then solicited their reactions, which not surprisingly were uniformly negative. Mark Keam and the other candidates running against Omeish in the June primary closely followed the controversy over his comments, but did not draw attention to them. John Carroll told a reporter for Fox News that most voters in the district were familiar with what Omeish had said, but then added, "He's about as nice a guy as you can meet. He's really championed health care for the uninsured."

Mark Keam easily triumphed in the June primary, with 55 percent of the total vote, needing only 3,653 votes for the win. Esam Omeish finished third, ahead of Roy Baldwin but slightly behind John Carroll. The recycling of his old "jihad" comments undoubtedly damaged his candidacy. *The Washington Post*, which endorsed Keam, said the Omeish comments nine years earlier about the Palestinian struggle "should be a disqualifier." Steven Emerson's Investigative Project on Terrorism, whose highlighting of the Jerusalem

Day speech had cost Omeish his seat on the immigration commission, once again took credit for his downfall. Emerson had reminded his readers of the comments, and he singled out the Omeish performance in his reporting on the primary race. "Omeish Campaign Crashes in VA Primary" was the headline. As a Muslim, it would have been hard for Omeish to win under any circumstances. A 2007 survey by the Pew Research Center found that being Muslim was a huge disadvantage for any political candidate. Of twenty-three character traits listed, "Muslim" ranked near the bottom in terms of attractiveness. Forty-six percent of the respondents said they would be "less likely" to support someone who was Muslim, against just one percent who said they would be "more likely." The only traits that ranked lower for a possible candidate were "doesn't believe in God" and "never held elected office."

Keam went on to win the general election, though by a narrow margin. Overall, his own political consultants were impressed by his performance. First-time candidates, inexperienced in the art of electioneering, sometimes aim too high, but Keam's decision to begin with a race for a state legislative seat was appropriate. He was rewarded for devoting full time to his campaign, though it involved considerable financial sacrifice and risk on his part. His targeted mailings probably contributed significantly to his triumph, at least in the primary race, given how few votes he needed.

Some analysts thought Esam Omeish might have been more successful if he had spoken more often of his immigrant heritage and if he had dealt preemptively with the "jihad" comments that he surely knew would be revived. He later acknowledged that his campaign effort could have been managed more effectively, but his duties as a physician could not be set aside as easily as Mark Keam's work. Omeish was gracious in defeat and warmly endorsed Keam's candidacy. "Today is a celebration of the diversity of our Virginia and the robustness of our great democracy," he said in his concession message. "People from all different communities came out to choose a more representative General Assembly to reflect the beautiful colors of Virginia." He did not abandon hopes of running for office again and kept his databases up to date and his campaign website active for years to come. Though he continued to give guest sermons at Friday prayer services around the D.C. area, including in the U.S. Congress, he no longer sought leadership positions in Muslim organizations.

Members of Virginia's House of Delegates earn $17,640 a year for their services, along with a meager $170 per diem for the time they have to spend in Richmond while the legislature is in session. Mark Keam took an unpaid leave of absence from Verizon for six months to run his primary campaign in 2009, another unpaid leave to prepare for the general election, and then a third for the opening of the legislative session in early 2010. During all that time and during other periods of Keam's political or legislative work, Alex was the family breadwinner, as well as the primary parent of their two children. As a staff attorney for the U.S. Patent and Trademark Office, Alex had the option of telecommuting from home, and that arrangement made it possible to handle all her responsibilities, but it was not easy. The death of her mother in 2004 had been a heavy blow. She had good reasons for reacting negatively to Mark's initial mention of a possible political career, but she was also proud of what he accomplished, especially as he became a celebrated figure in Korean American circles across the United States and even in South Korea. She knew her father supported Mark's political career, and after his death in 2010 she believed it was her duty to support her husband, just as her father had.

In Richmond, Keam was acutely aware of his status as one of just two Asian American legislators and the only Asian immigrant. The state capitol, where the House of Delegates and the Virginia Senate held their legislative sessions, dated from 1788, and it was where the Confederate States of America had convened their Congress during the Civil War. Keam preferred to think of it as a building designed by Thomas Jefferson. He was nevertheless gratified to be named to the Virginia Sesquicentennial of the American Civil War Commission, especially since it was committed to including African American and Union views on the war, in addition to the Confederate perspective. As a Democrat, he was in the minority in Richmond, and as one of the younger legislators in a chamber dominated by old white males, his influence was limited. The legislation he proposed was for the most part noncontroversial, focusing on transportation, education, public safety, and consumer issues. He was unopposed in his run for reelection in 2011, and with each year of additional seniority he had more opportunity to speak out on the issues on that mattered most to him.

In February 2012, Keam took to the floor in the House of Delegates in Richmond to make a speech. "I don't stand up a lot," he said, "because I have this mentality that anything I have to share you've probably heard before." But it was Black History Month, and he said he wanted to share his perspective on the occasion, "based on my experiences growing up here as an immigrant." He saluted the speaker of the house, William Howell, for appointing him to the Civil War Sesquicentennial Commission, noting that Howell said his role would be to represent "the new Virginia," and then he segued to the story of his family's arrival in the United States, tying it to the achievements of civil rights activists twenty years earlier. "It wasn't until they did their part that Congress passed the Immigration and Nationality Act in 1965," he said, "and that law was significant, because it was the first time that our immigration laws finally reflected the principle . . . that all people of all backgrounds, of all colors, of all origins from around the world can come here equally. I would not be standing here today if it weren't for that 1965 law," he concluded, "and that law would not have passed if it were not for the struggle of African Americans before. We really have to understand the history of how we all got here." To his surprise, the mostly conservative white legislators in the chamber gave him an ovation.

In July 2012, Barack Obama was on the campaign trail again, and he was back in Fairfax County, back among young people. On a muggy Saturday afternoon, he rallied a wildly cheering crowd in the Centreville High School gymnasium. Near the front were Abrar and Anwar Omeish, the daughters of Esam and Badria. Anwar, who was sixteen, had been volunteering at one of the local Obama campaign offices, preparing maps and packets for canvassers, helping with voter registration, and making phone calls. Those efforts got her and Abrar VIP passes to the Centreville rally, and when Obama moved into the crowd after the speech, Abrar managed to push Anwar to the front, directly facing the president. Both girls were wearing red, white, and blue American flag headscarves, and Obama walked right up to Anwar, clearly charmed.

"I love you!" she blurted, too nervous to say anything else and so excited that tears filled her eyes. Anwar later told a reporter for her high school newspaper that she'd been going to campaign rallies with her dad since she was four years old and that as a twelve-year-old during the 2008 election she had made phone calls for the Obama campaign. "I've been a Democrat since birth," she said.

The 2012 presidential results provided new evidence that the demographic changes in America were tilting the electorate in the Democrats' favor. The white share of the voting population was continuing to decline, as it had for twenty years, while the Hispanic and Asian-origin shares were rising, and both those groups went solidly for Obama. Exit polls in 2012 showed him getting 71 percent of the Hispanic vote and a stunning 73 percent of the Asian vote. The results set off alarm bells among Republican political analysts. When asked by a Fox News anchor why Republican Mitt Romney was unable to defeat Obama, conservative commentator Bill O'Reilly answered simply, "Because it's a changing country. It's not a traditional America anymore," apparently meaning that "traditional" America had been a whiter nation. Romney got just 17 percent of the nonwhite vote in 2012. Any future Republican candidate would have to do far better with those voters to win a general election, because the United States was on its way to becoming a nation in which non-Hispanic, native-born whites would be in the minority. (Two years later, the Census Bureau announced that this tipping point would come in 2045. By 2060, non-Hispanic whites would constitute just 44 percent of the total population.)

The declining fortunes of the Republicans and the ascendancy of the Democrats, however, had at least as much to do with positions the two parties took as it did with the changes in the electorate. For several years after 1965, Democrats were not necessarily seen as natural allies of immigrants. Organized labor was a key part of the Democrats' political base, and unions often saw immigrants as undercutting their interests, because of their apparent willingness to work for lower wages. It was only when union numbers went into sharp decline that labor leaders began to see immigrants as workers to be organized rather than as competitors to be shut out. With that new union perspective, the Democratic Party also became much more pro-immigrant. Republicans, meanwhile, having courted Hispanic voters with some success during the Reagan years, began taking a tougher line toward undocumented immigrants, and that cost them some support, at least with the Hispanic population.

During the 2012 campaign, Mitt Romney suggested that Latinos who were in the United States illegally should "self-deport," while other positions he took were unpopular with other immigrant groups. He bashed China repeatedly over trade issues, potentially angering some Asian American voters. Some Republicans, especially those associated with the Tea Party movement, engaged in anti-Muslim or anti-Islam rhetoric, further alienating a minority group that had previously voted in their favor. Republican attacks on Obamacare may have turned off both Hispanic voters, for whom better access to health care was a top concern, and Korean American workers, a quarter of whom are self-employed and therefore without employer-provided health insurance.

As the Republican Party moved to the right, its attitude toward immigrants became increasingly hostile. A Pew Research Center survey of political attitudes in 2014 identified a "Steadfast Conservative" group in the electorate that was "solidly Republican" and held clearly negative views of immigrants. Whereas 57 percent of the overall survey sample agreed with a statement that immigrants "strengthen our country through hard work and talents," the Steadfast Conservatives took the opposite view, with 73 percent saying immigrants "burden our country." Similarly, 59 percent of the respondents said the growing number of newcomers in the United States "strengthens American society," but 81 percent of the Steadfast Conservatives said the immigrant influx "threatens traditional American customs and values." Some moderate Republicans urged their party to be more accommodating of immigrants, but other analysts suggested that as long as mass immigration continued, Democrats stood to gain, no matter what position the Republicans took. A 2010 study sponsored by the Center for Immigration Studies found that immigration was causing "a steady drop in presidential Republican vote shares throughout the country" and dismissed the idea that there was much the party could do to bring about a different outcome. "The propensity for immigrants, and especially Latinos, to be swing voters has been wildly exaggerated by wishful-thinking Republican politicians and business-seeking pollsters who refuse to acknowledge the durability of individual party identification," the report concluded. If that were truly the case, the Republicans were definitely in trouble. A 2015 study by the analytic firm IHS, Inc., concluded that Hispanics in the U.S. workforce were replacing non-Hispanics at such a rate that they would claim more than 40 percent of the U.S. employment increase in the years leading up to 2020 and 75 percent by 2034.

In actual fact, the "durability" of an immigrant's party identification was highly questionable. In John Kennedy's time, the white "ethnic" vote was considered reliably Democratic, but Ronald Reagan captured it twenty years later. Cuban Americans were securely in the Republican column during many election cycles, but their party identification has loosened in recent years. Muslim voters and Asian Americans both switched allegiances in dramatic fashion, and there was no reason to think they could not switch again. Even in 2012, when three out of four Asian American voters went for Obama, a survey found that nearly half of them did not identify with either political party, and the number of undecided Asian American voters was three to four times the national average just one month before Election Day. The Center for Immigration Studies was an offshoot of the Federation for American Immigration Reform, which for thirty years had been promoting curbs on immigration. A CIS suggestion that the Republican Party had little hope of attracting immigrant voters may have not reflected sound political analysis as much as a desire to persuade Republicans that pro-immigration positions would not serve the Republican Party interest.

Evidence that immigrant voters could change their political preferences was not long in coming. In the 2014 midterm elections, exit polls suggested that Republicans made gains among both Hispanic and Asian voters in comparison to 2012. In Virginia's 10th Congressional District, which includes part of Fairfax County and areas beyond, Republican Barbara Comstock targeted Vietnamese, Chinese, Korean, Indian, and Filipino communities with outreach activities and won her race decisively. In the aftermath of the results, political consultant Anil Mammen, whose firm prepared the mailings that Mark Keam directed toward his Vietnamese, Korean, and Chinese constituents, warned his fellow Democrats not to take immigrant voters for granted.

"This is a constituency whose political alliances could shift dramatically over time," he argued, "particularly as some of these groups get more established, with higher income and more education. Once they develop a sense of economic confidence and their place in America, they lose that immigrant mentality, and then their partisanship will have more to do with economic status and educational attainment." Mammen, himself of South Asian origin, was one of the Democratic Party's leading experts on targeted mail campaigns. He challenged the candidates for whom he worked that the debate over immigration policy, including the challenge of handling undocumented newcomers, might not play out the way Democrats figured it would. Most Asian Americans, the fastest growing immigrant group in the United States, came to the country as a result of the 1965 Immigration Act, Mammen pointed out, not by sneaking into the country illegally. "That law allowed a lot of great things to happen for America," he said. "The American tradition is [represented by] this wonderful piece of legislation that was passed fifty years ago, but it was *a law*." Rather than focus on "amnesty" proposals, Mammen argued, the Democratic Party should commemorate the passage of the 1965 Act and other laws that facilitated increased immigration. "But that's not the Democratic Party's message today," he said. "Their message today seems to be that people who didn't respect the law should be given preference over people waiting in line, throughout Latin America, throughout Asia, throughout Africa."

For immigrant advocates, the ultimate goal was not affiliation with one party or another but empowerment. Despite their growing share of the U.S. population, the level of political participation among foreign-born U.S. citizens was lower than it was for U.S. natives. In 2012, only 56 percent of Asian American citizens and 59 percent of Hispanic citizens were registered to vote, compared to 72 percent of whites and 73 percent of African Americans. Their political representation was even weaker. A survey by the New American Leaders Project in 2014 reported that while Latinos and Asian Americans made up 22 percent of the U.S. population, they held fewer than 2 percent of elected positions nationwide, at all levels from local school boards to the U.S. Congress. The group's tally of immigrant members of state legislatures across the country found just four states—Hawaii, California, Arizona, and New Mexico—where Latino and Asian Americans were represented in numbers close to their share of the state populations. Eleven states were given an "F" grade by the group for not having a single Latino or Asian American state legislator. Virginia was one of eighteen states graded "D" for their immigrant representation. To reach parity with the immigrant share of their population, those eighteen states would need a sixfold increase in the combined number of Latino and Asian American state legislators. A separate study in 2010 found only ten Muslim state legislators in the entire country. The power of the foreign-born and their children had yet to be exercised and felt.

21

AMERICANIZATION

The ceremony in which Marta Quintanilla Call became a U.S. citizen was held in a cavernous high school auditorium in Oakton, Virginia. She and 499 other immigrants stood, put their hands on their hearts, and repeated the oath of allegiance, prompted by a woman on the stage. Next came a videotaped congratulatory message from President Obama and a slide show of American scenery accompanied by a recording of Lee Greenwood singing "God Bless the USA." The country hit, played incessantly on radio stations after the 9/11 attacks and again after Osama bin Laden was killed, would have struck some of the immigrant Americans as inappropriate if they knew what the songwriter actually thought about foreigners. "If America changes to the point that it is no longer a Christian nation and no longer protects itself from aliens who come and go," Greenwood said in 2010, "then it won't be America anymore." The new citizens nevertheless seemed to feel welcomed. At the end of the ceremony, they cheered and waved the little American flags they received with their naturalization certificate.

Though the ceremony was not personal or intimate (or culturally

328 A Nation of Nations

sensitive), its very size made it impressive, because of the diversity
on display. The people who filled the auditorium that morning in
August 2014 came from eighty-two countries (about half with a
non-Christian heritage) and represented nearly all the nationalities on the planet. Many of the women wore headscarves, and
some of the men wore skullcaps. Three of the top four countries
represented—India, Pakistan, and Ethiopia—had prior to 1965
been allocated only a few U.S. visa slots per year.

The fourth country was El Salvador, Marta Quintanilla's native land. Along with her, thirty-seven other Salvadorans took the
citizenship oath. For Marta, the ceremony was the culmination of
a sojourn in America that had begun twenty-two years earlier at a
detention center on the Texas-Mexico border. America to her was
the place where imagined futures did not seem hopelessly out of
reach, as they would have in the village where she was raised. She
wore a new black dress for the occasion and had her hair highlighted with a blond streak. A colleague from her Days Inn cleaning
job met her at the high school with a dozen red roses, which Marta
held throughout the ceremony. Her husband and their two young
children, Kimberly and Carlos, accompanied her to the ceremony,
as did Jonis, Marta's son from her first marriage. They celebrated
afterward at the International House of Pancakes. Erick and René,
the two sons from El Salvador, were still resentful of her and jealous
of Jonis, and they skipped the ceremony. Both nevertheless wanted
to follow in their mother's footsteps and intended to apply for citizenship themselves as soon as they could. René, the younger, said he
wanted to join the Army.

In theory, the decision to become a U.S. citizen separates migrants who want only to take advantage of economic opportunity
from those who are ready to acquire a new national identity. It suggests an ideological commitment that goes beyond the intent to
live and work in the United States simply for money. As a "legal
permanent resident," Marta Quintanilla Call could have stayed
in the United States indefinitely while retaining her Salvadoran

citizenship, but she was determined to vote in U.S. elections, carry a U.S. passport, and be as much a part of America as her husband and three U.S.-born children. One reason Chinese migrant workers encountered such hostility in the western U.S. in the nineteenth century was that they were not seen as coming to the country to start new lives. The men often journeyed alone, under labor contracts, and intended eventually to return to their families in China. The idealized immigration story is that people come to America freely, with a willingness to participate fully in the country's life.

A similar criticism was sometimes made of Hispanic immigration. A 2013 study by the Pew Hispanic Center found that people arriving from other parts of the world were almost twice as likely to become U.S. citizens as were those coming from Mexico or Central America. One possible explanation was the proximity of their homelands, which made it easier for these Hispanics to maintain old bonds that might otherwise be broken by the migration experience. Critics of Hispanic immigration also pointed to the prevalence of Spanish-speaking communities in the United States, suggesting that this showed that Hispanics were not assimilating. Samuel Huntington argued in his 2004 book *Who Are We?* that the scale and persistence of immigration from Mexico and the rest of Latin America, along with the widespread and continuing use of Spanish by immigrants from those countries, "could change America into a culturally bifurcated Anglo-Hispanic society with two national languages."

But the delay in Hispanic assimilation was also tied to other factors, notably poverty and low educational attainment, often associated with a lack of self-confidence. A 2000 survey of Salvadoran immigrant parents with children in Fairfax County public schools found that fewer than 30 percent had completed high school, and more than 80 percent reported household incomes of less than $40,000 per year. Marta Quintanilla could have applied for U.S. citizenship earlier than she did, but she did not feel ready. To become a citizen, she had to be able to speak, read, write, and understand basic

English and demonstrate some knowledge of U.S. government and history. Having reached only the fourth grade in her rural Salvadoran school, she was barely literate in Spanish, much less in English, and the burden of raising children and struggling constantly to make ends meet had left little time for education.

To prepare for the language and civic tests and learn more about the naturalization process, Marta attended nightly citizenship classes sponsored by Catholic Charities. Volunteer instructors tutored her and fellow immigrants on such matters as the number of senators and representatives in the Congress and the roles of the legislative, executive, and judicial branches of government. The immigrants needed to learn what led to the Declaration of Independence and what was in the U.S. Constitution. The students could continue in the class as long as they wanted, and Marta became one of the stalwarts, often reassuring others who were feeling overwhelmed by the material and the language barrier. "I was afraid to come to this class the first time," she told a Senegalese woman who was ready to give up. "I have been in this country for more than twenty years, but the first time I came to this class, it was like I was in the country for the first day."

A close evaluation of Hispanic acculturation data suggests there was scant reason to worry that their growing presence in the country would dilute America's national identity or lead to cultural separatism. The 2000 Fairfax County survey of Salvadoran immigrants like Marta Quintanilla found that while 83 percent had arrived in the United States with no English at all, most of their children by the time of the survey spoke English well enough to translate for them. In a 2007 article, four political scientists examined available data for Hispanic immigrants and found that they "acquire English and lose Spanish rapidly beginning with the second generation" and that their educational attainment and political attitudes suggest "a traditional pattern of political assimilation." A scholar at the RAND Corporation, after comparing the trajectories of various ethnic groups in America, found that "education advances made by Latinos are actually greater than those achieved by either Europeans or Asian migrants," meaning that as a group their educational attainment rose steadily from generation to generation. Hispanics were joining the American mainstream, just as previous immigrants had.

A broader and more difficult question was whether immigrants who became American citizens would genuinely embrace the American ideology. The woman from U.S. Citizenship and Immigration Services (USCIS) who presided at the naturalization ceremony at Oakton High School told the assembled immigrants to cheer as their origin countries were announced, and then she encouraged them to applaud again and wave their flags when they officially became Americans, as if they had been reborn. She said they should speak English whenever they could, take part in elections, and otherwise fulfill their civic responsibilities, but she also told them they should feel free to continue speaking their native language, celebrate their own cultural backgrounds, and stay true to their own religions.

The question of what it should actually mean to become American had been debated for decades. The term "assimilation" was resisted by some immigrant advocates because it suggested that people arriving from other lands were obliged to give up their distinctive histories and embrace the dominant culture in their new homeland. When almost all newcomers to America shared a European background, the question was less pressing, but that changed with the arrival of a much more diverse immigrant population after 1965. In 2006, the George W. Bush administration organized the Task Force on New Americans with representatives from twelve cabinet departments. In its report, "Building an Americanization Movement for the Twenty-first Century," the group attempted to balance the celebration of ethnic diversity and the promotion of national unity by distinguishing between the cultural and political aspects of a new citizen's identity. "The cultural sphere—traditions, religion—is up to the individual," it concluded. "The Task Force focuses on the shared common identity that binds us as Americans in the political sphere." Government policies, it said, should concern "not cultural but political assimilation," which the group defined as "embracing the principles of American democracy, identifying with U.S. history, and communicating in English."

Distinguishing between the political and cultural spheres of the American identity, however, did not address the question of whether the United States should have a common *political culture*, meaning the values, attitudes, and beliefs that shape the nation's approach to politics. Issues such as minority rights, civil liberties, the role of the state, and the place of religion in public life were largely unresolved. What, for example, was the significance of the national motto, *E pluribus unum*, which is usually translated as "Out of many, one"? One of the most provocative offerings about American identity came from the liberal historian Arthur Schlesinger, Jr., who claimed that a "cult of ethnicity has arisen among non-Anglo whites and among nonwhite minorities" and that it was endangering a distinctive American identity. "It belittles *unum* and glorifies *pluribus*," he wrote in his book *The Disuniting of America*. He detected a slackening commitment to America's unique goal, which he said "was not to preserve old cultures, but to forge a new American culture."

Schlesinger's critics countered that his "*unum*" was simply a white Anglo-Saxon construct reflective of an earlier, less diverse America, and that it could not possibly bind all Americans in the post-1965 period, whether laudable or not. "A nation of more than 130 cultural groups cannot hope to have all of them Anglo-Saxonized," wrote Molefi Kete Asante in his book *The Painful Demise of Eurocentrism*. Asante, a professor of African American Studies at Temple University, argued that Schlesinger and others who wrote critically of multiculturalism were not only out of touch with the contemporary U.S. reality but were actually advocating a vision that would divide Americans, not bring them together. "Since the American idea is not a static but a dynamic one," Asante said, "we must constantly reinvent ourselves in the light of our diverse experiences. One reason this nation works the way it does is our diversity. Try to make Africans and Asians copies of Europeans . . . and you will force the disunity Schlesinger fears."

Even the multiculturalists like Asante, however, recognized that "Americanization" brought certain obligations. Many immigrants were not accustomed to living in diverse communities, and accepting American values meant learning to respect people of different racial and cultural backgrounds. Americans of white Anglo-Saxon parentage had to appreciate the Asian or African experience, but Asians and Africans were also obliged to appreciate each other. The U.S. Commission on Immigration Reform chaired by Barbara Jordan of Texas devoted an entire chapter of its final report to "Americanization," focusing on the importance of "a covenant between immigrant and nation." The United States, the commission concluded, "assumes an obligation to those it admits, as immigrants assume an obligation to the country they chose." The commission emphasized that immigration is a voluntary act, and that those foreigners who choose to become U.S. citizens must necessarily accept certain principles, including the elevation of individual rights over collective rights. "Unlike other countries, including those from which many immigrants come," the commission said, "rights in the United States are not defined by ethnicity, religion, or membership in any group nor can immigrants be denied rights because they are members of a particular ethnic, religious, or political group." Whether such a formulation is inherently European or universal might be debated, but it would seem to put limits on the celebration of diversity per se. To adopt a position of pure cultural relativism would be to accept some customs or traditions that are antithetical to broadly accepted American values and norms. Forced marriage or genital mutilation are not to be tolerated, while freedom of expression and women's rights are not to be abridged, regardless of how other cultures or countries view such issues.

The elaboration of an American political culture that guarantees freedoms but also respects diversity is inevitably a challenge in an era when so many people of such different backgrounds are coming together. "The mutual antipathy of tribes is one of the oldest things in the world," Schlesinger observed. "Mass migrations produce mass antagonisms. The fear of the Other is among the most instinctive human reactions." While his detractors rejected Schlesinger's diagnosis of what ailed the American nation, they could not dispute the potential for conflict he identified in a more diverse America. The bigger questions were what diversity meant and how to deal with it. The critics of immigration regularly cited the prospect of increased ethnic conflict as a reason for limiting the foreign influx. Otis Graham, one of the founders of the modern restriction movement, highlighted the possibility of "weakening social cohesion, mounting class and ethnoracial division, and even regional separatism." Schlesinger argued that the multiculturalists were making things worse by not promoting commonality; the multiculturalists countered that the solution was to respect different cultural traditions.

Robert Putnam, a Harvard political scientist famous for his analysis of how and when Americans bond with each other, addressed the issue in a 2006 lecture he titled "E Pluribus Unum: Diversity and Community in the Twenty-first Century." Noting the increased ethnic diversity in the United States and other advanced countries due to rising immigration, Putnam said the consequence in the short run was reduced social solidarity. "New evidence from the U.S.," he wrote, "suggests that in ethnically diverse neighborhoods, residents of all races tend to 'hunker down.' Trust (even of one's own race) is lower, altruism and community cooperation rarer, friends fewer." But this was only a short-term phenomenon. "In the long run," he said, "successful immigrant societies have overcome such fragmentation by creating new, cross-cutting forms of solidarity and more encompassing identities." Social behavior in this vein featured what he called "bridging" interactions between individuals of different cultural backgrounds, and he saw this as an area that could be supported by public policy and institutions. "My hunch," he said, "is that at the end we shall see that the challenge is best met not by making 'them' like 'us,' but rather by creating a new, more capacious sense of 'we.'"

The foreign-born newcomers who settled in Fairfax County arrived with hopes and expectations that reflected the various circumstances driving their migrations. America came to mean different things to each of them, depending on the mind-sets they brought and the character of their immigration experience. Marta Quintanilla, coming from El Salvador, thought her life in America would be easier than it turned out to be. "It doesn't offer money," she said speaking more than twenty years after her arrival. "That's a lie. You have to work hard to live here." But after a childhood of poverty and violence, she found security in America, and that was what mattered most. "I come home from work. I park my car in the parking lot. I come into my apartment and lock the door, and I see my children sleeping," she says. "That's what America has given me. I can sleep peacefully here and not think somebody is going to come in the night. You just have to follow the rules. If I don't hang around with the gangs, nothing is going to happen to me."

For Un Joung Kim's parents, America was the place where they could be assured of the best treatment for their daughter's cerebral palsy. They had to spend several years in Argentina en route, but America was where they wanted to be. Victor Alarcón headed to the United States for the same reason his sister-in-law had come, because it offered someone with energy and initiative the chance to prosper. Abdul Shaheed Khan of Pakistan wanted to give his children the best education possible. When Esam Omeish, Alex Seong, Mark Keam, and their parents came to America, they found a country far less confining than the worlds they left behind, with more freedom and openness. Doris Meissner, a former commissioner of immigration in Washington, encountered a wide variety of immigrant experiences in her years of government service and saw a common theme. "Ultimately, it's a story of mobility," she recalled.

"People have different definitions of the American dream, but I think what runs through them all is the idea that there is an opportunity here through hard work to have a better life, for your children if not for yourself, and that it's worth the sacrifice. Wherever you came from, if you did the same amount of work, your children would be destined to follow in your footsteps. Here, they can be in a better place."

America offered big advantages over other countries, but in return the immigrants took on obligations. In some cases, it took a while to figure out exactly what was required of them. Alex Seong's mother used to tell her to keep a low profile and not make trouble. "Just be good people," she would say. "We came to this country; it's not our country. We are benefiting from the graciousness of this country, so we need to be the best people we can be." The problem with such advice is that it did not leave Alex feeling wholly American. Not until she moved to Fairfax and found herself surrounded by other people with varied backgrounds did she lose the self-consciousness she had felt as a child in rural Maryland.

Fairfax County, like other areas where immigrants settled in large numbers in the last years of the twentieth century, was a place where people of widely varying backgrounds could fit in. Un Joung Kim set out immediately to create a new American identity for herself. When her U.S. classmates and teachers tried to say "Un Joung," it always came out as "Onion," so she decided she needed a new name, just as Mark Keam and Alex Seong and other Korean youth had done. She heard of other kids called "Kim" and tried that for a while, but then she was Kim Kim, and again she got teased. Next she called herself "Cindy," a name many other Korean girls had taken, and for several years she was known as Cindy Kim. Still, she was not satisfied. "I wanted something unique," she recalled, "some name no one else had." One day, enchanted by a high school visit to an archaeological museum, she came up with Amber, after the fossil gem. "I thought, 'Amber sounds nice,'" she said. " 'Amber is going to be my name.'" So she went through yet another name change, and when she became an American citizen at the age of eighteen, her U.S. passport identified her officially as Amber Kim. The ease with which she chose new names and discarded others came from her immigrant experience; she had been straddling cultures her whole life.

Diversity in the student population in Fairfax County schools did produce conflict, but it also meant that youth became comfortable around classmates from other ethnic backgrounds. Amber Kim's boyfriend was from Peru. Álvaro Alarcón's best friend was Pakistani, and Álvaro ultimately married a girl from Jamaica. It seemed there was something about living in multicultural America that fostered more tolerant attitudes, if not in the first immigrant generation, then certainly in the second. A 2013 study by the Anti-Defamation League found that while 36 percent of Hispanic Americans born outside the United States harbored anti-Semitic views, the number dropped to 14 percent among those who were raised in the United States.

For Esam Omeish and his family, the challenge was to balance their Muslim faith with the responsibilities of American citizenship. They had the right to practice Islam freely and expect their religion to be respected, but they also had to recognize that America was organized on secular principles. Rather than separate from secular institutions, the Omeish family embraced them, especially when they reinforced their own Islamic values. When her daughters, Abrar and Anwar, transferred from an Islamic academy to Fairfax County public schools, Badria Omeish was concerned about it being difficult for them to meet new girls and decided to get them involved in Girl Scouts. She even became a troop leader. Abrar ultimately became a national delegate to the Girl Scout Council. "Girl Scout themes correlate with my faith," she told an interfaith group at the National Cathedral in May 2012. Citing the Girl Scout Law, which obliges them, among other things, to "make the world a better place and be a sister to every Girl Scout," Abrar then quoted a verse from the Quran: "O, mankind! We created you from a single pair of a male and a female and made you into nations and tribes, that ye may know each other, not that you may despise each other." As a high school sophomore, she cofounded a mentoring and tutoring program for low-income students, for which she was named a "Northern Virginian of the Year" in 2013.

Anwar Omeish, meanwhile, was inclined in a more activist direction. "It's impossible to grow up Muslim American and not have a political life," she often said. As a seven-year-old girl, she was asked to read an excerpt of a Martin Luther King speech on the Oprah Winfrey show. As a high school student, she wrote a long essay titled "I Found Him in the Ballot Box," tying together her observations of the Arab Spring, the Libyan revolution, Fourth of July celebrations in Washington, and Libyan exiles voting in their first free elections in more than four decades. On her Facebook page she described herself as "an individual, committed to social justice, inspired & frustrated & impassioned by everything. Everything is political. To think otherwise is a luxury. If you don't stand for something, you will fall for everything." Both she and her sister were top students in their schools. Abrar went to Yale, Anwar to Harvard.

Esam Omeish himself spent years reconciling the teachings of Islam, even as they apply to politics, with the American creed and U.S. political culture. Where there were contradictions, such as in the precise definition of human rights and the application of shariah law, he made clear in his sermons and speeches that in the United States the American approach necessarily trumped Islamist orthodoxy. With the 2011 Arab Spring uprising in the Middle East, Omeish turned his attention back to his native Libya, becoming a strong advocate for U.S. support of the anti-Qaddafi rebels. Esam was director of the Libyan Emergency Task Force, and the Omeishes organized a loose group of Libyan American doctors, businesspeople, and housewives who arranged for medical aid convoys, met with U.S. politicians, and held rallies and vigils in support of the Libyan revolution. In August, as rebel forces battled Qaddafi's remaining troops, Esam headed to Libya with $150,000 worth of surgical equipment and set up an emergency trauma center through the International Medical Corps at a hospital in Yefren, close to the zone of fighting. He spent three weeks treating devastating military injuries under primitive conditions. "I'm mirroring my passion about America in Libya," he said. He never reconsidered his earlier conclusion that Libya would never be home for him again, but that did not preclude him from having a role there. "Something in me longs to see Libya become like America," he said.

Most of the shops along Little River Turnpike on the eastern edge of Fairfax County have long been owned by Koreans, but the surrounding neighborhoods in recent years have attracted mostly Hispanic immigrants, and many of the people employed in the shops are Latinos. Ever enterprising, the Korean merchants realized their customer base was changing, so they adapted. One bakery that used to specialize in Korean sweets became Panadería Latina and switched to selling churros and pan dulce and tres leches cakes. The Korean owner was unfamiliar with the treats, but he let his Hispanic employees bake the pastries they knew would sell. The Korean barber down the street hung a sign in his window that promised, "Se Habla Español," and he hired Spanish-speaking employees to help him. The acculturation that took place along that stretch of Little River Turnpike was less from Korean to American than from Korean to Hispanic; more precisely, it was from Korean to a cultural mix that in an age of immigration was itself a new kind of American.

With the immigrant population dispersed throughout the county and no single group dominating, and with a progressive and well-resourced county government, Fairfax generally represented an example of successful immigrant integration. Still, there were exceptions to that pattern in some Fairfax immigrant neighborhoods, with gang violence, organized crime, and human trafficking.

Nationally, the story is also mixed. Growing inequality, racial alien-ation, and segmented acculturation—with immigrants integrated only within social class boundaries—are also realities. Whether the United States will always offer immigrants the same promise of up-ward mobility that it has in the past is becoming debatable.

One of the most alarming examples of failed acculturation was the case of the Tsarnaev brothers, the Chechen immigrants who were found to have planted the bombs that killed three people and injured more than 260 at the finish line of the Boston Mara-thon in April 2013. When it became apparent that Tamerlan and his brother, Dzhokhar, were the culprits, a stream of their friends, neighbors, and former classmates came forward to say how they had seemed to be relatively happy and well integrated into Ameri-can society. Alan Cullison, a *Wall Street Journal* reporter who knew Tamerlan, the older brother, recalled that he was an amateur boxer with big dreams. "He planned to box for the U.S. Olympic Team one day," Cullison wrote, "and he wanted to earn a degree, perhaps at Harvard or MIT and to hold a full-time job at the same time, so he could buy a house and a car."

Dzhokhar, a naturalized U.S. citizen, had seemed even more impressive. "Whether we were playing basketball or getting lunch, Dzhokhar never gave me a bad vibe," wrote a former classmate at Cambridge Rindge and Latin High School, Zolan Kanno-Youngs. "The Dzhokhar I knew was a young man who spent all night look-ing in his car for a new phone I clumsily lost. He left work early just to help me retrace my steps." Zolan's aunt, NPR host Robin Young, noted in a radio commentary how hard it was for people to hear that Dzhokhar was a popular kid. "What he's accused of," she said, "is monstrous. Evil. We want the perpetrator to fit the narrative of a loner, an outcast, an unassimilated immigrant. What Zolan did was write a new narrative, a more frightening one."

The Tsarnaev case showed that "assimilation" is not always as successful a process as it may appear on the surface. President Obama himself admitted to questions that he could not answer. "Why did young men who grew up and studied here, as part of our communities and our country, resort to such violence?" he asked in a speech to the nation four days after the bombings. For the advocates of more restricted immigration, the Tsarnaev story underscored their criticisms of the immigration system in the United States. Mark Krikorian, executive director of the Center for Immigration Studies, raised the Tsarnaev case during testimony at a Senate hearing on immigration reform. "What does it say about our broken patriotic assimilation system," he asked, "that legal, relatively privileged immigrant young people became so alienated that they engaged in this kind of mass murder against Americans?"

Up to that point, the debate in Washington over immigration policy had focused mainly on what should be done about people who were coming into the country illegally, but conservative commentator Ann Coulter cited the Boston bombings in making a larger argument. "The problem isn't just illegal immigration," she wrote in one of her typically provocative newspaper columns. "It's legal immigration, too." She even used the story of the Tsarnaev brothers to attack the nondiscriminatory premise of the 1965 immigration act. "My thought is, maybe we should consider admitting immigrants who can succeed in America, rather than deadbeats," she wrote. "But we're not allowed to 'discriminate' in favor of immigrants who would be good for America. Instead of helping America, our immigration policies are designed to help other countries solve their internal problems by shipping their losers to us. . . . Teddy Kennedy's 1965 Immigration Act so dramatically altered the kinds of immigrants America admits that, since 1969, about 85 percent of legal immigrants have come from the Third World. They bring Third World levels of poverty, fertility, illegitimacy and domestic violence with them. When they can't make it in America, they simply go on welfare and sometimes strike out at Americans."

As more details of the Tsarnaev brothers' lives became known, the evidence of their disaffection became more compelling. A five-month *Boston Globe* investigation led the *Globe* journalists to conclude that the Tsarnaev family had "imploded" within ten years after they arrived in America from their native Dagestan, with "each member marked by some personal failure within a culture they never fully understood or adapted to. . . . [As] the stress of life in their adopted country began to take its toll, the family turned to religion." Tamerlan spent more and more time on radical websites promoting violent jihad, and he shared them with his brother. They grew increasingly alienated, angry, and determined to cause pain. Acculturation, much less assimilation, never fully occurred.

Whether their case showed that the entire assimilation system in America was "broken," however, is another question. On the night they were cornered by the Boston police, the Tsarnaev brothers seized a car, holding the driver hostage. The man was able to escape and found refuge at a gas station, where the clerk called 911 and summoned the police. As it turned out, both the carjacking victim and the gas station clerk were themselves immigrants. The driver was from China, and the clerk, Tarek Ahmed, was from Egypt, and he was Muslim. "I love this country," he told a *New York Times* reporter. "My heart goes out to everybody who is affected by this." Two immigrant brothers had carried out an act of unspeakable violence, but it was two other foreign-born residents who helped to bring an end to the terrorism.

Sweeping generalizations about how well or poorly immigrants—Muslim immigrants in particular—are integrated in American society are unfounded. The 2010 U.S. Religion Census indicated that the number of Muslims in the United States more than doubled in the decade after the 9/11 attacks, precisely the period when counterterrorism policies were so controversial. Of the Muslim population in the United States in 2001, about one in four had immigrated in the previous ten years, and they seemed to be relatively happy. A 2011 Pew survey found 82 percent of U.S. Muslims expressing satisfaction with their American lives. Compared to the rest of the population, more than twice as many Muslims approved of "the way things are going" in the country.

For all its faults, the United States still represented opportunity and promise to people around the world. Gallup surveys in more than 150 countries over the last decade have shown that the United States is far and away the favored destination among those considering migration. The most recent survey projected that 138 million people worldwide would like to move permanently to the United States, more than three times the number who would choose the United Kingdom, the second most favored destination.

A hundred years ago, a young Harvard graduate by the name of Walter Lippmann wrote a book he called *A Preface to Politics*, the first of what would be many influential works of social and political criticism. Among his subjects was the challenge that immigration presented to the country, a development that he said brought with it "a thousand unforeseeable possibilities." At the time, the immigrants were almost entirely from Europe, but the influx was unprecedented, and for many Americans it was frightening. For Lippmann, it was exciting. "The great social adventure of America is no longer the conquest of the wilderness but the absorption of fifty different peoples," he wrote. "Immigration . . . may swamp us; it may, if we seize the opportunity, mean the impregnation of our national life with a new brilliancy." Another fifty years passed before America's leaders dared to embrace that "great social adventure" in its full breadth, and it is only in the half century after 1965, with a population connected to every corner of the globe, that the country has finally begun to demonstrate the exceptionalism it has long claimed for itself.

ACKNOWLEDGMENTS

This book relates the dramatic impact on America of the 1965 amendments to the Immigration and Nationality Act. In publishing terms, that meant it had to be ready for the 2015 anniversary of the legislation. Talk about a firm deadline. Bob Bender of Simon & Schuster wanted the book and made darn sure it was finished in time. I could not have managed without his guiding editorial hand along the way, including the criticisms he dared make when I had just a few weeks to go. He knew the manuscript could be improved, and he insisted on it. The book is much better for his input, and I am indebted to him and to his assistant, Johanna Li. We were connected only through the intervention of Gail Ross, my literary agent of two decades' standing. An author could not be better represented. Her partner Howard Yoon is a fast and insightful judge of rough drafts and set me straight from the outset on what this book needed to achieve in order to be successful. What a great team.

I have lost track of how many interviews I did in the course of reporting this story, and I apologize for not thanking all who helped me. Foremost among them were the immigrant families who were willing over many months to share their life stories with me: Victor and Rhina Alarcón and their son Álvaro; Mark and Alex Seong Keam; Esam and Badria Omeish and their daughters, Anwar and Abrar; Marta Quintanilla Call and her husband, Troy; and Amber

Kim, Brian Chun; and Fasih and Muzammil Khan. I was greatly helped in my reconstruction of the Fairfax County experience over the past several decades by Sharon Bulova, Penny Gross, Tom Davis III, Gerry Connolly, Anne Cahill, Suzanne Devlin, Robert Frye, and Ilryong Moon. The quality of governance in this remarkable county has been consistently exemplary. Kemal Kurspahić, whose courage and vision as a newspaper editor in wartime Sarajevo inspired my first book more than twenty years ago, is fighting the same fight today in the multiethnic world of suburban Virginia, and he was the first person I went to for advice when I took on this project.

Other Fairfax County notables who helped me were Sharon LeGrande, Meredith McKeen, Brooke Hammond-Perez, Dan Choi, Frederic Bemak, Gary Galluzzo, James Witte, Steve Thompson, Douglas Crooke, Michael Kwon, Toa Q. Do, and Tom Jackman. To the extent I was able to reconstruct the African American portion of Fairfax County history, I was guided by Elizabeth Hall, Juanita White, Wanda Johnson, Dennis Howard, and Naomi Sokol Zeavin. The story of J. E. B. Stuart High School came through interviews with Glynn Bates, Nancy Weisgerber, Thu Bui, Albert Santiago, and Stuart and Sherry Singer. At Dar Al-Hijrah, I was always welcomed by Imam Johari Abdul Malik and Samir Abo-Issa.

In reconstructing U.S. immigration history and the legislative story of the 1965 Act, I was assisted by Marian Smith, the incomparable historian in the offices of U.S. Citizenship and Immigration Services, by the staff of the John F. Kennedy Library in Boston, Massachusetts, and by several former staffers of Edward Kennedy, including Barbara Souliotis, George Abrams, and Peter Edelman. I also benefited from the counsel of some of the country's most esteemed immigration experts, including Demetrios G. Papademetriou, Doris Meissner, Muzaffar Chisti, and Michelle Mittelstadt of the Migration Policy Institute, Elizabeth M. Grieco of the U.S. Census Bureau, Douglas Massey of Princeton University, David Reimers of New York University, Hiroshi Motomura of the UCLA School of Law, Marilyn Halter of Boston University, and David

Choi of Loyola Marymount University. Roger Conner, Mickey Kaus, Dan Stein, and Mark Krikorian, all of whom have given deep thought to immigration issues, were good enough to share their perspectives with me.

Working against a tight deadline, I depended heavily on my team of researchers and editorial associates: Bridget Bowman, Carol Gould, Katherine Marsh, Victoria Ross, and Phyllis Travell. This was my third extended book-writing leave from NPR, and once again I enjoyed the support of my managers and colleagues there, especially Margaret Low Smith, Madhulika Sikka, Bruce Auster, Steve Drummond, and Vickie Walton. Special thanks to my fellow NPR correspondent Jennifer Ludden, whose early reporting on the 1965 Immigration Act gave me a head start and pointed me in the right direction when I had no idea what I was doing. Finally, I owe much to the support of my friends and family, beginning with my wife, Martha Raddatz, who knows better than anyone how to prod and encourage at the same time. She helped me identify the best stories that came my way and said, "Just do it," when that was what I most needed to hear.

I am dedicating this book to my granddaughter, Magnolia Williams, who came into this world just as I was embarking on this project and who inspired and entertained me day after day as I was toiling away. Magnolia shares her joy with whoever is lucky enough to be with her, and for the past two years I have been blessed with her regular company, thanks to her parents, Greta and Bailey. This book is as much about America's future as its past, and I hope Magnolia and her contemporaries will find it to be as generous a nation as I know it can be.

NOTES

All undocumented quotations are taken from interviews with the author.

PROLOGUE

1   *district known as Årdal:* There is more than one village in Norway named Årdal. This one is in Jølster municipality, in the county of Sogn og Fjordane, about forty miles inland from the southwest coast.

2   *Norway in the nineteenth century:* Sima Lieberman, "Norwegian Population Growth in the 19th Century," *Economy and History*, Vol. 2, No. 1, 1968.

2   *In each decade from 1860:* Roger Daniels, *Coming to America: A History of Immigration and Ethnicity in American Life* (New York: Harper Perennial, 2002), 164.

2   *Ole Rölvaag called it:* O. E. Rölvaag, *Giants in the Earth* (New York: Harper & Brothers, 1927).

3   *Samuel and Ole made their way:* The account of the Årdal Norwegians settling in America is drawn from "A History of Two Norwegian Communities in Northeastern North Dakota" by P. J. Olson (privately published) and from private correspondence.

4   As Per Hansa lay there dreaming: Rölvaag, *Giants in the Earth*, 46.

5   *the people came with the territory:* I credit this formulation to Aristide R. Zolberg, *A Nation by Design: Immigration Policy in the Fashioning of America* (New York: Russell Sage Foundation, 2006), 1.

5   *"They must look forward":* Quoted in ibid., 107, citing Max J. Kohler, *Immigration and Aliens in the United States* (New York: Bloch Publishing Co., 1936), 308.

5   *"new and unbounded":* Alexis de Tocqueville, *Democracy in America,* ed. Richard D. Heffner (New York: Signet Classics/ New American Library, 2001), 182.

5   *"where the inhabitants arrived":* Ibid., 115.

5   *"As no signs of incontestable":* Ibid., 164.

6   *"The position of the Americans":* Ibid., 183.

6   *"The bosom of America":* Address to the Members of the Volunteer Association and Other Inhabitants of the Kingdom of Ireland Who Have Lately Arrived in the City of New York, 2 December 1783," *The Writings of George Washington from the Original Manuscript Sources, 1745–1799,* Vol. 27, ed. John C. Fitzpatrick (Washington, DC: U.S. Government Printing Office, 1938), 254.

6   *"not by virtue of common descent":* Oscar Handlin, *A Pictorial History of Immigration* (New York: Crown, 1972), 70.

7   *"Do we want this country to be people":* Prescott F. Hall, "Immigration and the Educational Test," *North American Review,* October 1897, 395.

1: TWO FAMILIES FROM KOREA

15   *it was nearly impossible for Koreans:* According to the 1956 Annual Report of the U.S. Immigration and Naturalization Service, only 243 Koreans were naturalized as U.S. citizens in the year ending June 30, 1954, 295 in 1955, and 155 in 1956. The

1960 Census, counting citizens, permanent residents, and non-immigrant aliens, included just 11,171 persons born in Korea, out of a total U.S. population of 179 million.

15   *a quarter of the population was homeless:* Emerson Chapin, "Success Story in South Korea," *Foreign Affairs,* April 1969 http://www.foreignaffairs.com/articles/24078/emerson-chapin/success-story-in-south-korea.

15   *Of the 300,000 South Korean women:* "War Widows by Thousands Roam Korea," *Washington Post* (Reuters), April 2, 1954.

16   *By 1960, the annual per capita income:* World Bank figures.

2: A FAMILY FROM BOLIVIA

24   *Bolivia by then was facing:* The economic developments in Bolivia in the early 1980s are summarized in Jeffrey Sachs, "The Bolivian Hyperinflation and Stabilization," *American Economic Review: Papers and Proceedings*, Vol. 77, No. 2, May 1987.

3: OUT OF KOREA

28   *For a fee, Jeom Joo's brother-in-law:* Peter Pae, "Chicken Plant Jobs Open U.S. Doors for Koreans," *Washington Post*, December 1, 1999.

30   *Perdue Farms:* Peter Pae, "Perdue Ends Program for Korean Employees," *Washington Post*, February 25, 2000.

34   *"Our flag is red, white":* Jesse Jackson, Address to the Democratic National Convention, San Francisco, CA; July 16, 1984.

5: A FAMILY FROM LIBYA

47   *During Esam's years at J. E. B. Stuart:* Leah Y. Latimer, " 'Native Flight' Upsets Schools in N. Virginia," *Washington Post*, March 27, 1984; plus interviews.

6: CROSSROADS

52   *In 1950, fewer than 100,000 people:* U.S. Bureau of the Census, *U.S. Census of Population: 1950, Volume 2: Characteristics of the Population,* Part 46, Virginia, Chapter B, cited in Table 18, http://www.fairfaxcounty.gov/demogrph/fxprofile/profile _1973.pdf.

54   *By 1970, the county population:* U.S. Census Bureau, Decennial Censuses (1970–2000), cited in "Anticipating the Future: A Discussion of Trends in Fairfax County," Fairfax County Department of Systems Management for Human Services, March 2006, http://www.fairfaxcounty.gov/demogrph/archives/archive _general/anticipating_future.pdf.

54   *the foreign-born share during that period:* U.S. Census figures from Campbell Gibson and Kay Jung, "Historical Census Statistics on the Foreign-Born Population of the United States: 1850–2000," Population Division Working Paper No. 81, U.S. Census Bureau, February 2006; Fairfax County figures for 1970 from "Community Health Status Assessment," September 2011, http://www.fairfaxcounty.gov/hd/mapp/pdf /comm-health-assessment.pdf.

54   *The 1980 census showed:* "Anticipating the Future," Fairfax County.

54   *By 2000, one out of four:* Ibid.

54   *Up through the 1960s, African American:* Examples of racial discrimination in Fairfax County drawn from interviews with African American residents, plus Houston Summers, Jr., "The Family History of John Bell and Clarence Raymond Summers, Sr.," *Fairfax County Stories, 1607–2007* (County of Fairfax, Virginia, 2007); Nan Netherton et al., *Fairfax County, Virginia: A History* (Fairfax County Board of Supervisors, 1978); and Naomi Sokol Zeavin, *African-American History in Mason District*, Vols. 1 and 2, privately published.

56   *"If we can organize the southern states":* "Byrd Urges 'Massive'

Effort to Unite Against Integration," Associated Press, February 25, 1956.

57   *"The Southern people,"* *Smith said:* Charles Euchner, *Nobody Turn Me Around: A People's History of the 1963 March on Washington* (Boston: Beacon, 2010), 88.

57   the *"Southern Manifesto,"* *decrying: Congressional Record,* March 12, 1956, 4459–4460.

60   *"Do not underestimate the seriousness":* Speech to the American Legion Post 139, Arlington, Virginia, September 6, 1971, Joel T. Broyhill Papers, George Mason University, Special Collections and Archives.

61   *In an out-of-court settlement:* 571 F.2d 1299, *Fairfax Countywide Citizens Association v. County of Fairfax Virginia,* published on http://openjurist.org.

61   *A county survey carried out in 1975:* Cited in *Bailey's Neighborhood Improvement Program and Conservation Plan,* Fairfax County Department of Housing and Community Development, March 20, 1976.

65   *One Annandale resident wrote:* Paul Hodge, "Pagoda, Mosque Plans Upset Neighborhoods," *Washington Post,* April 5, 1984.

65   *"I really don't know much about them":* Barbara H. Blechman, "Druze Center Sparks Concern," *Washington Post,* July 11, 1985.

66   *in 1982, a group of radicals occupied:* Caryle Murphy, "Mosque Here Is Focus of Tug-of-War by Two World Visions of Islam," *Washington Post,* April 3, 1983.

67   *"may be the most peace-loving":* Hodge, "Pagoda, Mosque Plans Upset Neighborhoods."

7: A LIBYAN BOY IN AMERICA

71   *The staff that year documented eighteen:* "Ethnic Conflict in a U.S. High School," *Peace in Action,* January/February 1986.

8: GOOD IMMIGRANTS, BAD IMMIGRANTS

80   *in the words of historian Aristide Zolberg:* Aristede R. Zolberg, *A Nation by Design: Immigration Policy in the Fashioning of America* (New York: Russell Sage Foundation, 2006), 1.

80   *"generally of the most ignorant":* Benjamin Franklin, Letter to Peter Collinson, May 9, 1753, in Benjamin Franklin, *Writings* (New York: Literary Classics of the United States, 1987), 472.

80   *"by excluding all Blacks and Tawneys":* Benjamin Franklin, "Observations Concerning the Increase of Mankind, Peopling of Countries, etc.", in Franklin, *Writings,* 374.

81   *"wretchedness, beggary, drunkenness":* "The Material Condition of the People of Massachusetts," Fifteenth Report to the Legislature of Massachusetts by Francis De Witt, Secretary of the Commonwealth, published in *Christian Examiner,* 1858 Vol. 65, 53.

82   *1876 Democratic Party platform:* See the American Presidency Project, http://www.presidency.ucsb.edu/ws/?pid=29581.

82   *"the immigration of those races which":* Henry Cabot Lodge, "Lynch Law and Unrestricted Immigration," *North American Review,* May 1891, 606.

83   *In 1880, about 200,000 foreigners:* Oscar Handlin, *A Pictorial History of Immigration* (New York: Crown, 1972), 176; Zolberg, *A Nation by Design,* 229.

83   *By 1905, about a million:* Zolberg, *A Nation by Design,* 229.

84   *Hoar countered every argument:* Charles Frisbie Hoar, Speech on the floor of the U.S. Senate, February 28, 1882, reprinted in C. M. Whitman, *American Orators and Oratory* (Chicago: Fairbanks, Palmer & Company, 1884), 988–89.

84   *AFL president Samuel Gompers argued that:* "Gompers Cries for Less Immigration," *New York Times,* December 8, 1905.

85   *offered generalizations:* "Dictionary of Races or Peoples," United States Immigration Commission, 61st Congress, 3rd Session,

Document No. 602 (Washington, DC: U.S. Government Printing Office, 1911).

86   *characterizing them as "a race of soldiers":* Madison Grant, *The Passing of the Great Race*, 4th ed. (New York: Charles Scribner's Sons, 1916), 228.

86   *Celler recalled later, "you'd get up":* Maurice Carroll, "Emanuel Celler, Former Brooklyn Congressman, Dies at 92," *New York Times,* January 16, 1981.

86   *looking out "on a sea without a shore":* "Celler Becomes Dean of House, After Climbing 'the Greasy Pole,'" *New York Times,* January 5, 1965.

87   *"There were men older than I":* Emanuel Celler, *You Never Leave Brooklyn* (New York: John Day, 1953), 6–7.

87   *When he read in* The New York Times*:* "Immigration Record Broken as 11 Ships Race to Enter Port," *New York Times,* July 2, 1923.

88   *"There is no such thing as superior":* Emanuel Celler, "No Choice in Immigrants," Letter to the Editor, *New York Times,* July 6, 1923.

88   *In a column published in the:* "Calls Quota Law Cruel," *New York Times,* January 27, 1924.

88   *In February 1924, when Davis published:* James J. Davis, "One Hundred Years of Immigration," *New York Times,* February 17, 1924. Celler's response, "Interest in Citizenship," was published in the paper on February 20, 1924.

89   *"We have in America perhaps the largest":* Congressional Record, April 9, 1924, 5961–62.

89   *"I believe that not in the three decades":* Celler, *You Never Leave Brooklyn,* 80.

90   *Albert Johnson said the passage of:* "Applaud Alien Bill in D.A.R. Convention," *New York Times,* April 19, 1924.

90   *David Reed of Pennsylvania, explained:* David A. Reed, "America of the Melting Pot Comes to End," *New York Times,* April 27, 1924.

90   *Celler summarized:* Celler, *You Never Leave Brooklyn,* 4.

90   *"If America had any meaning at all":* Maurice Samuel, *You Gen-tiles* (New York: Harcourt, Brace, 1924), 218–19.

91   *Fewer than 300,000 people:* Census figures cited in Roger Dan-iels, *Guarding the Golden Door: American Immigration Policy and Immigrants Since 1882* (New York: Hill & Wang, 2004), 56–57.

91   *"The United States in effect proclaimed":* Zolberg, *A Nation by Design,* 9.

91   *"There were sporadic speeches":* Celler, *You Never Leave Brooklyn,* 86.

92   *When Celler asked that he be allowed:* Murray Marder, "Celler-McCarran Clash Opens Hearing on Immigration Laws," *Washington Post,* March 7, 1951.

93   *to preserve "the sociological and cultural":* Senate Report No. 1515, 81st Congress, 2nd Session, 1950, 455.

94   *"a slur on the patriotism, the capacity":* Harry S. Truman, Veto Message, June 25, 1952.

9: JFK

95   *Kennedy was walking down Hanover Street:* The account of JFK's 1946 congressional campaign comes from William De Marco and William Sutton oral histories at the John F. Ken-nedy Presidential Library and from Kenneth P. O'Donnell and David E. Powers with Joe McCarthy, *Johnny, We Hardly Knew Ye: Memories of John Fitzgerald Kennedy* (Boston: Little, Brown, 1972).

97   *He was outraged when Republican:* Doris Kearns Goodwin, *The Fitzgeralds and the Kennedys: An American Saga* (New York: Simon & Schuster, 1987), 102–3.

98   *"It is fashionable today to cry out":* Congressional Record, January 27, 1897, Appendix, pp. 467–49, quoted in ibid., 102.

98   *"You are an impudent young man":* John Henry Cutler, *"Honey*

Fitz": Three Steps to the White House (Indianapolis: Bobbs-Merrill, 1962), 64, quoted in Goodwin, *The Fitzgeralds and the Kennedys*, 102.

99   *perhaps helped a bit by his campaign:* Lewis H. Weinstein Oral History, June 3, 1982, JFK Library.

100   *"get out of the shadow":* Hubert H. Humphrey, Address to the Democratic National Convention, Philadelphia, PA, July 14, 1948.

100   *"There ought to be no place":* Oscar Handlin, "The Immigration Fight Has Only Begun," *Commentary*, July 1, 1952.

101   *the commission noted the broader discrimination: Whom We Shall Welcome*, Report of the President's Commission on Immigration and Naturalization (Washington, DC: U.S. Government Printing Office, 1953), xi.

101   *against "the non-white people":* Ibid., 53.

101   *"He would tell the southerners":* Harry McPherson Oral History Interview VI, Lyndon B. Johnson Presidential Library.

102   *Upon his return to the Senate:* Jethro K. Lieberman, *Are Americans Extinct?* (New York: Walker and Company, 1968), 116.

102   *Johnson personally arranged an immigrant:* Erich Leinsdorf, Oral History Interview, LBJ Library.

103   *two thirds of the immigrants:* Marion T. Bennett, "The Immigration and Nationality (McCarran-Walter) Act of 1952, as Amended to 1965," *The Annals of the American Academy of Political Science*, 1966, Vol. 367, No. 1, 134.

103   *at the suggestion of the Anti-Defamation League:* Mae M. Ngai, "Oscar Handlin and Immigration Policy Reform in the 1950s and 1960s," *Journal of American Ethnic History*, Vol. 32, No. 3, Spring 2013, 65.

103   *Myer Feldman, was later quoted:* Daniel J. Tichenor, *Dividing Lines: The Politics of Immigration Control in America* (Princeton: Princeton University Press 2002), 205; note 92, p. 343.

103   *The 1960 Democratic Party platform:* See the American Presidency Project, http://www.presidency.ucsb.edu/ws/?pid=29602.

104 *Michigan governor G. Mennen Williams:* G. Mennen Williams to Senator John F. Kennedy, July 26, 1960, JFK Library.

104 *regarded his mission as "almost hopeless":* Norbert A. Schlei, Oral History Interview, February 20, 1968, JFK Library.

105 *"I do not see why you should not submit":* Emanuel Celler to President Kennedy, June 24, 1963, JFK Library.

106 *grouped with the "right wing cranks":* "Immigration Reformer: Michael Aloysius Feighan," *New York Times,* August 25, 1965.

106 *Feighan "got his nose out of joint":* Lawrence F. O'Brien, Oral History Interview XII, July 25, 1986, LBJ Library; see also Norbert A. Schlei Oral History Interview, February 20, 1968, JFK Library.

106 *Feighan is said to have told guests:* Drew Pearson, "Feighan Roasted Kennedy Abroad," *Washington Post,* April 29, 1964.

10: THE 1965 REFORM

107 *Johnson found the human contact:* Harry McPherson, Oral History Interview I, December 5, 1968, LBJ Library; see also John P. Mackenzie, "President and Family Worship," *Washington Post,* November 25, 1963.

108 *"The ideas and the ideals":* Address Before a Joint Session of the Congress, November 27, 1963, *Public Papers of the Presidents: Lyndon B. Johnson, 1963–1964* (Washington, DC: U.S. Government Printing Office, 1965).

108 *speechwriter Harry McPherson said:* Harry McPherson, Oral History Interview I, LBJ Library.

108 *"He had no real priority among them":* Robert Dallek, *Flawed Giant: Lyndon Johnson and His Times, 1961–1973* (New York: Oxford University Press, 1998), 229.

109 *press secretary George Reedy said:* George E. Reedy, Oral History Interview XXVI, November 16, 1990, LBJ Library.

109 *the new president was "uninformed":* Irving Bernstein, *Guns or*

Butter: The Presidency of Lyndon Johnson (New York: Oxford University Press, 1996), 252.

109   *Feldman told one interviewer:* Daniel J. Tichenor, *Dividing Lines: The Politics of Immigration Control in America* (Princeton: Princeton University Press, 2002), 212.

109   *Schwartz, and other former Kennedy advisers:* Ibid., 212–13.

109   *eliminated "every trace of discrimination":* Lyndon B. Johnson, Address Before a Joint Session of Congress, November 27, 1963.

109   *a world "in which all men":* Annual Message to the Congress on the State of the Union, January 8, 1964, *Public Papers of the Presidents: Lyndon B. Johnson, 1963–1964.*

109   *He told them that he would be:* Tichenor, *Dividing Lines,* 213.

110   *look into the issue "expeditiously":* Tom Wicker, "President Urges a New Alien Law," *New York Times,* January 14, 1964; also, Tichenor, *Dividing Lines,* 213.

110   *After pushing a glass of scotch:* Kennedy relates the story of his encounter with Eastland in Edward M. Kennedy, *True Compass: A Memoir* (New York: Twelve, 2009), 193–95.

111   *"I'm mighty proud of you":* Telephone conversation with Rep. John McCormack and Rep. Emanuel Celler, February 10, 1964, LBJ Library.

111   *Celler reported that "our friend":* Telephone conversation with Rep. Emanuel Celler, May 5, 1964, LBJ Library.

112   *high-pressure LBJ "treatment":* Jack Valenti, Memorandum to Larry O'Brien, June 17, 1964, Adam Walinsky Personal Papers, Senate Subject Files, Box 23, "Immigration," JFK Library.

112   *Rusk seemed "unenthusiastic":* Abba P. Schwartz, *The Open Society* (New York: William Morrow, 1968), 119–120.

113   *Schwartz said afterward:* Ibid., 120.

113   *the 1960 census showed:* Census figures cited in Marion T. Bennett, "The Immigration and Nationality (McCarran-Walter) Act of 1952, as Amended to 1965," *The Annals of the American*

Academy of Political and Social Science, 1966, Vol. 367, No. 1, 134, note 9.

113 *would "open the floodgates":* Chalmers M. Roberts, "Miller Hits Immigration, Tariff Cuts as Job Perils," *Washington Post,* September 8, 1964.

114 *The prevailing sentiment in Congress:* Paul Duke and Stanley Meisler, "Immigration: Quotas vs. Quality," *The Reporter,* Vol. 32, No. 1, January 14, 1965, 30–32.

114 *"We have removed all elements":* Tichenor, Dividing Lines, 215, note 143, p. 346, citing Humphrey speech of April 29, 1965, Williamsburg, VA.

115 *the American belief "that a man":* Message from the President of the United States Relative to Changes on Our Immigration Laws, January 13, 1965.

116 *Bobby Kennedy "acted like he was":* Doris Kearns Goodwin, *Lyndon Johnson and the American Dream* (New York: St. Martin's, 1991), 200.

117 *"I've told you, call me anytime":* Telephone conversation with Sen. Edward M. Kennedy, March 8, 1965, LBJ Library.

117 *"Why can't we get that immigration bill out?":* Telephone conversation with Rep. Carl Albert, May 18, 1965, LBJ Library.

118 *John Trevor, Sr., was credited:* "Immigration," Hearings Before Subcommittee No. 1, Committee on the Judiciary, House of Representatives, May 20, 1965, 237.

119 *"The national origins provision":* "Immigration," Hearings Before Subcommittee No. 1, Committee on the Judiciary, House of Representatives, August 14, 1964, 798.

119 *"could result in further unemployment":* "Immigration," Hearings Before Subcommittee on Immigration and Naturalization, Committee on the Judiciary, United States Senate, June 25, 1965, 714.

120 *"I really believe that a people":* Hearings Before Subcommittee on Immigration and Naturalization, Committee on the Judiciary, United States Senate, Part 2, March 8, 1965, 423.

120 *"they gave us our language":* Hearings Before Subcommittee on Immigration and Naturalization, Committee on the Judiciary, United States Senate, Part 1, February 24, 1965, 62–63.

120 *In another hearing a week:* Hearings Before Subcommittee on Immigration and Naturalization, Committee on the Judiciary, United States Senate, Part I, March 1, 1965, 150.

120 *Holland of Florida asked, "Why, for the first time":* Congressional Record, September 22, 1965, 24776.

121 *Americans of African descent outnumbered Scandinavian:* "Race for the United States, Regions, Divisions, and States: 1960," U.S. Census Bureau; and Memorandum from Abba P. Schwartz to the Secretary of State, "Estimates of the National Origins of the 1960 U.S. Population" (citing Census Bureau data), February 13, 1963.

121 *because it "shifts the mainstream":* Congressional Record, August 25, 1965, 21773.

121 *would lead to "still more ghettoes":* Congressional Record, September 21, 1965, 24557.

121 *Kennedy promised "the ethnic mix":* Hearings Before Subcommittee on Immigration and Naturalization, Committee on the Judiciary, United States Senate, Part I, February 10, 1965, 2.

121 *"comparatively many Asians or Africans":* Congressional Record, August 25, 1965, 21577–78.

122 *only about 16,000 or 17,000 people would:* Hearings Before Subcommittee on Immigration and Naturalization, Committee on the Judiciary, United States Senate, Part I, February 24, 1965, 71.

122 *the State Department's "best information":* Ibid., 65.

122 *"Even if the national origins system":* "Quota Waiting Lists," Undated document, Adam Walinsky Personal Papers, Senate Subject Files, Box 23, "Immigration," JFK Library.

122 *Representative Spark Matsunaga of Hawaii:* Congressional Record, August 25, 1965, 21782.

122 *Peter Rodino of New Jersey, of Italian origin:* Congressional Record, August 24, 1965, 21594.

123　*a joke about an imaginary restaurant scene:* Congressional Record August 25, 1965, 21757.

123　*had been holding "reasonably steady":* "Immigration," Hearings Before Subcommittee No. 1, Committee on the Judiciary, House of Representatives, March 4, 1965, 42–44.

124　*A memorandum Henderson wrote:* "Foreign Students from Under-Developed Areas and US Immigration Policy," Memorandum from Gregory Henderson to Robert Kennedy, December 28, 1960, JFK Library.

124　*saying it was "a matter which you":* Memorandum from Arthur Schlesinger, Jr., to Byron White, Deputy Attorney General, February 4, 1961, JFK Library.

124　*officials at the State Department, who agreed:* Letter from Harris Huston, Acting Administrator of Bureau of Security and Consular Affairs, Department of State, to Joseph M. Swing, Commissioner of Immigration and Naturalization Service, February 8, 1961, JFK Library.

125　*Henderson wrote a former schoolmate:* Letter from Gregory Henderson, American Embassy, Seoul, Korea, to Burke Marshall, Department of Justice, June 2, 1961, JFK Library.

126　*In a February 1965 speech:* Michael Feighan, Address to the Thirty-sixth Annual Conference of the American Coalition of Patriotic Societies, Washington, DC, February 4, 1965 (copy of text in JFK Library).

126　*"devised a naturally operating national-origins system":* Deane and David Heller, "Our New Immigration Law," *American Legion Magazine,* February 1966, 8.

127　*"Thus," the league complained:* Reimers, *Still the Golden Door,* 73.

127　*a minority report saying "the possibility":* Congressional Record, August 25, 1965, 21811.

128　*"What are you going to do for me":* Telephone conversation with Nicholas Katzenbach, August 26, 1965, LBJ Library.

129　*Hart distanced himself from the legislation:* Mae M. Ngai, "The Unlovely Residue of Outworn Prejudices: The Hart-Celler Act and the Politics of Immigration Reform, 1945–1965," in *Americanism: New Perspectives on the History of an Ideal,* ed. Michael Kazin and Joseph A. McCartin (Chapel Hill: University of North Carolina Press, 2006), 126, note 31.

130 *"Had it not been for the tact":* Congressional Record, September 22, 1965, 24784.

130 *In future years, the advocates of tighter:* See, for example, Otis L. Graham, "Tracing Liberal Woes to '65 Immigration Act," *Christian Science Monitor,* December 28, 1995.

131 *"the brothers and sisters act":* Reimers, *Still the Golden Door,* 94.

131 *October 3 was a beautiful autumn day:* Carroll Kilpatrick, "Johnson Offers Haven to Cuban Refugees," *Washington Post,* October 4, 1965.

132 *"The bill that we sign today":* Remarks at the Signing of the Immigration Bill, October 3, 1965, Public Papers of the Presidents of the United States: Lyndon B. Johnson, 1965, Volume 2, 1037–40 (Washington, DC: U.S. Government Printing Office, 1966).

133 *Nine people were crowded into the car:* Erich Leinsdorf, Oral History Interview, March 18, 1969, LBJ Library.

11: TURNING POINT

138 *Foreign-Born as Percent of U.S. Population, 1900–2010:* Elizabeth M. Grieco et al., "The Size, Place of Birth, and Geographic Distribution of the Foreign-Born Population in the United States," Population Division Working Paper No. 96, U.S. Census Bureau, October 2012.

139 *Percent of Foreign-Born by Region of Birth, 1900–2010:* Campbell Gibson and Kay Jung, "Historical Census Statistics on the Foreign-Born Population of the United States: 1850–2000," Population Division Working Paper No. 81, U.S. Census Bureau, February 2006; and Grieco, et al.

139 *In 1960, barely 11,000 Koreans:* Immigration numbers for

Korea, Pakistan, India, and El Salvador come from these
sources: Campbell Gibson and Kay Jung; "Annual Report of
the Immigration and Naturalization Service," Department of
Justice, Washington, DC, 1965; "Regions of Birth for Immigrants in the United States, 1960–Present," Migration Policy
Institute Data Hub; http://www.migrationpolicy.org/programs
/data-hub/charts/regions-immigrant-birth-1960-present.

140   *the available slots were never completely filled:* Annual Reports of
the Immigration and Naturalization Service, 1951–1965.

140   *With decolonization, however:* Marilyn Halter, *African and
American* (New York: New York University Press, 2014), 15–16.

144   *Between 1990 and 2000:* "Anticipating the Future: A Discussion of Trends in Fairfax County," Fairfax County Department
of Systems Management for Human Services, 2006, 16 (citing U.S. Census Bureau Decennial Census data and American
Community Surveys).

144   *what human geographers called:* Marie Price and Audrey Singer,
"Edge Gateways: Immigrants, Suburbs, and the Politics of Reception in Metropolitan Washington," in Audrey Singer et al.,
eds., *Twenty-first Century Gateways: Immigrant Incorporation
in Suburban America* (Washington, DC: Brookings Institution
Press, 2008), 137–70.

145   *A* Washington Post *survey in 2010:* Carol Morello and Dan
Keating, "The New American Neighborhood," *Washington
Post,* October 30, 2011.

145   *a "diversity index" of 64:* "2010 Decennial Census Summaries,"
Fairfax County, http://www.fairfaxcounty.gov/demogrph/de
cennialcensus.htm.

146   *A community survey undertaken: A Community Sampler: Eight
Immigrant and Refugee Communities with Public School Children*
(Fairfax County, Virginia: Department of Systems Management for Human Services, 2000), 35–38, http://www.fairfax
county.gov/demogrph/archives/sampler/refugeerep.pdf.

147 *Harvard sociologist Nathan Glazer said:* Nathan Glazer, "Assimilation Today: Is One Identity Enough?," *Reinventing the Melting Pot,* ed. Tamar Jacoby (New York: Basic Books, 2004), 66.

147 *As Robert Byrd of West Virginia: Congressional Record,* September 14, 1965, 23793–95.

148 *Census data consistently showed:* See, for example: "Foreign-Born Workers: Labor Force Characteristics—2013," Bureau of Labor Statistics, May 2014; Dane Stangler and Jason Wiens, "The Economic Case for Welcoming Immigrant Entrepreneurs," Ewing Marion Kauffman Foundation, March 31, 2014; Steven F. Hipple, "Self-Employment in the United States," *Monthly Labor Review,* September 2010; Michael Greenstone and Adam Looney, "Ten Economic Facts About Immigration," Washington, DC: Brookings Institution Hamilton Project, September 2010; and Maude Toussaint-Comeau, "Self-Employed Immigrants: An Analysis of Recent Data," *Chicago Fed Letter,* No. 213, Federal Reserve Bank of Chicago, April 2005.

148 *with lower rates of divorce:* Data on immigrant families and language ability from Elizabeth M. Grieco et al., "The Foreign-Born Population in the United States: 2010," United States Census Bureau, May 2012.

148 *for second-generation immigrants good English:* Alejandro Portes and Rubén G. Rumbaut, *Legacies: The Story of the Immigrant Second Generation* (Berkeley: University of California Press, and New York: Russell Sage Foundation, 2001), 118–19.

148 *Douglas Massey tackled that question:* Douglas S. Massey, "The New Immigration and Ethnicity in the United States," *Population and Development Review,* Vol. 21, No. 3, September 1995.

150 *"Throughout American history," he wrote:* Samuel P. Huntington, *Who Are We? The Challenges to America's National Identity* (New York: Simon & Schuster, 2004), 61.

150   *"To what extent will these immigrants":* Ibid., 178.

151   *"It has been our fate as a nation":* Quoted in Hans Kohn, *American Nationalism: An Interpretive Essay* (New York: Macmillan Co, 1957), 13.

151   *Political scientist Seymour Martin Lipset:* Seymour Martin Lipset, *American Exceptionalism: A Double-Edged Sword* (New York: W. W. Norton, 1996), 18–19.

151   *this "assimilation contract," as some writers:* Peter D. Salins, "The Assimilation Contract: Endangered but Still Holding," in Jacoby, ed., *Reinventing the Melting Pot*, 99–109.

152   *because acculturation works in both directions:* David A. Gerber makes this point effectively in *American Immigration: A Very Short Introduction* (New York: Oxford University Press, 2011), 104.

153   *In comparison to other newcomers:* Grieco et al., "The Foreign-Born Population in the United States: 2010."

155   *The number of Salvadoran immigrants residing:* Aaron Terrazas, "Salvadoran Immigrants in the United States," Migration Policy Institute, 2010, http://www.migrationpolicy.org/article /salvadoran-immigrants-united-states.

12: MINORITIES

164   *"Whatever measure of power and influence":* Jack Miles, "Blacks vs. Browns, *The Atlantic,* October 1992.

165   *"We as Korea Americans must take charge":* Mark L. Keam, "Painful Memories . . . a Decade Later," *Goal IX,* Newsletter of the American Bar Association, Commission on Racial and Ethnic Diversity in the Profession, Vol. 8, No. 2, Spring 2002.

167   *Over the previous decade, at least fifteen: History of Korean Americans in the Washington Area, 1883–2005* (Alexandria, VA: Korean American Foundation), 226.

168   *Korean immigrants or their family members owned:* Joel Garreau, "A People Molded into Merchants," *Washington Post,* July 5, 1992.

13: DIVERSITY

174   *In 1983, three airlines at Washington's:* Caryle Murphy, "Market Tightens as Immigrants Fill Local Jobs," *Washington Post,* August 7, 1983.

174   *warned of latent tensions between immigrants:* Ibid.

175   *immigrants "often create new businesses":* Legal Immigration: Setting Priorities, U.S. Commission on Immigration Reform, 1995.

175   *Many economists hastened to argue:* See, for example, Gianmarco I. P. Ottaviano and Giovanni Peri, "Rethinking the Effect of Immigration on Wages," *Journal of the European Economic Association,* European Economic Association, Vol. 10, No. 1, 2012, 152–97.

175   *Harvard University economists Lawrence Katz and George Borjas:* George J. Borjas and Lawrence F. Katz, "The Evolution of the Mexican-Born Workforce in the United States," in George J. Borjas, ed., *Mexican Immigration to the United States* (Chicago: University of Chicago Press, 2007).

176   *Moreover, some economists who acknowledge:* Eduardo Porter, "Cost of Illegal Immigration May Be Less than Meets the Eye," *New York Times,* April 16, 2006.

176   *"I believe immigration on net":* Email from Lawrence Katz to author, February 9, 2015.

177   *just three of its 250 families:* "Reston to Observe First Birthday with Official Dedication May 21," *Washington Post,* May 1, 1966.

177   *"In our youth, you almost never went":* Oral History of Robert Frye, "Oral History Interviews and Written Memories: A Complete Compilation of Transcripts with Index," http://braddockheritage.org

177   *By that time, African Americans made up less:* U.S. Bureau of the Census, U.S. Census of Population: 1960, General Population Characteristics, Virginia, Final Report PC(1)-48B, Table 1,

cited in "Fairfax County Profile," Office of Research and Statistics, Research Branch, Fairfax County, November 1973, http://www.fairfaxcounty.gov/demograph/fxprofile/profile_1973.pdf.

179　*"The first time I suggested it":* Oral History of Robert Frye, "Oral History Interviews and Written Memories."

179　*"especially appropriate for this multi-ethnic community":* "Virginia Reel," *Washington Post,* November 13, 1980.

180　*"It seems like the Democrats are in decline":* Molly Moore, "Fairfax Democrats Concede Power Loss," *Washington Post,* November 8, 1984.

180　*"It's becoming a more conservative county":* Ibid.

14: MUSLIM AMERICANS

184　*A survey of Muslims residing in the United States:* "A Demographic Portrait of Muslim Americans," in *Muslim Americans: No Signs of Growth in Alienation or Support for Extremism* (Washington, DC: Pew Research Center, 2011), 13.

189　*Between 1990 and 2000, about 550,000 Muslim immigrants:* The 2011 Pew Research Center survey estimated that the U.S. Muslim population stood at 2.75 million and that 31 percent of the total had immigrated to the United States during the 1990s.

189　*Muslims constituted the fastest growing:* Data on the growth in Muslim congregants come from the online database "USA: Religion over Time," in Todd M. Johnson and Brian J. Grim, eds., *World Religion Database* (online by subscription), Boston: Brill.

190　*A strategy paper written by a Brotherhood:* "An Explanatory Memorandum on the General Strategic Goal for the Group in North America," published by the Investigative Project on Terrorism, http://www.investigativeproject.org/document/id/20.

191　*"I was horrified to hear a long procession":* Steven Emerson, *American Jihad: The Terrorists Living Among US* (New York: Free Press, 2002), 6.

15: INTEGRATION

201   *Thao said he intended "to bring":* Peter Baker, "In a First, Asian Is Named to Fairfax School Board," *Washington Post,* June 29, 1993.

204   *when she shot an African American man:* The account of the shooting incident is based on author interviews with Suzanne Devlin and Orvin Boyd, as well as "Fairfax Man Shot by Park Police," *Washington Evening Star,* December 10, 1980.

205   *"I've learned to see myself not just":* Carol Krucoff, "Tempering the Terror: The New Peacemakers," *Washington Post,* April 23, 1984.

208   *In 2001, five of the eleven homicide victims:* Tom Jackman, "Fairfax Police Hit Cultural Barriers," *Washington Post,* December 23, 2001.

213   *"I don't want to discriminate against anyone":* Peter Pae, "In Fairfax, an Uneasy Election," *Washington Post,* October 13, 1999.

214   *"This is our community," somebody said:* Recollections of Penny Gross and Toa Q. Do, in interviews with the author.

216   *"We've got to do something about":* Mike DeBonis, "Barry Chided for Remarks on Asians' 'Dirty Shops,'" *Washington Post,* April 6, 2012.

217   *condemned Barry's remarks as "racist":* Commentary quoted in its entirety by Mike DeBonis in his "District of DeBonis" blog, "Lessons from Marion Barry's Anti-Asian Comments," *Washington Post,* April 6, 2012, http://www.washingtonpost.com/blogs/mike-debonis/post/lessons-from-marion-barrys-anti-asian-comments/2012/04/06/gIQAzS33zS_blog.html.

16: INITIATIVE

220   *Immigrating can be seen as an entrepreneurial act:* Observation widely attributed to Edward B. Roberts, founder of the MIT Center for Entrepreneurship. See, for example, Matthew

Denhart, *Growth and Immigration: A Handbook of Vital Immi-gration and Economic Growth Statistics* (Dallas, TX: George W. Bush Institute, 2012), 5.

220 *U.S. census data show much higher self-employment:* "Why Do So Many Asians Own Their Own Businesses?" Data published on http://www.asian-nation.org/small-businesses.shtml cit-ing "Rates of Being Self-Employed, 2000, by Racial/Ethnic Group," Bureau of the Census, 5 percent Public Use Microdata Samples (PUMS).

227 *Koreans have one of the highest entrepreneurial scores:* Com-parisons are for immigrant groups with at least 20,000 self-employed persons. Sources: Bureau of the Census, 5 per cent Public Use Microdata Sample (PUMS), cited in Mary Dorinda Allard, "Asians in the U.S. Labor Force," *Monthly Labor Review,* Bureau of Labor Statistics, November 2011; Pyong Gap Min, "Korean Immigrants in the United States," *Handbook of Re-search on Ethnic Minority Entrepreneurship,* ed. Leo Paul Dana (Northampton, MA: Edward Elgar Publishing, 2007), 213; Alejandro Portes and Rubén G. Rumbaut, *Immigrant America,* 3rd ed. (Berkeley: University of California Press, 2006), 82–83.

228 *A joke in the Korean community:* Credit to David Choi, director of the Fred Kiesner Center for Entrepreneurship, Loyola Ma-rymount University.

228 *By 2012, nine out of ten dry cleaning:* A 2012 survey by the Ko-rean American Dry Cleaners Association of Greater Wash-ington (KADA) showed that 1,812 of 1,950 dry cleaning establishments in the D.C. metropolitan area were owned by Korean Americans, according to KADA president Jeff Ahn.

229 *"are partly inherited from the Confucian tradition":* Pyong Gap Min, "Korean Immigrant Entrepreneurship: A Multivariate Analysis," *Journal of Urban Affairs,* Vol. 10, No. 2, 1988, 199.

229 *As of 2009, foreign-born workers were slightly:* Steven F. Hipple, "Self-Employment in the United States," *Monthly Labor Re-view,* Bureau of Labor Statistics, September 2010, 24.

229 *argues that these data undercut the notion:* Steven A. Camarota, "Immigrants Neither More nor Less Entrepreneurial than the Native-Born," Blogpost, June 18, 2012, http://cis.org/a/immigrants-neither-more-nor-less-entrepreneurial-native-born.

229 *Data from the 2007 Survey of Business Owners:* See "Immigrant Small Business Owners: A Significant and Growing Part of the Economy," Fiscal Policy Institute, June 2012; and Robert W. Fairlie, "Immigrant Entrepreneurs and Small Business Owners, and Their Access to Financial Capital," Report to the U.S. Small Business Administration, May 2012.

230 *Research also makes clear that entrepreneurial:* See, e.g., Juan Holguin et al., "Challenges and Opportunities for Hispanic Entrepreneurs in the United States," in ed. Leo Paul Dana, *Handbook of Research on Ethnic Minority Entrepreneurship* (Northampton, MA: Edward Elgar Publishing, 2007); and Vicki Bogan and William Darity, Jr., "Culture and Entrepreneurship? African American and Immigrant Self-Employment in the United States," *The Journal of Socio-Economics,* Vol. 37, 2008, 1999–2019.

230 *One survey of engineering and technology: Then and Now: America's New Immigrant Entrepreneurs,* Part VII (Kansas City, MO: Ewing Marion Kauffman Foundation, October 2012).

17: BACKLASH

241 *"the gradual stabilization of our population":* Letter of Transmittal, Commission on Population Growth and the American Future, *Population and the American Future* (Washington, DC: U.S. Government Printing Office, 1972).

242 *"an expression of our interest in the population problem":* Oral History of John H. Tanton, MD, Otis Graham, Jr., Papers, Special Collections Research Center, Gelman Library, George Washington University, Washington, DC.

242 *"More children from the fit":* Quoted in David M. Kennedy, *Birth Control in America: The Career of Margaret Sanger* (New Haven: Yale University Press, 1970), 115.

243 *"To put it bluntly," Hardin argued:* C. Spencer, "Interview with Garrett Hardin," *Omni*, 14, 1992.

243 *"If the world is one great commons":* Garrett Hardin, "The Survival of Nations and Civilization," *Science,* Vol. 172, No. 3990, June 25, 1971.

244 *"Most people hadn't even noticed":* Oral History of John H. Tanton.

245 *One old friend told him:* Oral History of Roger Conner, Otis Graham, Jr., Papers.

245 *In a 1979 article for:* Otis L. Graham, Jr., "Illegal Immigration and the New Restrictionism," *Center Magazine,* Vol. 12, May/June 1979.

246 *The problem to be highlighted:* Otis L. Graham, Jr., *Immigration Reform and America's Unchosen Future* (Bloomington, IN: AuthorHouse, 2008), 58.

246 *"True, there are still with us those":* Otis L. Graham, Jr., "Illegal Immigration and the New Reform Movement," FAIR Immigration Paper II, February 1980.

246 *The three of them drafted a FAIR manifesto:* "Principles That Should Govern an Immigration Policy," unpublished draft paper, Otis Graham, Jr., Papers.

247 *"Our studies—as well as those of other students":* Anne and Paul Ehrlich, "Immigration in the Future," *The Mother Earth News,* January/February 1980, 150–51.

247 *"People with unsullied liberal credentials":* Roger Conner letter to Paul and Anne Ehrlich, June 13, 1980, Otis Graham, Jr., Papers.

248 *"John had become convinced":* Graham, Jr., *Immigration Reform and America's Unchosen Future,* 126.

248 *raised doubts about "the degree to which":* Quoted in Zolberg, *A Nation by Design,* 358.

249 *"If the only way to beat them":* Oral History of Roger Conner, Otis Graham, Jr., Papers.

249 *Speaking at the conference, Conner charged:* FAIR Press Release, January 19, 1984.

249 *Sociologist John Reid said the gains:* Ibid.

250 *Another Howard sociologist:* Ibid.

250 *within a year, Tanton's:* Otis L. Graham, Jr., *Immigration Reform and America's Unchosen Future,* 127.

251 *Bouvier had concluded that by 2010:* Leon F. Bouvier and Philip L. Martin, *Population Change and California's Future* (Washington, DC: Population Reference Bureau, 1985).

251 *In an accompanying memo, he said the time:* Archived in the Otis Graham, Jr., Papers.

251 *In an oral history interview he provided later:* Oral History of John H. Tanton, Otis Graham, Jr., Papers.

252 *what he called "the war against the white race:* Quoted in Dinesh D'Souza, "Racism: It's a White (and Black) Thing," *Washington Post,* September 24, 1995.

253 *"Is it not an inescapable conclusion":* Lawrence Auster, *The Path to National Suicide: An Essay on Immigration and Multiculturalism* (Monterey, VA: The American Immigration Control Foundation, 1990), 49.

253 *"a geometrically expanding chain":* "An Outline of a Rational Immigration Policy," FAIR, January 31, 1981, Otis L Graham Papers.

253 *include provisions for "reasonable discrimination:* Auster, *The Path to National Suicide,* 28.

254 *"the alteration of our demographic future":* Otis L. Graham, Jr., "Rethinking Purposes of Immigration Policy," Center for Immigration Studies, Paper No. 6, May 1991.

254 *"perhaps the single most nation-changing measure":* Otis L. Graham, Jr., "Tracing Liberal Woes to '65 Immigration Act," *Christian Science Monitor,* December 28, 1995.

255   *commission's report came as "a big surprise":* Dan Stein, Memorandum to FAIR Board of Directors, July 12, 1995, Otis Graham, Jr., Papers.

256   *"The chief difficulties that America faces":* Roy Beck, *The Case Against Immigration* (New York: W. W. Norton, 1996), 17.

256   *The right to migrate was supported by those:* This debate is explored by Mae M. Ngai in *Impossible Subjects: Illegal Aliens and the Making of Modern America* (Princeton: Princeton University Press, 2004).

257   *called the compromise bill "a shell of reform":* William Branigin, "Unusual Alliance Transformed Immigration Debate," *Washington Post*, March 23, 1996.

257   *"The racial and ethnic balance":* Peter Brimelow, *Alien Nation: Common Sense About America's Immigration Disaster* (New York: Random House, 1995), xvii.

258   *"The culture of a country":* Ibid., 180.

258   *Tanton projected that "U.S. immigration:* John Tanton, "The Color Line," *The Social Contract*, Summer 1998.

259   *sixteen Republican senators charged FAIR:* "Senators Sign Bennett Letter Condemning Tactics of Anti-immigration Group FAIR," Press Release, Office of U.S. Senator Robert F. Bennett, April 20, 1999.

259   *When* New York Times *reporter Jason DeParle:* Jason DeParle, "The Anti-Immigration Crusader," *New York Times*, April 17, 2011.

259   *"Tanton, who did more than anyone else":* "Deconstructing the New York Times," Jerry Kammer's Blog, April 22, 2011, CIS website http://cis.org/Kammer/Deconstructing-the-NYT.

260   *felt a certain "queasiness:* Letter from Arthur Schlesinger, Jr., to Otis Graham. Otis Graham, Jr. Papers.

260   *"The questions that Brimelow raises":* Michael Lind, "American by Invitation," *The New Yorker*, April 24, 1995.

260   *the 1965 Immigration Act was "an astonishing":* Brimelow, *Alien Nation*, 9.

260 *possibility of "an alternative form":* John Higham, *Strangers in the Land* (New Brunswick, NJ: Rutgers University Press, 2002), 334.

18: AFTER 9/11

265 *In his sermon three days later, Awlaki:* William Branigin, "When Terror Hits Close to Home," *Washington Post,* September 20, 2001.

265 *The Fairfax County chief of police:* Ibid.

266 *Two FBI agents showed up at the Dar Al-Hijrah mosque:* Reporting on Anwar al-Awlaki and the 9/11 hijackers is drawn from The National Commission on Terrorist Attacks Upon the United States, *The 9/11 Commission Report* (New York: W. W. Norton, 2004); Department of Justice documents obtained by Judicial Watch under a Freedom of Information Act request and published online at http://www.scribd.com/doc/149699460/1488-05312013; and from the "Unlocking 9-11" document archive maintained by intelwire.com and published online at http://intelfiles.egoplex.com/.

267 *The 9/11 Commission concluded: The 9/11/Commission Report,* 221.

267 *On the second Friday after the attacks:* Debbi Wilgoren and Ann O'Hanlon, "Mosques' Days of Worship and Worry," *Washington Post,* September 23, 2001.

267 *In an interview with* The New York Times: Laurie Goodstein, "A Nation Challenged: The American Muslims," *New York Times,* October 19, 2001.

269 *The director of the Graduate School:* "Federal Raids on Charities Anger U.S. Muslim Leaders," Knight-Ridder/Tribune News Service, March 22, 2002.

269 *The executive director of the Islamic Institute:* "U.S. Muslim Community Outraged by Raids on Muslim Offices and Homes," Agence France Presse, March 21, 2002.

270 *enough to get him listed as a defendant:* "Amended Complaint," Case No. 1:02CV01616, filed in the U.S. District Court for the District of Columbia, August 30, 2002.

271 *In a July 2005 press release:* "Treasury Designates MIRA for Support to Al Qaida," Press Release, Department of the Treasury, July 14, 2005. (MIRA was the Movement for Islamic Reform.)

271 *Through his attorneys Alamoudi:* Mary Beth Sheridan, "Government Links Activist to Al Qaeda Fundraising," *Washington Post,* July 16, 2005.

273 *whom he described as "a female of foreign origin":* Witness Statement, Baltimore County Police Officer Barry Sweitzer, August 20, 2004.

273 *"We had taped our whole vacation":* Jerry Markon and Eric Rich, "Va. Family Defends Video of Bay Bridge, *Washington Post,* August 26, 2004.

273 *"Suspected Terrorist Activity":* Officer Francis, "Incident Report," Maryland Transportation Authority Police Department, August 20, 2004, http://www.investigativeproject.org/documents/case_docs/1523.pdf.

275 *"If we really want to have a voice":* Michael Laris, "N. Va. Muslims Raising a Voice in Area Politics," *Washington Post,* June 16, 2003.

276 *"We are stepping up our civic participation":* Caryle Murphy, "Facing New Realities as Islamic Americans," *Washington Post,* September 12, 2004.

276 *The agents were served a dinner of lamb:* The account of the FBI town hall meeting at Dar Al-Hijrah is drawn from an interview with Esam Omeish, plus Caryle Murphy, "Protesters Seek Release of Saudi Prisoner," *Washington Post,* June 18, 2004; and Caryle Murphy, "Facing New Realities as Islamic Americans," *Washington Post,* September 12, 2004.

276 *"Sometimes you would go to":* William Wan, "An Uncomfortable Spotlight," *Washington Post,* September 19, 2011.

276 *"I didn't come here to be spoken to like that":* Ibid.

277 *he was accused by an anti-Islam weblog:* "Virginistan Follies," MilitantIslamMonitor.org, March 3, 2005, http://www.mili tantislammonitor.org/article/id/473.

277 The Washington Post *and the* Chicago Tribune *both published:* John Mintz and Douglas Farah, "In Search of Friends Among the Foes," *Washington Post,* September 11, 2004; Noreen S. Ahmed-Ullah et al., "A Rare Look at Secretive Brotherhood in America," *Chicago Tribune,* September 19, 2004.

277 *"falls short in many respects":* Unpublished letter provided to the author.

279 *"balanced mainstream advocacy of Islamic principles":* Paul Courson, "Muslim Groups Target Youths in Anti-Terror Campaign," cnn.com, http://www.cnn.com/2005/US/07/25/muslims.non violence/.

280 *"a kind of grand Jihad in eliminating":* "An Explanatory Memorandum On the General Strategic Goal for the Group In North America 5/22/1991," English translation of document seized in 2004 FBI raid, published online by Investigative Project on Terrorism, http://www.investigativeproject.org/documents/case_docs /445.pdf.

280 *"While some of these ideas were part":* Email from Esam Omeish to MAS chapter heads and board members, August 14, 2007, provided to the author.

281 *Awlaki prounounced it a "heroic act":* "Paths Crossed and Collided: Al-Awlaki Was Hasan Family Imam Years Before Fort Hood Massacre," *Dallas Morning News,* November 29, 2009, quoting Awlaki's weblog.

283 *claimed that Omeish was president of "a dangerous":* "Immigration Commissioner Quits," *Washington Times,* September 28, 2007.

283 *posted online a video of a speech:* http://www.investigativeproject. org/499/esam-omeish-jerusalem-day-rally-12-22-2000-full -speech.

284 *Governor Kaine learned of the video when:* "Immigration Commissioner Quits," *Washington Times*, September 28, 2007.

284 *"That is news to me, what you say":* "Va. Appointee Resigns After Videos," Associated Press, September 27, 2007.

284 *"I have been made aware":* "Muslim on Va. Commission Quits After Videos Surface," *Washington Post,* September 28, 2007.

284 *"The controversy that erupted around my appointment":* Esam Omeish, "Why I Resigned: The Ugliness of Intolerance in Virginia," *Washington Post,* October 21, 2007.

284 *In a press conference on the day following:* Tim Craig, "Muslim Activist Denies Urging Violence," *Washington Post,* September 29, 2007.

285 *When the FBI's Arthur:* Interview with the author.

285 *"It seems clear to us," the editor wrote:* Wayne Lutton, "A Note from the Editor," *The Social Contract,* Fall 2010.

19: THE SECOND GENERATION

289 *shift toward "a more militant reaffirmation":* Alejandro Portes and Rubén Rumbaut, *Legacies: The Story of the Immigrant Second Generation* (Berkeley: University of California Press, 2001), 157.

289 *"Groups subjected to extreme discrimination":* Ibid., 187.

289 *"The adaptation of the second generation":* Alejandro Portes, "Introduction: Immigration and Its Aftermath," in Alejandro Portes, ed., *The New Second Generation* (New York: Russell Sage Foundation, 1996).

304 *"one in which clusters of immigrants":* Marie Price and Audrey Singer, "Edge Gateways: Immigrants, Suburbs, and the Politics of Reception in Metropolitan Washington," in Audrey Singer et al., eds., *Twenty-first Century Gateways: Immigrant Incorporation in Suburban America* (Washington, DC: Brookings Institution Press, 2008), 138.

20: POLITICS

305   *"I learned to slip back and forth":* Barack Obama, *Dreams from My Father: A Story of Race and Inheritance* (New York: Crown 1995, 2004), 82.

307   *"This is unbelievable!":* "Obama Draws Large Crowd at College Rally," Associated Press, February 3, 2007.

307   *Obama defeated Clinton decisively:* "Obama, McCain Sweep the Vote Across Fairfax," Sun Gazette Newspapers, February 13, 2008; "Obama's Tidal Wave Puts Va. in Play for Dems if He Can Sustain It," Associated Press, February 13, 2008; "In Virginia, Results Signal a State in Play for November," *Washington Post,* February 13, 2008; "Democratic Duel Complicates Life Further down the Ticket," *Washington Post,* February 21, 2008.

308   *claimed to be registering four to five hundred:* Ian Urbina, "In Virginia, Large Voting Blocs for McCain and for Obama," *New York Times,* September 18, 2008.

308   *voting rates for Hispanics and Asian Americans:* "The Diversifying Electorate—Voting Rates by Race and Hispanic Origin in 2012 (and Other Recent Elections)," Current Population Survey, May 2013, U.S. Census Bureau.

308   *The 2010 census would show the Hispanic:* U.S. Census Bureau, Population of Virginia: Census 2010 and 2000.

308   *The number of Asian Americans registered: The New American Electorate: The Growing Power of Immigrants and Their Children* (Washington, DC: Immigration Policy Center, 2010). Based on research by Rob Paral and Associates.

308   *According to exit polls, Asian Americans:* "How Groups Voted . . ." Roper Center, University of Connecticut (reports from 1992, 1996, 2000, 2004, and 2008).

309   *A survey team from the Muslims in the American Public Square:* Cited in Farid Senzai, *Engaging American Muslims: Political*

Trends and Attitudes, Institute for Social Policy and Understanding, 2012.

309 *a survey by the Council on American–Islamic Relations:* CAIR News Release, "Muslims Congratulate President-Elect Bush," December 15, 2000.

309 *A frequent speaker at the ADAMS mosque:* DeNeen L. Brown, "Muslims Strive for Tolerance . . . and Voters," *Washington Post,* November 1, 2008.

310 *he won more than 80 percent of their vote:* "American Muslims Overwhelmingly Backed Obama," *Newsweek,* November 6, 2008, citing poll by the American Muslim Task Force on Civil Rights and Elections.

315 *Keam raised $194,000:* Campaign finance data from disclosure reports available on the Virginia Department of Elections voter information website, https://voterinfo.sbe.virginia.gov/.

316 *people of Asian ancestry made up about 16 percent:* "Voter Profile: Korean Americans," Connection Newspapers, October 22, 2008; Fairfax County Department of Neighborhood and Community Services.

316 *When asked by a suburban newspaper:* "Battle for 35th District," Connection Newspapers, June 3, 2009.

317 *"Our brave, selfless, and devoted":* www.omeish for delegate.com.

317 *He told a reporter that his resignation:* "Four Democrats Run for Shannon's Seat," Connection Newspapers, May 20, 2009.

317 The Washington Post's *Marc Fisher:* "From Fairfax to Richmond, 'The Jihad Way?,'" "Raw Fisher" (blog), April 29, 2009, http://voices.washingtonpost.com/rawfisher/2009/04/from _fairfax_to_richmond_the_i.html (accessed January 4, 2015).

317 *a reporter for* Washington Jewish Week: Adam Kredo, "Comments Dog VA Candidate," *Washington Jewish Week,* May 7, 2009.

317 *John Carroll told a reporter for Fox News:* "Clinton Invites Controversial Muslim Leader on Conference Call," FoxNews.Com, June 8, 2009.

317 *"should be a disqualifier":* "Northern Virginia Votes; Our Endorsements," *Washington Post,* May 31, 2009.

318 *"Omeish Campaign Crashes":* "Omeish Campaign Crashes in VA Primary," IPT News, June 9, 2009.

318 *A 2007 survey by the Pew Research Center:* "Candidate Traits and the '08 Campaign," Section III of Pew Report, "Voters Remain in Neutral as Presidential Campaign Moves into High Gear," Pew Research Center, February 23, 2007, http://www.people-press.org/2007/02/23/voters-remain-in-neutral-as-presidential-campaign-moves-into-high-gear/4/.

318 *"Today is a celebration":* Text of speech on website, www.omeishfordelegate.com.

320 *"I don't stand up a lot":* Keam's speech is archived at https://vimeo.com/36714299.

321 *Anwar later told a reporter for her high school newspaper:* "Omeish Volunteers for the Obama Campaign," *TJ Today,* October 12, 2012.

321 *The white share of the voting population:* "The Diversifying Electorate: Voting Rates by Race and Hispanic Origin in 2012," Current Population Survey, U.S. Census Bureau, May 2013.

321 *Exit polls in 2012 showed him:* "How Groups Voted in 2012," Public Opinion Archives, Roper Center, University of Connecticut.

321 *"Because it's a changing country":* Bill O'Reilly, interviewed during Fox News election night coverage by Megyn Kelly, November 6, 2012.

322 *(Two years later, the Census Bureau):* 2014 National Population Projections, U.S. Census Bureau.

323 *A Pew Research Center survey of political attitudes:* "Beyond Red vs. Blue: The Political Typology," Pew Research Center, June 26, 2014.

323 *Some moderate Republicans:* Michael Gerson, "A Coke Ad Crystallizes GOP's Immigration Problems," *Washington Post,* February 6, 2014.

323　*A 2010 study:* James G. Gimpel, "Immigration, Political Re-alignment, and the Demise of Republican Political Prospects," Center for Immigration Studies, February 2010, http://cis.org /republican-demise.

323　*A 2015 study by the analytic firm IHS, Inc.:* "Hispanics Will Account for More than 40 Percent of the Increase in U.S. Employment in the Next Five Years," Press Release, IHS, Inc., February 24, 2015.

324　*when three out of four Asian American voters:* "Behind the Numbers: Post-Election Survey of Asian American and Pacific Islander Voters in 2012," a collaborative project of the Asian American Justice Center, Asian and Pacific Islander American Vote, and the National Asian American Survey, April 2013.

324　*In the 2014 midterm elections:* Rosalind S. Helderman and Peyton Craighill, "GOP Gains Traction Among Hispanic Voters with Aggressive Outreach Campaigns," *Washington Post,* November 6, 2014; Lanhee Chen, "Republicans Courted Asians, and It Paid Off," Bloomberg View, November 5, 2014.

325　*In 2012, only 56 percent of Asian American:* "Reported Voting and Registration, by Race, Hispanic Origin, Sex, and Age, for the United States," November 2012, U.S. Census Bureau.

325　*A survey by the New American Leaders Project:* "Represent 2020: Toward a Better Vision for Democracy," New American Leaders Project, 2014.

326　*A separate study in 2010 found only ten Muslim:* Abdulkader H. Sinno, "Muslim Americans and the Political System," *Oxford Handbook of American Islam,* ed. Yvonne Y. Haddad and Jane I. Smith (New York: Oxford University Press, 2014), 332.

21: AMERICANIZATION

327　*"If America changes to the point":* Jeffrey Goldberg, "What's Your Problem?," *The Atlantic,* October 2010.

329　*A 2013 study by the Pew Hispanic Center:* "The Path Not Taken,"

Pew Hispanic Center/Pew Research Center, Washington, DC, February 2013.

329 *"could change America into a culturally"*: Samuel P. Huntington, *Who Are We? The Challenges to America's National Identity* (New York: Simon & Schuster, 2004), 221.

329 *A 2000 survey of Salvadoran immigrant parents:* "A Community Sampler: Salvadoran Households with Public School Children," Department of Systems Management for Human Services, Fairfax County, Virginia, http://www.fairfaxcounty .gov/demogrph/archives/sampler/salvadoran.pdf.

330 *while 83 percent had arrived:* "A Community Sampler: Eight Immigrant and Refugee Communities with Public School Children," Fairfax County, Virginia: Department of Systems Management for Human Services, 2000, Table 2-2 and Table 2-35.

330 *In a 2007 article, four political scientists:* Jack Citrin et al., "Testing Huntington: Is Hispanic Immigration a Threat to American Identity?", *Perspectives on Politics,* Vol. 5, No. 1, March 2007, 31.

330 *A scholar at the RAND Corporation:* James P. Smith, "Immigrants and the Labor Market," RAND Working Paper WR-321, November 2005.

331 *"Building an Americanization"*: U.S. Department of Homeland Security, Task Force on New Americans, *Building an Americanization Movement for the Twenty-first Century* (Washington, DC: U.S. Government Printing Office, 2008).

332 *a "cult of ethnicity has arisen"*: Arthur M. Schlesinger, Jr., *The Disuniting of America: Reflections on a Multicultural Society* (New York: W. W. Norton, 1998), 20.

332 *"It belittles unum"*: Ibid., 21.

332 *"was not to preserve old cultures"*: Ibid., 17.

332 *"A nation of more than 130 cultural groups"*: Molefi Kete Asante, *The Painful Demise of Eurocentrism* (Trenton, NJ: Africa World Press, 1999), 26.

332   *"Since the American idea"*: This quote from Asante appears in his review of the first edition of Schlesinger's book. It was published in *The World & I*, a monthly magazine published by the *Washington Times* in April 1992.

333   *"a covenant between immigrant and nation"*: U.S. Commission on Immigration Reform, *Becoming an American: Immigration and Immigrant Policy*, 1997 Report to Congress, 27.

334   *"The mutual antipathy of tribes"*: Arthur Schlesinger, Jr., "The Disuniting of America" (article adapted from book), *World & I* magazine, April 1992, 279.

334   *"weakening social cohesion"*: Graham, Jr., *Immigration Reform and America's Unchosen Future*, ix.

334   *addressed the issue in a 2006 lecture:* Robert D. Putnam, "E Pluribus Unum: Diversity and Community in the Twenty-first Century," *Scandinavian Political Studies*, Vol. 30, No. 2, 2007, 137–74.

337   *A 2013 study by the Anti-Defamation League:* "ADL Poll: Anti-Semitic Attitudes in America Decline 3 Percent," Press Release, October 28 2013, Anti-Defamation League, http://www.adl .org/press-center/press-releases/anti-semitism-usa/adl-poll-anti -semitic-attitudes-america-decline-3-percent.html.

338   *"O, mankind! We created you"*: Surah al-Hujurat, Verse 13.

339   *One bakery that used to specialize:* The story of the transformation of Korean-owned stores along Little River Turnpike is drawn from David Cho, "Commerce Connects Communities," *Washington Post*, February 12, 2004.

340   *"He planned to box for the U.S. Olympic Team"*: Alan Cullison, "A Family Terror: The Tsarnaevs and the Boston Bombing," *Wall Street Journal*, December 14, 2013.

340   *"Whether we were playing basketball"*: Zolan Kanno-Youngs, "Globe Correspondent Recalls Friendship with Boston Marathon Bombing Suspect," *Boston Globe* (online edition), April 20, 2013.

340   *"What he's accused of," she said:* "Here and Now," NPR News, April 22, 2013.

340 *"Why did young men who grew up"*: Statement by President Obama, April 19, 2013.

341 *"What does it say about our broken"*: Senate Judiciary Committee Hearing, "The Border Security, Economic Opportunity and Immigration Modernization Act," April 22, 2013.

341 *"The problem isn't just illegal immigration"*: Ann Coulter, "Legal Immigration Can Be Just as Big a Problem as Illegal," *Idaho Press-Tribune* (and other newspapers), April 28, 2013.

342 *the Tsarnaev family had "imploded"*: "The Fall of the House of Tsarnaev," *Boston Globe,* December 15, 2013, http://www.bostonglobe.com/Page/Boston/2011-2020/WebGraphics/Metro/BostonGlobe.com/2013/12/15tsarnaev/tsarnaev.html.

342 *"I love this country"*: Andrew Rosenthal, "The Boston Bombing and Immigration," *New York Times* (online), "Taking Note: The Editorial Page Editor's Blog," April 26, 2013.

342 *The 2010 U.S. Religion Census indicated:* The Association of Statisticians of American Religious Bodies, *2010 U.S. Religion Census: Religious Congregations and Membership Study.*

342 *about one in four had immigrated:* Pew Research Center, *Muslim Americans: No Signs of Growth in Alienation or Support for Extremism,* August 2011.

343 *Gallup surveys in more than 150 countries:* "More than 100 Million Worldwide Dream of a Life in the U.S.", Press Release on results of Gallup World Poll, March 21, 2013, http://www.gallup.com/poll/161435/100-million-worldwide-dream-life.aspx#.

343 *"a thousand unforeseeable possibilities"*: Walter Lippmann, *A Preface to Politics* (New York: Mitchell Kennerley, 1914), 190.

INDEX